W9-BNX-331

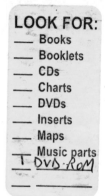
# READING
# RECONSIDERED

# READING
# RECONSIDERED

## A Practical Guide to Rigorous Literacy Instruction

## DOUG LEMOV
## COLLEEN DRIGGS
## ERICA WOOLWAY

Uncommon Schools | Change History.

JB JOSSEY-BASS™
A Wiley Brand

Published by Jossey-Bass
A Wiley Brand
One Montgomery Street, Suite 1000, San Francisco, CA 94104-4594—www.josseybass.com

Written by Doug Lemov, Colleen Driggs, and Erica Woolway

Credits continue on page 385.

Jossey-Bass books and products are available through most bookstores. To contact Jossey-Bass directly call our Customer Care Department within the U.S. at 800-956-7739, outside the U.S. at 317-572-3986, or fax 317-572-4002.

Wiley publishes in a variety of print and electronic formats and by print-on-demand. Some material included with standard print versions of this book may not be included in e-books or in print-on-demand. If this book refers to media such as a CD or DVD that is not included in the version you purchased, you may download this material at **http://booksupport.wiley.com**. For more information about Wiley products, visit **www.wiley.com**.

**Library of Congress Cataloging-in-Publication Data**

Names: Lemov, Doug, 1967- author. | Driggs, Colleen, author. |Woolway, Erica, 1979- author.
Title: Reading reconsidered : a practical guide to rigorous literacy instruction / Doug Lemov, Colleen Driggs, Erica Woolway.
Description: San Francisco, CA : Jossey-Bass & Pfeiffer Imprints, Wiley, 2016. | Includes bibliographical references and index.
Identifiers: LCCN 2015038419 (print) | LCCN 2015049348 (ebook) | ISBN 9781119104247 (paperback) | ISBN 9781119104346 (pdf) | ISBN 9781119104254 (epub)
Subjects: LCSH: Reading. | Reading comprehension. | Language arts–Correlation with content subjects. | BISAC: EDUCATION / Teaching Methods & Materials / Reading & Phonics.
Classification: LCC LB1050 .L44 2016 (print) | LCC LB1050 (ebook) | DDC 372.4–dc23
LC record available at http://lccn.loc.gov/2015038419

Cover design: Wiley
Cover image: ©kyoshino/Getty Images, Inc., ©marekuliasz/Shutterstock

Printed in the United States of America

FIRST EDITION

*PB Printing* 10 9 8 7 6 5 4 3 2 1

# Contents

# DVD Contents

These video clips and useful tools are also accessible via a login at

www.teachlikeachampion.com/yourlibrary

For instructions, please see How to Access the Online Contents in the back of the book.

## VIDEO CLIPS

### Close Reading (Chapter 2)

| Clip | Module | Teacher | Description |
|------|--------|---------|-------------|
| 1 | Layered Reading | Patrick Pastore | Patrick uses both contiguous reading and line-by-line reading as he and his students read "Occurrence at Owl Creek Bridge."* |
| 2 | Close Reading to Analyze Meaning | Rue Ratray | Rue reads for subtlety and author's craft by juxtaposing a line from *The Giver* with plausible alternatives. |
| 3 | Close Reading Bursts | Beth Verrilli | Beth and her students closely read a short and crucial moment in *Othello*. |

### Nonfiction (Chapter 3)

| Clip | Module | Teacher | Description |
|------|--------|---------|-------------|
| 4 | Embedding Texts | Colleen Driggs | Colleen makes the familiar more rigorous with an embedded text. |
| 5 | Embedding Texts | Patrick Pastore | Patrick embeds a short nonfiction piece on the Civil War to illuminate elements of a short story set in that time. ("Occurrence at Owl Creek Bridge") |

*For the video clips in which a specific text is highlighted, we've included the text title as an additional note.

| Clip | Module | Teacher | Description |
|------|--------|---------|-------------|
| 6 | Embedding Texts | Patrick Pastore | Patrick models rigorous character analysis with the help of an outside-the-bull's-eye embedded text. (*The Westing Game* and a description of histrionic personality disorder) |

**Writing for Reading (Chapter 4)**

| Clip | Module | Teacher | Description |
|------|--------|---------|-------------|
| 7 | Writing for Reading | Gillian Cartwright | Gillian builds student writing stamina and uses writing to support a high-quality discussion of *Fences*. |
| 8 | Reading Class Cycles | Kelsey Clark | Kelsey has systematized Stop and Jots that give her students multiple opportunities to reflect on their reading in writing. |
| 9 | Reading Class Cycles | Julia Goldenheim | Julia expands the Read-Write-Discuss cycle by having students revise based on insights gleaned from discussion of the text. (*The Winter of Our Discontent*) |
| 10 | Reading Class Cycles | Jessica Bracey | Jessica "re-cycles" to ensure that students frequently reflect on their reading through writing and to create the illusion of speed. |
| 11 | Writing Is Revising | Julie Miller | Julie carefully monitors student writing, then provides clear feedback based on her observations of students' writing. (*The Life and Times of Oscar Wao*) |
| 12 | Writing Is Revising | Julia Goldenheim | Julia quickly addresses a common error by Show Calling one student and soliciting constructive feedback from the class. |
| 13 | Building Stamina | Eric Diamon | Eric strategically helps students build their writing stamina. (*Baseball in April and Other Stories*) |
| 14 | Building Stamina | Lauren Latto | Lauren supports students' writing stamina by giving them a choice of three equally rigorous writing prompts for *Romeo and Juliet*. |

**Approaches to Reading (Chapter 5)**

| Clip | Module | Title | Description |
|------|--------|-------|-------------|
| 15 | Accountable Independent Reading | Patrick Pastore | Patrick encourages quality Accountable Independent Reading by giving students a clear focal point. (*Catcher in the Rye*) |
| 16 | Accountable Independent Reading | Daniel Cosgrove | Daniel uses a catchphrase to expand Accountable Independent Reading duration at low transaction cost. (*James and the Giant Peach*) |
| 17 | Control the Game | Nikki Frame | Nikki gently administers a consequence and positively brings an inattentive student back into the class's Control the Game reading of *A Single Shard.* |
| 18 | Control the Game | Jessica Bracey | Jessica masterfully Controls the Game during a Read-Aloud portion of her lesson. (*Circle of Gold*) |
| 19 | Control the Game | Rob De Leon | Rob bridges for his students as they finish a section of *The Mouse and the Motorcycle.* |
| 20 | Control the Game | Eric Snider | Eric prompts students to fill in missing words to ensure that the students are following along during a Control the Game reading. ("Dark They Were, and Golden-Eyed") |
| 21 | Control the Game | Patrick Pastore | Patrick names the sound and Punches the Error to minimize transaction costs and put the majority of decoding work on students. (*The Westing Game*) |
| 22 | Control the Game | Bridget McElduff | Bridget normalizes error and brings in the whole class to help a student correctly pronounce a word. |
| 23 | Read Aloud | Taylor Delhagen | Taylor injects life into reading aloud with drama and pizzazz. |
| 24 | Read Aloud | Maggie Johnson | Maggie asks for a little spunk, and gets some joy and laughter in return. (*To Kill a Mockingbird*) |

## Vocabulary (Chapter 6)

| Clip | Module | Teacher | Description |
|---|---|---|---|
| 25 | Explicit Vocabulary Instruction | Akilah Bond, Colleen Driggs, and Gillian Cartwright | Watch Akilah, Colleen, and Gillian demonstrate the importance of accurate and student-friendly definitions. |
| 26 | Implicit Vocabulary Instruction | Tondra Collins | Tondra turns one student's struggle into an opportunity for Implicit Vocabulary Instruction. (*Twelve Angry Men*) |
| 27 | Implicit Vocabulary Instruction | Nikki Frame and Patrick Pastore | Nikki and Patrick drop in definitions to support students' understanding of a text. (*Number the Stars* and *A Single Shard*) |
| 28 | Implicit Vocabulary Instruction | Jamie Davidson | Jamie projects a picture of a scalpel on the overhead to support a definition that's critical to understanding the text. (*Boy: Tales of Childhood*) |
| 29 | Implicit Vocabulary Instruction | Maura Faulkner | Maura, after quickly defining a key word, asks a series of application questions to increase rigor and support student mastery of the word. (*Number the Stars*) |
| 30 | Implicit Vocabulary Instruction | Erica Lim | Erica pushes students to use a tough vocabulary word, as well as identify nonexamples of it. (*The Itinerary of Benjamin of Tudela*) |
| 31 | Maintenance and Extension | Steve Chiger | Steve reviews and reinforces vocabulary words in his high school English class. |
| 32 | Maintenance and Extension | Beth Verrilli | Beth reviews the word *exploited* as it relates to *Macbeth* through a series of Cold Calls. |

**Reading Systems (Chapter 7)**

| Clip | Module | Teacher | Description |
|---|---|---|---|
| 33 | Phases of Implementation | Patrick Pastore | Patrick rolls out and models Interactive Reading for his students. (*Miracle's Boys*) |
| 34 | Phases of Implementation | Kim Nicoll | Kim models elements of Interactive Reading like labeling and writing margin notes. (*The Watsons Go to Birmingham – 1963*) |
| 35 | Phases of Implementation | Amy Parsons | Students in Amy's class autonomously annotate as they read *Forgotten Fire.* |
| 36 | Interactive Reading System | Alex Bronson | Alex highlights a student's Interactive Reading notes in her science class as a model for the rest of the class. |
| 37 | Discussion Systems | Erica Lim | Erica encourages the use of nonverbals like eye contact and strong voice in her class discussion. |
| 38 | Discussion Systems | Erica Lim | Students in Erica's class hold a rigorous discussion with little prompting. |
| 39 | Discussion Systems | Erin Krafft | Erin installs a system that students can use to respectfully agree or disagree with their partner during their Turn and Talks. |
| 40 | Discussion Systems | Eric Snider | Eric uses multiple Turn and Talks while reading a short story, "Dark They Were, and Golden-Eyed," to check for comprehension and keep engagement high. |
| 41 | Discussion Systems | Laura Fern | Laura's class engages in an impeccable Turn and Talk supported by strong systems she's established. |

**Toward Intellectual Autonomy (Chapter 8)**

| Clip | Module | Teacher | Description |
|------|--------|---------|-------------|
| 42 | Toward Intellectual Autonomy | Maggie Johnson | Maggie facilitates a discussion based on phrases students have autonomously identified as important during independent reading of *To Kill a Mockingbird*. |
| 43 | Autonomous Discussion Structures | Beth Verrilli | Beth clearly lays out the frame for a class discussion to support a rigorous and student-driven conversation about *The Great Gatsby*. |
| 44 | Autonomous Discussion Structures | Ryan Miller | Ryan models for students replicable actions of higher-level discussion as he facilitates a peer-to-peer conversation in his history class. |

## USEFUL TOOLS

**Reading Nonfiction (Chapter 3)**

- Ideas for Meta-Embedding
- Unit Plan with Embedded Texts: Rue Ratray and *The Giver*
- Embedding Nonfiction: Quality-Control Checklist

**Writing for Reading (Chapter 4)**

- Read-Write-Discuss-Revise Cycle Template

**Vocabulary Instruction (Chapter 6)**

- Sample Vocabulary Rollout Script

**Toward Intellectual Autonomy (Chapter 8)**

- Reader's Response Journal Template
- Literary Terms and Definitions

*To our kids, with whom we have 16,000 more nights*
*to read—not nearly enough*

# About the Authors

**Doug Lemov** is a managing director of Uncommon Schools and leads its Teach Like a Champion team, designing and implementing teacher training based on the study of high-performing teachers. He was formerly the managing director for Uncommon's upstate New York schools. Before that he was vice president for accountability at the State University of New York Charter Schools Institute and was a founder, teacher, and principal of the Academy of the Pacific Rim charter school in Boston. He has taught English and history at the university, high school, and middle school levels. He holds a BA from Hamilton College, an MA from Indiana University, and an MBA from the Harvard Business School. Visit him at www.teachlikeachampion.com.

**Colleen Driggs** is a director of professional development for the Teach Like a Champion team at Uncommon Schools. Alongside Erica and Doug, she works to train thousands of high-performing teachers and school leaders across the country each year—reaching over one million students. Colleen is also an adjunct professor for Relay Graduate School of Education's National Principals Academy Fellowship. Before joining the Teach Like a Champion team, she taught middle school science in New York City; middle school science and literacy in New Haven, Connecticut; and middle school literacy in Rochester, New York. In Rochester, she served as the chair of the Reading Department, coaching literacy teachers and developing curriculum and assessments, at Rochester Prep Middle School. Colleen received her BA in psychology and education from Hamilton College and a master of education degree from Pace University.

**Erica Woolway** is the chief academic officer for the Teach Like a Champion team at Uncommon Schools. In this role, she works with the team to train thousands of high-performing teachers and school leaders across the country each year—reaching over one million students. Prior to becoming CAO, she served as both dean of students and director of staff development at Uncommon Schools and as an adjunct literacy instructor at Relay Graduate School of Education. Erica began her career in education as a kindergarten teacher and then worked as a school counselor. She received her BA in psychology and Spanish from Duke University, an MA and master of education degree from Teachers College in school counseling, and an MA in school leadership from National Lewis University. She is a coauthor of *Practice Perfect* with Doug Lemov and Katie Yezzi. She currently lives in New York City with her husband and their three boys.

# About Uncommon Schools

At Uncommon Schools, our mission is to start and manage outstanding urban public schools that close the achievement gap and prepare low-income scholars to enter, succeed in, and graduate from college. For nearly twenty years, through trial and error, we have learned countless lessons about what works in classrooms. Not surprisingly, we have found that success in the classroom is closely linked to our ability to hire, develop, and retain great teachers and leaders. That has prompted us to invest heavily in training educators and building systems that help leaders to lead, teachers to teach, and students to learn. We are passionate about finding new ways for our scholars to learn more today than they did yesterday, and to do so, we work hard to ensure that every minute matters.

We know that many educators, schools, and school systems are interested in the same things we are interested in: practical solutions for classrooms and schools that work, can be performed at scale, and are accessible to anyone. We are fortunate to have had the opportunity to observe and learn from outstanding educators—both within our schools and from across the United States—who help all students achieve at high levels. Watching these educators at work has allowed us to derive, codify, and film a series of concrete and practical findings about what enables great instruction. We have been excited to share these findings in such books as *Teach Like a Champion* (and the companion *Field Guide*), *Practice Perfect, Driven by Data, Leverage Leadership,* and *Great Habits, Great Readers*.

Since the release of the original *Teach Like a Champion*, Doug Lemov and Uncommon's Teach Like a Champion (TLaC) team have continued to study educators who are generating remarkable results across Uncommon, at partner organizations, and at schools throughout the country. Through countless hours of observation, Doug and the TLaC team have further refined and codified the tangible best practices that the most effective teachers have in common. *Teach Like a Champion 2.0* builds off the groundbreaking work of the original *Teach Like a Champion* book and shares it with teachers and leaders who are committed to changing the trajectory of students' lives.

We thank Doug and the TLaC team for their tireless efforts to support teachers everywhere. We hope our efforts to share what we have learned will help you, your scholars, and our collective communities.

Brett Peiser
Chief Executive Officer
Uncommon Schools

Uncommon Schools is a nonprofit network of forty-four high-performing urban public charter schools that prepare more than fourteen thousand low-income K–12 students in New York, New Jersey, and Massachusetts to graduate from college. A 2013 CREDO study found that for low-income students who attend Uncommon Schools, Uncommon "completely cancel[s] out the negative effect associated with being a student in poverty." In July 2013, Uncommon Schools was named the winner of the national 2013 Broad Prize for Public Charter Schools for demonstrating "the most outstanding overall student performance and improvement in the nation in recent years while reducing achievement gaps for low-income students and students of color." To learn more about Uncommon Schools, please visit our website at http://uncommonschools.org. You can also follow us on Facebook at www.facebook.com/uncommonschools, and on Twitter and Instagram at @uncommonschools.

# Acknowledgments

Having seen this book through to reality demands of us many heartfelt thanks to a great many people. We start with our team: John Costello, Dan Cotton, Joaquin Hernandez, Derek Hines, Maggie Johnson, Jennifer Kim, Tracey Koren, Hilary Lewis, and Rob Richard. Writing this book wouldn't have been possible without your superb analysis and insights, your relentlessness about honoring teachers with deep study of their work, and your great camaraderie. We love coming to work because of the joy that you all bring to it, and that helps us do our best thinking and writing.

We are especially grateful to Rob and John, who happily granted every request in order to edit and produce all of the invaluable videos of teachers you see here and to Maggie, our reading content specialist, who generously devoted hundreds of hours sharing anecdotes and examples from her own teaching experiences, provided feedback on drafts, and offered thoughtful ways to frame some of the key ideas in the book. If she sees her thinking in this book, we are honored.

Without knowing it, we started drafting this book five years ago with our colleagues in the 5–8 Reading Working Group at Uncommon Schools: Kelly Dowling, Mabel Lajes-Guiteras, J. T. Leaird, Amy Parsons, Patrick Pastore, Serena Savarirayan, Hannah Solomon, and Lauren Vance. Your collective wisdom about literacy instruction is the foundation of this book, and the talented teachers you lead continue to inform and shape our understanding of excellent reading instruction. A special thanks to Evan Rudall, former CEO of Uncommon Schools, who originally gave us the overwhelming and incredible task of helping Uncommon "do reading" better. We'll try not to hold it against you!

Thank you, perhaps most of all, to the teachers who graciously allowed us to observe and videotape their instruction, who responded to emails and requests for phone conversations even at the end of long workdays, and who shared student work samples as well as the templates they've created in hours of careful planning. Teachers do the most important work in our society, we believe, and they do it with insight, passion, and skill. We are grateful to you all for doing that and for sharing what you've learned with us.

And there's the original literacy team at Rochester Prep, with whom Colleen worked and learned much of her craft. Thank you to Stacey Shells, Patrick Pastore, and Jaimie Brillante for helping pilot some of the early ideas for this book and for your constant feedback in helping make those ideas better.

An incredible thank you, also, to Christy Lundy and Stephen Chiger, both leaders of literacy at Uncommon Schools and trusted thought partners. Steve, thank you for your eloquent contributions, your sagacious feedback on drafts, and for your incredible spirit of collaboration and humility. The good news is, we owe you a pony. The bad news is, we are going to keep promising it at the next get-together so you keep coming to talk reading with us. Thank you to Katie Yezzi, Sam DeLuke, and Emily Hoefling for thoughtful feedback on our drafts using your experienced elementary school lens, and to all of the school leaders within Uncommon with whom we work, for your leadership generally and for your insight on teaching reading. Of course, all of the work at Uncommon Schools is possible only because of the support and guidance of our leadership: Brett Peiser, Julie Jackson, and Paul Bambrick-Santoyo.

There are also many friends outside of Uncommon to whom we owe a great deal of thanks: David Didau and Judith Hochman for significantly informing our discussion of writing, Sara Yu for her depth of knowledge about books and youth fiction in particular, David Coleman for taking the time to meet with us to discuss the vision behind the Common Core, Jessica Petrencsik for reviewing early drafts, and professor Patricia O'Neill for her comments in the Text Selection chapter.

Thanks to our agent, Rafe Sagalyn, for your leadership, guidance, and keeping us in line most of the time. A huge thanks to the team at Jossey-Bass who have supported us through the entire process, including Nic Albert, whose writing was a major asset to both the content and organization of this book; Michele Jones, whose careful edits ensured at least some clarity of ideas; and our editor, Kate Gagnon, whose constant support made this project possible.

Finally and most of all, thank you to our families: to our spouses, who put up with quite a bit even without the strain of a manuscript to write when there are bedtimes looming; and to our children, whom we adore beyond words and who we hope will forgive us for experimenting wildly on them with ideas from this book in our nightly reading with them.

# READING
# RECONSIDERED

# Introduction

# Reading Reconsidered

This book is about the enduring power of reading to shape and develop minds, both in the classroom and, ultimately, outside of it. Of the subjects taught in school, reading is first among equals—the most singular in importance because all others rely on it. Excellence in almost any academic subject requires strong reading. This applies to the history, math, science, arts, and other subjects that students study in their K–12 years, as well as the behavioral economics, organic chemistry, or ancient religious history they will pursue at the university level (to say nothing of the intellectual pursuits of their private and professional lives).

One of the core requirements of reading beyond the K–12 level is the ability to make meaning from the literature of a discipline: often dense and arcane, and where grasping the main idea—*this is a document about the rights of citizens!*—is insufficient. The specifics must be mastered—which rights, say, as defined how and by whom. Getting the gist is not enough. Academic success often means a student with a challenging text—sometimes at the margins of his comfort level—that he must read and master, alone. It's not *all* challenging reading—there will surely be fantastic lectures and labs and discussions, but even then, what a student is able to contribute to or take from those activities will depend heavily on what she took from the hundred pages of dense critical theory, case law, restoration drama or metastudies she sat down with the night before. The farther students advance, the more demanding the reading required of them.

If our hopes and expectations for our students stretch far—to the highest levels of accomplishment and learning—then our responsibility includes preparing them to read with rigor, independence, precision, and insight in the long run. However, it is important to remember that the journey and the destination do not always look the same.

Consider the case of Xavier University of Louisiana's premed program. Though you've probably never heard of it, you could argue that it's the most successful premed program in the country. Certainly it is the most effective at closing the preparation gap for students not born to privilege. Why do we say that? Well, consider that it is tiny, unheralded Xavier—with an enrollment of just under three thousand students, most of whom are first in their family to go to college and many of whom grew up with limited financial resources and attended high schools that did not prepare them for advanced STEM work—that produces the largest number of black medical school students in the country.[1] Yes, you read that correctly. More black students make it to med school from Xavier than from any Ivy League school or any flagship state university with an enrollment ten times Xavier's. Why? Xavier seeks to reverse-engineer the skills and knowledge required in med school and ensures that every student masters those elements systematically in the first years of the program. The school prepares students for autonomy, independence, and problem solving through a program that not only offers practice at autonomy, independence, and problem solving but also ensures that every foundational skill on which they rely is robustly developed.

The reading teacher's job is similar: to ensure that each and every student—privileged in knowledge and skills or not, motivated (at first) or not—moves steadily and reliably toward mastery of advanced, complex skills. This requires understanding how such skills are built, not just hoping they will bloom. K–12 reading teachers, in short, must prepare students for college and university with intentionality and backwards design. This book proposes how to do that.

Once, a century-and-a-half ago, before compulsory schooling was universal, the beliefs of the English-speaking world were shaped by the words of writers like Charles Dickens, Frederick Douglass, Charles Darwin, and Jane Austen, and those four visionary nineteenth-century thinkers have at least this in common: all four were educated primarily outside of any formal schooling system, via deep and constant reading. In part or in totality, books were their teachers, and they were able to shape the world's opinions based on what they read while working in a boot-blacking factory (Dickens) or under the lash of enslavement (Douglass). They show us that an exceptional reader can learn to do anything, no matter where those first pages of text reach him or her, no matter how long the journey to mastery. The power of their ideas reminds us that a well-read citizen can do anything.

Our argument is not, of course, that the way to educate the greatest number of future scholars to excellence is therefore to let them read on their own and hope for the best. Certainly, with that approach, some would rise to the top—but many more would sink. No, what brilliant self-educated readers teach us has to do with the power of reading. Words, especially the written variety, remain the primary currency of ideas, and the diligent study of reading is the diligent study of idea creation and development, so the urgency of making the teaching of reading in American schools as effective and rigorous as it can be must always be at the forefront of the work—and every teacher plays a role. Every student must glimpse, as much as possible, the power that comes from the world that reading can bring to light.

## "FIGURING OUT" READING

A few years ago, the head of Uncommon Schools, the nonprofit where we work and which runs forty-four high-performing urban charter schools, turned to us in the midst of an otherwise ordinary meeting and asked us to "figure out" reading. By "figure out," he meant for us to go and analyze what we (our schools and teachers) were doing in our reading classrooms and determine what we needed to do more or less of. In other words, we were tasked with finding better ways to reach a consistently higher reading standard—to better prepare our students to succeed in college and in their lives beyond. We received this mandate despite the fact that, by most people's measures, we were succeeding in our ELA classrooms. Our students were consistently able to significantly outperform "expectations" as defined by what other similar populations of kids were able to achieve and what schools in similar neighborhoods did.[2] Internally, however, we knew that it wasn't good enough to do better than a standard that was not nearly high enough; we needed to find a way to help our kids outperform students born to privilege and the lifetime of implicit benefits to literacy that come with it.

Our standard had to be true and enduring excellence, and there we fell short.[3] Whereas in math and other subjects we would close the gap between our kids and those of privilege in just a year or two, our best schools took three and four years to do so in ELA. Some of them never did. Whereas our math results were consistent, those in ELA were far less predictable. Further, our first rounds of graduates brought back tales from college that were not always the march of triumph we'd expected. We'd sent 100 percent of our graduates on to college, but in many cases 150 pages of reading a night in texts of dizzying complexity had left our students overwhelmed by the challenge.

The charge to figure out reading was relatively terrifying. Our first thought was, "What if we can't think of anything to say?" But we set out to solve the problem in the way we've become accustomed to: by watching and learning from what successful teachers do and by doing our best to figure out what, among those things, works best.

Even before we started to develop thoughts about solutions, we noticed a lot about the challenge. For example, we noticed that "what we did" in our ELA classrooms could roughly be described as "just about everything." There was a daunting breadth of skills and knowledge teachers were setting out to ensure that students mastered in a typical ELA classroom: learn to use hundreds of new words, develop the ability to comprehend texts in multiple genres, interpret texts in discussion with peers — and independently. Develop clear and evocative prose. Love and celebrate books. Know deeply some of the best ones that had been written. In some cases, the list included teaching those things to students who arrived in fifth grade not yet able to decode reliably. Oh, is *that* all?

But we noticed, also, that teachers did "just about everything" in another way, too. There was an immense inconsistency in the methods used by teachers across our network, even in comparison to the diverse approaches used by teachers in other disciplines. Our teachers, we sometimes thought, not only used every approach and ascribed to every philosophy under the sun but also often saw their chosen approach — to a degree far more evident than in our math or science classrooms, say — as something more than practical. The way they taught ELA was an expression of themselves, of their most deeply held beliefs. They were not necessarily going to relish suggestions that they make changes to that, we thought.

Our journey, several years in the making, began with that initial request to "figure it out," but it was refined and focused with even greater urgency soon after, in response to another clarion call, this one directly from teachers and sounded in reaction to the phrase *Common Core*. At that point, no one had yet written standards or promulgated a test or tied that test to the lives of teachers and students in a variety of useful and not-so-useful ways. But teachers knew there would be changes, challenging ones, and they wanted their students to succeed with them. And with some anxiety, they knew they would be measured on something they did not yet fully understand. As information trickled out, we strove to combine what we were learning about teaching reading with what the Common Core required—or at least with the best arguments it was making—and how we saw teachers making those changes.

Because our work is informed in part by the phrase Common Core and because that phrase is fraught for many teachers, let us reflect on it for a moment. First, we want to observe that there are two levels on which teachers can react to the Common Core: the practical and the philosophical.

On the practical level, teachers have to consider the sorts of questions their students will have to be able to answer, about what kinds of texts, in what kinds of formats when they (both students *and* teachers) are formally assessed. They have to place bets to some degree: what the assessments will ask them to read and do is not always transparent, even though they understand that they will be evaluated for their success in preparing students for them. Teachers must make a "best guess" or, alternatively, bet in a different way and choose *not* to consider the assessments, continuing to teach in the manner they think is right and rigorous and true, no matter how reading is measured. These practical challenges are real, and we do not intend to minimize how stressful they can be for teachers. On a practical level, how rigorous, fair, accurate, and worthy those assessments turn out to be and how much teachers should adapt their teaching to them are questions we cannot answer.

But no matter how teachers may feel about the practical realities of assessment and implementation, it is also important for teachers to engage the questions the Common Core seeks to raise at the philosophical level. What is it that it asks teachers to do? Why? Are they good ideas, even if the pragmatics of the implementation are messy?

## THE CORE OF THE CORE

To that last question, we think the answer is a clear "Yes"—particularly if one were to try to simplify the changes the Common Core asks of teachers to focus on a few most important ideas and then think about how to execute them, regardless of how they are measured. We tried to do that and distilled from the Common Core four very clear and, we think, very good ideas. Those four ideas make up what we think of as the *Core of the Core*:

1. Read harder texts
2. "Close read" texts rigorously and intentionally
3. Read more nonfiction more effectively
4. Write more effectively in direct response to texts

When we discuss the Common Core in this book, it is, for the most part, these four ideas that we focus on. We of course discuss other topics as well: the end goal of autonomous reading, and a variety of foundational aspects of reading instruction, such as developing vocabulary. But the rationale behind these four Common Core ideas is, we think, sound and addresses some of the most important gaps in current reading instruction. So no matter what happens to the Common Core on the practical side—how it is assessed and implemented by districts and states, and so on—making those four changes and making them well is likely to ensure that students are better prepared for college and life. Therefore, we put aside the pragmatic questions we cannot answer, to focus instead on the ideas that are powerful, rigorous, and worthwhile. If, as an ancillary bonus, focusing on them also means that students will succeed on assessments, then hooray.

So why do we think these four ideas, which we discuss directly in the first four chapters of the book, make so much sense? We discuss the rationale more deeply in the chapters themselves, but offer a brief defense of each of them here.

## Reading Harder Texts

Arriving at college means making adaptations: to dorms and meal halls (usually), to bigger classes, to managing time. But it also means encountering science classes that require the reading of highly technical abstracts and dense textbooks; social sciences courses that tend to transition from using secondary sources (discussion of a document in a textbook, say) to primary sources (reading the document itself, be it by Freud or Darwin, or the Declaration of Independence); and English classes that introduce texts that deliberately resist easy meaning-making by readers: John Donne, Ralph Ellison, William Faulkner, Gabriel García Márquez. To send students who are unfamiliar with the struggle of challenging text—never mind having never read a book more than a hundred years old—to this environment is to send them unprepared. A steady exposure over the years leading up to college both to harder texts specifically and to the experience of struggling with the challenge of difficult text is critical to success on campus.

The SAT is an instructive source of data on this topic. Where once the average American SAT reading score exceeded the average math score, the reverse is now true. As illustrated in Figure I.1, in 1986, the average Critical Reading score on the SAT was 507, and the average math score was 501. In the intervening years, Critical Reading scores have gone steadily down (to 495 in 2015) while math scores have gone steadily up (to 511 in 2015).[4] At some point in the early-1990s, their trajectories crossed. Math was no longer the bigger challenge; reading was. ELA scores are in "relative decline," and

**Figure I.1**  Mean SAT Scores by Year

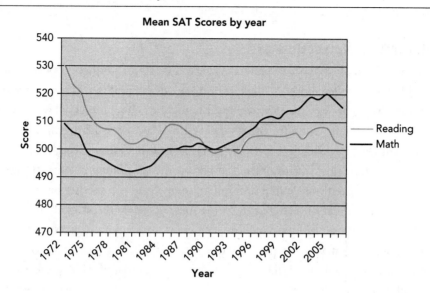

whatever scholastic or demographic or instructional trends have pushed SAT scores downward have affected reading more negatively than math, a fact which suggests that the most common explanation cited—that a wider percentage of U.S. students now take the test—is probably insufficient. Something else is happening to reading skills in the United States. One clue may lie in Marilyn Jager Adams's observation that the scores of the top 10 percent of test takers have dropped the most.[5] Her argument, that this statistic indicts a lack of preparation for the notoriously challenging level of text difficulty on the SAT, is compelling, and one of many arguments for reading harder texts in school.

## Close Reading

If success in college demands of students the ability to read successfully above their comfort zone, then the importance of teaching students how to struggle with challenging text is another good argument both for reading more challenging texts and for "Close Reading," which is, as we define it, the set of tools readers use to "solve" text when it is challenging and out of their comfort zone. It involves strategies of both rereading and analysis—ways of unlocking the densest, most challenging lines of text, and in so doing learning how language works. It is the study of the mechanics of meaning-making, a topic that will serve students well everywhere they go and, in addition, teach them to be poised and composed in the face of struggle.

## Reading More Nonfiction

Reading more nonfiction more effectively is wise advice too. Nonfiction poses a special set of challenges. It relies more on background knowledge and is among the most useful tools in building background knowledge, a happy fact if one is blessed with excellent knowledge to start, but which for others can result in a downward spiral of less comprehension and less knowledge, especially given that most students read less nonfiction than they do fiction. This, in and of itself, is yet another challenge, as nonfiction has its own distinctive conventions. When unfamiliar, they create yet another barrier to comprehension. And nonfiction is dense, information packed, and less likely to try to sell the reader on its own engaging storytelling style as it is to make its case straight up and using a stay-with-me-if-you-can prose style. Certainly much of the nonfiction that students read in college will be of that type. And, crucially, most of what students read in college will be nonfiction, which stands in stark contrast to the balance of what most probably read during their K–12 years (and certainly in reading and English classes), which tends to be overwhelmingly fiction and narrative nonfiction. So a shift in the balance of text to more—and more intentional—nonfiction will help students not only prepare for what they'll read in college but also build the knowledge they'll need to get there. And with a few clever tricks, we think teachers can do this engagingly and still teach all of the novels and stories they love so well. In fact, as we'll explain in the chapter, we think nonfiction can help you teach that literature better.

## Writing for Reading

Finally there is the topic we define as "writing for reading." Writing, we note, is the "coin of the realm," the currency in which ideas are most widely circulated and valued. If you cannot put it in writing, you aren't assured of full credit—and in that statement we are referring to both school and life. Every act of textual interpretation may not have to be set down on paper to be fully credible, but the student, the thinker, who cannot get those interpretations onto paper operates at a massive handicap. What is written is permanent, enduring, recorded. True, learning to write directly in response to texts is a unique art worthy of practice; true, the experience, when focused on most intently, develops an affinity for language and its forms, but more urgently, we think, there are deep synergies between learning to read well and learning to write well, so the way students write in reading and English classes influences a lot more than just what they put on paper. It shapes what they take from their reading. Nothing for example, helps a student decipher a sentence of complex, thorny syntax like having sought to use complex syntax to capture complex ideas herself. One of our goals in this book then is to be more intentional about plumbing the synergies between reading and writing.

## HOW TO USE THIS BOOK

To make the material presented easier to navigate and digest, we've broken each of the following chapters into a series of shorter modules. The broader structure of the book reflects our belief in the four core ideas we've just described. As noted earlier, we address them in the first four chapters.

Chapter 1 addresses text selection, the idea that what you choose to read matters as much as how you read it. This sounds obvious, but we argue that in many classrooms, teachers have, without even realizing it, come to assume that reading is *how* one reads. We propose a set of qualitative measures of text complexity that can be used for choosing text. We also discuss hidden benefits of coordinated text selection among teachers.

Chapter 2 takes on one of the most critical and, at the same time, poorly defined ideas from the Common Core: Close Reading. We start by defining it, then provide a set of tools that can help teachers Close Read with rigor and insight.

Chapter 3 addresses the importance of nonfiction. The challenges of reading nonfiction are many; this is both a cause and an effect of the knowledge deficit. Therefore, we set out to examine ways to ensure that teachers can use reading of nonfiction, especially, to build knowledge.

Chapter 4 takes on the topic of writing for reading. Both writing and reading are not only critically important but also deeply synergistic. Teaching writing in specific ways, we think, can help students read more effectively.

The next four chapters address what we think of as the "fundamentals" — core elements of literacy instruction important in their own right that also offer deep synergy with the four Core of the Core Ideas.

Chapter 5, Approaches to Reading, focuses on ensuring that students read a lot and read in a variety of ways: reading silently, reading aloud, and being read to. We also address the often hidden challenges of reinforcing fluency and building decoding skills; we refer to them as "hidden" because we think many students struggle with them well beyond the early elementary grades, after which those skills are often no longer taught or reinforced.

Chapter 6 takes on vocabulary, something that almost every teacher addresses and that, in part because of its overwhelming familiarity and apparent mundanity, we think presents an opportunity for study. (At least watching great teachers at work makes us think that's so.) We propose a two-part approach that focuses on building both depth and breadth of word knowledge via both explicit and implicit vocabulary instruction.

Chapter 7, Reading Systems, focuses on consistent ways to approach key activities in the literacy classroom to make them more efficient, productive, and autonomous. For example, we discuss how to make text markup during reading—what we call Interactive Reading—as productive as possible, and how to motivate and monitor independent reading.

Chapter 8 addresses the ultimate goal of reading instruction: intellectual autonomy. Intellectual autonomy has to do with developing readers who are able not just to understand but also to critique and provide thoughtful answers to our questions and their own. This kind of autonomy doesn't happen by magic, so we propose ways to build the skills that will ultimately sustain students in developing their own ideas and interpretations about what they read.

## NOTES

1. The school's premed preparation program was profiled for its accomplishments in the September 9, 2015 issue of the *New York Times Magazine.*

2. More than 80 percent of Uncommon Schools students live beneath the poverty line.

3. Nor do we claim to be at that high standard yet.

4. U.S. Department of Education, National Center for Education Statistics, "Fast Facts: SAT Scores," https://nces.ed.gov/fastfacts/display.asp?id=171; "Average SAT Scores of College-Bound Seniors (1952–Present)," http://www.erikthered.com/tutor/historical-average-SAT-scores.pdf.

5. Marilyn Jager Adams, "Advancing Our Students' Language and Literacy: The Challenge of Complex Texts," *American Educator,* Winter 2010–2011, 3–11, 53, http://www.aft.org/sites/default/files/periodicals/Adams.pdf.

# Part

# The Core of the Core

IN THE INTRODUCTION, we briefly discussed four core elements of the Common Core—reading harder texts, Close Reading, reading more nonfiction, and writing in direct response to texts—that we think are especially enduring and valuable and that we see reflected in the teaching of our strongest peers. We dub them the Core of the Core, and discuss each in turn in the four chapters that follow, studying how these ideas can play out in the sometimes hectic, sometimes messy, almost always short-on-time reality of the classroom.

Chapter 1

# Text Selection

## MODULE 1.1: THE DECLINE OF THE CANON

The books you choose to teach are just as important as how you teach them.

## MODULE 1.2: TEXT ATTRIBUTES AND LEVELING SYSTEMS

Leveling systems can be inconsistent, especially in terms of the qualitative complexity of texts.

## MODULE 1.3: THE FIVE PLAGUES OF THE DEVELOPING READER

It is imperative to expose students to a broad and deep list of difficult texts.

## MODULE 1.4: BOOK CHOICE

Including the totality of a text is important for providing literary utility, cultural capital, knowledge development, and disciplinary literacy.

## MODULE 1.5: MANAGING SELECTION

Managing selection and establishing a schoolwide canon improve intertextual discussion, as well as teacher knowledge and workload.

# Chapter 1

# Text Selection

One of the most important topics in teaching reading is text selection, the process by which teachers choose what their students will read. Yet the importance of this topic remains partially invisible to many educators. This might seem at first to be a strange statement. Naturally, every teacher is aware of the text he or she is teaching. Of course, every teacher selects texts (or oversees students selecting them) carefully, right?

The reality, however, is that in teaching reading, many educators have come to believe that the goal is to teach students a set of skills — "how to read" — that are applicable to any text. Teach a book, almost any book, the "right way" — by fostering rich discussion, say, and drawing students' awareness to depth of characterization and the role of figurative language — and students will learn to read any text well.

The million-dollar question is, of course, "What is the right way?" Once that is settled, for many teachers, text selection can boil down to choosing something relatively engaging for kids to read. If there's buy-in and students like a book, there's a viable platform for practicing the skills of reading in whatever manner a teacher defines them. Assuming there's reasonable diversity in genres and authors, that's probably enough.

But in fact, *what* students read shapes how and how well they learn to read in far more ways than what might at first seem obvious.

A closer look at this famous scene from *Oliver Twist* suggests a few of the reasons why.

> Oliver Twist and his companions suffered the tortures of slow starvation for three months: at last they got so voracious and wild with hunger, that one boy, who was tall for his age, and hadn't been used to that sort of thing (for his father had kept a small cookshop), hinted darkly to his companions, that unless he had another basin of gruel per diem, he was afraid he might some night happen to eat the boy who slept next him, who happened to be a weakly youth of tender age. He had a wild, hungry eye; and they implicitly believed him. A council was held; lots were cast who should walk up to the master after supper that evening, and ask for more; and it fell to Oliver Twist.
>
> The evening arrived; the boys took their places. The master, in his cook's uniform, stationed himself at the copper; his pauper assistants ranged themselves behind him; the gruel was served out; and a long grace was said over the short commons. The gruel disappeared; the boys whispered to each other, and winked at Oliver; while his next neighbours nudged him. Child as he was, he was desperate with hunger, and reckless with misery. He rose from the table; and advancing to the master, basin and spoon in hand, said: somewhat alarmed at his own temerity:
>
> "Please, sir, I want some more."
>
> The master was a fat, healthy man; but he turned very pale. He gazed in stupefied astonishment on the small rebel for some seconds, and then clung for support to the copper. The assistants were paralysed with wonder; the boys with fear.
>
> "What!" said the master at length, in a faint voice.
>
> "Please, sir," replied Oliver, "I want some more."

Imagine a typical student, a ninth-grader perhaps, reading this passage and struggling. Let's say the student failed to realize that young Oliver was goaded into his actions—that they were not characteristic of his true gentleness of character. Let's say that our high school student failed to hear Dickens's sardonic, narrative voice exaggerating the cruelty of Oliver's wards.

Let's also consider just as plausibly that our student might struggle to follow the basic action—that "child as he was" means "because he was a child," that a "copper" is a pot, the "commons" was their meal, that "lots were cast" means they decided by drawing straws, that "it fell to Oliver" means he lost, and that when the master "gazed in stupefied astonishment on the small rebel," Dickens means he was looking at Oliver. Maybe our student would simply have run out of steam and given up somewhere in the maze of Dickens's thirty-seven-word first sentence!

The cause of the debacle is unlikely to be that our student lacks practice in common reading skills, such as making inferences or assessing character motivation. It's far more likely that our student can't execute those skills—or even achieve basic comprehension—with a complex text, specifically one full of lengthy, multi-clausal sentences written in nineteenth-century syntax and relying on knowledge of nineteenth-century society.

Quite plausibly, prior to *Oliver Twist*, our student might have been almost exclusively exposed to benignly appealing youth fiction written after 1980, chosen *specifically because of its easy accessibility. Of course* many high school students struggle to read Dickens. A huge number have never read anything older or more disorienting than *Tuck Everlasting*. And although we tend to assume that a basic skill like assessing character motivation is fungible across books, it is not necessarily true that assessing Winnie's motivation in fifteen scenes from *Tuck Everlasting* will set a student on a course to understand Oliver Twist's.

The "skills" of reading, in other words, may not be so universally applicable. They are applied in a setting, and the details of the setting—what we read—matter immensely. Almost anyone can make accurate character inferences about Curious George. Making them in a George Elliott novel is tougher. A systematic exposure to certain types of text experiences is at least as necessary in determining a student's ability to read widely and successfully as a systematic exposure to certain kinds of skill-based questions.

Choosing harder texts, as we will discuss, is one element necessary to preparing students for success in college. But more than that, students need to wrestle with *specific types* of challenges posed by a rich array of challenging texts, systematically introduced starting in elementary school.

In this chapter, we will reflect on factors teachers can consider in deciding what students read—what, for example, they can be reading in fifth grade to help ensure later success with *Oliver Twist*. The goal is to make choices as rigorous as possible—in a balanced way that still allows for *Tuck Everlasting*—and to think about how the texts students read now can contribute to their success in and love for reading later on.

In many schools, reading has come to be tacitly defined as "the act of asking and answering questions about a text." Depending on what philosophy of reading you choose, it consists, at its core, of asking students to demonstrate a specific vision of skills inherent in readership. There are different visions of what constitutes these skills, and their adherents disagree, often vociferously, on which is best. Even so, almost all of them agree that there are indeed universal and fungible skills, applicable and applied to almost any text in a consistent way, and that they are the core of the discipline of reading. This is a big assumption, however; and, as Daniel Willingham, E. D. Hirsch, and others have suggested, even if reading relies on "skills," it also depends heavily on knowledge. Choosing what we read is one of the most important ways we build that knowledge for students.

## "THE BEST THAT HAS BEEN THOUGHT AND SAID"

Seen historically, the prioritization of how we read over what we read may be more divergence than norm. For much of its history, the profession of teaching has been at least as concerned with *what* books students read as how they read them. More specifically, it has been concerned with making sure they read the *important* books and were familiar with their arguments. The purpose of reading *Paradise Lost* as a student in the nineteenth century was probably at least as much that of being familiar with the story and being able to refer to it on the right occasion as it was to develop a unique and trenchant interpretation of it.[1] The job was in understanding Milton's purpose of "justify[ing] the ways of God to men" more than it was in critiquing it.

More broadly, much of the point of schooling was to have read a corpus of great books and to be able to participate in a conversation about them. To a degree that was certainly more than trivial, the ability to do so marked your status as "well educated" in a way that revealed a different purpose than ours today. That is, the purpose of education was—in some places, still is—more to preserve class distinctions than to erode them.

By the second half of the nineteenth century, arguments for more universal access to education began to abound. Social critics like Matthew Arnold, a former school inspector, argued in favor of more students reading "the best which has been thought and said in the world." Reading the best texts—and having all "educated" citizens read them—had the benefit, he argued in *Culture and Anarchy* (1869), of "turning a stream of fresh and free thought upon our stock notions and habits, which we now follow staunchly but mechanically."[2] If we all read the important books, the argument went, we could all talk about them.

Arnold's argument and others like it framed the way reading was taught for much of the ensuing century. The idea that being educated was about reading and discussing a relatively finite corpus of "best" texts was an old one. Arnold's argument that the benefit of reading "the best that has been thought and said" should be made available to more than just the elite was new. We could democratize society by allowing more people to participate in discussions previously reserved for the elite—discussions concerned with critiquing or reinforcing our core intellectual premises.

## READING IN READERS

The growing American republic was more democratic yet. Laura Ingalls Wilder describes her peripatetic childhood there, in fictionalized form, in the volumes of the Little House on the Prairie series. The books feature Laura moving from town to town and school to school in Wisconsin, Kansas, Minnesota, Iowa, South Dakota, and Missouri. At each school, the core of the curriculum is a "reader." It's the one consistency to her schooling on the American frontier. New place, new teacher, new classmates, but predictable schooling and consistent texts.

The ubiquity of "readers" probably wasn't fictionalized much. As access to education became democratized through more universal public schooling, students often did the lion's share of their reading from these relatively standardized collections of readings intended to introduce reading, as well as a certain set of moral and cultural influences.

---

### The McGuffey Reader

According to some histories,* the McGuffey Reader, the most common of the genre, sold over 120 million copies in the United States. To put that number in perspective, it exceeds that of nearly every other book, ever, save the Bible and the dictionary.

*(Continued)*

---

(*Continued*)

A McGuffey Reader was an eclectic array of short pieces that both introduced reading and set out to "present the best specimens of style...insure interest in the subjects...impart valuable information and...exert a decided and healthful moral influence," in the words of the preface to *McGuffey's Fifth Reader*, a volume that offered 117 two- or three-page selections by such authors as Hawthorne, Dickens, Alcott, Longfellow, and dozens of now lesser-known authors such as Dr. John Todd and William Wirt.

*National Park Service, "William Holmes McGuffey and His Readers," *Museum Gazette*, January 1993, http://www.nps.gov/jeff/learn/historyculture/upload/mcguffey.pdf.

How students read texts in their readers was likely different from how we would read them today. There was probably less emphasis on asking, "What words characterize the blacksmith's motivation in Longfellow's poem?" than there was "Recite the first ten lines of *The Blacksmith*, please, John." The idea was that the texts showed students how to be successful citizens, gave them practice reading, and let them participate in civil discourse. The task was to understand; interpretation was probably more optional. Besides, you often got only enough to accomplish the most basic reading. In the McGuffey Reader, students didn't get *Hamlet* in five acts, they got "Hamlet" as a five-page excerpt with a brief introduction that observed, "Shakespeare's works consisted chiefly of plays and sonnets. They show a wonderful knowledge of human nature, expressed in language remarkable for its point and beauty." And that was that.

By the twentieth century, American society was changing even more rapidly in structure and demography—and, by the second half of the century, even in its perception of itself. Citizens became increasingly less inclined to accept authorities because they were authorities. An approach to reading that was based on a straightforward gloss of a text chosen by a wise but invisible hand was by this time unsustainable.

Before we continue, we would like to emphasize, lest our comments be misinterpreted, that in describing historical changes in education and reading, we are not arguing in favor of the systems and beliefs of the past. Our goal is to consider how past perspectives can help us understand decision making within the framework of our current—and rightly very different—beliefs about reading and learning today.

## FLATTENING THE TEXTUAL HIERARCHY

The word *canon*, many readers will know, refers to an authoritative group of "best" books that are deemed central to a culture's tradition — or at least are the most important to read within it. In *Post-War British Women Novelists and the Canon*, Nick Turner writes that the birth of the term in its present meaning can be traced back to the 1980s.[3] It emerged both to describe and dismantle the notion — now incommensurate with a complex, polyglot society drawing on multiple traditions — that there was a single, finite list of what needed to be read to participate in society. The word made explicit that such a thing existed at exactly the time it fell out of sync with society.

Knowing that there was such a thing as a canon — and that it was implicit in so many decisions about what we valued and read — inexorably led to all sorts of thorny questions. Was the authority implicit in canon selection wise or sinister? On what grounds could one evaluate quality objectively? Were the books in it "best" in quality, or merely reflective of the values of those in power? And why were a supermajority of the authors from the Western European tradition? Were the implicit decisions about who was a "classic" author inherently racist? Classist? Sexist? Elitist? The now mildly ironic phrase "dead white males," used to impugn things that are old, out-of-date, or indicative of past values that are just as well passed, derives from the debate about the canon. It was not ironic then.

In short, the word *canon* described an idea that was, to many people, past its use-by date. Though some still advocated in favor of its traditional and established books, teachers were evidently among the skeptics. *Walden*, *The Scarlet Letter*, and the like went from bulwarks to museum pieces, replaced by a hundred examples of more contemporary writing, including, especially, a great deal more youth fiction.

---

## YA Fiction Explosion

According to a recent article in *The Atlantic* magazine "Young-adult fiction, commonly called 'YA fiction,' has exploded over the past decade or so: the number of YA titles published grew more than 120 percent between 2002 and 2012, and other estimates say that between 1997 and 2009, that figure was closer to 900 percent" — this amid what are probably declining overall teenage reading rates.*

*Nolan Feeney, "The 8 Habits of Highly Successful Young Adult Fiction Authors," *Atlantic*, October 22, 2013, http://www.theatlantic.com/entertainment/archive/2013/10/the-8-habits-of-highly-successful-young-adult-fiction-authors/280722/.

---

Without a default list of "right" books from which to choose, teachers increasingly fell back on more personal choices: what inspired them, what was new, what they liked to teach, what their students liked to read. In many schools, the idea of a shared book disappeared. Each student read his or her own book and wrote or reflected on it more or less independently.

There are clear positives implicit in the decline of the canon. One is that, having been allowed as a profession to choose which texts to study, teachers have unlocked the insight and power in hundreds of books they hadn't previously considered teaching. It turns out that "worth reading" is a term for which there are lots of contenders; considering them expands our definition of worth. Teachers almost assuredly also ended up teaching texts that showed us a more accurate and diverse version of our society as a result—one that valued more perspectives and voices, one that noticed how a perspective can exclude others to our collective detriment. Among other benefits, this has probably made for better and more observant readers—readers who better understand perspective and its subjectivities.

At the same time, there are negatives, too, stemming from the decline of the canon, though, fortunately, much of the loss can be recouped within a more contemporary and flexible approach to deciding what to read. One lost benefit is the Arnoldian notion of shared discourse—the idea that part of the value of reading is to be able to read and talk about important books that almost everyone else has read. When a student makes reference to a similarity between a scene her class has just read and a scene in another book, the power of that moment is magnified a hundredfold if everyone has also read that other book. Intertextuality—discussing the ways that different texts treat similar problems or tell similar stories—works only when students have read some texts in common. Schools now embrace a world with a much more fractured reading base. To find a single shared text outside of your own class's reading is often all but impossible—what text could you or a student refer to as an example of plot or theme or character and know that the great majority of the class would be familiar with it?

Another loss is the erosion of the democratizing influence of "cultural capital." Members of the upper and upper-middle classes often take for granted knowledge that marks them as educated and sophisticated. They can hear a reference to *Hamlet* or Dickens or Zora Neale Hurston (in a classroom, a coffee shop, or a book) and join the conversation. They know at least that Dickens is English and wrote about a time that was, well, *Dickensian*—when children labored in factories and Scrooges refused to share the wealth. They know these things—and things about Marx and Monet and many more—without really knowing how they know them or what it is like *not* to know them. This knowledge of common cultural touchstones lets them — and others who have it — feel as though they belong. Indeed it helps them belong. Knowledge of the books that educated society takes its familiarity with for granted is a powerful tool, though perhaps only *not* having it would help you realize that. A culture of reading that doesn't consider this cultural importance has a disparate impact on those who are less likely to acquire cultural knowledge by other means. It is their best chance to be included in the secret conversations of opportunity.

Finally, there are the aspirational effects of reading texts that are "great." If we are all supposed to read a book because it is uniquely great, then the fact that it is also difficult becomes a hurdle to be overcome by good teaching, not an argument against reading it. It is commonplace in schools to hear that students should never read a book that is "too hard." When the criterion is solely accessibility and not greatness, the result is that students who start out as weak readers almost never study the same rigorous texts that imply our highest expectations, are almost never offered the opportunity to read and master what's truly considered great, and are rarely asked to push themselves and find that they are indeed capable of bringing great insight to even the most challenging situations.

Fortunately, as we'll discuss later on, schools and teachers can take specific actions to address these challenges and also retain the benefits of our postcanonical world. Schools can, for example, establish an "internal canon" — a common base of books all students read for shared reference, and these books can be far more diverse and representative than was the canon of yore. Schools can set out to determine locally what books are "great" without being tied to the traditional canon, and thereby read with aspiration and ambition. They can make the planning and balancing of books a more explicit part of the conversation within the instructional staff so that reading what students or their teacher like is balanced with at least some cultural capital. We further discuss these ideas later in this chapter.

| MODULE 1.2 | Text Attributes and Leveling Systems |
|---|---|

One of the first factors many teachers consider in choosing what to read is the text's *attributes* — its sentence length and complexity, for example, or the difficulty of its vocabulary. These and other measures are often used to determine whether a text will be beneficial and accessible to students. They are usually applied via one of two systems, the Lexile framework or Fountas and Pinnell's Guided Reading Levels.

Now firmly ensconced within the *lingua franca* of teachers, these systems are almost assured to increase in influence as the designers of the Common Core emphasize the importance of students' reading harder texts, measured explicitly via Lexiles. Generally, the emphasis on harder texts is beneficial and the need for a simple, quantifiable tool understandable, but there's a lot more to determining how difficult a text is than leveling.

## *THE GIVER*: MORE THAN THE SUM OF ITS LEXILES

Consider Lois Lowry's *The Giver* and Andrew Clements's *The School Story*. Both score 760 according to the Lexile framework, so some teachers might view them as interchangeable. In fact, some would argue to let their students choose which to read — then they would read more happily and with greater engagement, right? But ask us — and many of the top teachers we've observed — and we would instantly choose *The Giver*. A brief digression into our reasoning may illustrate some of the reasons why text attributes alone are insufficient for making strong text choices.

*The Giver* is a dystopian novel, and reading it would give our students context when, later on, they read other examples of this important genre (*Animal Farm, Brave New World, Fahrenheit 451, A Clockwork Orange*). Further, the true dystopian nature of the book's society is only gradually revealed over the course of the book — things look pretty nice in "the Community" at first. This strategic manipulation of the reader's knowledge makes it not only a great read but a *useful* read, providing students with tools for looking at how books and narration work — tools that they can apply time and again. In the future, they will know to ask, "Is this narrator holding back information from me? Is my perception being manipulated?" A book like *The Giver* brings that sort of issue to the fore.

In literature, conventions are the powerful but unstated ways that we come to expect stories to unfold. *The Giver* is important because it both challenges conventions and, in so doing, reveals them in a way that the more predictable *School Story* does not. For example, a convention in storytelling — not only in novels but also in memoir, movies, and so on — is that "problems" raised in the course of the narrative are resolved; at the end, a measure of "order" is restored; good is rewarded; bad is punished, defeated, or at least understood. Justice is served. *The Giver*'s ending, however, is unresolved. What is it that Jonas sees in the distance in the final lines of the novel: the faint lights of a civilization that might represent salvation, or his last hunger-ravaged hallucinations before death? An ending that does not tidily restore order is rare, especially in *children's* literature. Not only is it intellectually challenging, but it also allows students to begin discussing the nature of resolution in other texts. *The Giver* thus allows students to participate in discussions about storytelling—how it works and its relationship to society—more than other books.

Text selection, then, means looking at more than just the *quantitative* aspects of language—the attributes of a text distilled into a number. It means taking account of the importance of a text in other ways as it informs a student's interactions with literature. Another way of thinking about this is that a book like *The Giver* builds students' knowledge base about books and storytelling in a way that will be useful to them in understanding how texts work, throughout a lifetime of reading. That sort of knowledge is worth looking for explicitly, especially because there are only so many books students will read in school. Choices matter.

---

## In Defense of the Book

One of the most important aspects of choosing texts is choosing the *types* of texts—most important, books, plenty of them, rather than a constant diet of excerpts, passages, and other selections. We are strong believers in "the power of the book," of students building a sustained relationship with a text over time and coming to understand its perspective and mode(s) of narration—and how they shift. In fact, only by glimpsing these changes and variations as part of a sustained relationship between reader and text can students really learn to read. This was one of our first realizations when we began studying successful teachers. Even in an era of test-based accountability, the most successful schools and teachers consistently opt, in our observations, for books—and books of substance—as the core of their instructional choices. Of course, they include passages, articles, and other forms of texts as well, but the year is built around books—long and sustained engagements with an author, a set of characters, a perspective, and a voice.

---

## LESSONS IN TEXT LEVELING

We should state that we didn't start out skeptical of text attributes.

In fact, we were excited when the designers of the Common Core announced that they would use Lexile scores to assess the difficulty of text. To us this meant a drive toward both a higher standard and a clearer measure of what students should read. Our interest was more than theoretical: if we could infer what the expectation looked like at each grade level, we could make sure that students across Uncommon Schools were reading sufficiently demanding texts. We set out to generate useful data to help us shape decision making.

For starters, we took exemplar texts that Common Core recommended, and assessed their Lexile levels. This would tell us more about what the target Lexile level was for each grade. We could chart this and see the overall trend, then adjust the texts we read accordingly, choosing texts within the target range, dropping those that were too easy, and maybe even shooting to get above the target range as our students grew. When we graphed the result, we got a pretty clear "target range" (Figure 1.1). Now we could make sure we were asking our students to read texts that overall were sufficiently challenging.

We decided to go a step further and superimpose some of our core texts from across Uncommon Schools on the graph to see how we were measuring up. We chose books that our teachers most often read and valued highly. The findings were surprising (Figure 1.2).

**Figure 1.1**  Common Core Exemplars by Lexile and Grade Estimate

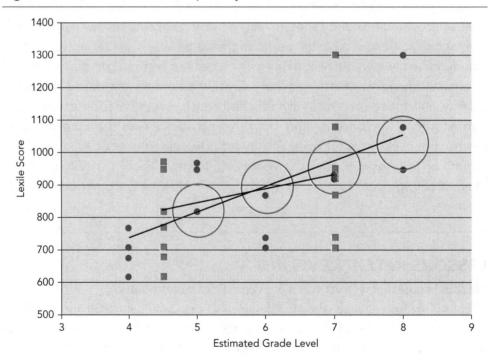

**Figure 1.2**  Uncommon Schools Canon vs. Common Core Exemplars by Lexile

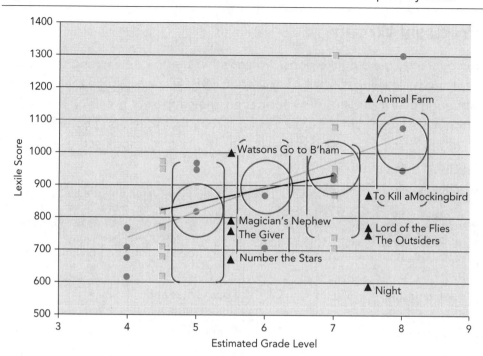

It wasn't just that so many of the books we thought of as rigorous did not appear to match the implied targets. We were prepared for that; we were comfortable saying that a certain book didn't reach the targeted Lexile level but was still something students should read. What we struggled with was the perversity of some of the scores. The places where books fell when we graphed them didn't seem in accord with our sense of what students really found difficult. This is best shown in the nearly equivalent Lexile scores given to *Lord of the Flies* and *The Outsiders*. They are, according to the graph, all but interchangeable. In terms of our students' experiences reading them, however, they couldn't be more different. One was among the most challenging books our seventh graders read, while the other was among the easiest. If you're a middle school teacher, we almost assuredly don't have to tell you which was which. (If you're not, *Lord of the Flies* is several times more challenging than *The Outsiders*.)

Our next thought was to consult Fountas and Pinnell's Guided Reading Levels (often referred to as F&P Levels); perhaps it would provide a rationalizing data point. It didn't. F&P rates *The Outsiders* at Guided Reading level Z—the same as *The Adventures of Huckleberry Finn* and *Animal Farm,* an argument that we, and our teachers, found even more far-fetched than equating it with *Lord of the Flies.*

# Precisely Wrong

Accountants, the old joke goes, would rather be precisely wrong than generally right. Leveling tools like Lexiles and F&P Levels would do them proud. Although they include useful information, their apparent precision belies the often more significant differences in difficulty that they don't contemplate. Here are some examples of books that the two methods score as being roughly equivalent in difficulty.

| Books at or about Lexile 760 | | | Books at or about F&P Guided Reading Level R | | |
|---|---|---|---|---|---|
| Title | Lexile | F&P Level | Title | F&P Level | Lexile |
| The People of Sparks | 760 | U | Circle of Gold | R | 610 |
| Tuck Everlasting | 770 | V | Pocahontas and the Strangers | R | 370 |
| Walk Two Moons | 770 | W | Sarah, Plain and Tall | R | 560 |
| Indian in the Cupboard | 780 | R | Brian's Winter | R | 1140 |

Beyond discrepancies between leveling tools, these scales often contain discrepancies within themselves. We call these Perverse Pairings—instances where books are scored closely together when their difficulties are disparate, or when objectively difficult books are scored as easier than their actually easier counterparts. Here are some examples.

| Lexile Perverse Pairings | | F&P Perverse Pairings | |
|---|---|---|---|
| The Giver (760) | A Bear Called Paddington (750) | The Wind in the Willows (Q) | The True Story of the Three Little Pigs (Q) |
| Where the Wild Things Are (740) | Tuck Everlasting (720) | Number the Stars (U) | A Christmas Carol (U) |
| Esperanza Rising (750) | Grapes of Wrath (680) | To Kill a Mockingbird (Z) | The Outsiders (Z) |

So if the two texts were so hugely different in difficulty, as our teachers knew, what were the features that made *Lord of the Flies* so much more difficult than *The Outsiders*? Could we, through reading specific text segments and analyzing why students struggled with them, identify what made a page from *Lord of the Flies* harder for students to read, and use that to better assess what made text complex?

We used analyses like these to try to discern what the real barriers to student understanding were — not just to state emphatically that a system that equated *The Outsiders* with *Huck Finn* or *Lord of the Flies* was missing something but to identify what those characteristics might be so that teachers could choose texts (and adapt their teaching) to address them. Our intention is that these additional measures of text complexity be used alongside existing quantitative measures like Lexiles and guided reading levels. And because we like a bit of august and epic-sounding prose, we decided to call these qualitative measures "plagues." In the next module, we'll tackle the Five Plagues of the Developing Reader, one by one.

| MODULE 1.3 | The Five Plagues of the Developing Reader |
|---|---|

We describe here five unique challenges (the term *plague* being tongue-in-cheek) of complex texts. To paraphrase George Orwell, though, while all plagues are equal, some plagues are more equal than others. In other words, although developing readers should be prepared for each of the challenges, not all of those challenges require the same amount of time or attention or number of selections. Whereas some probably require specific book choices, others might be addressed by teaching books differently (highlighting archaic or nonlinear sections, for example) or choosing ancillary texts (short additional readings) to augment a main text.

## PLAGUE 1: ARCHAIC TEXT

Authors wrote differently fifty, one hundred, and two hundred years ago. People spoke differently too. They used different words, in different sequences, within different syntactical structures.

Consider, for example, this text, written in 1859:

> This Abstract, which I now publish, must necessarily be imperfect. I cannot here give references and authorities for my several statements; and I

must trust to the reader reposing some confidence in my accuracy. No doubt errors will have crept in though I hope I have always been cautious in trusting to good authorities alone. I can here give only the general conclusions at which I have arrived, with a few facts in illustration, but which, I hope, in most cases will suffice. No one can feel more sensible than I do of the necessity of hereafter publishing in detail all the facts, with references, on which my conclusions have been grounded; and I hope in a future work to do this.

You probably noticed that the author of the passage uses syntax and vocabulary that have passed out of common use. Table 1.1 lists some examples and some plausible modern equivalents that match the tone of the original.

With each passing year, this text and dozens like it become a little less familiar to, a little more distant from, readers who have never experienced such dated forms of discourse. And no steady diet of twenty-first-century youth fiction will bring them any closer.

Why does that even matter? you might ask. There's plenty to read that's more recent and, frankly, more lively. Perhaps the source of this passage will help explain the importance. Did you recognize it? It's from the introduction to Charles Darwin's *On the Origin of Species,* and this is no trivial fact. It is one of the three or four most foundational texts in shaping ideas and discourse in contemporary society. It is a constant part of conversations about and conceptions of the world today.

The question, then, is: Who should be able to read it? Does it matter whether students graduate from our schools able to read Darwin comfortably, fluently, and not overwhelmed just figuring out what is being said at the most basic level? Similarly,

**Table 1.1**  Modern Equivalents of Archaic Language

| The Language Used in the 1859 Text… | …Would Probably Be Something Like This Today |
| --- | --- |
| *This Abstract, which I now publish, must necessarily be imperfect.* | *The essay I am publishing is of course imperfect.* |
| *I must trust to the reader reposing some confidence in my accuracy.* | *I hope readers will have confidence in my accuracy.* |
| *I have always been cautious in trusting to good authorities alone.* | *I have always been cautious in assuming the accuracy of any one source.* |
| *No one can feel more sensible than I do of the necessity of hereafter publishing in detail all the facts, with references.* | *I fully understand the importance of publishing all of the data as soon as possible.* |

does it matter who can read other aging but still foundational texts of our society: *The Declaration of Independence*, Frederick Douglass's *Narrative of the Life of a Slave*, Mary Wollstonecraft's *Vindication of the Rights of Women*, Mary Shelley's *Frankenstein*, and the works of Shakespeare? Do we wish for a future when only antiquarian specialists (perhaps the elite of the elite) read these texts and pass along their interpretations to the rest of society, as if from on high? These issues are critical in ensuring that schools prepare students for university and, more broadly, for their roles in society. How do you sustain democracy in a culture where the majority of its citizens can't read its founding documents?

Reading archaic text, in short, is necessary to a full education, but it is unrealistic to think that students will do so without having practiced reading older texts in a steady, intentional, and, especially, incremental way. Fortunately, the goal of strategically exposing students to archaic text need not imply a third-grade reading of John Donne.

## Pre-Complex Texts

Recall our earlier reflection on the plight of a high school student who struggled to read *Oliver Twist*. One thing that might have helped that student succeed with Dickens would have been steady and incremental reading in texts that included simpler versions of some of the challenges of Dickens's writing, a diet rich in books like C. S. Lewis's *The Magician's Nephew*, say. This engaging text, written to appeal to the imaginations of young readers, is more than sixty years old and uses formal and slightly dated diction and syntax in sentences—sentences that aren't quite Dickensian, but are longer and more dated than those in most comparable books. *The Magician's Nephew* is, in short, a starter kit for students who aspire to one day read Dickens.

Consider these lines, an exchange between Jadis, the White Witch, and Digory, the child protagonist of *The Magician's Nephew*.

> "You are no magician. The mark of it is not on you. You must be only the servant of a magician. It is on another's Magic that you have travelled here."
>
> "It was my Uncle Andrew," said Digory.
>
> At the moment, not in the room itself but from somewhere very close, there came, first a rumbling, then a creaking, and then a roar of falling masonry, and the floor shook.

Like the lines from Darwin's introduction, these lines contain archaic structures. We would write them differently today, even if, as Lewis was, we were trying to capture the tone of royalty in the queen's voice.

Or consider this passage, about Polly, also a protagonist, in the same book:

> Then she was given dinner with all the nice parts left out and sent to bed for two solid hours. It was a thing that happened to one quite often in those days.

The line uses the pronoun "one" instead of "you" or the noun "children." This linguistic structure remains fairly common today in academic discourse. If one has seen it with some frequency before, one hardly notices it and leaps right over it in engaging a text. However, if the construction is foreign to a reader—and if it is embedded in a larger framework of linguistic structures, such as, say, the sort of complex sentence structure common to Victorian prose—a device like the impersonal pronoun *one* can disrupt one's entire conception of a sentence, be it Lewis's or the sentences in this very paragraph.

There may be a temptation, at first, to think of these differences as merely quaint. Some might even see them as a negative—will it keep students from enjoying the text if it sounds "funny"? In fact, this is how students are introduced to the language of the past. First, in reading *The Magician's Nephew* they are alerted to the fact that people spoke differently then. Over time they begin to pick up some of its rhythm and quirks, but at an accessible scale and wrapped in a story that is engaging—it has endured in the hearts, minds, and bookcases of families for sixty or so years for a reason. Perhaps later they read something written fifty years before that. And so it goes. It is the first step in a process that gives students access over the long run to the texts of the past.

In this way, *The Magician's Nephew* serves a useful function to reading teachers. It's what we call a *pre-complex text,* a text that provides readers with practical experience with a simpler version of the ultimate challenges posed by complex texts. This prepares them to someday tackle books by the likes of Darwin and Dickens. In this case, our example addresses the issue of archaic language specifically, but as you will see, pre-complex texts can help prepare readers to be more familiar and comfortable with a variety of forms of complexity.

## Growing Up Archaic

The following are examples of pre-complex texts that introduce some degree of archaic diction and syntax and are likely to help prepare young readers for archaic texts when they get older. Because some of them are challenging, consider reading them aloud.

| Title | Author |
|---|---|
| The Tale of Peter Rabbit | Potter, Beatrix |
| The Wind in the Willows | Grahame, Kenneth |
| The Velveteen Rabbit | Williams, Margery |
| Little House on the Prairie | Wilder, Laura Ingalls |
| A Bear Called Paddington | Bond, Michael |
| Winnie the Pooh | Milne, A. A. |
| Mary Poppins | Travers, P. L. |
| Black Beauty: The Autobiography of a Horse | Sewall, Anna |
| The Secret Garden | Burnett, Frances Hodgson |
| The Wonderful Wizard of Oz | Baum, L. Frank |
| The Merry Adventures of Robin Hood | Pyle, Howard |

## PLAGUE 2: NONLINEAR TIME SEQUENCE

Written roughly for second graders, Donald Crews's book, *Bigmama's,* is a meditation on the nature of memory and time. It's a beautiful read, but if you were to ask many students, even strong readers, basic comprehension questions about the story, they might struggle to answer. Their difficulties would not be because they were not observant readers, but because the book manipulates time in subtle, unorthodox ways—ways that make it hard to discern, for example, what happened when. In *Bigmama's,* time is nonlinear, sometimes leaving it unclear when an event actually happened or which ones occurred in what order. It's an easy book to get the "gist" of, but it's a hard book to follow precisely.

In that sense, *Bigmama's* is an example of the way a book's complex treatment of time can be a hidden challenge to readers. But it also shows how a teacher's careful selection of texts, even texts written for relatively young readers, can prepare students to be successful when faced with increasingly challenging and increasingly prevalent examples of nonlinear time sequencing in the texts they read.

What are some examples of *Bigmama's* nonlinear time sequence? And what do we mean when we say that Donald Crews manipulates time in subtle and unorthodox ways?

Here's the opening:

> "Did you see her? Did you see Bigmama?"
>
> We called our Grandma Bigmama. Not that she was big, but she was Mama's Mama.
>
> Every summer we went to see her—Mama, my sisters, my brother, and me. Daddy had to work. He'd come later. It took three days and two nights on the train. Now we were nearly there.
>
> "Cottondale. Cottondale. Next station stop, Cottondale," yelled the conductor to the nearly empty train. "Don't leave no babies on this train." He made the same joke year after year.

As you may have noticed, the narrative subtly switches back and forth between recollection of a specific trip to Cottondale and recollections of a series of visits made over the course of several years in the narrator's childhood. It's the similarities of those trips—and just maybe the way the memory of them all blends into one—that interest him. So, for example, on a trip to Cottondale one specific year in the past, call it X, someone spoke the first line, "Did you see her?" as they arrived. The next line, "We called our Grandma Bigmama," is spoken from the present, reflecting back on those times. Then the narrator describes the details of a series of trips made across many years. When he writes, "Daddy had to work," he means not during the one summer he was just describing but during all (or most) of the summers in his memory. It always took three days and two nights, he notes, making that a recollection of many years. Already there are three times to keep straight: the "now" from which the narrator is remembering events, a specific "then" that was one trip he remembers well, and a more general "then" that encompasses many trips.

The narrative continues to shift among these times. "Now we were nearly there" describes, again, the specific "then." But the conductor's words to the passengers are a mix. He says "next station stop, Cottondale" in the specific then, but "don't leave no babies on this train" in the general then. Perhaps this is the point of the book—the narrator can perhaps never quite recollect on which specific trip certain things happened. Memory is like that.

If you asked students how often the narrator went to his grandmother's or when the conductor made his joke, however, they might struggle; doubly so if you asked them about what the narrator was recollecting: a series of summers that had melded together in his mind. As with *Oliver Twist,* their struggles would probably not indict poor skills generally but a lack of experience executing those skills with a specific kind of complex text — one that made time and its passage hard to trace. Only experience with texts that use time in unorthodox ways would prepare them to "follow" the narrative as they faced increasingly complex iterations of this challenge.

Many people tend to think of nonlinear narrative sequence as consisting primarily of flashbacks, flash-forwards, and other more obvious movements in time. Of course, these devices are common. Depending on an author's treatment of them — they can be clearly demarcated in the text or can occur subtly, even stealthily — these can be simple or challenging for a young reader to follow. Generally, however, the most challenging — and perhaps most important — aspects of nonlinear time sequence are subtler. The following paragraphs briefly describe some of these less obvious time-shifting tactics.

### Unclear Timing of an Event

When describing an event, a narrator has no obligation to specify when it happened. In fact, many narrators leave this ambiguous. For example, an author might make reference to an event that happened at one time, then just after describe an event that happened at another time, without explicitly telling readers that the two events did not happen in the same time frame. A good reader has to infer the change in time — or become confused.

### Shifts in Fixity of Time

Narration can shift from the depiction of a single incident in time ("Atticus stood in the garden telling Jem to be a gentleman") to a description of multiple moments that occurred and reoccurred periodically ("He often did as much but rarely with such vigor"). The first sentence describes a single event; the second summarizes multiple events to which the single event is contrasted. In many cases, the cues (the word *often*, for example) are missing, making the shift in and out of a narration of recurring events difficult to catch.

### Layers of Memory

A character remembers remembering an event. In the critical scene of *To Kill a Mockingbird*, for example, Scout recalls that while the jury was deliberating, she remembered a "cold morning in February when the mockingbirds were still." It's not necessarily simple for readers to understand that the courtroom scene is taking place in the summer and that this caused the narrator to recall a separate February morning — a memory within a memory. If they don't recognize this, it's a very confusing read!

## Shifts in Rate of Time Elapsing

One of the most common clichés in movies is the idea of "time slowing down." We use that cliché to simulate the hyperfocus we feel in critical moments. As a player slides into home plate, or a mother runs to save her child from an oncoming vehicle, details are presented in a manner that is hyperreal—one that always seems to involve slow-motion photography.

Written narratives use a similar trope and presume our understanding of such devices—that we know time isn't really slowing down, but is rather perceived to do so. In cases like these, the slowing down indicates the importance of an event. Thus a reader must understand that (1) sometimes there is a change in the rate at which someone perceives time to be passing, (2) the rate at which "real" time is passing has not changed, and (3) this tells us to attend very carefully to the events described because they are important.

Authors can also shift the rate at which time elapses in the opposite manner, by breezing unexpectedly through the critical moment—as Virginia Woolf does in *To the Lighthouse*—referring to the death of a character in parenthesis:

> (Mr. Ramsay, stumbling along a passage one dark morning, stretched his arms out, but Mrs. Ramsay having died rather suddenly the night before, his arms, though stretched out, remained empty.)
>
> (Prue Ramsay died that summer in some illness connected with childbirth, which was indeed a tragedy, people said, everything, they said, had promised so well.)

Even experienced readers may stop to go back. *Did that really just happen?* But to a reader unprepared to attend to manipulations of time, such narrative tricks can be land mines; students can spend a hundred pages wondering whether Mrs. Ramsay is alive or not.

## Recurrence of Events

An event can happen only once in real life. But anyone who has a certain uncle knows that a story can be retold and revisited time and time again—in the same or slightly different versions. A narrative that revisits and retells an event multiple times can disorient a reader.

In short, storytelling doesn't obey any rules in terms of how time elapses. The manipulation of time is one of the primary tools authors use to shape a reader's perception of events—and can be a primary source of confusion for students. For these reasons, it's important to ensure that students gain experience with texts that manipulate time.

## Out of Order! Texts with Nonlinear Time Sequence

Here are a few favorites for introducing nonlinear time sequence.

| Title | Author |
|---|---|
| One Candle | Bunting, Eve |
| The Barn | Avi |
| Putnam and Pennyroyal | Jennings, Patrick |
| Farm Boy | Morpurgo, Michael |
| Holes | Sachar, Louis |
| Time Pieces: The Book of Times | Hamilton, Virginia |
| Three Brave Women | Martin, C.L.G. |
| Alice's Adventures in Wonderland | Carroll, Lewis |
| The Summer My Father Was Ten | Brisson, Pat |
| Walk Two Moons | Creech, Sharon |
| The Chocolate War | Cormier, Robert |
| The Time Traveler's Wife | Niffenegger, Audrey |
| The Great Gatsby | Fitzgerald, F. Scott |
| Slaughterhouse-Five | Vonnegut, Kurt |
| A Christmas Carol | Dickens, Charles |
| Catch-22 | Heller, Joseph |

## PLAGUE 3: COMPLEXITY OF NARRATOR

R. J. Palacio's popular 2012 youth novel, *Wonder,* uses six different narrators to tell its story. One of them is the protagonist, Auggie, a middle school student with severe craniofacial disfigurement, but he narrates just three of the chapters. Five other characters narrate a chapter each—each one in a different voice, and with one of them, Justin, telling his version without uppercase letters and with idiosyncratic punctuation. It's a useful book, first and foremost, as an object lesson in kindness and understanding;

but it's also a starter kit for understanding books whose narration is complex and potentially confusing.

The challenges that narrators present can be tricky and, like the other plagues of complex text, can result in failed comprehension regardless of the degree of a student's skills. Books can have multiple narrators, nonhuman narrators, unreliable and even deceitful narrators. They can have narrators whose role or identity is unclear—is the narrator the author? They can, like E. L. Konigsberg's *From the Mixed-Up Files of Mrs. Basil E. Frankweiler*, suddenly and inexplicable begin referring directly to an unknown person (Saxonberg) as if the narrator were talking to him.

Or they can have narrators who self-consciously narrate the story, as in Lemony Snicket's book series *A Series of Unfortunate Events,* in which the narrator persistently interrupts the story to address readers directly. In one scene, for example, when the three siblings who are the books' protagonists find themselves misunderstood and ignored in a time of danger, the narrator breaks in to opine upon the meaning of the word *literally*:

> Violet stared up at the sky " . . . Perhaps we can stop and see Justice Strauss."
> "But you said she wouldn't help us," Klaus said.
> "Not for help," Violet said, "for books."
> It is very useful, when one is young, to learn the difference between "literally" and "figuratively." If something happens literally, it actually happens; if something happens figuratively, it *feels like* it's happening. If you are literally jumping for joy, for instance, it means you are leaping in the air because you are very happy. If you are figuratively jumping for joy, it means you are so happy that you *could* jump for joy, but are saving your energy for other matters. The Baudelaire orphans walked back to Count Olaf's neighborhood and stopped at the home of Justice Strauss, who welcomed them inside and let them choose books from the library.

It's fun and engaging when you are prepared for and familiar with a bit of self-consciously absurd narration, but very, very disorienting if you've never seen or imagined a narrator like this before.

Narrative complexity can be trickier yet as students engage increasingly complex texts, such as Edgar Allen Poe's short story "The Tell-Tale Heart," a story told by a narrator who is insane. But there's crazy (*Boy, he rants a lot*) and there's *crazy*: he is fundamentally detached from reality, and events he describes as having transpired may not in fact have happened at all! It's a difficult story anyway—the prose is archaic, and the ravings are, well, ravings—but the difficulty level is doubled for readers who have never read a book with an unreliable narrator and thus may fail even to consider that a narrator could be lying or hallucinating. Miss that and you miss most of the story. It's important for students to experience a wide variety of narrators throughout their schooling so that they are prepared when they encounter texts like "The Tell-Tale Heart" in high school and college.

Complex narration is often used when writers attempt to tell a story for which they find traditional narration insufficient. They present — to the reader who is able to come to terms with them — distinctive perspectives that stretch the range of storytelling. In Mark Haddon's *The Curious Incident of the Dog in the Night-time,* for example, an autistic narrator is characterized in part by what he perceives and, as an astute reader recognizes, what he does not. Through his distinctive perceptions, a condition like autism becomes, for the first time, narratable — a fascinating literary development that is, unfortunately, inaccessible to readers who aren't prepared for its complexity.

## Complex Voice: Complex Narration for Different Grades

What follows here is a list of texts showcasing a variety of complex narrators. As with other texts in this chapter, if read aloud by an adult, a number of these can be introduced earlier than the recommended grade level.

| Title | Author |
| --- | --- |
| And the Dish Ran Away with the Spoon | Stevens, Janet |
| The True Story of the Three Little Pigs | Scieszka, Jon |
| The Three Little Wolves and the Big Bad Pig | Trivizas, Eugene |
| A Tale Dark and Grimm | Gidwitz, Adam |
| Wonder | Palacio, R. J. |
| The Underneath | Appelt, Kathi |
| The Curious Incident of the Dog in the Night-time | Haddon, Mark |
| The Book Thief | Zusak, Markus |
| A Series of Unfortunate Events [series] | Snicket, Lemony |
| The Bluest Eye | Morrison, Toni |
| Ghost Hawk | Cooper, Susan |
| As I Lay Dying | Faulkner, William |

# PLAGUE 4: COMPLEXITY OF STORY (PLOT AND SYMBOLISM)

To prepare students to read successfully, teachers must also expose them to texts with multifarious and complex plot structures. To point out the obvious, following multiple plots and multiple interwoven plots is harder than following a single plot. Disorientation as to how the pieces of a story fit together can cause students to miss inferences they are supposed to make, to not understand who is and isn't in the room when character Y is speaking. This is exponentially true when the interweaving is not clearly demarcated by the author or when the distinctions in plot lines are hard to discern.

Our colleague Daisy Christodoulou found this out recently during a unit on *A Midsummer Night's Dream*. Reading papers over several school years gave Daisy and her colleagues at ARK schools in England the hunch that a deep-lying haziness about plot elements — what exactly happened to whom, when — resulted in muddied analysis. They decided to make absolutely certain that students could disentangle the interwoven plots of Shakespeare's comedy — with a thoroughness they had never attempted before. Only then did they ask for analytical essays on the topic of whether Demetrius's free will is taken away by the fact that the love potion is not removed from his eyes. Daisy noted, "In order to discuss this, you have to be really clear about the fact that Demetrius is in love with Hermia at the start but Helena at the end. If you can't grasp the plot, you can't start to discuss the big issues about what true love and free will are."

But their effort to tame the complexity of the play's plot paid off. "The final essays were brilliant, totally unlike previous years." Sophisticated analysis was grounded in the ability to track and unwind a complex plot.

Grace Lin's Newberry Award–winning novel, *Where the Mountain Meets the Moon,* is a modern story that melds the tradition of Chinese folk tales with a western journey-of-discovery narrative. It's a bit like *The Wizard of Oz* retold as a Chinese fairy tale, Lin has observed. However, *Where the Mountain Meets the Moon* is more complex than that; it weaves fairy tales into the plot of the book. Characters tell other characters stories, and those stories are inserted within the novel for readers as well — texts within a text.

Not only that, but the characters in the book, who are imagined to hear the fairy tales as the reader reads them, often react to the tales, and this shapes the plot. It's recursive: the tales change the story; the book reacts to itself. In the end, its theme probably has to do with the way stories and real life become intertwined in the consciousness. Only through these complex plot devices can the book challenge readers' conception of how storytelling works; but before that, it challenges their basic comprehension. For that reason, it's an outstanding text to read with students. It's simple and accessible in some ways—perfect for a fourth grader, perhaps—and also a book that teaches students how to manage complex and unconventional plots. It's both a complex and a pre-complex text at the same time.

But complex plots aren't the only way that story elements can make a text hard for readers to follow. The use of symbolism is essentially a way to add a plot layer. And we're not just talking about pulling out and examining individual symbols that might be tangential to the plot. Often a network of symbols is foundational to understanding a story. For example, *Animal Farm,* most readers know, is a retelling of the communist revolution in the guise of a story about pigs who take over a farm; each character is a symbol for one of the historic figures involved in the events in Russia. All of a sudden, there is a second story line to follow and make sense of.

*Lord of the Flies* is similarly full of layers of symbolism. It's a narrative full of hints and allusions, but one more disjointed and harder to follow than *Animal Farm.* Unpacking what *all those symbols* are trying to convey is one of the primary tasks of reading the book. Intentionally exposing students to a book like that—a case study in symbolism—is a powerful tool they will leverage throughout their reading careers.

## PLAGUE 5: RESISTANT TEXT

Some texts set out to be difficult to understand, often because part of the point is that the story cannot be told simply. Telling it stretches the bounds of the tools storytellers have available. To cause a reader to struggle to make sense of a story is to communicate the struggle of making sense of it as a writer. Sometimes the gaps in meaning are part of the meaning. It takes a sophisticated reader, however, to both recognize when a text is deliberately resisting comprehension and understand how to make meaning from that lack of meaning.

Consider the beginning of Kurt Vonnegut's novel *Slaughterhouse-Five,* written in the form of a memoir of a fictional writer who, like Vonnegut himself, was taken prisoner in World War II and experienced the fire-bombing of Dresden firsthand, and has set out to tell the story of that destruction, but struggles to do so.

The book begins:

> All this happened, more or less. The war parts anyway, are pretty much true. One guy I knew really was shot in Dresden for taking a teapot that wasn't his. Another guy I knew really did threaten to have his personal enemies killed by hired gunmen after the war. And so on. I've changed all the names.

I really did go back to Dresden with Guggenheim money (God love it) in 1967. It looked a lot like Dayton, Ohio, more open spaces than Dayton has. There must be tons of human bone meal in the ground.

The book's first sentence vouches for the truthfulness of the narrative. Its second sentence immediately undercuts this alleged truthfulness when the narrator promises that, well, at least the war parts are "pretty much true." Not exactly a high bar for trustworthiness. Then the third sentence makes reference to key events in the story as if the reader knew the story already, which of course cannot be true. His storytelling is out of order. You can't rely on time, and you can't trust your narrator.

The narrator sets out to describe a historical event, yet eventually he travels in time and into outer space, blending historical fiction and memoir with science fiction. Even syntax falls apart. The sentence "It looked a lot like Dayton, Ohio, more open spaces than Dayton has" is not misprinted here. It is missing a verb in the book, too. To capture the absurdity of the events he describes, Vonnegut makes his storytelling inscrutable. Even the degree to which Vonnegut's thoughts and his narrator's overlap is unclear. The book is resistant to simple meaning-making in almost every way.

Many readers find Vonnegut exhilarating precisely because of these elements. They create a thrilling narrative unbounded by traditional rules. But a confused reader—a reader unaware that a text might deliberate try to disorient him, a reader who has never struggled with that disorientation—may in fact be confused by the premise, not comprehend that he is not supposed to comprehend, and fail to follow or perhaps even give up on the narrative.

Reading such texts can be a huge challenge, but an important one. College is full of the most boundary-pushing texts, often precisely because they push boundaries. Three key actions can prepare students to read resistant text successfully.

First, as the example of *Slaughterhouse-Five* suggests, highly resistant texts are often made resistant by the use of a combination of the other four plagues. Exposure to those elements will help students unpack even the densest texts—*The Sound and the Fury, Portrait of the Artist as a Young Man, Cane, The Things They Carried,* and so on.

Second, poetry frequently does not ascribe to the "expectation of logic" that is characteristic of (most) prose. In fact, we use the term *poetic license* to refer to the OK-ness of breaking rules in the name of art; but the real license in poetry is to be as allusive or illusive as the writer wishes. Because of this, poetry can be an outstanding tool for preparing students for resistant prose. Imagine the benefits of a lighthearted reading of

Lewis Carroll's "Jabberwocky," a primer in filling in the gaps between tiny islands of meaning in a text, as a prelude to reading *Slaughterhouse-Five*.

Third, closely reading and unpacking very short examples of resistant text are great ways to expose students to intense challenges without overwhelming them—or committing to several hundred pages of it. Many novels and stories are full of resistant moments that can be studied to gain critical experience with resistant text.

## A BIT OF PERSPECTIVE: THE PLAGUES IN PRACTICE

In the preceding pages, we've gone pretty deep in studying the factors that make complex text difficult for students. Now is a good time to step back and see the forest for the trees, and share further thoughts as to how the plagues should—and should not—affect the decisions about what to read in the classroom.

We think that the Common Core's suggestion (its designers are certainly not the only people offering it) that students should frequently read harder texts is worth heeding, but please understand that we are *not* arguing that every text you read with students needs to specifically address these plagues. A world in which students did nothing but slog through hundreds of pages of Dickens would be a pretty dark and Dickensian one. Our advice is to address the plagues with balance and judiciousness. Should you read some texts just for the sheer joy of them? Or for the power of the story a certain book tells about the world? Of course! You don't need us to tell you there are lots of other reasons to choose books than text complexity, no matter how much it helps prepare students for college. In fact, we'll discuss some of them in the next section of this chapter.

Bring harder text into your classrooms with some frequency and when you do, make it strategic—that's the point. Complex text doesn't always have to be book length, either—lots of exposure spread out over the year in small bursts is likely to help quite a bit. Just make sure that when you do the hard work of reading harder text, you do so in a way that prepares students for success. To that end, we find standard complexity algorithms (Lexiles and the like) useful but incomplete, and addressing the plagues can help you get more out of the time you invest.

Some teachers might also argue for the need to embrace the opposite of complexity and to level texts to the individual reader's skill level. We think there's value to leveling texts—at times. It certainly makes sense when you are working with students on decoding or fluency, for example. Similarly, if students are reading a book on their own, perhaps you might well want to ratchet back the difficulty level a bit to ensure success, and then steadily add challenge. But also remember that these are not either-or choices. You could let students read one text at their instructional level and another above it that poses a distinct and unique challenge. The second might require more support, but it's also critically important because low readers in particular are often balkanized to reading only lower-level books. Fed on a diet of only what's "accessible" to them—but which is also often insufficient to prepare them for college—they are consigned to lower standards from the outset by our very efforts to help them. So the question for harder text should not be whether but how, in addition to what.

You can also be strategic about how much and when you address the plagues. We want students to have lots of experiences that prepare them for the real challenges of reading, but these might be small experiences or big ones. It could be that you read *The Magician's Nephew*. It could be that you bring in snippets of challenging text of different stripes and varieties or that you use a combination of Read-Aloud, shared reading, and silent reading (we discuss this more in chapter 5, Approaches to Reading), or that you are merely especially attentive when elements of the plagues emerge in what you're already reading.

Finally, we should note that there is clearly a sixth "plague"—a further area of difficulty—and that is nonfiction. Our five plagues deal almost exclusively with fiction or narrative nonfiction (biography, memoir); nonnarrative nonfiction, we note, is at least as challenging to young readers: densely packed with information, full of unique conventions that students are far less familiar with. So important is this topic that we have given it its own full discussion in chapter 3.

With that said, some discipline is required because many of the incentives are stacked against seeking long-run benefits. To truly ensure our students' success, we must expose them to complex (or at least pre-complex) texts relatively early and relatively often, including during their elementary and middle school years, while there is time to steadily and gradually develop their comfort and skill with the various types of challenge these texts create. There is little immediate incentive to choose a tricky text with an unreliable narrator or archaic language, say, over something easier or more popular. The absence would likely go unnoticed and the short-term benefits—"Hey, we're reading *Hunger Games*!"—would be obvious. It is quite possible that only years later, long after our students have passed on down the years, would they reap the deferred rewards of a decision by their teacher to teach complex texts.

So far, in discussing choices about what to read, we have for the most part focused on text generally, especially on technical elements that make its specific passages challenging. We have assumed that the texts would often be books, but they don't necessarily need to be. In this module, we turn to the topic of books and consider aspects of the whole, rather than the parts. We believe in books, great ones, read cover to cover, and we think most great teachers do too.

It is important to recognize that the books students read and study in school are finite—a scarce and valuable resource. From middle school through twelfth grade, a typical student might read and intentionally study forty or fifty books in English classes (assuming five or six books per year from fifth through twelfth grade)—we hope more, but some students surely will read fewer. These few books form the foundation of their knowledge of how literature works within and interacts with society, so teachers must select them like the precious resource they are. Teachers should consider not just whether each book their students read is "good" but also what the totality of the texts they choose for students accomplishes as part of their broader education.

Such scarcity implies the importance of mediated book choice. Of course students should have a book that they are reading on their own. And occasionally it's surely fine for students to read their own book choices in class. But there is power in shared reading in the classroom—power that is generally underrated.

## Other Text Choices

While we make the case here for reading books as frequently as possible, text selection should also include plays, poems, short stories, and articles. Here are a few thoughts on each:

### *Short stories*

Short stories are low-risk ways to introduce daring texts; when making bold experiments in expanding students' range in and exposure to different types of text complexity, fifteen-page experiments are often more forgiving than three-hundred-page experiments.

*(Continued)*

*(Continued)*

You can also study a short story in a few days versus a novel's few weeks. That shorter duration often makes it easier to see its narrative structure and more viable to reread it, allowing students to glimpse the development of ideas and themes with the beneficial knowledge of how everything ends up. Nothing builds meta-awareness of how narratives work like rereading a full narrative. Because they can demonstrate an aspect of theme and structure in such a short space, stories can be especially powerful when paired: two examples of satire; two unreliable narrators; two third-person narratives with different degrees of omniscience.

Read more about the particular benefits of short stories on Doug's *Field Notes* blog here: http://teachlikeachampion.com/blog/particular-benefits-short-stories/.

## Poetry

As we noted earlier, poetry is frequently resistant. That it is often about its own resistance to meaning makes poetry a great tool for familiarizing students with the experience of reading challenging text, of filling in the gaps around what you know. It's also ideal for establishing meaning with very challenging language. Like short stories, poetry can let you dive into intensely challenging text without committing to three hundred or so pages of *Autumn of the Patriarch*.

## Articles, essays, and excerpts

Articles and excerpts are at their best when connected and often compared to a book (more on this topic in our chapter on nonfiction). It's worth noting here, however, just how many types of articles and excerpts there are. Consider the book review, for example—how often our students approximate its forms while rarely, if ever, seeing a professional example of the form. Consider, also, the lowly obituary. Our colleague Peter Sipe, at Boston Collegiate High School, reads an obituary with his class every Friday. "An obituary," he notes, "is the story of a life; death is just the detail that gets it printed." "It's real character education, the past made present," he adds, and his students have studied the lives of the famous, the infamous, and the unknown alike.

One of the greatest gifts a teacher can give students is a book they might never have considered or known, brought to life through great teaching. Yet we often find ourselves reading blog posts with titles like "How to Get Kids to Read—Let Them Pick Their Own Damn Books" and "Why Do We Force Students to Read Shakespeare?"[4] It is to us a form of low expectations to assume that students will not find that they like what they knew nothing about, or presumed they wouldn't like, before they began reading it. For example, Doug recently visited a school for elite athletes where the students chose their own books, and many were reading—surprise!—biographies of elite athletes. Why? Good intentions: the school wanted them to love what they read. But must we assume that what they know they already like (at age fourteen, say) is all they are capable of liking or learning valuable things from? We can each name a handful of texts we read against our better teenage judgment (infallible though it seemed at the time), but that turned out to be transformative—instantly in many cases, years later in others. The world of experience turned out to be slightly broader than our wizened teenage frameworks quite contemplated. We argue, therefore, for unrepentant teacher guidance on what to read—not necessarily on every book, but with frequency.

Another loss, for those elite athletes reading their chosen books, was that they read their books in isolation. They never heard anyone else's interpretation of their books; they never were pushed to rethink what they first assumed. We see this trend frequently. There seem to us to be an increasing number of classrooms in which teachers let their students decide what to read, not just for independent reading but for their class work. "Read a book and respond to these questions about it." "Read a book and write a journal entry about it." In either case, the assumption is that the process of describing your own reflections is the primary work of the classroom, rather than refining ideas in discussion with others and making sense of different readings of a book. In fact, there is power in shared text, and there are a number of important factors to consider in choosing books. We look at these in the next several sections.

## LITERARY UTILITY

Some books pay it forward in the literary sense. They help students read and understand other books. For example, a book might provide an especially clear model of an idea (satire) or a common structural element (first-person narrative voice). Or a book might break a convention. *All Quiet on the Western Front* tells the compelling story of its protagonist Paul's coming of age, and disillusionment, as a soldier. He's a character readers come to know deeply and to respect. They see the world through his eyes. All of this is characteristic of the subgenre of war (or antiwar) novels—though one could argue that *All Quiet* is among the high-water marks of them. However, in a short coda on the last page, Paul is killed. This is not the way stories are supposed to proceed: the main character, the protagonist, is supposed to live to the end and share what he's learned amid the travail. The book manages to challenge a key convention of storytelling, which makes it an ideal tool for analyzing texts thereafter. Students will have reason to reflect on each ending they read and see it as a decision with alternatives they'd never contemplated before. The coda also reminds us of an important benefit of shared text in the classroom. One child of a colleague read *All Quiet* on his own and did not notice the last page. For weeks after, he had no idea that the novel ended with the protagonists' death or indeed that this was the point of the novel. Shared discussion mitigates the risk of misreading.

## LITERARY SIGNIFICANCE AND CULTURAL CAPITAL

Besides functioning as tools to help students understand other books or aspects of storytelling, many titles are significant for their own sake. Knowing them gives the reader a certain amount of cultural capital.

Consider this scene from Ron Suskind's *A Hope in the Unseen*, the story of Cedric Jennings, who makes it to the Ivy League from a struggling high school in Washington DC where few male students even graduate, never mind go on to college. Cedric arrives at Brown University and finds himself in the bookstore, trying to select his courses.

> He begins to wander, gazing at titles and authors: Sylvia Plath's *The Bell Jar*, Hemingway's *For Whom the Bell Tolls*, a biography of Theodore Roosevelt, another of Woodrow Wilson. All people from another country. Some of the names sound vaguely familiar. Most draw a blank . . .
>
> He looks to his left. Martin Gilbert's new biography *Churchill, A Life* is piled five feet high . . .
>
> Oh god, he thinks. I should know who that is.[5]

Later, Cedric has a similar experience with Virginia Woolf, Karl Marx, and other intellectuals of western culture with whom children of privilege are familiar, able to make casual reference to without knowing how they know. Cedric becomes painfully aware that he is unable to participate in any of these conversations, not to mention class discussions, because he is cut off from the cultural allusions the rest of the students take for granted. He doesn't know there's a canon to critique, scorn, consider, or what-have-you, and this, more than anything else, sets him up as an outsider.

On the same theme, here is an excerpt from a piece by James Theobald, a teacher in the United Kingdom and one of our favorite bloggers. It describes the first steps in his journey to university, having grown up in a family where further study was not the expectation.

> I was in the bottom set. The head of English knocked on the door and said that a few people from the class were going to have to move from this class to the top set. The top set wasn't very full and this bottom set class was bursting at the seams. They asked for volunteers. I turned to a mate who was sat in my row: he nodded at me and we put our hands up. I think about 4 or 5 of us went. I don't know if anyone else volunteered, but we were pointed at, asked to grab our stuff and we left the lads to whatever it is those lads did for the next two years. We were going to the top set.
>
> What I really remember is the reading. We read texts from cover to cover. And we read lots. We read 'To Kill a Mockingbird'; we read 'Macbeth' and 'Romeo and Juliet'; we read 'The Mayor of Casterbridge.' And we talked about what we were reading. And something happened to me: I found out I loved reading. I didn't always understand everything that I was reading (I was lower ability) and I didn't always enjoy the texts that I was reading. But I enjoyed learning from them. And I learned lots. I can remember really disliking Hardy at the time, but I also can recall learning all about fate and determinism and how interesting it was. Years later, at university, it was this formative experience that allowed me to flourish in reading texts within a critical context.
>
> I'm not from a family that placed any emphasis on higher education. I was encouraged to go out to work after finishing A levels. And go out to work is what I did. And then, in my late 20s, I decided to go to university. I worked 4 days a week whilst also studying full-time for my degree. It was a bit unfashionable to do so, but I read everything they put on my reading lists. The bottom set pupil. Who hated reading.
>
> The one single thing that got me where I am today is the cultural capital I was endowed with in being made to read Hardy and Shakespeare from cover to cover. So, please don't tell me it is elitist to teach pupils great works of 19th century literature. It's elitist NOT to teach these texts to everyone. It's elitist to leave these to the top set pupils or those pupils whose parents buy them an expensive education.[6]

The fact is that some books matter more than others, get discussed more than others, both in life and by other texts. Only those who already know those books can afford the luxury of dismissing this fact. Our purpose is not to suggest that every book students read has to be a classic in the traditional sense, but rather that students who use education to gain access to new opportunities are most likely to rely exclusively on school for the cultural knowledge that will serve them in that journey.

## KNOWLEDGE DEVELOPMENT

"The brain," notes cognitive scientist Annie Murphy Paul in her piece "What Happens in Our Brains as We Read," "does not make much of a distinction between reading about an experience and encountering it in real life; in each case, the same neurological regions are stimulated."[7] This is a fascinating observation—and one that Murphy Paul has followed up on to show a variety of applications. For example, in her article for *Time* called "Reading Literature Makes Us Smarter and Nicer," Murphy Paul explains that reading, it turns out, builds empathy in students who read frequently and deeply (for long, steady, uninterrupted periods—the opposite of how you read online, by the way). These readers act as if they had lived through the experiences they read about. The brain does not distinguish.[8]

One further application of this idea is in the area of knowledge development. As cognitive scientist Daniel Willingham pointed out in his piece called "School Time, Knowledge, and Reading Comprehension," one of the strongest drivers of reading ability is prior knowledge:

> Once kids are fluent decoders, much of the difference among readers is not due to whether you're a "good reader" or "bad reader" (meaning you have good or bad reading skills). Much of the difference among readers is due to how wide a range of knowledge they have. If you hand me a reading test and the text is on a subject I happen to know a bit about, I'll do better than if it happens to be on a subject I know nothing about . . . Teaching content IS teaching reading.[9]

Although it appears to be true that studying subjects like science and history, especially in a content-rich manner, results in stronger reading achievement, it is also true that one of the ways that students gain knowledge is by reading deeply and widely. Not all reading develops knowledge in readers at the same rate, because of both how we read (a topic we take up in our chapter on nonfiction) and what we read. Reading lots of historical fiction—good historical fiction, that is—builds knowledge, as does reading about cultures and settings unfamiliar to you. So ensuring that students read widely and read about things constructively unfamiliar to them is something teachers should take seriously.

Consider, for example, this vignette about the principal of a school we knew with a population of almost entirely urban minority kids and unusually high reading results. When we visited her, she made a comment that seemed odd at first: "I won't stand for my teachers assigning books over and over with narrators who are minority kids living in the city," she said.

This was a surprise. She was passionate about the lives of urban and minority kids. She called developing minority scholars her family business. (Her mother had been the first Black school administrator in a major city.) What was she doing advocating for fewer protagonists who were instantly accessible to her students? She went on: "They *know* that world already. They live it every day. One or two books like that a year is enough. Then they need to read about the rest of the world. They need to read about protagonists who lived in Germany during the Holocaust. They need to read science fiction, just like other kids. They need to see themselves in the worlds of powerful narrators, not just disempowered ones. They need to read Greek myths."

Later that day, we observed her teaching a model lesson for her teachers. Her eighth graders were reading *The Great Gatsby*.

## DISCIPLINARY LITERACY

A small, final point, mostly for high school teachers: literature is a discipline. It has a history—one of which writers are hyperaware. Mark Twain wrote the way he did because Chaucer wrote the way he did, both of them relying on a slightly shocking folksy vernacular, the latter influencing the former to adapt his style five hundred years later. And Hemingway wrote the way he did because he loved Twain's direct and realistic language. He believed that American literature started with *The Adventures of Huckleberry Finn,* and sought to emulate it, this time more like fifty years later.

Perhaps this notion of influence sounds like something from a bygone era. Consider, then, the comment of 2015 Man Booker Prize winner Marlon James. *The Economist* described his winning novel *A Brief History of Seven Killings* as one that "retells the story of this near-mythic assassination attempt [on singer Bob Marley] through myriad voices . . . to create a rich, polyphonic study of violence, politics and the musical legacy of Kingston of the 1970s." Could there be a more postmodern novel? Could there be a more complex narrative voice? Of his writing, James observed, "I still consider myself a Dickensian."[10] To understand writers and their texts, even today, one must be at least somewhat aware of the way authors inherit ideas from one another. There is value in teaching texts in chronological order and letting students glimpse how ideas develop and are passed down.

| MODULE 1.5 | Managing Selection |
|---|---|

We've spent most of this chapter describing factors teachers should consider when selecting texts, and one takeaway might be that it's challenging business: there are so many factors to consider and manage across one teacher's or multiple teachers' reading choices, and the decisions require so much knowledge of so many texts. In this module, we discuss something that can help address those challenges: how you or your school thinks about the selection *process*. Managing the selection and, especially, involving teams of teachers in the task can make choosing result in higher-quality texts, more coordination across a school, better teacher development opportunities, and a more sustainable workload for individuals.

## THE INTERNAL CANON

One of the most important things you can do to get the most out of text selection is coordinate. A cultural canon may be obsolete, but a schoolwide canon—a set of best books read across classrooms so all teachers can refer back to it, with "best" defined as a rich, diverse sampling of engaging and useful books that serve students over time—is an idea that is quite practicable. And its benefits are myriad.

First, teachers and students can reliably refer to a body of other texts and know that others in the room will have read them. They can be rigorously intertextual.

Also, teachers don't have to decide all by themselves what's best to teach. They can get together and decide as a group, sharing the intellectual load and perhaps leveraging the wisdom of crowds, knowing that as a group they will likely choose the best books.

Of course, this canon does not have to encompass every book teachers teach in a given year. You could decide that the internal canon within your school would specify two shared books a year, say. The rest of the books are theirs to choose.

Beyond the classroom, shared selection of books has two very large benefits for teachers—benefits that should not be overlooked.

First, it allows *teachers* to have conversations about books. If everyone is reading *Lord of the Flies,* there are people with whom to discuss interpreting the book for and with students. Perhaps you missed the symbolism in the first lines. At least some of your peers probably did not. One of the best ways to help students learn to Close Read difficult texts (more in the next chapter) is for teachers to get together and practice doing so themselves.

Having shared texts also helps improve teacher training by making it text-specific. All of us getting together to script great writing prompts from the novels we're teaching is good professional development. But *great* professional development is all of us getting together to script great writing prompts about the same novel, which we all are teaching. We could share great ideas, understand them better, and borrow and adapt one another's questions. We could share the workload and mutually plan lessons. Experienced teachers could share lesson plans with their junior colleagues so that they wouldn't have to reinvent the wheel—especially while still learning the ropes of the classroom. These are no small things.

## TEXT SELECTION PROCESS

In many schools, it has become a teacher's prerogative alone to choose what he or she wishes to read with students. In many cases, this is not something that the school even manages. Rarely does a teacher, say, present a list of his books for the year to his department head and ask, "Is this a good list?" Even more rarely do teachers get together and say, "Let's all teach these books in the seventh grade this year." Even more rarely yet does a school say, "These are some books we'd like all of our seventh-grade teachers to read." Text selection is increasingly personal and not something that schools and districts conceive of as being appropriate to manage.

---

## Giving Up Autonomy Once You've Had It

In a world where text selection is increasingly not managed, it can be tricky to get teachers to come around to giving up autonomy. But as shared texts can be so immensely valuable, it's worth thinking a bit more about how to accomplish such a shift. For a better sense of what such a process might

*(Continued)*

---

(Continued)

look like, we asked Alex Quigley, director of learning at Huntington School in York, England, and David Noah, principal of Success Academy Harlem East—schools with impressive reading results—to tell us about the process.

"Was it hard to get teachers to be comfortable giving up their right to read whatever they wanted?"

"Yes," they both answered emphatically, but both also persevered and were glad they did. Ultimately, so were most of the teachers.

Alex wanted students to experience at least some of their texts each year in chronological order so that students could understand the historical context of each book—how it was developing or rejecting what came before. He also wanted to be more intentional about ensuring that students were exposed in a systematic way to specific genres and styles. He asked teachers at each grade level to teach the same books and to coordinate across grade levels. He let teachers work in groups to choose the actual books, but they had to agree to select as a group and with his sign-off.

In David's network, an English team chooses books and maps the daily lessons. Lesson planning for teachers is deciding how to adapt the lesson plan to their specific students—and what data from previous lessons revealed about what the students knew (and didn't). David's check-ins with teachers were backwards from what most school leaders do: instead of meeting after a lesson to give teachers feedback, he met with them before the lesson. They framed exactly how they would address the skill or knowledge they were working to build. They rehearsed, making the actual lesson better before it even went live. That's a powerful professional development insight in and of itself. But it's worth noting that only the fact that all of his ELA teachers were working on the same books—books he could read over the summer to ensure that he was prepared to lead them in teaching—enabled him to use this approach.

What students read is among the most important considerations a school can address. As such, the decision, even if it is made independently by each teacher, deserves to be managed. This might take a variety of forms. It might involve a teacher merely asking for feedback from others. It might involve a school setting goals and asking for a response. It could involve vesting teachers to make shared decisions. It could involve constrained choice. It could involve increasing levels of autonomy for more experienced teachers and more prescriptiveness for younger teachers. It could involve working, individually or in groups, with a set of text selection guidelines or reflection questions—for example, "What kinds of complex texts will your students see over the course of the year?"—that requires analysis and assessment of books. Or it could involve a fixed curriculum.

Whatever way text selection is managed, it's simply too important not to manage. And if it's done well, management of text selection can serve teachers by developing their knowledge and insight through reflection and feedback.

## Text Selection, Reconsidered

If teachers want to ensure maximum achievement in reading and maximum readiness for college, text selection deserves greater attention and intentionality. This does not mean that every book needs to be selected using a "maximum value for learning" calculation. Some should be; we hope many will. Choosing others sheerly for the pleasure of it or on a lark is fine as long as the overall portfolio of books is intentional and balanced. Thinking more deeply about aspects of the texts we choose for students does not exclude enjoyment as a criterion— even a major one. With study and reflection, these categories need not be mutually exclusive; part of the joy of teaching, in fact, is seeing the joy students derive unexpectedly from texts that surprise them.

With the hurdle of text selection cleared, the next step is, of course, reading itself. In much the same way that not all texts are created equal, neither are all types of reading. In the next chapter, we'll take a look at one way to get the most out of your in-class reading time and in particular to address the challenges posed by complex texts: Close Reading.

## NOTES

1. The National Rading Panel's April 2000 report, *Teaching Children to Read: An Evidence-Based Assessment of the Scientific Research Literature on Reading and Its Implications* (http://www.nichd.nih.gov/publications/pubs/nrp/documents/report.pdf) observes that the belief that reading is "the construction of the meaning of a written text through a reciprocal interchange of ideas between the reader and...a particular text," as opposed to a less reciprocal process of

meaning-making wherein, say, the reader's task is to understand an author's intended argument, can be traced to one of the "important developments" around 1970. In other words, the conception of the purpose reading as developing your own interpretation rather than understanding what you were intended to understand is a late-twentieth-century notion. The panel continues: "The explicit teaching of text comprehension before the 1970s was done largely in content areas and not in the formal context of reading instruction" (4–39).

2. Matthew Arnold, *Culture and Anarchy* (London: Smith, Elder, 1869), viii.

3. Nick Turner, *Post-War British Women Novelists and the Canon* (London: Continuum, 2010). Chapter 1 of Turner's book, "Theories of the Canon," is an outstanding extended discussion of the history of the word *canon* and its application. The specific reference to the advent of the current meaning in the 1980s is discussed on page 11.

4. Lauren Katz, "How to Get Kids to Read—Let Them Pick Their Own Damn Books," *Vox Xpress,* April 30, 2015, http://www.vox.com/2015/1/15/7545757/kids-books; Rajat Bhageria, "Why Do We Force Kids to Read Shakespeare?" *The Blog, Huff Post Education,* January 13, 2015, http://www.huffingtonpost.com/rajat-bhageria/why-do-our-schools-force-_b_6443672.html.

5. Ron Suskind, *A Hope in the Unseen* (New York: Crown/Archetype, 2010), 184.

6. James Theobald, "'Elitism'? Be Careful How You Use That Word," *Othmar's Trombone* (blog), March 6, 2012, https://othmarstrombone.wordpress.com/2014/03/06/elitism-be-careful-how-you-use-that-word/.

7. Annie Murphy Paul, "What Happens in Our Brains as We Read," *The Brilliant Blog,* April 21, 2014, http://anniemurphypaul.com/2014/04/what-happens-in-our-brains-as-we-read/.

8. Annie Murphy Paul, "Reading Literature Makes Us Smarter and Nicer," *Time,* June 3, 2013, http://ideas.time.com/2013/06/03/why-we-should-read-literature/.

9. Daniel Willingham, "School Time, Knowledge, and Reading Comprehension," *Daniel Willingham* (blog), March 7, 2012, http://www.danielwillingham.com/daniel-willingham-science-and-education-blog/school-time-knowledge-and-reading-comprehension.

10. "A Big Win for Marlon James," *Prospero* (blog), *Economist,* October 13, 2015, http://www.economist.com/blogs/prospero/2015/10/man-booker-prize.

# Close Reading

## MODULE 2.1: LAYERED READING

Great teachers show students how to strategically get the most out of complex passages.

## MODULE 2.2: ESTABLISH MEANING VIA TEXT-DEPENDENT QUESTIONS

The rigor and value of establishing meaning correlate to the rigor and value of the text.

## MODULE 2.3: CLOSE READING TO ANALYZE MEANING

True analysis is text focused and evidence based.

## MODULE 2.4: PROCESSING IDEAS AND INSIGHTS IN WRITING, AND THE POWER OF CLEAR FOCUS

Writing and a reading focus can up the rigor and value of Close Reading lessons.

## MODULE 2.5: CLOSE READING BURSTS

Bursts of Close Reading make for frequent practice and foster independence.

# Chapter 2

# Close Reading

In the Introduction, we identified the four key ideas that make up the Core of the Core:

1. Read harder texts

2. Read more nonfiction

3. Write in direct response to texts

4. "Close read" texts frequently

It's pretty clear what the first three mean in a day-to-day sense. However, among the four, Close Reading stands out, both because it is the most difficult to define clearly and because it is so important. One of the end goals of teaching is to instill in students the ability to wrestle with the most demanding texts, interpret them independently, and understand why and how they mean what they do. Close Reading does this, and that makes it critically important.

Still, important but undefined ideas are at risk of falling victim to cognitive bias and the inertia of doing what we've always done. One common definition of Close

Reading says, "Close reading means reading to uncover layers of meaning that lead to deep comprehension."[1] What teacher doesn't believe that she already does that? Then again, who wouldn't be inclined not to change much when asked to make a somewhat ill-defined change *and being measured doing it*? Of course teachers are tempted to fall back on what they know best! Without clarity around what to do or how to do it, the incentives are stacked against substantive change.

So what exactly is Close Reading? How do you do it? Why do you do it? And what separates magnificent from mundane? This chapter sets out to answer these questions. To begin, let's take a look at why Close Reading is so important. There are three especially compelling reasons.

First, Close Reading helps defend against "gist" readings—interpretations and discussions that are "based on" the text, but not grounded in a comprehensive understanding of it. Students will not succeed if they can observe in only a general sense that Hamlet is unhappy, or summarize the Bill of Rights broadly but not understand the specific language used to frame each individual right, or understand, generally, that glucose levels in the blood affect health, but not how. Close Reading ensures that students are able to glean specific and comprehensive understanding from even very difficult texts.

Second, Close Reading is the tool that allows students to read text that is over their heads—one of the fundamental experiences of attending (or preparing for) college. Reading that is frequently demanding and often done alone, generally without the safety net of peers to discuss it, is the way much learning takes place there. If students can read and learn from what is challenging and unfamiliar, the world is open to them; if they are intimidated by challenging texts, their horizons are limited. Even though it can be difficult to teach students to read outside their comfort zone, it is folly not to.

Finally, Close Reading develops "language sense." It develops in students an "ear" for word, syntax, rhythm, and structure that is applicable across texts. The ear for satire you sharpen in reading Roald Dahl helps you read Jonathan Swift years later.

## CLOSE READING DEFINED

Arriving at a definition of Close Reading is no simple task, however. As with any carefully wrought text in which the author feels strongly about an idea, the language of our definition has shifted and evolved over time. After discussing and refining it through dozens of conversations with colleagues, we arrived here:

**Close Reading is the methodical breaking down of the language and structure of a complex passage to establish and analyze its meaning. Teaching students to do it requires layered reading and asking sequenced, text-dependent questions; and it should end whenever possible with mastery expressed through writing.**

We hope this definition proves sturdy and useful and that by the end of the chapter, it can serve to guide your implementation of Close Reading, but in the meantime, the definition itself may require a bit of close reading of its own. Here is an unpacking of some of its key terms.

**Close Reading is:**

*methodical* ... This word communicates the thoroughness implicit in Close Reading a segment of text. To Close Read is to study both the parts that fascinate readers right away and those that may escape initial notice; it is to work diligently to make sense of the parts that resist meaning-making even after several passes.

*breaking down* ... If you work with engines, you must be able to take one apart to understand how fuel enters the cylinder, expands, drives the piston, and moves the crankshaft. Close Reading involves taking apart a complex passage to understand how a sequence of specific words takes on a biting irony and hints at a character's true nature.

*of the language and structure* ... Close Reading includes the study of language — the denotation and connotation of words, the meaning of phrases both formal and idiomatic, the subtleties of subordination in sentences — and the study of structure: how the elements of language are placed near to or far from each other, the way they repeat or echo one another, the way they build or break a rhythm.

*of a complex passage* ... Close Reading is a set of tools for unlocking complex texts. Challenge is a part of the formula. If the text being read closely isn't difficult, a primary rationale is missing. There is no reason to methodically break down an easy text, and trying will likely leave the endeavor appearing to be without value. The proof lies in the flash of insight gleaned from what once seemed a thicket of words, impenetrable like brambles.

*to establish and analyze its meaning.* Establishing meaning is locking down an argument or narrative thoroughly and with precision. It explains: here is what the passage says, all of it — even when it's very hard to determine. Analyzing meaning explains how that argument is formed, what forces shape it, and how those forces can be used to build disciplined, text-based interpretation. The tasks of establishing and analyzing meaning are *equally critical* and require one another. A quality analysis requires careful establishment of meaning; establishing meaning is sustainable only if it leads, ultimately, to student insights and epiphanies.

*It requires layered readings*... Students need to read a challenging text more than once. Ideally, each reading would be *different,* with the changes in approach modeling the kind of problem solving implicit in deciding *how* to reread a passage when it proves difficult.

*and asking sequenced, text-dependent questions*... Asking readers of Martin Luther King's "Letter from Birmingham Jail," "Do you agree that injustice anywhere is an affront to justice everywhere?" is a worthy question, but teachers also should recognize a question that savvy, well-informed students can answer whether or not they have read and understood the depth of Dr. King's arguments. Text-dependent questions are specific and can be answered only when students have read carefully and understood an author's specific arguments. They do not preclude other worthy questions; in fact they often precede them.

*and...with mastery expressed through writing.* Asking students to write causes them to express their opinions in the most rigorous and important format in which society expresses its ideas. And writing has permanence: it can be revised, and referred to again and again, used to show students the development of their ideas over time. And at the end of a lesson, having asked your students to write allows you to assess not only whether the class *generally* understood the text but also whether *each student* was able to make sense of it.

## Two Tracks to Close Reading

There are two primary ways to bring Close Reading into your classroom: a Close Reading lesson and a Close Reading "burst." In a Close Reading lesson, you select a passage of substantive length—perhaps a paragraph, perhaps several. For advanced Close Readers, you might perhaps choose an essay with certain sections read with intense focus. A Close Reading lesson has four parts—four tasks you should ask students to do in methodically breaking down challenging text—and you commit the better part of an hour to them. The four parts are as follows:

1. Use layered readings to read the text multiple times.

2. Establish meaning via text-dependent questions.

3.  Analyze meaning also via text-dependent questions.

4.  Process insights in writing.

Although the four parts often occur roughly in the order we've listed, they need not necessarily; even when they do, the parts almost always overlap. In short, we deliberately call the elements of a Close Reading lesson "parts," not "steps."

But Close Reading is also a skill that can be practiced in units of shorter duration; such practice can take place when you recognize that a line or two from a text requires greater focus. Although these moments can be planned in advance, they can also happen spontaneously. A challenging sentence — one you had not realized would be so tricky — suddenly reveals itself in class. You pause and unleash your Close Reading tools upon the challenge. Whether planned or impromptu, these Close Reading bursts are short but intensive studies of a more limited section of text.

In this chapter, we'll look at both approaches in greater detail. Each of the first four modules looks closely at a key part of a Close Reading lesson; the last module tackles Close Reading bursts.

| MODULE 2.1 | Layered Reading |
| --- | --- |

As a student, you faced a crisis, during college or in the school that prepared you to go there. Late at night, perhaps, holed up on the top floor of the library, you had William Faulkner or Ralph Ellison or Mary Wollstonecraft in front of you. On first reading, it was a mystery. Let's say it was Ellison. You read: "That invisibility to which I refer occurs because of a peculiar disposition of the eyes of those with whom I come in contact. A matter of the construction of their inner eyes, those eyes with which they look through their physical eyes upon reality."[2]

Huh?

You had to read it again. Even more than that, you had to figure out *how* to read it again — deciding, at the end of those sentences, whether to go back and reread or to forge onward and hope that Ellison's next lines would elucidate a bit of those ornate, beautiful, and confounding sentences. If you decided to double back, did that mean rereading the previous sentence, or the whole previous paragraph? Or did it mean scanning backward for a line that felt relevant, that explained the idea of not being seen?

Wasn't there something about that before? Ah, yes: "I am invisible, understand, simply because people refuse to see me." That helps.

If you forged ahead, you also faced choices: you could read sentence by sentence, pausing to wrestle with Ellison's meaning each step of the way, or you could jump in and start swimming, knowing that the text was a river of ideas you would never grasp fully at first. You could read for a bit, let the ideas wash over you, get your bearings, and then come back and make better sense of it the second time through. In short, you didn't just read and reread, you adapted the way you reread to the challenges of the text. For each text, and each passage, the solution was a bit different.

The process of reading and rereading is a form of problem solving, though we don't always think of it this way. We advise students to reread difficult texts, but it's rereading a text strategically, to engage it in *different* ways that makes the difference. *What kind* of rereading should they use? when? with what purpose? We call this process of strategic rereading **layered reading**, and observing great teachers has shown us at least three ways to attack complex passages: the contiguous read, the line-by-line read, and the leapfrog read. These approaches are not mutually exclusive and are generally used in different combinations to unlock different texts in different situations.

## THE CONTIGUOUS READ

In a contiguous read, students read a passage with the fewest possible interruptions or stoppages. The idea is to experience the text as a whole, to glimpse its broad context, to hear its voice. It can be an ideal way to introduce a text—the most common way that a text is read the first time in Close Reading lessons—but it can also be a superb last step, one that allows students to see the pieces they've analyzed come together as a whole.

### Kicking Off with a Contiguous Read

Typically, a teacher might use a contiguous read to begin a Close Read, asking his students to read for broad context and make general observations about narrative voice before going back to unpack complexities, nuances, and thorny syntax. Starting with a contiguous read is what one of Doug's favorite professors advised regarding especially resistant novels: "Sometimes you just have to jump in and start swimming; with time, you will come to understand more about what you did not know you were reading about. Then you can circle back." In fact, it can be an especially empowering experience for students to struggle with a text's seeming impenetrability, then watch as its mysteries are revealed by careful study.

Colleen chose to start this way on a recent *Grapes of Wrath* Close Reading lesson. The first paragraphs of the book form a sort of prose poem—a sweeping impressionist description of Oklahoma just before the dust bowl. Colleen wanted her students to get a feel for the passage before she dug in deep. She also chose to start with a contiguous read because so much of Steinbeck's meaning in the passage is communicated with subtlety. She wanted students to read it, think they "got it," and then go back through and be blown away by how much more was there.

Colleen had her students read the passage aloud, Control the Game style (see Module 5.3), stepping in from time to time to bridge and model fluent, expressive reading. She wanted to hear students read so that she could better assess how much they seemed to be picking up on the nuances of the text—whether or not they could express meaning in their oral reading. As they read, she didn't stop much to ask questions, merely to define a few key vocabulary words that she had students note in their texts so that they could use them later on.

As Colleen's approach shows, a contiguous read also often works well as a form of Check for Understanding (CFU). Just after the contiguous read is an ideal time to gauge student understanding, especially by asking students to respond in writing, though often even their oral reading can be a valuable and revealing source of data: Were they able to invest the text with a bit of expression and emphasis to show they understood, or were they just trying to untangle its phrases? Either way, a relatively unmediated read—with few teacher hints and little or no discussion—gives you a strong indication of how much students got (or didn't get) on their own. For this reason, the sequence of events in many Close Reading lessons is (1) contiguous read, (2) initial writing to CFU, (3) reread with text-dependent questions, (4) final writing.

## Contiguous Read as Closer

A contiguous read also works well as an opportunity for synthesis after more deliberate analysis. Having ended a sequence in which you explicate each line and allusion in a passage with your students, for example, you might then go back and use a contiguous read to allow students to experience how the pieces come together, this time without interruption. You might even combine two contiguous reads: the first to experience the text and all of its mysteries, the second, after deeper analysis, to read it "as if for the first time" to "see how much more we understand."

Either way, a contiguous read can take different formats. It can feature students reading silently and independently, students reading the text aloud, stretches of the teacher reading aloud to students, or a combination of these formats. You might hear, for example, a teacher reading the first few lines of a text to model an unusual or challenging narrative voice. Then the teacher might ask students to read independently for a stretch to rehearse before reading aloud as a group.

## THE LINE-BY-LINE READ

In a line-by-line read, pauses for discussion and analysis are frequent: you and your class read a line and then stop to make sense of it, unpacking, explicating, and analyzing before moving on. In this way, students build up their understanding of the argument in a methodical way as they read. As they read "Letter from Birmingham Jail," for example, you might ask students to stop and paraphrase and reflect on the argument every few sentences. You might do this not only because his text is full of important allusions and complex syntax but also because his argument builds so systematically and logically from each previous point.

The name *line-by-line* can perhaps be deceiving. Although it may mean unpacking or paraphrasing every single line, as you might with a soliloquy from *Hamlet* or a sonnet, a line-by-line read could just as easily let students encounter two or three sentences at once, followed by their pausing and examining them as a group. It could also gloss over some less thorny segments while pausing at the most prickly. You don't need to stop after *every single line* to do a line-by-line read.

For example, take Colleen's *Grapes of Wrath* lesson. She used a line-by-line read after her contiguous read. Here are her notes on the beginning of the passage:

**Read:** "To the red country and part of the gray country of Oklahoma, the last rains came gently, and they did not cut the scarred earth."

**Questions:** Last rains: What does this mean? Are the rains probably a good thing/bad thing? "They did not cut the scarred earth." Who or what is "they"? What does it mean that the rains did *not* "cut the scarred earth"? Why does Steinbeck describe the earth as scarred?

**Read:** "The plows crossed and recrossed the rivulet marks."

**Questions:** If a rivulet is a small stream, what might a rivulet *mark* be? What does the author show is *not* there? By the way, who's driving the plows? In other words, what's the hidden subject of this sentence? We will come back to this at the end of the passage, but for now think: Why would the author leave out the people driving the plows?

Colleen didn't stop after every single line the whole way through as she does in this short segment, though you could if you wanted to. The idea here is to show that a text builds up meaning in intentional ways—ways that require focus and attention at the micro level. In a way, this is learning to read in a whole new way—learning to read deeply and attentively as if for the first time.

## THE LEAPFROG READ

A leapfrog read follows an image, phrase, or idea through a passage. This means leaping over some parts of the passage to glimpse, in close proximity, the related images or phrases in others—hence the name. Colleen's goal in reading the first paragraphs of *Grapes of Wrath*, for example, was to highlight the role of the sun, which does not project the bright and hopeful image it does in most texts, but is a relentless antagonist attacking the land and creating a drought. The nameless farmers of Oklahoma are caught in the middle of this battle between earth and sky—a key insight into Steinbeck's portrayal of them, and an insight begun by tracing the three references to the sun spread throughout the first two paragraphs. We've extracted them from the narrative here and put in close proximity to emphasize the point:

- "The sun flared down on the growing corn day after day until a line of brown spread along the edge of each green bayonet."

- "And as the sharp sun struck day after day, the leaves of the young corn became less stiff and erect; they bent in a curve at first, and then, as the central ribs of strength grew weak, each leaf tilted downward."

- "Then it was June, and the sun shone more fiercely."

The paragraphs describe a brutal, inexorable sun at war with the earth, but this point would be easy to miss without looking at all three references in close proximity. So Colleen did just that; she asked students to find the first reference to the sun; asked them to read and interpret the line; asked them to skip ahead and find the next reference to the sun; asked them to read and interpret that; asked them to find the third and do the same; and finally asked them to make sense of the imagery of the sun as a whole (see "Colleen's Leapfrog Read").

# Colleen's Leapfrog Read

Here are the questions Colleen used in her leapfrog read:

1. Scan the passage and find the first place that you notice the sun mentioned.

> "The sun flared down on the growing corn day after day until a line of brown spread along the edge of each green bayonet."

- What is it doing? Underline the phrase *the sun flared down.* Normally when the sun is out, is it positive or negative? Let's find out from the text whether that holds true in this case . . .
- What's the sun flaring down on?
- What's starting to happen to the corn as a result?
- If it's getting brown lines, that means it's drying out. What happens to plants if they get too dry?
- What's being described as a "green bayonet"? Given me one literal and one figurative reason why the author would describe the leaves of the corn plants that way.

[Note in margin to summarize: "Sun at war with earth" or similar.]

2. Find the second mention of the sun.

> "And as the sharp sun struck day after day, the leaves of the young corn became less stiff and erect; they bent in a curve at first, and then, as the central ribs of strength grew weak, each leaf tilted downward."

- Underline the phrase "sharp sun struck day after day."
- The author could have used any adjective and verb to describe the sun, but he chose *sharp* and *strike.* How would the effect have been different had he said, "The bright sun shone . . . "?
- What kinds of objects usually are sharp and strike?
- What is the author implying?
- Why does the author say "day after day"?

- What's it striking down on?

- Underline the rest of that sentence and paraphrase.

  [Note in margin to summarize: "Battle ongoing; sun is winning," or similar.]

3. There's one more mention of the sun. Find it and keep your pencil by it.

   "Then it was June, and the sun shone more fiercely."

- Underline the phrase "sun shone more fiercely."

- More fiercely than what?

- (If needed, Break It Down): The last time the sun was mentioned it was like a...? More fiercely than a sword?

- So now we're sure that the sun is like a weapon. What's it doing?

**Stop and Jot:** In your notes packet, briefly describe the role of the sun. This is going to help us to better understand the rest of the passage.

Of course, a leapfrog read could just as easily look at an important phrase as at a recurring image. Mark Antony's speech in *Julius Caesar*, "Friends, Romans, countrymen, lend me your ears," refers four times to Brutus as "an honorable man." Yet each time Antony uses the phrase, its meaning changes. It's practically begging for a leapfrog read.

And of course, leapfrog reads — and all of the methods of reading — are not relevant only to the advanced texts of Shakespeare and Steinbeck. Consider the power of examining both the repetition of and changes in the similar phrases Donald Crews uses to describe visiting his grandmother's house in *Bigmama's*, a pre-complex text you might read in second grade:

- First, when they arrive: "Then off with our socks and shoes. We wouldn't need them much in the next few weeks. Now to see that nothing had changed."

- Later, after casing the farm: "We stood on tiptoe to watch the bucket go down and fill with water so that we could have a drink from the dipper that hung nearby. Everything was just the same."

- In the middle of the visit: "Plenty of water for fishing and swimming this year. Everything was just as it should be."

Tracking the differences in these similar phrases would help students understand how Crews expresses the comforting timelessness of his visits. Having students find and then study the lines one after the other in close proximity is, if not the only way, probably the best way to help them see it.

## COMBINING READS

As the example of a leapfrog read from *Bigmama's* suggests, part of the power of the three types of reading lies in the combinations. You'd get more out of your leapfrog read if, for example, students knew the story and had a sense of it; in this light, you might want to make it your second read. But should the first read be a line-by-line or a contiguous read? The story has challenging parts, but is not dense enough syntactically to warrant a line-by-line read. Perhaps it's better to start with a contiguous read. At the same time, the narrator's voice might be hard for some students to hear, so maybe it would be better to start with the teacher reading the first half of the text aloud, transitioning to students reading the second half, and then circle back and leapfrog through Crews's phrases about timelessness. Of course, there are a variety of ways you could combine reads to unlock a text's unique challenges or to respond to your students' skills and needs as readers. That's the point.

We recently observed Patrick Pastore combine two types of reading with his eighth-grade students. They were reading Ambrose Bierce's 1890 short story "Occurrence at Owl Creek Bridge." The text is dauntingly complex (kudos to Patrick for choosing it!) and requires not only the ability to read archaic text but also a sound knowledge of the Civil War and its vocabulary.

His students were surprised when he passed it around. They'd rarely read texts written before 1900. "It sounds old school," one student commented. "Yes, anything that's been around that long and is still read is going to be worth it," Patrick said with a smile, before starting in on a contiguous read of the first paragraph. He asked students to read parts aloud, but he also read some himself, modeling the cadence of Bierce's prose. "Pause there," he said at the end of the first paragraph. "We're going to restart from the top. You didn't do anything wrong, but this is worth reading twice." This time, Patrick used a careful and methodical line-by-line read to unpack the complex elements in the first paragraph. Which side did it mean you were on if you were in the Federal army? What did it mean to be at a "short remove" from something? What did it imply that a man who suggested to the protagonist that he try to wreck a bridge had been wearing grey? The read was methodical and technical—but necessary to understanding the story.

Next, Patrick returned to contiguous reading. The class read through a critical scene when it is very subtly revealed that the protagonist had been entrapped by a Union spy. Then Patrick slowed again to reread the relevant line methodically—a one-line line-by-line read. There was a gasp among the students as the realization hit them—the protagonist had been set up, framed, and was going to be hanged. Now Patrick and his students pushed ahead again. It was time for a contiguous read with speed and energy to let the drama unfold of its own accord.

## See It in Action

In clip 1 at teachlikeachampion.com/yourlibrary, watch Patrick Pastore teach "Occurrence at Owl Creek Bridge" to his eighth graders.

As we mentioned earlier, deciding how to read is a form of problem solving. The way teachers use the three types of layered reading is a key application of that idea. The number of reads, which forms of reading you choose, and the order of reads are all tools that help shape a reader's strategy. In the next module, we'll look at ways to establish meaning through the text-dependent questions you ask during those readings.

## MODULE 2.2 — Establish Meaning via Text-Dependent Questions

Too often, conversations about literature, from the elementary to the college level, are "gist" conversations—conversations wherein readers understand a text at a broad and general level and proceed to develop and share opinions about it despite an incomplete understanding. Teachers start a discussion assuming that students understood all of the text because they are able to provide or recognize a general summary. The assumption is that, because students have gotten the main idea, they know the text comprehensively. Of course, this is not true. There is much more to a text than a pithy statement of its general argument. Sometimes such a "gist phrase" can even crowd out reading:

Teacher: What is Shakespeare saying about love in the sonnet?
Student: That it doesn't last.

Teacher: Can anyone develop that?

Student: It's like a flower. It blooms and then fades.

Teacher: Yes, love, to Shakespeare, is fleeting like a flower. Do you agree?

A discussion about the idea of love being fleeting then ensues. Such a discussion is not without value—it engages students and can be high in Participation Ratio, the proportion of the cognitive work students do—but it's less demanding in many ways than the careful work of unpacking text. It's an easy shortcut compared to the harder work of unpacking a thicket of signifiers, or of understanding what else Shakespeare's language choices reveal about the nature of love's temporality.

## MORE THAN "MAIN IDEA"

Unless the conversation starts with a deep understanding of the specifics of what Shakespeare wrote rather than some generalized proximity of it, the discussion is not an exercise in reading. It is a substitute activity—a philosophical discussion about issues raised in a text, one that competes with careful reading for time and energy in the classroom. This isn't to say you should never do it; but such discussions don't generally teach students to read deeply.

Close Reading then starts with establishing meaning via sustained and methodical attention to what the text says, a task that can be immensely challenging—and immensely worthwhile in a variety of often overlooked ways. Consider for a moment how rigorous it can be simply to paraphrase a rich and complex passage from a work of literature. Take this one, for example, from *To Kill a Mockingbird*, which Maggie Johnson used for a Close Reading with her eighth graders in a recent lesson. The narrator, of course, is Scout Finch:

> Somewhere, I had received the impression that Fine Folks were people who did the best they could with the sense they had, but Aunt Alexandra was of the opinion, obliquely expressed, that the longer a family had been squatting on one patch of land the finer it was.

A paraphrase, remember, is different from a summary. It is a restatement of the sentence in simpler and clarified terms that still capture all of the explicit meaning and as much of the connotation as possible. "Scout is reflecting on her interpretation of how class was determined, as contrasted to that of her Aunt Alexandra" is not a paraphrase but rather a summary description of the passage. A paraphrase would be written in the first person and take on Scout's point of view. It might start: "Somehow I had come to believe that respectable people were . . . "

If you've read *To Kill a Mockingbird*, try your hand at a paraphrase right now. Here's some space. Give it a try. We won't collect it:

_____

_____

_____

_____

How'd you do? There's no single right answer, but if nothing else, checking yourself against our best effort makes it clear that there are a lot of ideas in that one little sentence:

> **Paraphrase:** I had come to believe, though I'm not sure when [or possibly how], that people of stature were those who lived as wisely and well as they could given their circumstances, but Aunt Alexandra believed, though she wouldn't come out and say it directly, that status was based on how long you had been living on your land.

The ideas here are interwoven and complex and relate to the important themes in the book. Just unwinding them all is challenging. There's Aunt Alexandra's belief that status is conferred by heredity, the implicit connection of that issue to race and class, and the fact that Aunt Alexandra would never just come out and say what she felt (that is, her feelings were "obliquely expressed").

After paraphrasing, perhaps students could analyze Aunt Alexandra's "obliqueness"—was she being, as she might have put it, tactful and "ladylike," or was her obliqueness actually a means of quietly reinforcing the racial caste system—to speak in code to remind those who ascribed to her set of beliefs of their importance while keeping those same beliefs invisible to others who might be angered by them or, like Scout, not understand them? Answering that question would fall in the next step of a Close Reading lesson: analyzing meaning. However, before analyzing meaning, students would first need to understand what it means to express an opinion obliquely and exactly what opinions about class Alexandra expressed in this manner. They would need to understand how Harper Lee used relatively low, uncouth diction—"squatting"—to describe the fundamental premise of Alexandra's worldview, to subtly mock it. You cannot truly analyze meaning unless you can also diligently first establish it.

The synergies between establishing meaning and analyzing it run even deeper. Establishing meaning often identifies key issues worthy of analysis. Imagine how you could push students into analysis once they'd captured the overall meaning of our sentence from *To Kill a Mockingbird*, for example:

Q: Why is "Fine Folks" capitalized in these lines?

A: Maybe it's a common phrase that gets said all the time around Scout?

Q: By whom?

A: By the people Scout most often hears talking, people like Alexandra, white people of middle to upper status?

Q: Why might they say it all the time?

A: *(eventually, with a bit of discussion or during some writing)* It was capitalized because, like Democracy, which is also sometimes capitalized, it is a proper noun in people's minds. That is, it was deeply enshrined in the belief systems of the South.

Q: So, given our discussion, why would Lee capitalize these words in the text? What message is she conveying?

Paraphrasing might seem to some like the most straightforward and mundane of activities—banal, even. But as this line from *To Kill a Mockingbird* shows, paraphrasing a worthy segment of complex text is a rigorous task. As an aside, the fact that *To Kill a Mockingbird* responds so richly to text-dependent questions is both a reminder that trying to Close Read with insufficiently complex text is not likely to yield successful lessons: the value of establishing meaning correlates to the rigor of the text.

## Close Reading, Professional Development, and the Importance of Subject Knowledge in ELA

We recently asked a roomful of teachers at one of our workshops to take a shot at paraphrasing the sentence from *To Kill a Mockingbird* described earlier. Many of them acknowledged that they struggled. They hadn't done much of this as students! Many wrote summaries instead of paraphrases. Many teachers who were ultimately very insightful in our discussion began with paraphrases for which they might not give full credit to their students. In other words, it's hard work and takes practice.

This underscores for us that the first step in making sure students can Close Read is the intellectual preparation of teachers. Having teachers sitting down with key sections from a book they are teaching, reading them closely, discussing how they'd interpret them and (only) then how they'd teach them is one of the key pieces often missing from professional development. In short, a great PD would be to practice Close Reading a series of key sentences from *To Kill a Mockingbird*, both to prepare students to execute effective paraphrases and to allow teachers to more deeply reflect on the book and different readings of it. The importance of knowledge of the text you teach cannot be overemphasized. Sharing text among teachers and choosing texts as a team within a school allows for text-based PD that moves training to a higher level of practicality and rigor by focusing teachers on both developing knowledge about and teaching texts.

So how does one establish meaning? Let us begin by looking at one of the key ideas in this book: the importance of *text-dependent questions (TDQs)*.

## TEXT-DEPENDENT QUESTIONS: UNLOCKING THE POWER OF THE MICROSCOPE

TDQs are those that cannot be answered without firm knowledge of the text itself. They cannot be faked by carefully listening to the discussion, for example, or by conducting an earnest but inexact reading of the chapter. They cannot be answered by recalling yesterday's reading or by having a strong background knowledge of the subject. To answer TDQs requires attentive reading. Nothing else will do.

To gaze through a telescope is to look at the universe at its broadest. This can be inspiring. To look through a microscope, in contrast, is to see the universe at its smallest—and its views, though not perhaps as grand at first as those seen through a telescope, are just as critical. They show the hidden units of structure that shape the interactions of the larger world.

When seeking rigor in reading with students, teachers often seek it through the telescope: with broad, sweeping, grand questions. "What is William Golding's vision of the 'natural' state of humanity in *Lord of the Flies*? Do you agree with him?"

TDQs, in contrast, help us unlock the power of the microscope; they focus in on small moments that are revealing and rigorous, and that recur again and again in the texts we

**Table 2.1** Levels and Purposes of TDQs

| Text-Dependent Questions | Questions to Establish Meaning | Questions to Analyze Meaning |
|---|---|---|
| Word- or phrase-level questions | | |
| Sentence- or line-level questions | | |
| Paragraph- or stanza-level questions | | |

read. "What does the description of the boy 'clambering heavily among the creepers and broken trunks' in the first paragraph of *Lord of the Flies* suggest about William Golding's view of the state of nature?" (Hint: when the flora is made up of creepers and broken trunks, you are probably not in paradise.)

To help teachers conceptualize what those questions are and how they can work in different settings, we will build here a map of different types of TDQs, including both definitions and examples.

Our map divides TDQs into two columns, differentiating those that establish meaning from those that analyze it. Further, the map is divided into rows. These rows represent the idea that TDQs can focus on analytical units of different size within the text: words and phrases, sentences and lines, paragraphs and stanzas. Each of the columns is thus subdivided into three levels, as shown in Table 2.1.

Questions focusing on each of these three levels are equally important and rigorous. Though some teachers may be slightly inclined to consider questions more rigorous when they encompass broader content, and therefore tend to privilege paragraph-level questions over word-level questions, this is not necessarily the case. Students need to work with challenging questions at both larger and smaller units of analysis; the most rigorous teacher is she who asks all three types of questions.

## Word- and Phrase-Level Questions to Establish Meaning

Explaining the vocabulary in a passage certainly matters, but there's more to understanding words and phrases than that. Students need to understand how words and phrases relate and refer to one another—what they mean *in a specific instance,* and even how their meaning changes with the situation. Consider this apparently very mundane example from Langston Hughes's *A Dream Deferred*, which, you may recall, begins like this:

What happens to a dream deferred?

Does it dry up
like a raisin in the sun?
Or fester like a sore—
And then run?
Does it stink like rotten meat?

Many students read the second line of the poem and think "it" must be something mysterious or hypothetical, that Hughes is being vague on purpose; they think maybe poetry just works that way and that we are supposed to wonder about the many things that might dry up in the sun. And they could be excused for doing so. Readers often expect poetry to defy logic and convention. Besides, the second line of the poem is separated from the first by a stanza break, making it easy to think that the sentences are not related. Students could spend a lot of time talking about the poem without realizing that the second stanza consists of Hughes's descriptions of things that happen to dreams when they are deferred and that this is what "it" refers to. The entire poem, in fact, is a meditation on what happens to "it." Imagine trying to understand the poem without knowing what "it" is. Asking, "What is 'it' in the second line?" or "Who can read that line replacing the pronoun 'it' with the noun it refers to?" can help ensure that your deep discussion of the poem is founded on a solid reading. It's a basic question, so many teachers might overlook it. But for a third grader reading outside her comfort zone, it is a critical question.

Here are three specific types of word- or phrase-level questions that you can ask. For each, examples come from the first paragraphs of *The Grapes of Wrath*. In several cases, the questions that establish meaning presage a question to analyze that meaning more deeply. Some possible follow-up questions are included in italics.

## Referent Questions

A **referent question** asks what a word, often a pronoun, refers to. Asking what Langston Hughes's "it" refers to is one example. If you were reading the first two paragraphs of *The Grapes of Wrath*, you might ask:

Steinbeck writes, "and in a while, they did not try anymore." Who are "they," and what are "they" no longer trying to do? [Answer: The clouds (not the farmers); they no longer tried to protect the land from the sun.]

## Denotation Questions

A **denotation question** asks about the meaning of a specific word or phrase. Often it focuses on distinctive or unusual constructs, or those that take on a unique meaning in the specific setting. If you were reading the first two paragraphs of *The Grapes of Wrath*, you might ask:

If a rivulet is a small stream, what might a "rivulet mark" be? *What would have to be true for there to be a rivulet mark on the ground?* [Answer: the lack of water; a state of drought]

What are "weed colonies"? How are they different from just "weeds"? [Answer: They are clustered together possibly for strength; possibly to "colonize" new land.] *What might that show about the setting?*

## Explanation Questions

An **explanation question** asks what a word or phrase means *in this setting*. It emphasizes understanding which of several possible usages of a word is relevant, or how its nuance or implication is perhaps different than usual. This type of question can also examine how the presence of a word changes a sentence, often by asking how the sentence would read without it. If you were reading the first two paragraphs of *The Grapes of Wrath*, you might ask about the phrase "last rains." The first time students read that phrase, it probably appears to mean something quaint and pleasant—the last rains before the sun came out. By the time they are midway through a Close Read, however, they should have come to see that "last rains" has a darker tinge to it: it refers to the last rain before a deadly drought.

[First time through the passage] What does the phrase "the last rains" seem to mean?

[Second time through the passage] What does the phrase seem to mean now, and how is it different from what you thought?

---

## They Could Not Take It

Think that referent and other word- and phrase-level questions that "merely establish meaning" are simplistic? Take this small test, using a sixth-grade Common Core sample passage from New York. It was shared with teachers to help them understand what sorts of passages and tasks their students would need to be able to read and complete. We've bolded and numbered thirteen pronouns. Read the passage and number a sheet of paper 1–13, identifying for each what the pronoun refers to.

The Greeks besieged the city of Troy for nearly ten years. **They (1)** could not take **it (2)** because the walls were so high and strong—some said that

---

they (3) had been built by the hands of gods — but they (4) kept the Trojans inside. This (5) had not always been so. There had been a time when the Trojans had gone out and fought with their (6) enemies on the plain, sometimes they (7) had beaten them (8) in battle, and once they (9) had very nearly burnt their (10) ships. But this (11) was all changed. They (12) had lost some of the bravest of their chiefs, such as Hector, the best of the sons of Priam, and Paris the great archer, and many great princes, who had come from the countries round about to help them (13).

Trickier than you thought? Consider, then, how hard it would be for sixth graders, especially sixth graders already confused by the fact that, say, the word "Trojans" refers to people from Troy (now there's a good referent question), and that the phrase "they could not take it" doesn't mean, as it does in modern parlance, "they couldn't put up with it anymore," but rather "they could not capture it via military action." You'd definitely want to focus a denotation question on that phrase. Anyway, here's our best shot at an answer key:

1.  The Greeks
2.  The city of Troy
3.  The walls around Troy
4.  The walls around Troy (or possibly the Greeks?)
5.  The state of besiegement wherein the Trojans were trapped inside their own walls
6.  The Trojans'
7.  The Trojans
8.  Their historical enemies (various, unnamed)
9.  The Trojans
10. Their historical enemies, but in this case hinting at an action against specific enemies, probably the Achaeans
11. The state of existence wherein the Trojans were brave warriors who went out on conquests
12. The Trojans
13. The Trojans

(Continued)

(Continued)

Notice answers 5 and 11. A full and fairly complex sentence is required to describe what the pronouns are referring to. As we hope is now clear, without skill and practice at tracking pronoun references, kids wouldn't have a chance reading this passage.

## Sentence- and Line-Level Questions to Establish Meaning

Sentences are the basis of idea-formation—complete thoughts. But sentences are complex and thorny and don't always yield their meaning simply. Students will often grasp part of an idea from a complex sentence but miss other ideas, or will understand a portion of a sentence but not a subsequent portion that contradicts or undercuts its meaning. In this light, it is important for students to practice reading challenging sentences attentively and technically to understand how they create meaning.

Here are four specific types of sentence-level questions that you can ask. Each includes examples, in this case from a variety of texts that lend themselves to Close Reading.

### Paraphrase Questions

As we've discussed, a **paraphrase question** asks a student to restate a line of text in simplified language to express its meaning clearly. It takes the point of view and perspective of the original and, unlike a summary (explained in Table 2.2), glosses all key parts of the original.

**Table 2.2** Paraphrase versus Summary

| Paraphrase | Summary |
|---|---|
| • Is a restatement of the text as if from the narrator's perspective. Matches the tense and syntax of the original | • Is a statement about the text from the observer's perspective |
| • Uses more simplified language than the original | • Often but not necessarily uses more simplified language than the original |
| • Is intended to capture the full extent of the passage and all of its arguments and pieces | • Is intended to shorten and prioritize the elements of a passage to focus on what's most relevant |
| • Is most often applied to a single sentence | • Is most often applied to a sentence or a longer passage |

If you were reading from *To Kill a Mockingbird,* you might ask:

Paraphrase the sentence, "Somewhere, I had received the impression that Fine Folks were people who did the best they could with the sense they had, but Aunt Alexandra was of the opinion, obliquely expressed, that the longer a family had been squatting on one patch of land the finer it was." Be sure to gloss all of the segments of the sentence. Write your paraphrase in the first person.

### Key Line Questions

A **key line question** asks about the connotation or denotation of a key line or sentence. Sometimes it asks what role it plays in a paragraph. If you were reading *Animal Farm,* you might ask:

Orwell writes, "Squealer, who happened to be passing at this moment, *attended by two or three dogs,* was able to put the whole matter in its proper perspective" (italics ours). What does this sentence tell us probably happened between Squealer and Clover, and why is that important?

### Reference Questions

A **reference question** asks who or what a sentence refers to, especially whom characters are talking about, who spoke a certain line, or what event they are referring to. If you were reading *Othello,* you might ask:

Iago says, "For I mine own gain'd knowledge should profane / If I would time expend with such a snipe, / But for my sport and profit." Who is Iago talking about?

### Sentence Structure Questions

A **sentence structure question** asks how the syntax of a sentence affects meaning. If you were reading Donald Crews's *Bigmama's,* you might ask:

Crews writes, "We talked about what we did last year. We talked about what we were going to do this year. We talked so much we hardly had time to eat." Why does the author repeat the phrase "we talked" at the beginning of each sentence?

## Paragraph- and Stanza-Level Questions to Establish Meaning

Words, phrases, and sentences are powerful units of analysis for studying how language works. They allow students to see in hyperfocus how ideas come together. Paragraphs (and stanzas in the case of poetry) are also rich fodder for Close Reading; they, too, rely on distinctive forms and structures to create or nuance meaning. Here are four specific types of word- or phrase-level questions that you can ask.

### Summary Questions

A **summary question** asks students to distill the elements of a block of text and reduce it in scope to its most important ideas. In other words, a summary inherently asks students to prioritize what is most important or germane. Because summarizing can allow students to skip discussing parts of a paragraph they may not have understood, teachers often use, in addition to a general summary, a "targeted" summary: a summary that asks students to focus on something specific. For example, if you were reading Martin Luther King's "Letter from Birmingham Jail," you might ask:

> Summarize King's explanation, in the early paragraphs, of the difference between a just and unjust law.

In this way, the task of summarizing can be trained on an important idea, image, or theme, within a block of text.

### Delineation Questions

A **delineation question** is similar to a targeted summary in that it asks students to trace the elements of an author's argument or the sequence of events in a narrative. To return to "Letter from Birmingham Jail," you might ask:

> Trace all of King's references to children in the paragraph beginning, "We have waited for more than three hundred and forty years." Where and why does he discuss their perspectives on racism?

### Finite Evidence Questions

A **finite evidence question** asks students to track evidence comprehensively throughout a section of text. It requires students to find multiple pieces of evidence (or all the evidence, or a fixed number of pieces of evidence) from a particular section. This prevents students from finding just the low-hanging fruit—the most obvious pieces of evidence—and forces them to grapple with the evidence in its totality: Is it clean and tidy and all of a piece, or is some of it questionable, hidden, contradictory even? Asking a finite evidence question is often more rigorous than asking for a single piece of evidence, because it causes students to read more carefully (often for what they didn't see the first time around) and because it prepares students to turn isolated pieces of evidence into a compelling argument. So if you were reading Jared Diamond's essay "The Worst Mistake in the History of the Human Race," you might ask:

> Diamond gives us three key reasons why the dominance of agriculture has been negative for humanity. What are they?

This would prepare you for a more thorough discussion of the article. Or, if you were reading *Number the Stars*, you might ask:

> Find all the evidence in the passage that shows us that the little sister, Kirsti, fails to perceive the threat of the German soldiers.

As we noted earlier, regardless of what line(s) of questioning you choose to employ in a particular lesson, trying to Close Read with insufficiently complex text is unlikely to succeed. The rigor and value of establishing meaning correlate to the rigor and value of the text.

The synergies between establishing meaning and analyzing it, we have noted, run deep. Establishing meaning often identifies key issues worthy of analysis. In the next module, we move on to analyzing.

| MODULE 2.3 | Close Reading to Analyze Meaning |
|---|---|

To ask students to analyze meaning is to ask them to explain how and why the elements of a passage mean what they do, and how they contribute to the passage's overall meaning. It's an activity that prepares students for independent autonomous interpretations of the text (see chapter 8, Intellectual Autonomy, for more), and it operates in deep synergy with the second part of a Close Reading lesson, establishing meaning.

Simply put, the two parts need each other. Successfully analyzing meaning requires a solid grasp of the argument; and establishing meaning requires the epiphanies of insight that come from subsequent analysis to justify it. Why ask students to evaluate what Claudius's speech at the beginning of act 1, scene 2 of *Hamlet* reveals about his character before you are sure that they understand what he is claiming (that he is able to mourn the king's death and celebrate marrying his widow at the same time)? When asked this question, we have observed students to suggest that the speech shows Claudius's generosity and wisdom, their having not perceived his hypocrisy and self-serving manipulation. Establishing the meaning of his lines

> Have we, as 'twere with a defeated joy,—
> with an auspicious and dropping eye,
> with mirth in funeral and with dirge in marriage
> in equal scale weighing delight and dole

must come first.

## TEXT-DEPENDENT QUESTIONS AND ANALYZING MEANING

Establishing meaning and analyzing meaning are connected in another more practical way: they both rely on text-dependent questioning. The analyzing meaning part of Close Reading is not a mere discussion of a book. It remains text focused and evidenced based. Like establishing meaning, analyzing meaning hinges on the exact manner in which the text is worded and structured. Fittingly, TDQs are organized into the same three levels we looked at when we discussed establishing meaning. Similarly here, word- and phrase-level questions are especially important and surprisingly rigorous, and can be easily overlooked in the rush to talk big picture.

As you fill in Table 2.1 with specific types of questions, you will notice the parity between many of the question types on the left and right sides of the chart. It is not an accident that the line-level question is a category on both sides, or that word-level denotation questions in the Establish Meaning column are in parallel with word-level connotation questions in the Analyze Meaning column. In fact, this parallel structure allows a teacher to quickly and easily move back and forth between establishing and analyzing meaning throughout a lesson, a process we call **toggling**.

Before we discuss toggling, let's look at some of the kinds of questions that teachers can leverage to analyze meaning.

### Word- and Phrase-Level Questions to Analyze Meaning

In parallel with text-dependent word- and phrase-level questions to establish meaning, there are a number of different word- and phrase-level questions teachers can use to establish meaning. Here are some of the most effective.

## Word Pattern Questions

A **word pattern question** asks about a pattern that is set up (or sometimes broken) by repeated words, and how this pattern contributes to meaning. If you were reading Winston Churchill's "We Shall Fight on the Beaches" speech, for example, you would almost certainly want to ask about the striking anaphora (repetition of words) beginning the most famous lines:

> Churchill wrote, "We shall not flag or fail. We shall go on to the end. We shall fight in France, we shall fight on the seas and oceans, we shall fight with growing confidence and growing strength in the air, we shall defend our island, whatever the cost may be, we shall fight on the beaches, we shall fight on the landing grounds, we shall fight in the fields and in the streets, we shall fight in the hills. We shall never surrender." Why does Churchill repeat the phrase "we shall" over and over? What effect do you think he intended such repetition to have on his listeners?

## Connotation Questions

A **connotation question** asks about the implied meaning of words based on their associations, and how this affects meaning or tone. If you were reading the opening paragraphs of *The Grapes of Wrath,* particularly the line reading "The sun flared down on the growing corn day after day until a line of brown spread along the edge of each green bayonet," you might ask:

> Where do we usually read about bayonets? What might Steinbeck's word choice in his description be suggesting about the setting?

## Figurative/Literal Meaning Questions

A **figurative/literal meaning question** asks students to clarify figurative meaning, often by comparing it to potential literal interpretation of the same passage. Alternately, teachers might ask why a certain type of figurative language or image was used: Why personification here? Why a simile comparing him to a worm rather than to, say, a snake? You might use such a question to analyze the meaning of the same line from *The Grapes of Wrath* as in the previous example:

> Explain one figurative and one literal reason why Steinbeck would describe the leaves of the corn plants as looking like bayonets. [Answer: They were literally shaped like bayonets; they symbolized the war between the sun and the earth.]

It is important to note that just because a question asks about figurative language does not make it a TDQ that supports Close Reading. Merely asking students, "What type of figurative language do we see there?" does not in and of itself foster Close Reading. A good Close Reading figurative/literal meaning question asks *why* and *how* and delves into specific language.

### Sensitivity Analyses

A **sensitivity analysis** asks students to consider how the text would read differently if the author had chosen a different word in a specific place. For example:

> Steinbeck writes, "The sharp sun struck day after day." How does that suggest something different than if he'd said, "The sharp sun shone down day after day?" Or "The sharp sun blared down day after day?"

## See It in Action

Clip 2 at teachlikeachampion.com/yourlibrary shows Rue Ratray at Brooke East Boston examining a single sentence from *The Giver* in comparison to two other plausible alternatives. The result is an epiphany for his students about how the subtleties of language reveal the depth of the father's character. Of course, his students aren't just learning about the father in *The Giver* and how Lois Lowry deftly characterizes him; they are learning sensitivity to language and understanding how tiny changes have profound effects on meaning. Over time, this sort of reading for subtlety will build in students a tremendous "ear" for language—an ear that they can apply to whatever they read.

### Missing Word Analyses

A **missing word analysis** is similar to a sensitivity analysis except that it asks about words that are notably *missing*. In other words, the focus is on words or phrases that would or might ordinarily be included in such a passage, but are not. Colleen used such a question in her reading of *The Grapes of Wrath*. Specifically, she wanted students to notice that Steinbeck is describing an epic battle between forces of nature wherein people are lesser participants—hapless victims of larger forces, if you will. So, reading the sentence "The plows crossed and recrossed the rivulet marks," she asked, "Who was driving the plows in that sentence?" [Answer: farmers] This question established meaning. Her next question, "Why *wouldn't* Steinbeck mention them in the sentence? The plows didn't drive themselves!" allowed Colleen to have students analyze the subtle choice Steinbeck made, as well as its ramifications in terms of meaning and interpretation. What wasn't said mattered as much as what was.

## Line- and Sentence-Level Questions to Analyze Meaning

Myriad insights can come out of focused word- and phrase-level questions. Students can derive similar benefits from TDQs that analyze the next-larger units of language: lines and sentences. Here are four kinds of line- and sentence-level TDQs that can be used for analysis.

### Key Line Questions

A **key line question** asks about the role a sentence plays in a passage and, often, about situations where similar sentences have played a similar role. As we described earlier, the following is one example of a key line question that establishes meaning:

> Orwell writes, "Squealer, who happened to be passing at this moment, attended by two or three dogs, was able to put the whole matter in its proper perspective." What does this sentence tell us probably happened between Squealer and Clover?

A key line question that analyzes meaning might then ask:

> What might it accomplish to express the idea with such subtlety? What other similar lines in the novel should this recall for us? Why would Orwell keep so many important events hidden in a novel like this?

### Allusion Questions

An **allusion question** asks students to analyze an indirect reference to another text or to an important scene in the text they are reading. If you were reading *The Giver,* which contains a large amount of biblical imagery and allusions, you might ask, of the critical scene in which Jonas first gains the knowledge that colors exist,

> Why is Jonas playing catch with an apple in this line instead of, say, a ball? What other famous book might this call our attention to, and why?

### Figurative Language Questions

A **figurative language question** at the sentence level asks about the meaning of imagery or nonliteral language in the text (simile, metaphor, symbolism, analogy, and so on) and how it functions at a sentence level. For example, if you were reading *Animal Farm,* you might ask:

> Orwell writes, "Squealer, who happened to be passing at this moment, attended by two or three dogs, was able to put the whole matter in its proper perspective." Given other information in the sentence [that Squealer had dogs with him], what does "put the whole matter into its proper perspective" imply happened between Squealer and Clover? What type of figurative language is used to suggest that? [Answer: understatement]

### Pattern Questions

A **pattern question** at the sentence level is similar to a pattern question at the word and phrase level except that it asks about a pattern in structure, syntax, or sound and how that affects meaning. If you were reading Donald Crews's *Bigmama's,* you might ask:

> We've seen several similar sentences now: "Now to see that nothing had changed," "Everything was just the same," and then, "Everything was just as it should be." Why does Donald Crews keep mentioning this idea, and why does he do it in different ways?

Or if you were reading Ann McGovern's *Robin Hood of Sherwood Forest,* you might ask:

> The text relates, "Now he whistled; now he sang; now he leapt across the brook, taking care that his stout bow and score of arrows would not tumble as he ran free as the King's deer in the forest." How does the way this sentence is written help us understand the progression of time in this scene? [Answer: The relation of three distinct actions using three short, quick independent clauses condenses the time span of the actions.]

## Paragraph- and Stanza-Level Questions to Analyze Meaning

Because most Close Reading focuses on distinct and defined blocks of text, paragraph- or stanza-level questions are critical. These questions can help tie an analysis together. (Of course, such questions can also be applied to segments of text longer than the single paragraph.) Of the many types of paragraph-level TDQs, here are three that have proven effective in a number of classrooms.

## Paragraph Function Questions

**A paragraph function question** asks students about the role of paragraphs in a text or how paragraphs build on one another. If you were reading Martin Luther King's "Letter from Birmingham Jail," you might ask:

> Look carefully at paragraphs 5 and 6. How has King shifted his use of logos, ethos, and pathos and the degree to which he is arguing using logic, justice, or compassion? Why is he making this shift? How do these choices build off of his approach in the previous paragraph?

You also might use such a question to ask about intended audience. If, alternately, you were reading King's "Eulogy for the Martyred Children," you might ask, at the outset of the sixth paragraph,

> Who is King's audience in this paragraph? How is it different from his audience in the rest of the eulogy so far? What is King's purpose in speaking directly to multiple audiences?

## Dramatic Irony Questions

**A dramatic irony question** asks students to identify and analyze the difference between their own knowledge about events within a text and that of characters or people described within the narrative. Returning to a line from *Animal Farm* mentioned earlier, you might ask:

> The text says, "Curiously enough, Clover had not remembered that the Fourth Commandment mentioned sheets; but as it was there on the wall, it must have done so. And Squealer, who happened to be passing at this moment, attended by two or three dogs, was able to put the whole matter in its proper perspective." What do we know there that Clover does not? And why wouldn't Orwell simply tell us that fact?

## Extended Metaphor/Allegory Questions

**An extended metaphor/allegory question** asks students to trace a metaphor across multiple lines of text. For the opening passages of *Grapes of Wrath*, you might ask:

> What evidence is there in these passages about the relationship between the sun and the earth? Reread them paying close attention to their imagery and figurative language and explain what extended metaphor Steinbeck might be using to portray that relationship, and why that matters.

## ADDITIONS TO THE MAP OF TEXT-DEPENDENT QUESTIONS: TOGGLING AND ZOOMING

Now that we've discussed types and examples of TDQs at each of the levels of text, we can represent them as shown in Table 2.3. Surely there are other types of questions; if you have a few in your pocket (or as new types emerge in your classroom), add them.

To be complete, the TDQ map requires two more pieces of shared vocabulary. The first, mentioned earlier in this module, is toggling.

### Toggling

Toggling, when you are Close Reading, is shifting back and forth between the two columns—between reading to establish meaning and reading to analyze it. As mentioned earlier, the two tasks are inextricably intertwined. Although it is important to think about them separately in order to make sure both halves receive the attention they are due, the ultimate goal is to link them by moving back and forth between them. Sometimes analysis requires toggling back to a closer examination for a few moments of what the text actually means. This might happen just before the analysis—to see how the text created the conditions for such-and-such a reading—or just afterwards,

**Table 2.3**  Updated Map of TDQs

| Text-Dependent Questions | Questions to Establish Meaning | Questions to Analyze Meaning |
|---|---|---|
| Word- or phrase-level questions | Referent<br>Denotation<br>Explanation | Word pattern<br>Connotation<br>Figurative/literal meaning<br>Sensitivity analysis<br>Missing word analysis |
| Sentence- or line-level questions | Paraphrase<br>Key line<br>Reference<br>Syntax or sentence structure | Key line<br>Allusion<br>Figurative language<br>Pattern |
| Paragraph- or stanza-level questions | Summary (and targeted summary)<br>Delineation<br>Finite evidence | Paragraph function<br>Dramatic irony<br>Extended metaphor/allegory |

to reconsider certain lines in the wake of an "aha!" of analysis. Sometimes the rationale for establishing meaning of a passage becomes suddenly clear if a teacher briefly asks why and how a certain word choice is so important from a broader perspective. In short, *Good Close Reading requires toggling both ways.*

Toggling, as you have surely begun to reflect, requires some strategy. Here are two different models of how you might toggle during a reading of the opening sequence of *The Grapes of Wrath,* for example. In the first instance, you might proceed to establish meaning line by line, unpacking the depth of meaning potentially hidden in each sentence. You might then analyze each sentence as you go.

[Establish meaning in sentence 1]: What does it mean that the earth is "scarred" in the first sentence?

[Analyze meaning in sentence 1]: What might that mean both literally and figuratively? Why would Steinbeck not tell us why it was scarred?

[Establish meaning in sentence 2]: Good; next sentence: What, in sentence 2, are rivulet marks? If a rivulet is a small stream, what is a rivulet *mark*? What does this tell us is probably happening? Great. Steinbeck writes that the plows crossed and recrossed those rivulet marks. Who is driving the plows?

[Analyze meaning in sentence 2]: Why would Steinbeck make inanimate objects the subject of this sentence? I mean, why not "The farmers drove their plows back and forth across the rivulet marks"? There are no farmers in Steinbeck's narrative. But it's supposed to be a book about the farmers. Why would that be? What does it tell us?

[Establish meaning in sentence 3]: OK; next sentence. Steinbeck describes the "last rains" coming. We also saw that phrase in the first sentence. What does it mean?

[Analyze meaning in sentence 3]: Let's focus on the word "last." Last before what? And what are some possible connotations of "last rains"?

In this model, the toggling is fast: Read a sentence. Establish its meaning. Analyze it. Alternatively, however, you might choose to establish the meaning of several sentences at once and then analyze them as a group. For example:

[Establish meaning]: OK, let's look closely at this first paragraph. What does it mean that the earth is "scarred" in the first sentence? Good. Now what, in sentence 2, might a rivulet mark be? If a rivulet is a small stream, what is a rivulet *mark*? Great. Steinbeck writes that the plows crossed and recrossed those rivulet marks. Who is driving the plows? Interesting. Now, in the next sentence, Steinbeck describes the "last rains" coming. We also saw that phrase in the first sentence. What does it mean?

[Analyze meaning]: OK, so let's look at some of the things we established in those first sentences. A first paragraph often sets the stage: so tell me how the stage is being set here. OK, good points. But let's keep going. What's unusual about how Steinbeck is setting the stage? For example, who is the main character?

In this second model, the teacher still toggles between establishing and analyzing meaning, but she does so in larger-grain sizes, letting the text's meaning build up a bit more. In short, the rate at which you toggle is a key factor in your Close Reading lessons.

Needless to say, there isn't really a best way to choose a "toggling rate." The particulars of the text and your students will help determine what works best—as will your desire to manage a key challenge in Close Reading: pacing. Sometimes, the fast back-and-forth will help. Sometimes, letting a bit of suspense build up will be better.

As a reminder to work strategically back and forth, it helps to add "Toggling" to the top of our map, as shown in Table 2.4.

**Table 2.4** Completed Map of TDQs

| | Text-Dependent Questions | ← Toggling → Questions to Establish Meaning | Questions to Analyze Meaning |
|---|---|---|---|
| *Zooming* ↕ | | Referent<br>Denotation<br>Explanation | Word pattern<br>Connotation<br>Figurative/literal meaning<br>Sensitivity analysis<br>Missing word analysis |
| | Sentence or line level questions | Paraphrase<br>Key line<br>Reference<br>Syntax or sentence structure | Key line<br>Allusion<br>Figurative language<br>Pattern |
| | Paragraph or stanza level questions | Summary (and targeted summary)<br>Delineation<br>Finite evidence | Paragraph function<br>Dramatic irony<br>Extended metaphor/allegory |

You may notice another word we've added on the left-hand side: **zooming**. This refers to a second strategic decision implicit in establishing and analyzing meaning: moving back and forth between smaller and larger units of text.

## Zooming

Sequencing TDQs, and doing that sequencing in a way that unlocks maximum value, is the final step to developing powerful Close Reading lessons. It's a challenging step. In the face of this challenge, our colleagues at Uncommon Schools formed a working group to study it. What they developed was powerful: a process called zooming in and out of text. Essentially, analysis is a function of moving closer to the word level (zooming in) and all the way out to discuss the author's purpose (zooming out). Consider this exchange focused on a sentence from *The Grapes of Wrath*, "The sun flared down on the growing corn day after day until a line of brown spread along the edge of each green bayonet."

A teacher might first zoom in:

Let's zoom in on the imagery here. How is the grass described? [Answer: As green bayonets]

Unpack "bayonet" for me. [Bayonets are used in war; they are weapons; they are used for fighting and stabbing.]

Then she might toggle from establishing meaning to analyzing it:

Interesting! How would the text be different if Steinbeck had said "each green stalk"? That would still mean the same thing, right? [No — you'd lose the connotation of violence.]

So, then, why would Steinbeck have chosen this *particular* language? [Steinbeck is reinforcing the notion that the earth and sky are somehow at war with each other. His violent imagery underscores this point.]

She might then zoom out again, first toggling to the left to establish meaning:

OK, let's step back. Where *else* do we see violent, warlike imagery here?

and then back to the right to analyze:

So what can we start to conclude from this idea that the "sharp" sun is "striking" down on bayonets of corn over and over?

What's key here is not just the use of zooming but the friction that is created by zooming in and out—moving between language study and the author's larger purpose. These sequences are what make a Close Reading lesson come to life. It's also what gets teachers beyond asking good questions (which many have been doing for years) to pushing students down a path that will allow them to analyze text in a new way.

---

## It's Not Just the Questions, It's the Sequence

by Stephen Chiger, Director of 5–12 Literacy, North Star Academies

Close reading instruction may hinge on great questions, but great questions alone won't make a class powerful. Decisions about sequencing often boil down to deciding when to toggle or zoom; they create a road map for how to think about text.

Here's a series of questions from a lesson by Megan Fernando and Julia Goldenheim on John Steinbeck's *The Pearl*, in which Steinbeck introduces a smug, self-centered doctor who casually exploits the protagonist's village. Steinbeck writes:

> His eyes rested in puffy little hammocks of flesh and his mouth drooped with discontent.

Megan and Julia prepared a series of questions designed to help students analyze the imagery in "puffy little hammocks of flesh" and a mouth that "drooped with discontent." Their first question established meaning:

> Let's look more closely at the image of "puffy little hammocks of flesh." What does this mean the doctor looked like? Can you describe him?

Next, they toggled over to the analysis side of the chart and zoomed in tight on the text:

> What ideas do we typically associate with hammocks?

> Steinbeck could have chosen something else; he could have said "puffy little *cradles* of flesh." Instead, he said "hammocks." Why? What does this specific choice of words add to the text?

---

Then:

> Can anyone suggest another piece of loaded diction for us to unpack?

After that, they zoomed out slightly, asking students to begin to construct an interpretation based on other language choices:

> What about "drooped"? Does this word support or challenge our hypothesis about the doctor's characterization?

Finally they zoomed out even more broadly:

> Now let's look at Steinbeck's diction across the whole passage introducing the doctor. How does his imagery characterize the doctor? What is Steinbeck telling us?

It's worth noticing that Megan and Julia zoom in and out of the text to push students to consider specific language choices, *and then connect them to Steinbeck's larger purpose or the effect he creates.*

The process of zooming in and out is often implicit in what teachers want students to do when asking students to analyze texts. Their ability to make meaning comes from the continual process of reflecting deeply on an author's choices, scrutinizing them, and considering the implications of those decisions. Zoom in to language and zoom out to author's purpose: it's the friction that makes the fire.

## AFTERWARD: GLOBAL-LEVEL TEXT-DEPENDENT QUESTIONS

Having added toggling and zooming, we complete the map of TDQs with one final addition: global-level questions. Global-level questions are those that come as an "afterward" to the Close Reading analysis—questions that ask students to extrapolate the insights they've gleaned from the passage and apply them either to the text as a whole or to a large section (say, a chapter). Here are some types and examples.

### Convention Alignment Analyses

**Convention alignment analysis** asks students to identify how a piece conforms to or diverges from what readers can expect from the form of a genre (for example, a sonnet, an editorial) and how those divergences or conformities create meaning. For example:

How does our reading suggest that Claudius's soliloquy in act 1, scene 2, "with mirth in funeral dirge in marriage" is like or unlike what we've come to expect from a soliloquy in a Shakespearean tragedy?

## Intratextual Motifs and Discourse

**Intratextual motifs and discourse** ask students to analyze the connection between different parts of a text or how a motif shows up elsewhere. For example:

Where else do we see images of violent struggle among the forces of nature—especially ordinarily positively portrayed forces of nature like the sun—like those we see in the first chapter of *Grapes of Wrath*?

## Intertextual Discourse

**Intertextual discourse** asks students to analyze the explicit or implicit connection between a given text and others. For example:

Where else do we see allusions to Moses's journey across the desert in *Grapes of Wrath*? How is their presence in this scene typical of the connections Steinbeck sees?

## Ambiguity Questions

**Ambiguity questions** at the global level ask students to analyze what is left unstated or unresolved by the passage you've read closely, and why. For example:

The line from the nonsensical limerick, "My name is Yon Yonson, I come from Wisconsin," appears not only in this passage but throughout *Slaughterhouse-Five*—over and over, in fact. Why would the author repeat an apparently meaningless line over and over without explanation?

## Part-to-Whole Questions

**Part-to-whole questions** ask what role this scene/chapter/excerpt plays in the context of the larger work from which it comes. For example:

Why would Steinbeck choose to divide his long, plot-driven novel with a series of prose poems like this first chapter that are completely different in style from the rest of the book?

The majority of this chapter has looked at the different ways teachers and students can highlight, excavate, and analyze meaning from given texts, most often verbally. In the next module, we'll look at processing ideas in writing—and the power of having a focus up front.

| MODULE 2.4 | Processing Ideas and Insights in Writing, and the Power of Clear Focus |
|---|---|

The final piece of a Close Reading lesson is to require students to do plenty of written processing, particularly after the first reading but also at the end of the lesson as a summative activity. Although the process of asking TDQs can include questioning, writing, and discussion in a variety of combinations, the last part must focus on writing—on taking the analysis and hammering it into a clear argument. Not only is writing the format that will be required of students in college—and not only is writing an idea the most rigorous and demanding way to express it—but (1) writing also requires every student to independently complete the analysis that synthesizes the lesson, and (2) writing makes thinking permanent; it allows teachers to assess effectively—to Check for Understanding. We'll get more broadly into the role of writing in chapter 4; our discussion here is limited to the role of writing in Close Reading lessons.

## On Writing, Revision, and Close Reading

By Stephen Chiger, Director of 5–12 Literacy, North Star Academies

Beginning your Close Reading lesson with writing is a powerful way to begin with reflection—by all students. It also allows you to see what students are able to do from the get-go. Best of all, if you start your class with writing, you can end it with revision, creating a feedback loop that helps students improve, not just day to day, but moment to moment.

Hadley Roach, a seventh-grade teacher who planned a lesson on the first page of Mario Vargas Llosa's *Feast of the Goat*, recently began her class by establishing meaning—ensuring her students' literal understanding

*(Continued)*

(Continued)

of the text—and moving into analysis. She wanted students to see the patterns in Vargas Llosa's diction: the violent words that established the narrator's disdain for a return to the Dominican Republic, and a more subtle pattern that revealed the disdain to be closer, perhaps, to ambivalence.

Hadley began by having students write, asking them to explain what patterns they could find in the diction and what those patterns suggested about the author. She then began moving about the room to collect data on her students' writing. Observing carefully, she was able to make a decision about her next instructional step.

Think about that for a moment. How often do we bemoan the lack of attention and care students give to our writing feedback—feedback that we spend hours generating? It's hard to blame students too much. For them, a paper they wrote a week ago may feel as though it was written last year. It's an artifact.

But if we respond to student writing in the moment, we create something rare and powerful: a shortened instructional feedback loop that makes feedback relevant and urgent.

As it turns out, Hadley's students found the pattern of diction she was hoping they'd see (sounds "assault" ears and "assail" each other; the city is an "explosion of savage life"), but they weren't quite sure about what it meant. They knew there was *something* happening, but they couldn't explain how word choice affected meaning.

Great teaching begins at the moment learning breaks down, and Hadley began her text-dependent questioning there, zooming in with students on specific words and helping them assess the connotations individually with TDQs. Gradually, they appeared to see how the text worked.

When she finished her questioning, Hadley had students revise their work, asking for a very specific change: "In your revision, I want you to include a breakdown of the word *savage* as part of your writing." *That's* the moment of change. Hadley targeted an error, remediated it through questioning, and sent students to fix it. Not for homework. Not on a paper she'd get to on the next weekend. She did it right then.

Hadley monitored again to see if students could demonstrate mastery. Students' writing is the key to seeing this growth. Great literature discussions too often give teachers a false positive. Teachers hear a few students sharing insights and assume everyone is at their level. Hadley needed to be sure that everyone could make the change.

On this particular day, it turns out that one of Hadley's classes fully grasped the text, but the other didn't. So she showed them a piece of strong student writing, asked the class to analyze what made it effective, and then had students revise yet again. Her feedback loop was fast, targeted, and conducted in response to real-time data.

Her teaching—and use of writing—should remind teachers that students don't need innate talent to become masterful at their craft. They simply need patience, practice, loads of revision, and coaching toward mastery, one small detail at a time.

## THE POWER OF A READING FOCUS

There's one final factor you'll want to consider in ensuring a successful Close Reading lesson: having a clear "focus." A focus is similar to the objective you would use for your lesson—a Close Reading lesson or any other—but is not quite the same. Here's how it's different:

When you identify a focus for your Close Reading lesson, you clarify what you are reading for. This is critical. In a rich text, there is often an almost unlimited supply of imagery, word, and structural choices to discuss. A surfeit, sometimes, and that can make the lesson—and the endeavor of Close Reading—seem scattershot, haphazard. You ask one minute about one thing and the next moment about another, with everything fair and equal fodder for discussion. It's all breadth but no depth; that's not usually superproductive.

A key aspect of Close Reading, ultimately, is identifying and attending to a line of inquiry. It's what you do when you write a paper about a text. So it is often helpful to know before you start what idea you want students to read a text for. This does not have to mean there is a "right answer" so much as a consistent area of focus—a line of inquiry you will follow. Often this means modeling how to "argue a line," tracing a theme, a motif, a conflict, or an image through the complexity of a text. Other times, it could mean asking students to identify the "line" they find most interesting. That's great too—especially if they've seen you model how to do it right. Either way, your focus remains different from your lesson objective. It is more specific and identifies the most important things you want to track in a specific portion of text. For a simple comparison:

Lesson Objective: To describe the setting of *The Grapes of Wrath* by reading—and Close Reading—the first chapter.

Close Reading Focus:

*Text:* the first two paragraphs of the chapter.

*Focus:* establish meaning by ensuring student attentiveness to constant symbolism; then unpack imagery of violence used to describe the sun and the earth. Determine why it is so prevalent.

Consider here that you might Close Read two sections of text during a lesson, focusing on slightly different aspects of each. You'd have a focus for each but still a unified lesson objective.

## Focus and the Close Reading Lesson

By Maggie Johnson, former reading teacher, currently Reading Content Specialist at Uncommon Schools' *Teach Like a Champion* team

Great literature is usually created with tremendous intentionality. Word choice and plot elements are spun together meticulously, and uniquely, in every text. This is one of the reasons Close Reading is such a valuable exercise, but it is also one of the great challenges of teaching Close Reading.

Great texts—and great readers—are rebellious. Interpretations refuse to stay simple or universal; alternatives are forever emerging from the frayed pages of a great novel. This creates a challenge for teachers planning Close Reading. Analyzing a character is likely to take you on a very different journey if you are reading *The Sound and The Fury*, say, as opposed to *The Catcher in the Rye*. This is why it's difficult to give students simplistic formulas for identifying or interpreting literary elements across texts. Reading literature requires problem solving.

Another challenge is that a good text can go in any number of directions. Going off in an unexpected direction can be a nice outcome of Close Reading skills, but it's not always the best way to teach them. For a great Close Reading to be cohesive, comprehensive, and intentional, and to show students how an argument is created out of words and phrases and lines and stanzas, a teacher must have a focus—something she wants to help her students see. Something she wants to teach them how to see in a given text. This task—framing a Close Reading focus—is one of the hardest parts.

It's often useful to begin by reading and marking up the passage organically, without prejudgment, much as one might have done in preparation for a discussion in college. It can help to reread several times a text you plan to teach, adding more detail to your notations with each pass. As your familiarity grows, you'll likely be better able to tease out the unifying threads woven into the passage—the threads that contribute to its meaning. It is from these threads that a teacher is able to establish a thesis of sorts, or an understanding of the text to guide students through their fastidious reading. This involves de-emphasizing certain aspects of the text to facilitate achieving depth of a chosen line of analysis. In some cases, it may involve revisiting the text again with a new goal.

In order to test the quality and clarity of a tentative Close Reading focus, translate it into a writing prompt and "live the learning" by composing an ideal response. For example, after reading Dr. Martin Luther King Jr.'s "Letter from a Birmingham Jail" with an eighth-grade class, you might want students to understand that Dr. King justifies his presence in Birmingham to fellow clergymen who consider him an agitator by developing a theory of human interrelatedness. This idea is epitomized in his famous quote from the letter, "injustice anywhere is a threat to justice everywhere." The prompt you might practice responding to (and eventually expect your students to answer), then, is "How does Dr. Martin Luther King Jr. justify traveling to Birmingham in April of 1963?"

To explain how King uses ethos and descriptive imagery to argue that the collective fate of humans holds us accountable for one another's suffering, a good response involves explicating multiple key lines from the letter, such as "We are caught in an inescapable network of mutuality, tied in a single

(Continued)

garment of destiny." Answering this question as a student allows a teacher not only to pressure-test the feasibility of its focus but also to identify the key lines and phrases crucial for analysis. If you're unable to answer a question by analyzing specific details from the text, that should be a signal to revise your focus well before bringing it live to students.

Holding yourself accountable for avoiding tangential questioning and maintaining a laserlike focus on essential aspects of the text are vital to fostering the shared understanding you want your students to achieve. In teaching Close Reading, choosing your destination is often the best place to begin.

We've just spent the better part of a chapter talking about the design and execution of Close Reading lessons, which require careful planning and preparation on the teacher's part. The value of teaching students how to read complex text through such lessons is obvious, but Close Reading does not only take place as a full lesson. It can and should also be "activated" in small units of just a few minutes' duration. In fact, given that the planning burden is significant for a strong Close Reading lesson, such lessons cannot be taught as often as some might like. It's necessary to ensure that Close Reading is done in smaller units—"bursts"—in the midst of other types of work with texts. In the next module, we'll look at those bursts.

| MODULE 2.5 | Close Reading Bursts |
|---|---|

Close Reading bursts allow students to practice Close Reading frequently, often in quick, dynamic iterations, and in many cases to understand the decision making they will ultimately use in determining when to use their Close Reading skills on their own. For example, it is important to use Close Reading skills in response to both challenge ("Wow, that is really hard; I'm going to go back through and tear it apart until I get what she means") and opportunity ("Wow, that imagery is so striking; I'm going to go back through and make sense of why it seems so important"). Bursts model this.

Unlike full Close Reading lessons, Close Reading bursts can be planned or unplanned. A burst might come about due to your decision during planning that students will need to delve deeper into a particular line to have the highest-quality discussion during class. Your burst, then, could be ten minutes spent unlocking the nuances of two lines as a preliminary activity to a student-led seminar.

## See It in Action

Watch an example of a Close Reading burst in Beth Verrilli's AP English class in clip 3 at teachlikeachampion.com/yourlibrary. In a recent lesson, Beth asked two of her AP English students to do a dramatic reading of a short excerpt from *Othello*. She praised the students for a beautiful reading and then dove into a Close Reading burst, starting with the question, " What did we notice about Amelia that can say something about her character?" The first student Beth called on, Hamiya, pointed out Emilia's repetition of the phrase, "My husband" and her show of "surprise or bewilderment about finding this [Iago's malevolent plotting ] out about her husband." Beth made note of Hamiya's observation and then called on a second student who'd read it differently—he believed that Emilia knew the truth about her husband all along.

With two contradictory interpretations, Beth called on the class to weigh in—asking them to decide which argument they agreed with ("shock and surprise" versus "Emilia's known all along"). One student opined in support of Hamiya's argument that Emilia was expressing shock and surprise at Othello's actions, but Beth wanted students to focus on Iago, so she went back to the text doing a leapfrog read of Emilia's lines. She continued to probe into Emilia's reaction to news about her husband, directing students back to the text to looking for more evidence in support of the shock-and-surprise argument. Students knew that Iago was shocked and surprised, but Beth wanted them to be sure that they understood why. And she wanted them to derive their understanding directly from Shakespeare's words. She reread for them Emilia's lines "My husband? That she was false to wedlock? My husband? My husband! My husband say she was false!" Beth then asked a student to read another excerpt directly from the text—starting with the lines just after Emilia seems to understand what Othello is telling her about her husband. Then Beth probed further: "Anything here about her understanding of her husband?" A student responded, "We saw heavenly diction coupled with the word 'pernicious,' so we know that she knows her husband's true nature now that Othello has shed light on it." In order to confirm and solidify their understanding, Beth asks yet another text-based question: "How do we know she knows it now and not before?" as a finale to the class's Close Reading burst.

---

There are also times, though, when you stumble on a passage unexpectedly, in the middle of class. Maybe you had not anticipated a certain line to be so tricky. Your students are stumped. "Pause," you might say. "It looks like there's a lot in the last two sentences of this paragraph that we need to pull out. Let's do a bit of Close Reading here to make sure we're getting everything we need and then we'll come back to our discussion." You dig in for a few minutes of Close Reading and then it's on to other things.

You might think about it this way, then: that there are four types of Close Reading bursts, as illustrated in Table 2.5.

In all four cases, bursts are characterized by their comparative brevity—in terms of both duration and text length. Typically, bursts focus on a sentence or two of text; they might involve extended discussion or a sequence of just four or five TDQs, for example. Toggling and zooming still apply to bursts. As Steve Chiger observes, it's important that teachers still think about the sequence of questions strategically, understanding that you can't really Close Read with just one question.

The notion of a burst in reaction to challenging—often unexpectedly challenging—text suggests that the Close Reading tools outlined in this chapter can be thought of,

**Table 2.5**   The Four Types of Close Reading Bursts

|  | Planned | Unplanned |
|---|---|---|
| Difficult Text | You prepare the burst in advance in order to delve into key lines that are especially tricky and hard to understand. | You begin a burst in reaction to important lines or what happens during class, working with lines that are especially tricky and hard to understand. |
| Critical or Striking Passage | You prepare the burst in advance in order to delve into key lines that are or will be especially important or memorable. | You begin a burst in reaction to important lines or what happens during class, working with lines that are or will be especially important or memorable. |

quite usefully, as a means of reacting to evidence of incomplete mastery in reading, one of the trickiest challenges in the critical task of Checking for Understanding. Teaching students how to circle back and solve the text when it resists easy understanding is preferable to explaining to students what they missed. And in the end, if we are reading challenging texts, we will *always* be faced with moments of special depth and incomplete initial understanding. This is supposed to happen when we read widely and well. So Close Reading bursts model comfort and poise in that situation.

## CHOOSING LINES FOR CLOSE READING BURSTS

There are several benefits to Close Reading in short, portable bursts. One of the simplest and most obvious is one of the most important: you can usually execute it within whatever novel or text you are already reading and in the context of whatever else you might be doing with the day's lesson.

Generally, for a full Close Reading *lesson,* you will choose a specific text for the occasion. You will spend your forty-five or fifty-five minutes or one hour studying a speech or an essay that you have chosen specifically as a device to allow you to practice Close Reading; or perhaps the lesson comes from a short story that, although not chosen exclusively for a single Close Reading, is dense and challenging enough that it allows for plenty of Close Reading.

But a burst can come from any text, even a novel that is generally less complex and more accessible to students. Remember that a text's difficulty level—it's Lexile score, say—is an *average.* The book is actually made up of passages slightly—or significantly—above and below the mean. The outlier passages, which can be complex for any of the reasons discussed in the chapter on text selection—are likely shorter in length. They can arrive suddenly and even unannounced. And it is a critical skill to recognize them—to be self-aware enough to say, "Whoa, I have to slow down here" or "Whoa, there's something deep here"—and know how to make sense of them. Close Reading in bursts derived from your class novel allows you to model that aspect of successful reading.

Recently, eighth-grade English teacher Ellie Strand of Troy Prep put this idea to work. Even though she was doing only a short burst of Close Reading, her lesson involved layered readings and rereadings much like the kind described in the section on Close Reading lessons.

In the course of reading *Animal Farm* with her class, Ellie identified a single critical sentence from a section they'd recently read and dug into deeply. Her Close Reading burst was retrospective. Students went back to the previous day's reading to study it even deeper. As it turns out, they reread it another three times.

The first time, Ellie led a Control the Game reading during which she paused briefly to define three vocabulary words and instructed students to underline key lines that they'd revisit later in the class. Next, Ellie asked students to reread the passage again, this time independently—with the goal of annotating the text and formulating a hypothesis about the central idea/theme of the passage. After they'd done so, Ellie asked them to interpret the central idea of the text in writing. Ellie then brought the class back together to study just one sentence with deep focus:

> Again the animals seemed to remember that a resolution against this had been passed in the early days, and again Squealer was able to convince them this was not the case.

Through a series of TDQs, in ten sharp minutes, she modeled how to read a single critical sentence with depth and insight. She then zoomed out and asked her students how their new understanding of the line changed their understanding of the passage as a whole—a key line (analyze meaning) question.

---

## Epigraphs and Close Reading

Laurie Halse Anderson's novel *Chains* is set in the years of the American Revolution. It views the events of the Revolution through the eyes of a protagonist who is enslaved for much of the novel. Almost every chapter begins with an epigraph taken from a contemporary text and providing context, background, or perspective on the larger narrative. This of course is the purpose of epigraphs. (They are, in fact, a perfect, naturally occurring example of embedded nonfiction, discussed in chapter 3.) But Anderson's approach raises the question: Do most students read epigraphs? If they do, is it merely at a glance, or do they reflect on them and their relevance with care? Or do they skip over them, missing the depth and perspective they provide?

Epigraphs such as Anderson's, which often use short and especially challenging or allusive texts to put the events in a chapter or book in broader perspective, are ideal for Close Reading bursts. Here, for example, are the epigraphs Anderson chose to begin chapters 9 and 10, which take place after the protagonist, Isabel, has moved to New York at a time when it is riven with tension between Tories and patriots.

> Hundreds in this [New York] Colony are active against us and such is the weakness of the Government, (if it can deserve the Name) that Tories openly profess their sentiments in Favour of the Enemy, and live unpunished.
>
> —Letter of William Tudor, Washington's Chief Legal officer,
> to John Adams

> The people (of New York)—why the people are magnificent; in their carriages, which are numerous, in their house furniture, which is fine, in their pride and conceit, which are inimitable, in their profaneness, which is intolerable, in the want of principle, which is prevalent, and In their Toryism, which is insufferable.
>
> —Letter from Henry Knox to his wife, Lucy

Imagine the benefits of ten short minutes digging deeply into these lines—unpacking their archaic text, the subtle positioning on the events of the time their word choices reveal—not just as an exercise in reading challenging text with precision but for the benefit it would provide to reading the rest of the novel. Further, the epigraphs allow you to ask the natural question: Why would the author think it was important enough to use this exact passage as an epigraph? A little bit of spinach to build reading muscle at the start of every engaging chapter. It's a novel almost built for Close Reading.

## ANATOMY OF A BURST

Earlier in this chapter, we shared a video clip of Rue Ratray's reading a critical scene in Lois Lowry's *The Giver* with his students. Lets return to it now to study it a bit more deeply; it provides an outstanding example of a Close Reading burst.

In the clip, Rue is preparing his students to discuss the scene where Jonas learns what "release" is and the extent of his father's participation in it. [Spoiler alert: Release is state-sponsored killing of citizens who are believed to be unproductive.] He wanted his students to spend the rest of class discussing whether the father in *The Giver* was a cruel character, so Rue began class by Close Reading two revealing lines from the novel. His burst began class and started with his putting the lines on the board and asking students to read them:

> Jonas watched as his father bent over the squirming newchild on the bed. "And you, little guy, you're only five pounds ten ounces. A shrimp!"

Then he used a Turn and Talk:

> "Based upon *just* this sentence, as it's written, what can we infer about how Jonas's father feels about what he did?"

What Rue wanted students to recognize was how the father used the same loving "baby-talk" voice with the child he was about to "release" that he used with a beloved child he had adopted at home. Rue wanted his students to hear the unself-conscious singsong in the father's voice, how the use of the playful, loving terms of affection "little guy" and "shrimp" was the way Lowry demonstrated that the father had little awareness of what he was doing—and how she expressed the deep dissonance Jonas felt.

It takes a special intuition for how words work, an affinity for the hidden language of tone and word choice to pick up on these things. Call that "language sense." Rue's approach to developing it focused on sensitivity analysis. He asked students to read two near-parallel sentences he'd constructed in which he'd inserted minor changes from the original. He asked his students to evaluate how the changes affected the value of the overall expression. First they read the original.

Then this:

> Jonas watched as his father bent over the squirming newchild on the bed. "And you, you're only five pounds ten ounces. A shrimp."

Then this:

> Jonas watched as his father bent over the squirming newchild on the bed. "And you, little guy, you're only five pounds ten ounces. A baby."

Rue was removing and substituting (and adding back) slight variations: just the pet names Jonas's father used. The idea was to help students see how the sentence communicated ideas differently with just a tiny change, how the tone of a single word sent the entire sentence spinning off in a new direction. Not only was it an incredibly useful ten minutes—a "burst" of Close Reading that would pay dividends a thousand times by developing students' ear for language—but it worked in perfect synergy with the rest of the lesson, a discussion of the father's character and the degree to which he was aware of and culpable for his actions.

## READING BURSTS AND CONSISTENT PRACTICE

One of the other benefits of Close Reading bursts has to do with the power of consistent practice. Think for a minute about the similarities between Close Reading and another act of attentive and often intense interpretation: studying music. Musicians know that success comes from practicing regularly; sometimes the goal is to practice widely applicable skills for a short period of time almost every day. You do your scales and exercises for ten minutes and then go on to the piece you are playing and interpreting. You do this no matter how good you are. You know you will apply the fluidity and dexterity you develop in your exercises to every piece you play.

There's a good argument to be made in favor of the power of learning more by doing a little bit of something every day. In the end, would you learn more by spending a full and intense hour Close Reading a passage once every week or by spending ten to twelve minutes Close Reading the most important couple of lines from whatever you were reading that day? It's impossible to say, but it can't hurt to leverage the benefits of both approaches.

## READING BURSTS AND SOLOING

A final benefit of Close Reading bursts is the independence they can help foster. Close Reading teaches students the skills and sensitivities that lead, ultimately, to the ability to fly solo: to step out of the nest and confidently develop sturdy and autonomous interpretations of texts on their own. The short blocks of text implicit in bursts make them the ideal time to experiment with freedom and autonomy, to say something like "Explain and analyze this passage from *Animal Farm*" for the first time. Students can "solo" not only more simply but also more successfully that way, and that small fact is highly important.

One of the keys to practicing something effectively, Erica and Doug found in the course of writing (along with Troy Prep principal Katie Yezzi) *Practice Perfect: 42 Rules for Getting Better at Getting Better,* is to encode success. Only by practicing at highest quality do you get better at executing at highest quality. This was the rationale for the approach the great cellist Yo-Yo Ma's parents took to his early training in music. Rather than long practices where his energy and focus would fade, they began teaching him in five-, ten-, and fifteen-minute bursts of intense, high-quality playing. Then he would stop before his execution began to waver. Gradually, over time, the length of his intensive practice increased.

Reading closely in short bursts can offer similar benefits. To have students do it well for a short period of time and then stop before they struggle to maintain their focus makes the whole process feel less daunting. To have students succeed (or fail) in deciding effectively, over and over in small, frequent, low-risk iterations, which of the *many* tools for text analysis to use *when no one tells them what tools to use* is a key to success.

## On Soloing

By Maggie Johnson, former reading teacher, currently Reading Content Specialist at Uncommon Schools' *Teach Like a Champion* team

There comes a time when every student is asked to wade through a formidable piece of literature companionless. The importance of this inevitable moment would nag me every time I sat down to plan a Close Reading lesson. I was confident my students were accessing with great success the texts we read together, but I questioned whether they were internalizing the habits of Close Reading we practiced so diligently. If they weren't, I worried, all of our hard work would be for naught.

I needed to gradually release students to practice more and more autonomous bouts of Close Reading. So I began asking them to "solo," with one line or phrase at a time. Oftentimes this line would be embedded within a longer passage worthy of Close Reading, and in some cases it would be emblematic of the passage itself. Take the following line from *The Great Gatsby*, for example: "I was within and without, simultaneously enchanted and repelled by the inexhaustible variety of life." The line is rich but difficult, and its brevity helps facilitate students' careful dissection of its parts, without compromising rigor or exhausting their willpower.

I would often backstop soloing by adding one or two questions for students to answer after annotating the line, as a sort of accountability check for students and a tool for me to gather data. For this line I might ask, "Who is the speaker? How do you know?" and "Summarize the line." As students experienced success, I would ask them to solo with more complex lines, subsections, or sets of paired lines. The questions I asked scaled back in explicitness as well. Oftentimes it would simply be "What do you make of this line?" or "Why is this important?" In their answers, students began to sort of Close Read aloud, explicating the meaning of a line in the course of their analysis. As students grew increasingly confident (and accurate), they began to identify lines worthy of Close Reading themselves and cultivated engaging, text-based discussions with less and less intervention from me.

## Close Reading, Reconsidered

Close Reading, well defined and carefully executed, is arguably one of the most important sets of skills and habits teachers can instill in their students. Working through Close Reading in class is the bridge between reading with "training wheels" and successful, competent independent reading. Through layered reading, text-dependent questions to establish and analyze meaning, working through texts in writing, and Close Reading bursts, teachers can help build up the problem-solving skills so essential to autonomous reading—the kind of reading students will need to master to be successful in college, let alone life beyond grade school.

In the next chapter, we'll turn to the third portion of the Core of the Core: nonfiction.

## NOTES

1.  Nancy Boyles, "Closing In on Close Reading," *Educational Leadership* 70, no. 4 (2013): 36–41, http://www.ascd.org/publications/educational-leadership/dec12/vol70/num04/Closing-in-on-Close-Reading.aspx.

2.  Ralph Ellison, *Invisible Man* (New York: Random House, 1980), 3.

# Reading Nonfiction, and the Challenge of Background Knowledge

## MODULE 3.1: THE KEY CHALLENGE: BACKGROUND KNOWLEDGE

The more knowledge students have up front, the more they are likely to get out of their interaction with a text.

## MODULE 3.2: ABSORPTION RATE

Teachers must manage reading both fiction and nonfiction strategically, as not all students process material at the same rate based on their background knowledge.

## MODULE 3.3: EMBEDDING TEXTS TO INCREASE ABSORPTION RATE AND BUILD BACKGROUND KNOWLEDGE

Whether complementary texts are intended to support basic understanding of a primary text or to force students to look at a primary text more rigorously, synergies go both ways.

## MODULE 3.4: OTHER WAYS TO BUILD BACKGROUND KNOWLEDGE

Teachers can deliberately maximize the value of nonfiction through highlighting cross-textual connections, leveraging fiction and nonprinted texts, and posing connecting questions.

## MODULE 3.5: SOME UNIQUE CHALLENGES OF NONFICTION

Nonlinear text layouts, as well as obscure formats and micro rules, present special challenges to developing readers.

# Chapter 3

# Reading Nonfiction, and the Challenge of Background Knowledge

Reading nonfiction poses a double challenge for most students. Comprehension of nonfiction often demands a strong base of prior knowledge, but reading nonfiction is also one of the primary ways such a base of knowledge is built. Nonfiction, in other words, both relies on and develops knowledge, and the significance of this paradox is far reaching.

We can start with the practical. One of the most forceful arguments in the Common Core is that students should read significantly more nonfiction than most currently do. This argument is intended to address a gap in preparation. Much of what many students must read in college is nonfiction—often complex and dense nonfiction—but their reading during their middle and high school years is usually heavily weighted toward fiction, often, as we discussed in chapter 1, insufficiently complex fiction. Thus students arrive on campus unprepared to read what is required of them.

So students need to read more nonfiction to be ready for college. And they will need to be able to read more of it for the gateway assessments that will get them there, not only any Common Core assessments but the redesigned SAT, which will focus intensively—even more so than in the past—on cross-disciplinary reading from the sciences, social sciences, and history, and which will include at least one excerpt from a key founding document of the United States every year.[1]

But even beyond these pragmatic arguments, success in middle and high school demands that students "read to learn." They must glean knowledge from articles, textbooks, essays, research summaries, and the like to thrive in both social and hard sciences. And of course a broad and deep base of knowledge doesn't just assist students in reading nonfiction texts: it makes successful readers of fiction too, just as the knowledge that students derive from reading isn't exclusively from nonfiction. No matter how you feel about assessments like the Common Core and the SAT, this broader urgency of preparation drives their design.

So it is important not only to read plenty of nonfiction and to read it in a way that adds as efficiently as possible to a student's knowledge base but also to read fiction in the same way. But we note a further challenge here. Students often like reading nonfiction less because it's less engaging. We think it's also worth reflecting on how we can help them enjoy it more, and our reflections on these challenges form the basis of this chapter.

Before we look at the connection between knowledge and reading comprehension, we should parse some terms. It's not just nonfiction that students need more of. It's *nonnarrative* nonfiction. Despite its terrible name, this term makes a critical distinction. Nonnarrative nonfiction (NNNF) is nonfiction that *does not tell a story*, as memoir and biography do. Rather, the main goal of NNNF is to disseminate information, as an article would, or present an argument, as an essay would. It's the difference between reading "Letter from Birmingham Jail" and reading *The Autobiography of Malcolm X*. We use the term deliberately and in place of the more common term "expository" writing because to us it encompasses a wider array of texts, many of which are growing in relevance and importance with the rise of electronic media: interviews, speeches, opinion pieces (including op-eds and columns but also blog posts and less formal writing), letters, and primary historical documents, for example.

When teachers decide to read nonfiction in class, they most often read its narrative forms, precisely because of their accessibility. Reading narrative nonfiction is important. Much of our compendium of personal favorites—to read and to teach—is made up of memoir and biography, but it is also worth noting that these are the forms of nonfiction that *most closely resemble fiction* and therefore are most intuitive to students already. They have been familiarized with basic narrative conventions since the earliest stories they have heard, and this familiarity is reinforced with every movie or sitcom they watch. Less familiar forms of nonfiction—ones that lack a beginning, middle, and end or an identifiable storyteller, or that employ different organizing principles, for example—pose much bigger challenges. Thus, in this chapter, we place particular emphasis on tools teachers can use to read nonfiction's nonnarrative forms more frequently, engagingly, and successfully.

MODULE
3.1

## The Key Challenge: Background Knowledge

One reason why the fact that nonfiction texts both build and rely on background knowledge is so critical for teachers to consider is the tendency for its effects to compound over time. In reading, the more you know, the more you learn. Educators often refer to this as the Matthew Effect, in reference to a line in the Bible that details the rich getting richer and the poor getting poorer. In reading, it means that when you know a little about a topic going in, the text adds more knowledge and detail to your framework—easily and naturally deepening your understanding and building connections to existing knowledge while still leaving you enough processing capacity to be able to reflect on the nature of the ideas in the text.

This is great news if you start out with broad and deep knowledge, but less positive if you don't. When you know very little about a topic, it's easy to be confused or overwhelmed by new information. You can hold just a small fraction of it in your working memory, but you don't really know enough to decide what's most important and worth prioritizing. What you attend to is likely to be a combination of signal and noise. The new knowledge can easily become a morass of disjointed facts too daunting to prioritize or weave together in a cohesive way. Instead of comprehending an argument as a whole, you'd risk remembering a random detail here or maybe confusing two facts there. Or you'd just miss things. You might finish not much further along than you started.

Consider this sentence:

> As the desert sun climbs overhead, the kangaroo rat burrows deep in the sand and rests until evening.

For a reader with the background knowledge to know that the desert sun's "climbing" implies that it is moving toward the point where it is hottest and where that heat is deadly to mammals, there is not much of an inference to make—survival demands that the rat hide until the sun goes down. But if the reader merely knows that deserts are hot—not deadly hot—or that we are talking about the scorching midday sun, then the rat's behavior is, if not inexplicable, at least subject to multiple interpretations. Maybe the rat is afraid. The passage loses its intended meaning. An uninformed reader is misunderstanding as much as failing to understand.

And there are even subtler knowledge requirements implied by the sentence. A reader familiar with the conventions of species naming is likely to recognize instantly (that is, in the time it takes to process it while decoding the sentence) that the kangaroo rat is a species of rat, not a creature that's half kangaroo and half rat, and that it doesn't look like a kangaroo. Its name is metaphorical, not literal, and given merely because it can jump far. Worse, uninformed readers are likely to suffer these misunderstandings in silence. The passage seems "obvious" to those who have the necessary knowledge, and the barriers to meaning to those who lack that knowledge are both inscrutable and often invisible, so misunderstandings are likely to endure.

Research bears this out. Cognitive psychologist Daniel Willingham notes that a student's background knowledge is among the strongest factors predicting his or her reading comprehension. As he wrote recently in his blog, "Once kids are fluent decoders, much of the difference among readers is not due to whether [they're] a 'good reader' or 'bad reader' (meaning [they] have good or bad reading skills). Much of the difference among readers is due to how wide a range of knowledge they have. If you hand me a reading test and the text is on a subject I happen to know a bit about, I'll do better than if it happens to be on a subject I know nothing about."[2]

A 1988 study by Recht and Leslie is often cited as a compelling bit of proof. The researchers divided a group of young readers into two groups. One half of the readers had been shown by previous assessments to have strong reading skills—from decoding to comprehension—but they knew little about baseball. A second group comprised students with much lower reading skills, but with solid baseball knowledge. Both groups were given a passage about a baseball game to read and asked a series of comprehension questions. The result was that "weaker" readers with baseball knowledge outperformed the "good" readers without it.[3] They simply had the context to understand what was happening when, let's say, "Roberts sacrificed Martin to second." For them, Martin was now in scoring position, and Roberts was in the dugout. But this was not clear to their peers. As perspicacious as their reading might have been, their lack of knowledge betrayed them. What they needed to know was left unsaid.

"Every passage that you read omits information," Willingham writes. "All of this omitted information must be brought to the text by the reader. Otherwise the passage will be puzzling, or only partly understood."[4] And of course this is particularly obvious with passages about baseball, but it's just as true of passages about kangaroo rats in the deserts or about life in Colonial times or even *Tuck Everlasting*.

Teachers often refer to the process of figuring out what's left unsaid as *making inferences*. We see colleagues practicing this "skill" to help students get good at it. But no amount of inferencing practice—no amount of asking students to combine what they know with a conjecture about what they don't—would have helped those high readers without baseball knowledge as they sought to grasp what they did not know was missing. In fact, as we will discuss in a moment, it may be that inferencing is not a skill. If it is, it is a skill that is *also* predicated on students having knowledge to enable it to take place.

A paper by Cunningham and Stanovich went further in studying the connection between knowledge and reading. It took results for eleventh graders on an established reading comprehension test and assessed their correlation to several measures of their general knowledge, *not knowledge specific to the passages on the test* as the baseball study had done.[5] There was a "remarkably high correlation between reading comprehension and the measures of cultural knowledge," Willingham noted.[6] Correlation isn't cause, of course—a point we make throughout this book—so it's possible that the good readers in this second study simply knew more by the time they were tested, but given the relationship between knowledge and reading, that's sort of the point. Whether the knowledge caused the reading comprehension or the reading comprehension caused the knowledge, or both, it is still clear that reading and knowledge are linked in important ways.

Let's return for a moment to the idea of practicing inferencing to help students get better at it. Every text requires constant inference on the part of the reader. However, the size of the inferences students must make varies with the depth of their prior knowledge about what they are reading. This discrepancy in the size and number of inferences—a sort of regressive tax on lack of knowledge—is likely one of the key reasons that knowledge influences comprehension so deeply.

In *The Knowledge Deficit*, E. D. Hirsch Jr. argues that the ability to make inferences is not actually a formal skill.[7] Although this point may sound abstract, its ramifications aren't. If making inferences isn't a skill—that is, if practicing making inferences in one setting won't necessarily increase the likelihood of your making successful inferences elsewhere—then repetition is of limited value. If you make inferences based in large part on your existing knowledge, making a leap might not be the problem; knowing enough to know where and how to jump might be.

Consider that even the weakest readers have no trouble making inferences about the movies and television shows they watch as part of their constant interaction with popular culture. The problem then clearly isn't with those students' ability to make inferences. In a familiar context, they "get" what's unsaid. Rather, the difficulty must lie in the setting—at least in most cases: the students cannot process the text with enough cognitive bandwidth left over to make inferences, or they lack the vocabulary to follow the narrative, or they lack knowledge. They don't know what it means to burrow or what a climbing sun implies. Yes, it could be that there are also specific cognitive processes that make inferences work differently when made from text rather than visually, but even if that were true, knowledge would almost assuredly be a significant compounding factor. So in all likelihood, making inferences requires both background knowledge and experience thinking about what's missing from a text—in fact, we'd argue, knowing what sorts of things are often missing in a text is a sort of tacit knowledge that comes from experience. By itself though, a strategy-based approach to practicing making inferences is at least insufficient. Building background knowledge is necessary—and possibly primarily necessary—for students to make effective inferences.

The importance of background knowledge raises a chicken-or-egg type of problem for teachers. Students lack content knowledge in part because they don't read nonfiction well, and they don't read nonfiction well because they lack content knowledge. If we need background knowledge to build background knowledge, where and how do we start?

In the next module, we'll begin to answer the question by defining one of the key ideas in this chapter: **absorption rate**.

| MODULE 3.2 | Absorption Rate |
|---|---|

When students read, it's not just the fact that they comprehend the text at different levels that matters. If part of reading's long-term benefit is its capacity to build students' knowledge base, differences in how much knowledge they acquire from reading also has decisive long-term consequences. **Absorption rate** is a term we use to describe how quickly students assimilate new knowledge as they read. We use the term because absorption rate is not necessarily uniform. It can be different among the various students reading a given text, and it can be different for a single student as he or she engages different texts.

Two students reading the earlier sentence about the kangaroo rat might have understood it equally—the desert-dwelling rat hides from the hot sun—but one imagines the hiding creature to be a giant half-kangaroo half-rat and the other a tiny rat that can jump. One perhaps understands that the rat hides because it must adapt to its living conditions; the other just knows that it hides. The first has a useful idea to which she can connect other examples of adaptation in other texts. The other does not. One of a teacher's key tasks when reading nonfiction in particular, then, is to strategically manage absorption rate and take steps to ensure that the absorption rate is as high as possible for as many students as possible. Doing so is critical to students' long-term success.

So we support the idea that students should read more nonfiction, as long as they also continue to also read plenty of great fiction (as we discussed extensively in chapter 1). But as important as reading *more* nonfiction is reading nonfiction *more effectively*—in a way that unlocks knowledge and increases engagement and appreciation. Fortunately, part of the solution involves the synergy between reading nonfiction and fiction.

One simple change to increase absorption rate is to change what we read when. For example, teachers are often encouraged to teach nonfiction in isolation. In English or reading classes, that might mean a separate, stand-alone unit on nonfiction in which students read a series of articles, one after the other, studying their text features and structural elements. What do captions do? What are subheadings? The problem with this approach is that they cause students to encounter nonfiction texts devoid of context. One day it's an article about the naked mole rat, and the next it's another article with similar structural features, but this time about the American Revolution. The result is a situation where absorption rate is likely to be lowest—engagement too, possibly.

If a person gathers more knowledge on a given topic when he or she knows more about it, then students will absorb more when they read their third article about topics related to desert ecosystems, for example. So it can often be useful to have students read multiple texts on a topic so that their reading will result in a crescendo of knowledge absorption. Or, even better, to have them read an article that gives context to or elaborates on ideas from a novel in which they are deeply engaged. If you are reading *My Brother Sam Is Dead* and encounter an article on the armaments used in the Revolution, you have more context to help you absorb the information—how heavy the rifles were, for example. And you have more motivation too. The article helps you understand Tim, whom presumably students have come to care about. We call this idea **embedding nonfiction**, and we will come back to it in a moment.

First, though, let's define two more important and relatively simple terms: primary and secondary texts.

In many reading classes, we focus on a **primary text**. We don't mean primary text in the sense that it necessarily needs to be primary source material—like the Bible or the Declaration of Independence or any other original, historical document. Here, when we say primary text, we mean primary in the sense that the text is chosen as the principal reading material for a particular class. It is often a book-length text, usually a novel, on which a teacher focuses the majority of instruction. It might be a whole-class text or a series of guided reading texts, read over the course of several weeks, say, building familiarity and an ongoing relationship between students and an engaging and important story.

A powerful, rigorous, and engaging primary text is one of the key drivers of successful literacy instruction, but it is also useful to think about the additional shorter texts that relate to the primary text in some way. These **secondary texts** could give context, provide background, show a contrast, or develop a useful idea that helps students better engage the primary text. Nonfiction, we argue, is ideal as a secondary text.

For example, Dave Javsicas, seventh-grade reading teacher at Troy Prep, was teaching *Lord of the Flies* as a primary text. Early into their work with the novel, Dave presented his students with a scientific article that detailed the climate and layers of a tropical rainforest. In addition to gaining background knowledge that would help them access the dense descriptions of setting throughout *Lord of the Flies,* he also had the opportunity to ask, "How do you think it felt to be living in a place like this in your woolen school uniform, after having lived in England all your life? How might this contribute to character mood and interactions?" After reading a few hundred words clearly describing the jungle setting, Dave's class was already set up to engage Golding's dystopia in a far more meaningful way than they would have been without such context.

In the next module, we'll look at ways to strategically embed a variety of secondary nonfiction texts to help students get the most out of both them and their primary text.

# Embedding Texts to Increase Absorption Rate and Build Background Knowledge

Embedding nonfiction is the process of pairing secondary nonfiction texts (often NNNF) with a primary text in an intentional and strategic way. When it comes to embedding texts, there are two main categories: inside-the-bull's-eye secondary texts containing content necessary to support basic understanding of the primary text; outside-the-bull's-eye texts causing students to look at the primary text in a new and unexpected or more rigorous way. They deepen and expand rather than support meaning.

## INSIDE THE BULL'S-EYE

Text pairings that fall inside the bull's-eye can maximize synergy and best harness the Matthew Effect. If you know a little at the start, you pick up the signs and symbols and hints in a book faster than if you know nothing. The more you know about the Nazis—especially the difference between a Nazi and a mere "enemy soldier"—the more you read the scene in the first chapter of *Number the Stars*, where Annemarie and Ellen encounter two occupying Nazi soldiers, differently than a student who knows little.

By the time an unknowing student has been told how malevolent the soldiers are, much of the richness and tension of the scene will have already passed him by. And a student who is never told this—whose knowledge of Nazis is left to chance—misses the power of the scene almost entirely. When students start from a base of knowledge, their inferences allow them to engage the text with much greater depth—to learn from what they read as efficiently as possible. They're more attentive, both to the emotions of the characters and to the factual information presented in the fictional text. They connect the dots.

Reading secondary nonfiction texts in combination with a primary text almost certainly increases the absorption rate of students reading that text. So, as many teachers have recognized, it can be immensely valuable to start *Number the Stars* with an article about what Nazi soldiers were like.

On the flip side, the secondary text is also framed by the primary text. *When texts are paired, the absorption rate of both texts goes up,* and that's the best part. Colleen discovered this during a unit on *Lily's Crossing,* a novel set in New York during World War II that examines both "European" issues of the war (Nazism, appeasement, and persecution) and "domestic" issues of the war (rationing, shortages, migration, and immigration).

To contextualize *Lily's Crossing*, Colleen decided to use sections of articles a history teacher had shared with her earlier in the year—adapted to correspond to key issues in the book—as secondary text. But instead of reading all the nonfiction first, as she'd originally planned, Colleen decided to read the novel for several days before pausing to read the nonfiction.

After four class periods and twenty-three pages of *Lily's Crossing*, Colleen interrupted the novel to read a secondary nonfiction text she'd prepared on the topic of rationing during wartime. The result was both powerful and revealing. The nonfiction text helped her students understand and absorb more of the novel. She was able to pose questions about the historical concept ("What does rationing mean?") and also its application to the novel ("How did rationing affect the characters in our novel?"). Her students better connected the background material to the story; the primary text started to come alive and make sense: there were things they could not buy because no one was allowed to. The fact that the students had started the novel—and knew something about the setting in which they would be applying what they learned from the secondary text—made that learning stick more. Colleen's students already knew Lily, so what she was living through seemed more real to them—it mattered to them.

The inferential leaps the novel required were still there, but the lengths were more achievable. Because of their nonfiction reading, the book was a richer experience and students could infer independently without Colleen's support; she didn't need to fill in the knowledge gaps.

## SYNERGY RUNS BOTH WAYS

But something else happened that surprised Colleen even more. She found that while the background article was helping her students better read the novel, having started the novel was in turn *helping her students absorb more of the secondary nonfiction passage.* Students got more out of the secondary text when they could apply it to people they were interested in and felt a connection to—even if they were fictional characters. Students realized that these events really affected the lives of people during World War II—they weren't just mundane, isolated facts in an article. They were parts of the experience of a "real" person like Lily. Reading some of the fiction first, then reading nonfiction, greatly increased their absorption rate of the nonfiction article.

Not only were the two texts on World War II (the novel and the article) mutually beneficial, but *there was also synergy specifically in the difference of the genres.* The connection to characters from the novel made the facts in the secondary text real; the facts from the nonfiction helped students understand the situations the characters encountered in the primary text. Reading across genres on the same topic created additional value.

Colleen's insight provides a guide to more systematically leveraging the Matthew Effect in classrooms. Because texts can work in synergy to increase their mutual absorption rates, *reading multiple texts on a given topic is a worthwhile investment.* If you paired two articles on frogs, say, or the American Revolution, students' absorption rate would increase for both texts — simply by virtue of the additional knowledge and context they brought to each. They would, on net, know more than if you read one article about frogs and one about the American Revolution, and this suggests that an inclination to cover a wide breadth can keep us from getting the most out of our reading.

When we teach nonfiction as a unit, we often choose articles and texts with the specific goal of covering different genres, styles, formats, or text features. Our choices have less to do with topic than format. If we do consider topics, we typically choose texts assuming that we are helping our students fill in knowledge gaps by covering as many things as we can, but this results in nonfiction that constantly appears out of context and, frankly, begs the question of why people read it at all. For Colleen's students, the answer to why you would read an article about rationing was answered by its effectiveness in helping them unlock more about Lily's life. Embedding, pairing nonfiction with related fiction, brings both to life. To be abundantly clear, this is not an argument against reading widely; it is essential for students to be exposed to a broad range of texts. It is, however, a cautionary note — *if students read too thinly, they are less likely to remember what they've read* — and a reminder of the immense opportunity the texts we are already reading provide to increase students' absorption rate.

## EMBEDDING OUTSIDE THE BULL'S-EYE

Embedding outside the bull's-eye takes a similar approach, pairing nonfiction with a primary text, but it seeks to help students better analyze texts by modeling for them how to apply an analytical framework to a given text or multiple texts. As an additional benefit, outside-the-bull's-eye texts help you increase the breadth of nonfiction topics to which students are exposed, helping them better understand the world generally.

Not too long ago, Colleen was planning lessons on S. E. Hinton's *The Outsiders.* Instead of planning embedded texts to provide context and background, Colleen instead set out to use paired texts to cast the story in a new and more challenging light.

Her reflection began with a sense of limitation. The story itself was already pretty familiar to her students. There wasn't a ton of background knowledge to fill in on a book about teenagers and social cliques. In many cases, that familiarity is exactly why teachers choose the story. From a knowledge-deficit perspective, *The Outsiders* is not an ideal primary text. But Colleen began to reflect on how a college class might frame the familiar aspects of the book.

She hit on a couple of promising ideas for broadening the context and giving a potentially light read a bit more heft. Two hidden themes of the novel were the power of class and caste, and the influence of male bonding. For the former, she considered articles on class and caste systems in cultures around the world. She could, she realized, have students talk about whether the characters in the book are part of a caste and how it affected their lives. Or she could ask students how the characters themselves might see it. Ultimately, though, she ended up going in another direction.

---

## See It in Action

Watch as Colleen and her students read and analyze an outside-the-bull's-eye nonfiction article about the social behaviors of male elephants from *Smithsonian* magazine in clip 4 at teachlikeachampion.com/yourlibrary.

---

Colleen found an article from *Smithsonian* magazine describing research into male elephants—specifically, how younger male elephants learn their social behaviors by watching and modeling slightly older peers. This of course is a constant element in the story of *The Outsiders,* though students likely would not realize it without a bit of prompting. The article, Colleen realized, could do that. She read the article and asked questions that caused students to understand the author's interest in the hierarchy of male elephants in the wild. She then asked her classes to apply terms like *hierarchy* to *The Outsiders* as well—to find evidence that the social structures of the Greasers and Socs weren't necessarily unique to humans, but were actually similar to those of the rest of the animal kingdom.

In the end, the embedded text ended up performing a function different from what we usually ask it to do: instead of trying to make the unfamiliar familiar, it made the familiar more rigorous. It forced students to see interactions in the novel as part of the systems of behavior common to all social beings. They read much of the book through that framework, studying its hierarchies and using scientific descriptions of them to explain in a new way what was familiar. While reading about elephants certainly built background knowledge, it also elevated the rigor of the lesson, as one of Colleen's postreading questions revealed: "How are the social structures of the Greasers similar to those of the bull elephants? Be sure to include their typical interactions and a description of their actions before and after the 'showdown.'" Not only that, but it probably gave her students a useful glimpse into the "why" behind scientific studies. Why would someone spend their days on the African savannah studying how elephants get along? Because it helps us see how people are like or unlike the rest of the natural world. And of course there was an additional benefit to Colleen's choice of the elephants article: they could use their newfound understanding of hierarchies not only to understand the characters in *The Outsiders* but also to discuss almost any text, which in fact they did as the read other novels throughout the year.

## AIMING INSIDE AND OUTSIDE THE BULL'S-EYE

Giving students historical context on the setting of a novel is productive and logical — it falls right inside the bull's-eye; but remember, when choosing secondary texts, that you can complement that sort of embedding with texts that cause students to connect ideas that don't obviously go together, and give them "aha" moments.

---

## Nonfiction for *A Single Shard*

At a recent reading workshop, we asked participants to brainstorm ideas for nonfiction articles to embed in various novels. The results were pretty incredible. We were especially struck by the ideas teachers came up with for articles to embed in *A Single Shard*. It's the story of an orphaned, homeless boy in thirteenth-century Korea, Tree-ear, who yearns to be an apprentice to a master potter, Min.

We think the ideas are useful and illustrate a range of outside-the-bull's-eye nonfiction you can embed in one novel. The experience also illustrates the power of collaborating with colleagues to generate ideas for embedding.

*(Continued)*

---

*(Continued)*

Here are four ideas for embedded nonfiction that participants shared with us:

1. Rachel D'Addabo from **Jubilee Public Schools** pointed out that Tree-ear is obsessed with rice. It's not just what he eats; it's also a currency. Having it is a psychological factor. She suggested reading an article on the economics of rice and its importance in Korean culture to understand why it was so fundamental to the narrative.

2. Lindsay Allan from **Coney Island Prep** suggested reading an article on the tree-ear mushroom. The mushroom, she noted, "survives because it's rootless—a perfect analogy for the wandering homeless narrator. Reading about it would help students understand the connection and the symbolism."

3. Amanda Henry from **De La Salle Middle School** in St. Louis observed that Min battles with what appears to be depression throughout the book. She proposed reading an article on depression (its causes and manifestations), both to better understand Min as a character and to cause them to recognize cause and effect—the mood disorder that Min may have suffered from after losing his son.

4. Amanda Phelan from **Charlotte Mecklenberg School District** in North Carolina suggested reading an article on homelessness, given that Tree-ear lives under a bridge throughout much of the novel. It would be fascinating to compare the causes and psychological effects of homelessness today with Tree-ear's story.

In a recent lesson with his eighth-grade students at Rochester Prep, Patrick Pastore embedded inside-the-bull's-eye nonfiction to support and expand his students' understanding of the challlenging, "An Occurrence at Owl Creek Bridge," a short story written in 1890 by Ambrose Bierce that we discussed in chapter 2. The story, you will recall, is set in the Civil War, and its protagonist is a Southern planter who is about to be hanged for sabotage.

## See It in Action

Watch Patrick Pastore embed inside and outside the bull's-eye in clips 5 and 6 at teachlikeachampion.com/yourlibrary.

As they read, students learned the circumstances that led to the hanging — the protagonist was framed by a Northern spy. Understanding this relies on the reader's ability to make inferences based on subtle cues in the text. Patrick therefore started with a short nonfiction text about the Civil War that students read independently. It framed key vocabulary — who the Federalists were, for example — and ensured a basic knowledge of its events. Before starting the short story, Patrick and his students reviewed questions about this secondary text that Patrick described to his students as "basic but important":

- According to the text, how did the Civil War bring the North and South together?
- What was another name for Confederate army soldiers?
- What was another name for Union army soldiers?
- What did Southerners and Democrats believe about states' rights? How did this change postwar?

Although Patrick's students had studied the Civil War in history class, the nonfiction text helped them access and solidify knowledge that would be necessary simply to make sense of the short story, and Patrick used his questions to focus on key terms that he knew would become relevant in Bierce's narrative.

Then they began reading the short story. As they read, Patrick paused frequently to reinforce understanding of the text. In the first paragraph, students read the following sentence:

> Some loose boards laid upon the sleepers supporting the metals supplied a footing for him and his executioners — two private soldiers of the Federal Army, directed by a sergeant who in civil life may have been a deputy sheriff.

Patrick asked, "What do we know about the people who are about to kill him [main character]?" When a student responded, "Soldiers," he probed further, "Soldiers of which army?" After the student replied, "The Federalists," Patrick inquired, "Does this mean the soldier is from the North or the South?" Another student chimed in to say, "from the North," and Patrick followed up with an inferential question: "So what do we now know about [the main character]?" A student correctly responded, "He's most likely from the South." Patrick pointed out that the questions he asked were about lines from the story that were easy to gloss over but that were, in fact, central to understanding the story.

Without the knowledge students had obtained through the inside-the-bull's-eye non-fiction reading at the beginning of class, they might have been confused about or indeed simply not understood key aspects of the story, leaving them little chance to make the inferential leaps that Bierce required of his readers, especially because they were reading the story over one hundred years after it was written.

In another lesson, we observed Patrick embed an outside-the-bull's-eye secondary nonfiction text with his sixth-grade students as they read the novel *The Westing Game* by Ellen Raskin. The novel itself, a mystery in which sixteen heirs are challenged to figure out the circumstances of the death of a newly deceased millionaire in order to win his fortune, did not pose a significant challenge for his students to comprehend. So Patrick embedded nonfiction that caused students to read the novel with a more rigorous lens. For homework, Patrick assigned an article from a psychology manual describing "histrionic personality disorder." In class, Patrick asked his students several questions to ensure general understanding of the psychiatric disorder (for example, "What are the symptoms of histrionic personality disorder?" "How is it treated?").

Then Patrick turned the conversation back to the novel: "What heir from our book would most likely be diagnosed with histrionic personality disorder?" The question was simple but significant. It wasn't necessary for basic understanding of the novel, but it deepened students' understanding of the characters (especially Sydelle Pulaski, the character they decided would most likely be diagnosed with the disorder) by providing a lens for character analysis. In order to answer the question, students had to provide multiple pieces of evidence about Sydelle's actions and words to support their "diagnosis." Was she just strange, or did she have a psychological condition? Never, perhaps, had sixth graders read so enthusiastically the pages of a dry psychology manual, absorbing as they did so the unique style and conventions of the sort of social science text they would be required to read again and again in college. Patrick broadened his students' knowledge base dramatically and, what's more, modeled for them new ways to think about analyzing characters in texts. Perhaps this was the first time they had considered that a person's actions could be the result not so much of their being "strange" but of mental illness. This, like Colleen's introduction of the idea of hierarchy, was a framework they could apply to text after text.

# LESSONS ON MAXIMIZING EMBEDDED NONFICTION

When choosing secondary texts to pair with a primary text—whether inside or outside the bull's-eye—there are a number of ways you can maximize their value for your class. Some of these additional tips come from Colleen's unit on *Lily's Crossing*, and still more come from years of observing great teachers.

## Cutting and Adapting

Because the purpose of the secondary text is often to build context for and maximize the absorption rate of the primary text, it's worth prioritizing and shaping its content so as to create maximum value. In other words, there's nothing that prevents you from excerpting (and sometimes rewriting) carefully chosen sections of text to increase clarity, or introducing facts from multiple sources that are especially relevant. For example, in preparing students to read both *Lily's Crossing* and *Number the Stars*, Colleen used several articles—but only relevant sections of each one—in order to refresh students on some basics on World War II itself and highlight information that aligned to what they were reading in their novel.

It's not always our first instinct to shorten an article and remove parts of comparatively low value, or to combine texts or rewrite things that don't work, but sometimes, particularly with younger students, it's productive to distill key information by assembling difficult pieces of text from multiple sources. With older students, perhaps from grades 8 and onwards, however, we are less inclined to do this sort of collaging, as one of the skills they will need to master is finding relevant information in a broader text *not* tailored to their particular needs.

## Overlapping Questions

To make the connections between primary and secondary texts even more salient for students, it can help to deliberately ask questions that cause them to connect the secondary and primary texts. We call these **overlapping questions**. Having read, as a secondary text, an article describing the conditions that would be considered unfair child labor during your study of *Esperanza Rising*, for example, you might ask, as Maggie Johnson did, whether Esperanza's experience would be considered "unfair" according to experts. And of course you could ask questions like this while reading either text. You could, in the midst of your novel, ask a question that referred back to your nonfiction secondary text or, while reading the secondary text, ask students to apply it to previous scenes from the novel. This could cause students to engage the details of both texts—to grasp the framework from the secondary text and apply it to the specific context of the primary text, thus allowing you to maximize the rigor and engagement of both texts, particularly the nonfiction article, and to boost the absorption rate of knowledge among your students. Applying the knowledge would cause them to remember it better and make it more relevant and useful. Such synergies, of course, need not be left to accident.

It's worth noting that overlapping questions can be asked anytime, not just on the day you are reading the relevant secondary text. Take, for example, these lines from *Lily's Crossing*: "Strange that Mr. Orban was using his last drop of gas. He had sworn to hold onto it until the day the war was over in Europe." Perhaps you'd read your article on rationing several days or even weeks earlier. All the more reason to ask: "Why does Mr. Orban have only a 'last drop of gas'? Why had he sworn to hold on to it until the end of the war? Remind me: Was this typical of the responses to rationing we read about last week?" Asking students these questions throughout their experience in the text requires them to recall and apply the knowledge they acquired in their nonfiction reading repeatedly in a variety of settings. This kind of ongoing use of information is far more likely to drive it into long-term memory.

## Frequent Embedding

Teachers tend to embed nonfiction in their primary texts most often at the beginning, but if embedding secondary nonfiction in your reading of a primary text can help bring richness and depth to it and help increase absorption rate of knowledge from both texts, there's no reason not to do it frequently. That is, you could embed six, eight, or even ten diverse examples of nonfiction in the course of reading a book like *Number the Stars*. This would not only allow your students to experience the quantity of nonfiction they need to be exposed to, in a wide variety of formats and with increased interest, but also model intellectual curiosity for them — build a habit of it, even. You would show that a book does not live in isolation. Good readers unlock its depths by engaging the questions it raises with further study. There is a world of questions implicit in a great book and a world of information we can access to answer them.

Embedding secondary texts multiple times in the reading of a novel leverages the opportunity to compound increases in absorption rate as students read. As students get more and more out of a book, they read with increasing depth and understanding, ultimately "studying" it as much as "reading" it. Further, embedding secondary texts in our study of a primary text models what mature readers do when they read in their outside lives (their "real" lives, their "college" and "grad school" lives). Mature readers not only ask questions, as students are socialized to do, but also answer them by stopping to find additional sources of information: Is this part of the story true? Did the king really say that? Did this battle really take place? Can dogs really be trained to hunt like that?

As our collective relationship to information changes and access to contextualizing information becomes easier (talking about the Internet here), embedding texts throughout becomes more critical. The more teachers bring background to a text via nonfiction readings, the more they socialize students to copy that valuable process—and to do it repeatedly as they read. For an idea of what embedding secondary texts multiple times across a novel might look like, take a page out of Dave Javsicas's unit on *Lord of the Flies* (see "Sample Embedded Outline").

## Sample Embedded Outline

Here is an outline of the embedded nonfiction topics and texts that Dave Javsicas and his seventh graders read as part of their novel unit on *Lord of the Flies*. For another example, this time from Rue Ratray's class, see the appendix or teachlikeachampion.com/yourlibrary.

| Embedded Nonfiction Topic | Purpose for Embedding |
|---|---|
| Culture of English boarding schools in the 1940s | • Becoming familiar with where the characters had been before the beginning of the story |
| Article on rainforests and jungles | • Gaining background knowledge to understand the setting of the story |
| British evacuation of children during World War II | • Explaining why the boys were on the plane leaving England |
| Definition of *herd mentality* and an article titled "Why Do People Follow the Crowd?" | • Using herd mentality to explain Ralph's behavior during the slaughtering of the pig<br>• Explaining why Ralph acted in a way that violated his civilized tendencies |
| Summary of the Milgram experiments | • Explaining what implications the findings from the Milgram experiments might have for characters in *Lord of the Flies* |
| Biography of William Golding | • Focusing on the roots of Golding's "dark perspective" on human nature, particularly the idea of "civilized" people being capable of savagery |

*(Continued)*

(Continued)

| Embedded Nonfiction Topic | Purpose for Embedding |
| --- | --- |
| Article on Chilean miners | • Understanding how the miners responded to crisis and avoided descent into savagery |
| Aftermath of Hurricane Katrina (the truth vs. hysteria of individuals and the media) | • Explaining the difference between real fear and perceived fear<br>• Explaining the impact that fear had on the emergency response following Hurricane Katrina<br>• Comparing the impact of fear following Katrina to the impact of fear on the boys in *Lord of the Flies* |
| Articles on Puritans and the Salem Witch Trials compared to the views of the Quakers ("There is that of God in everyone.") | • Comparing different views on human nature |
| Excerpt from and discussion of *The Coral Island*, a work of English literature that ascribed to British cultural superiority (Golding may have written *Lord of the Flies*, in part, to refute these ideas) | • Comparing and contrasting Golding's view of the British with that of the author of *The Coral Island* |

Rereading texts (both primary and secondary) a second time during a novel unit may also be a worthwhile activity. That is, you might read part of a secondary text and then continue with your primary text, only to reread the secondary text after the primary text has given students a fuller and deeper perspective. Or you could reread a short story, picture book, or excerpt from your novel after you've read the secondary text. In either case, the goal is to have students recognize how much more deeply they understand the text because of embedding—the "Oh, *now* I see!" moment.

## Embedding with Other Genres

We describe embedding here primarily as a tool to read more nonfiction in your classes and to read that nonfiction in a way that makes it relevant and engaging, and, most of all, to increase the amount of knowledge students absorb from reading it. That said, the power of embedding transcends nonfiction texts. We have observed teachers embedding, with great effect, poetry, song lyrics, and excerpts from other (more challenging) fiction texts as secondary texts to support and extend students' understanding of their primary text. For example, in a reading of *Number the Stars* by Lois Lowry, you might embed diary excerpts from *The Diary of Anne Frank*. This would give students the opportunity to read a more complex and challenging text and provide them with multiple presentations of the topic, almost certainly yielding rich comparisons.

## Meta-Embedding

Here's one last idea that we've seen great teachers employ when embedding texts. We call the use and reuse of embedded articles as tools or frameworks for interpreting multiple texts **meta-embedding**. Examples include texts that explain how literature works, such as articles defining the "tragic hero," defining the elements that make a novel dystopian, or explicating ten or so classic themes in literature. Having read such an article, you would refer to it again and again throughout the year, linking the primary texts together in terms of their treatment of the key ideas from your meta-texts.

As part of her unit on *Chains*, Laurie Halse Anderson's novel about a young girl in the Revolutionary War era, a former slave, who is orphaned and sold back into slavery, Maggie Johnson asked her sixth graders to read an article about the prevalence of orphans in children's literature. The article described how the absence of parents naturally presents young characters with a key conflict, testing their resilience in a way that wouldn't be possible had they been under parental protection, and it suggested that this was particularly appealing to young readers who faced the question of how to define themselves in the world. Being parentless allowed young readers to consider how characters, and therefore perhaps themselves, might invent themselves in a completely autonomous way.

Maggie deliberately embedded this text in the first novel of the year to equip her students with a lens for analyzing subsequent novels—like *Esperanza Rising*, *The Outsiders*, *Miracle's Boys*, and *The Diary of Anne Frank*. Although her chosen texts didn't always include actual orphans (*The Diary of Anne Frank*), the article still presented a frame for students to analyze characters who had similar characteristics of resilience and autonomy. This enabled her students to be self-reflective about how different characters reflected the core ideas in the article and why they personally found certain characters interesting. It was, as Maggie put it, "a kind of literary theory for sixth graders."

Students not only referred back to the reading of their own volition throughout the course of the year but also began to understand literary archetypes and the impact that different versions of those archetypes had on them as readers. The article lifted the curtain to reveal the careful and intentional decisions of authors when it comes to crafting characters, particularly main characters. Not only that but, as Maggie related, it made teaching the novels especially new and interesting *to her*, and she found that this engaged her even more in their discussions. In the appendix (and on teachlikeachampion.com), you will find a table with additional ideas for meta-embedding.

---

## Keys to Planning for Embedding Nonfiction

- *Choose your spot.* It may not always make sense to use a secondary text at the beginning of a novel. Consider other times when synergies may be strongest.

- *Create synergy.* Use interlocking questions to enhance synergies between texts. (Ask questions about the secondary text that refer to the primary text, and vice versa.)

- *Adapt, combine, and amend* nonfiction articles in fifth and sixth grade to enhance their applicability to primary texts. We don't recommend doing this after sixth grade.

- *Excerpt.* When your focus for the class period is on a secondary nonfiction text, excerpt relevant sections from your primary text while reading the secondary text. This is really important for helping students build an explicit connection to knowledge that they already have from a primary text.

Check out the appendix (or teachlikeachampion.com) for a table with more examples of embedding ideas (and a checklist to help you make sure that the ideas are strong).

---

In this module, we've looked in detail at the different ways teachers can embed different types of texts to enhance both background knowledge and absorption rate. In the next module, we'll look at ways champion teachers work to leverage different types of "texts" in their classrooms.

# Other Ways to Build Background Knowledge

Many teachers are aware of the important role of background knowledge in learning, but the most frequently cited antidote to the knowledge gap—a coherent, sequential knowledge-rich curriculum delivered every year from kindergarten onwards—is beyond the purview of most teachers, who often don't have much say in coordinating the sequence of curriculum that students in their school or district encounter from grades K through 12. The question for a teacher who realizes that knowledge acquisition is a critical issue, if sometimes a bit of a blind spot, is, "What can *I* do about it, here in my classroom and in my daily approach to teaching?"

Reading more nonfiction and reading it better via embedding is one way to address the knowledge deficit. In this module, we discuss other ways to address background knowledge gaps during reading.

## USING FICTION TO BUILD BACKGROUND KNOWLEDGE

Knowledge built through reading, we noted in the beginning of this chapter, is not built solely through the reading of nonfiction. The choice of what fiction to read and even decisions about how to read it are also important factors. Consider the choice between reading *Number the Stars* and *Tuck Everlasting* in your fourth- or fifth-grade reading class. Both are wonderful novels, artfully written, with engaging stories and memorable characters. In many ways it is a lifelong gift to students to read either one (or both!). But after the book is done and you've moved on to the next near-perfect read, it's worth noting that *Number the Stars* may continue paying dividends that *Tuck Everlasting* will not. In grappling with *Number the Stars*, students will come to understand something about World War II, about occupation and resistance, about the geography of Denmark, about the Nazi reign, and even something about milking cows, as they continue their studies. It normalizes for students the process of inferring facts about the world from fiction reading. Now, this definitely doesn't mean you can't or shouldn't read *Tuck Everlasting*. It's a wonderful read, but you wouldn't want to read *only* books like *Tuck* without reflecting on their value in terms of building background knowledge. Perhaps a bit of embedding could bring out some key areas of knowledge to make it also serve to address the knowledge deficit. Or perhaps you'd want to balance *Tuck* with *Number the Stars.*

Whatever books you choose, your approach to questions, even when reading fiction, can build knowledge more intentionally and productively. This is probably easiest to do with historical fiction like *Number the Stars,* but a clever teacher could probably also pull it off with books less clearly useful from a knowledge perspective.

One of our colleagues was recently struck by the homework assignment a teacher gave to her first-grade students at a school she was visiting—a highly successful school with exemplary results that was especially committed to addressing knowledge issues starting in kindergarten. The teacher had read a book about frogs aloud while the students followed along, looking at a copy of the book even though most could only read parts of it. The teacher asked them to take it home.

However, instead of asking students to read the book to their parents and practice decoding, as many teachers would, she chose a different approach: she asked them to retell to their parents what they remembered, even if they could not read the actual text. She wanted them to describe the contents, emphasizing knowledge development (retelling the facts) over skill development (practice decoding). It's a very unconventional approach, but just may be very powerful. The message was that what the class had learned about frogs was important—that the book was more than just a vehicle for practicing decoding skills and familiarizing students with nonfiction. Each time they read, instilling the knowledge they took away was an important goal. Inside reading classrooms, however, teachers often ask skill-based questions exclusively, at the expense of fact-based questions. Is it possible that the lack of factual knowledge keeps our kids from being able to use their reading skills?

Doug was reflecting on this a few weeks later while reading a historical novel, *Behind Rebel Lines,* with his daughter. The novel is about a young woman who disguises herself as a man and goes behind Confederate lines during the Civil War. In a chapter they read together, Emma, the protagonist, disguises herself as an itinerant peddler. Having been dropped near Cold Harbor battlefield, she sets off on a "mission." She enters an abandoned house to seek shelter during a rainstorm and finds a dying Confederate soldier. He has typhoid fever, she realizes. Emma stays for a day or so to comfort him until he dies. He asks her to take a gold watch to a general as his dying wish—a request that shapes the plot of the novel as she sets out to meet the general.

As he read with his daughter, Doug thought about the types of questions he'd been trained to ask as an English teacher:

- What motivates Emma to aid the Confederate soldier? [Answer: her sense of duty and humanity]

- What does she learn about herself? [Answer: that her loyalty to the human race is stronger than her loyalty to the Union]

- Who else feels a strong sense of duty to someone else in the book?

Indeed, those questions would have made for an interesting and worthwhile discussion. But he had been thinking about his friend's visit to the first-grade classroom and found himself wondering if it would be possible to replace a purely skills-based approach to reading with a more knowledge-based approach. He sketched out how he might have done that and came up with questions like these:

- "What does Emma tell us about how soldiers died during the Civil War? Is it surprising in any way?" [Answer: Emma notes that far more soldiers died from disease than battle, and typhoid fever was a leading killer. Most people think more about more dramatic combat deaths, but this is true about almost every war.]

- "Is there anything in the text that tells us why so many soldiers might have died from disease so often during the Civil War?" [Answer: Alan, the soldier, recalls how when he started to get weak and could not keep up with his regiment, he was left behind with no food or shelter to care for himself. Further, Emma observes that there is nothing she can do but comfort Alan—there is medicinal cure as we might hope there would be today.]

Doug was surprised by the questions. They weren't simplistic, and they didn't involve empty or simplistic recall as he had often been warned questions about "mere facts" would. Thinking about his daughter's development, he found himself wanting to use those questions instead. Not exclusively perhaps, but with frequency. Without them, he would be leaving to chance whether his daughter actually learned any history from the historical fiction she'd chosen. And, more broadly, he'd miss the opportunity to socialize her to seek to unlock bits of knowledge from what she read. She could analyze a text with rigor and still build her knowledge.

In the classroom, asking a few of these questions each day would eat away at the knowledge deficit and teach students how to attend to important facts and reflect on them as they read. This might cause them to absorb more both in the moment and as they read on their own.

It's also interesting to note that asking knowledge-based questions about fiction texts might influence your choice of which texts to teach. There is, a colleague of ours noted, a wide variety of commitment to knowledge within the genre of historical fiction. Some is rich in knowledge and factual detail; some is content-light and essentially offers a pleasant setting and perhaps a unique problem for a story that really could be set anywhere or in any time period. Seeking to ask knowledge-based questions as much as skill-based questions would cause teachers to better appreciate quality in the historical fiction they choose — or indeed any fiction.

## EMBEDDING NONPRINTED TEXTS

Reading is not the only means by which knowledge is generated, of course, and many of the other ways that knowledge is transmitted can be especially productive when used in synergy with reading; and just as an embedded secondary text can unlock the depth of a primary text, a nonprinted text — a brief video, a series of photographs, perhaps aided by short targeted teacher presentation and questioning — can also be immensely useful. But why bother calling a video or a set of photos a "nonprinted text"? you might ask. We use the term to emphasize that, to use them correctly, teachers should approach multimedia much as they would printed texts. They should "read" them in short chunks, stopping frequently to ask questions and causing students to engage actively and prioritize information. They should push students to process them through writing, just as they would do with a written text. And as we hope you are already thinking, they can be embedded throughout a primary text, as either inside- or outside-the-bull's-eye texts and at various points in the narrative.

We note, though, that video in particular is an especially complex form of text, a form that usually features multiple narratives and lots of images to attend to. It is easy to assume that students are attending to the most valuable elements, but of course they may not be. Teachers can often help students attend to the most important points by using overlapping questions in much the same manner that they would with a written text, and emphasizing precise and focused ideas from the text so that students can refer to them in processing the primary text.

Video is often best approached as one would any complex text: as something to be "read" carefully in short bites, reinforced by Close Reading and evidence-based questions, and processed in writing to inscribe and analyze key learning points. This may sound obvious, but we often see teachers simply sit back and let the video roll, forgetting that even though its delivery is different, it is still a text.

## EMBEDDING OUT LOUD

Another opportunity to embed nonfiction is by reading it aloud. We all know that having a parent read aloud from an early age allows some students to assimilate knowledge very efficiently when they become readers. Nonfiction has a different rhythm, or cadence, than fiction. Students need to hear this aloud to be able to "hear it" when reading silently.

Because secondary texts are usually shorter—meaning you read them for closer to a day than a month—they are in some ways easier to use, especially when it comes to exposing students to difficult text, the likes of which they will ultimately need to learn to handle but that is presently above their reading level. A teacher could, in short, choose a very difficult secondary text and read all or part of it aloud to students (with students reading it themselves a second time through in some cases), in order to increase students' familiarity with a topic—and, in turn, their absorption rate. While we often think of reading aloud as the sole purview of elementary school teachers (and as appropriate only for fiction), it can be a highly effective way to model nonfiction reading—not to mention accelerate the absorption of contextualizing background knowledge.

## BATCH PROCESSING

The synergistic quality of overlapping texts may also apply to nonreading classes. Science classes and history classes could increase absorption rate by reading two or three articles on a single topic. In many of our classes, we shoot for the broadest possible survey of knowledge, whereas it might actually be more productive to read multiple texts on a slightly more limited range of topics.

---

### Batch-Processed Texts

Imagine including articles/excerpts on the following topics on predators and prey, instead of a sample of relatively random topics.

- How a lion stalks its prey
- Cats mimicking lions in stalking their prey
- Frogs stalking flies
- How carnivorous dinosaurs hunted their prey

*(Continued)*

---

(*Continued*)

- Ways that prey defend themselves (for example, camouflage)
- Adaptation of species

Over time, students would use knowledge from an article about predators stalking their prey to absorb knowledge more rapidly. For example, knowledge about how predators stalk their prey would help students better (and more quickly) understand information on defense mechanisms and adaptation.

Again, we can increase absorption rate by reading nonfiction texts not in isolation but *alongside* primary texts or "grouped" in bunches—for example, three articles in a row on desert ecosystems with the understanding that by the third article on the topic, students will be absorbing at a faster rate than they were when reading the first article or articles on a variety of topics.

## Action Steps for Addressing the Background Knowledge Challenge

- *Embed nonfiction throughout your primary texts.* Embed secondary nonfiction texts *multiple times* in your primary texts to increase absorption rate.

- *Ask overlapping questions* to build on the synergies between primary and secondary texts.

- *Use knowledge-based analytical questions* to allow fiction to build background knowledge too.

- *Use grouping.* When you read nonfiction without a primary text, consider reading in batches or themes (that is, three or four texts on a single topic) rather than reading texts on isolated topics.

- *Try other formats.* You can embed fiction too. Or consider embedding nonprinted texts that you "read" diligently and intentionally, just as if they were written texts. Also consider reading complex nonfiction aloud with students.

Our primary suggestion for getting the most out of nonfiction in this chapter so far involves ensuring that students read more NNNF by embedding it with primary texts to increase absorption rate. This is also likely to make the nonfiction more engaging and relevant for students. We have also proposed ways to read fiction texts more intentionally to build background knowledge that will be useful in reading nonfiction. But getting the most out of nonfiction is not always as easy as that. Nonfiction can be a stew of stylistic tropes—structures, conventions, and flourishes unique to the format. An experienced reader understands and absorbs content presented via these tropes with ease, but a lack of tacit knowledge about how to read informative texts can be deeply challenging to the uninitiated—and can interfere with meaning-making.

## MODULE 3.5 — Some Unique Challenges of Nonfiction

Some of the conventions that make nonfiction different from, and often more challenging than, fiction are structural—the use of different text features, for example. But there are other conventions of nonfiction that are subtler and harder to spot. These often occur at the sentence level and as a result can be especially disruptive to students' comprehension.

Doug discovered this recently when reading with his youngest daughter. She was seven at the time, and they were enjoying reading a short nonfiction treatment of dolphins together. His daughter was reading happily through a passage about how dolphins hear and see the world when she came upon a phrase in parentheses, full of capital letters and dashes like nothing she'd ever seen before. It was, as frequent readers of nonfiction would know, a pronunciation guide, in this case for the word *echolocation*. It looked like this: (EK-oh-lo-KAY-shun), and it stopped her in her tracks. "It's telling you how to pronounce the word," Doug whispered. "You can skip over it."

As an experienced reader you know at a glance what such a parenthetical does, just from the look of it (all those capitals and dashes), and you decide in a flash whether to focus on pronunciation at that moment or not. If not—if you are deeply engaged in absorbing details about the lives of dolphins, say—you skip over it at a gallop, perhaps coming back to consider pronunciation after you've finished a sentence or paragraph. The pronunciation guide, after all, will always be there, and although there's no data on this, we suspect most readers either glance very quickly if they can absorb such information rapidly or skip it and come back at an opportune moment. But new readers do not know this, and the strain of reading a pronunciation guide is much greater for them than for a fluent adult. This can be immensely disruptive.

Even with an experienced reader to tell her that the parenthesis was optional, for example, Doug's daughter was thrown off. The parenthetical was like nothing she'd ever seen and she had to figure out what "it" was that she was allowed to skip and how much of it she was skipping. Probably, she wondered why it was there and why it looked so strange. Maybe she began starting to decode it as she did with other words she didn't know right away. It disrupted her focus on and processing of the passage about the dolphins, a disruption that would probably cause her to absorb less and a disruption that surely would have been far greater if she'd been reading on her own, without an adult right there to whisper that she could skip it.

Nonfiction, it turns out, is full of what we call **micro rules**: tiny conventions in the way the text is written or presented. For the most part they are distinctive to NNNF and therefore especially unfamiliar to students who don't read a lot of it. And because they often occur midsentence, they can be especially disruptive to students' comprehension and absorption.

In this last module of the chapter, we'll look at some of the micro rules that can make NNNF so challenging. We'll also briefly examine two other potentially hidden difficulties associated with nonfiction: unique formatting challenges and micro genres—that is, the many forms of nonfiction, often with distinctive rules. These are relevant, we think, because they can disrupt meaning-making for readers new to nonfiction while remaining almost completely invisible, as a source of difficulty, to experienced readers who are more familiar with them.

## MICRO RULES

So what are these micro rules, the tiny conventions and quirks of writing that can disrupt comprehension of nonfiction? Consider the following lines from a typical article about foxes:

> The Arctic fox will generally eat any meat it can find, including lemmings, Arctic Hare, reptiles and amphibians, eggs, and carrion. Lemmings are the most common prey. A family of foxes can eat dozens of lemmings each day. During April and May the Arctic fox also preys on ringed seal kits when the young animals are confined to a snow den and are relatively helpless.[8]

## The Universal Article

In almost every case where it appears in narrative text, the definite article *the* refers to a single creature, as it does in the sentence, "Hearing a dog barking, the fox raced to safety inside its den." There's one fox in that sentence, that's all. However, in scientific articles and other forms of nonfiction, a definite article can refer to an entire species, as in, "The fox, like the dog, has specialized smelling skills to help it survive." In this case, as is obvious to experienced readers, there are an unlimited number of foxes (and dogs) — the reference is to the entire species. Imagine yourself unaware of this convention, however, and things become confusing. You might well fail to recognize that "The fox, like the dog, has specialized smelling skills" is telling you about all foxes and all dogs. And you might spend precious time and energy trying to make sense of what has now become nonsensical syntax: *Which* fox has specialized smelling skills? Which dog? In other words the failure to follow the convention would cause not just lack of understanding of the intended meaning but additional and distracting misperceptions.

This can be compounded further by the juxtaposition within a single passage of references to the fox using a universal article and the plural, as in the following:

> The fox, like the dog, has specialized smelling skills to help it survive, but foxes have an even greater advantage over their canine cousins.

A variation of the universal article is the use of the pronoun *we* to refer to society as a whole, as in the line from an article titled "Tech Trash Tragedy," "Each year we throw away 12 million computers."[9] Know this rule, and it's obvious that we're talking about society. If not, you're left wondering who these people are with their piles of trash.

## The Artful Synonym

Look again at this sentence:

> The fox, like the dog, has specialized smelling skills to help it survive, but foxes have an even greater advantage over their canine cousins.

There's a second trouble spot for nonfiction novices here. Can you spot it?

Nonfiction writing often requires repetition of key nouns. The word "fox" or "dog" might appear twenty times in an article comparing their sensory apparatus. At some point, that gets boring, both for readers and for writers, who begin to yearn for some word-use variety.

Because so much NNNF is written for publication in newspapers and journals, NNNF writers routinely coin artful synonyms for recurring nouns — the sole purpose of which is to come up with temporary, distinctive, and sometimes even hokey ways to avoid using the same word for a recurring noun. In this example, the dog becomes the fox's "canine cousin." Another article on pets might throw in the odd "four-legged friend" to describe dogs or cats, while another on evolution might refer to humanity's "aquatic ancestors." Almost every experienced reader recognizes such elaborate synonyms as contrivances. They refer back to the recently used familiar noun; they are often tongue in cheek and understood to be "disposable," never to recur, not worth remembering — a form of single-use pronoun. The stranger and more hokey — full of alliteration, for example — the more obvious the artifice is to initiated readers. At the same time, these bizarre phrases can be a source of confusion for readers who know nothing of the convention. In fact, these readers can end up spending critical bandwidth processing these complex but disposable phrases.

## The Optional Parenthetical

Reading about dolphins, Doug's daughter stumbled on one form of optional information in nonfiction texts — a description of how to pronounce a word. But pronunciation guides are just one example of information that is frequently included in nonfiction with the tacit understanding between author and reader that it will be used by a few and ignored by others. Here's another example:

The gray wolf (*Canis lupus*) is a native to remote areas of North America.

For the great majority of readers, the Latin is there to be referenced later (if at all); and for readers getting their feet wet in nonfiction, it is probably best ignored. They not only don't benefit much from the Latin, but slogging through decoding it and wondering how it makes sense syntactically is likely to result in the almost assured disruption of comprehension.

Nonfiction, unlike fiction, is often meant to be read at different levels by different readers. For example, footnotes or citations of other research are intended for those readers who may wish to do more research, but, the author knows, such information will probably be ignored by most — unless, of course, those readers do not know they are supposed to ignore them. What's more, NNNF is also often meant to be a reference that readers can refer back to, from which they can access certain critical information later on after they have read and absorbed it — thus the Latin names for species. Fiction generally is not used this way. And scientific writers simply observe certain traditions to signal the seriousness and legitimacy of their writing. All of these factors result in the inclusion of a great deal more optional information in texts—and in potentially disrupting the comprehension of students who do not understand these traditions.

## The Throwaway Reference

In an article written for a newspaper, magazine, or journal, every single quote gets attributed to somebody, even when who said it is not that important or the individual speaking is unlikely to factor in the story again. The rule of universal attribution exists as much for legal reasons as for literary ones. If an article features an interview with a "man in the street" who is merely an example of a typical perspective, that person still gets named and described, as in: "One reader, John Jones, a reading teacher from Detroit, agreed, 'That *Reading Reconsidered* is a heck of a book!'" This does not necessarily signal John's importance to the article. You're not really supposed to try to remember his name. Knowing that helps students separate wheat from chaff. But an inexperienced reader might laboriously decode and read the appositive, giving it his or her full attention and becoming distracted from the meaning of the sentence, whereas the savvy reader glances at John's name and decides to ignore him.

A variation of the throwaway reference is the "shifting name." Because names also repeat tediously throughout NNNF texts, authors reference the same person in a variety of ways. If you don't know that, you won't understand that in the article "Living the Wild Life," Dr. Smith, Doug Smith, and "the eminent scientist" are the same person.[10]

## The Generic Number

If you are an experienced reader, you make strategic decisions about the numbers you encounter. Often they are specific—to understand the article, you need to know how much of something there is or how much it's growing or declining in a quantifiable way—for example, when one of the main points of an article is that the growth rate of the population of China has gone down by half in the last twenty years. But sometimes numbers demonstrate a general point—there is a lot or a little of something—and a discussion of why or what that means begins. Experienced readers know they can selectively attend to those generic numbers. You read "There are an estimated 254.4 million registered passenger vehicles in the United States," and you know you don't really have to focus on that number specifically. The article is going to be about the ramifications of having a lot of cars, not the ramifications of having 254.4 million specifically. Essentially you save your attention and cognitive processing for other things. This may seem trivial to you, but to a young reader, the distraction of reading and thinking about 254.4 million might take more focus than it does for you or me. It also matters because some 365,000 texts per year include numbers that really aren't specifically important and just signal a general point. We call these kinds of numbers generic numbers, and spotting them can help students get through a swampy section of text quickly and attend to more important matters, even if they later go back and track the numbers more carefully.

The micro rules we've described here are examples of some of the ways nonfiction is written differently, even at the sentence level. Experienced readers have the knowledge, based on experience, to know how to navigate them. Inexperienced readers do not. And for the most part, this sort of tacit knowledge about how to read informative texts is invisible to those who have it, which means that these hidden barriers are rarely analyzed or discussed. Please note that we are not necessarily saying that teachers need to address these challenges by teaching them to students. The first step is to be aware of them, as they are often hidden causes of struggle for students unfamiliar with nonfiction. From there we can imagine a variety of productive ways to address the challenge.

## MICRO GENRES AND NONLINEAR FORMATS

That the stylistic conventions we have been describing are unexpected and confusing to new readers is important. Readers have a limited amount of bandwidth with which to process what they read. Just as for the student whose decoding is so weak that he uses all of his bandwidth to sound out words and has nothing left for comprehension, so too can the confusing and arcane conventions of NNNF soak up valuable bandwidth until little remains. Here are two more common obstacles that can trip up a still-learning reader.

### Micro Genres

Much of what students read through, say, sixth grade is written for students and school settings. Even if it mimics the tropes of real-world nonfiction, it has been adapted and made more accessible for students in a variety of ways. As students get older, particularly in upper middle and high school, they should more frequently encounter texts *not* written exclusively for students. Such texts are different from "made-for-school" texts in a variety of ways. They are, for example, less shy about using technical vocabulary, and more inclined to assume a minimum level of familiarity among readers. They are also far more diverse, serving focused interests and communities. Further, the degree to which additional, diverse forms of nonfiction are emerging and growing in importance is probably accelerated by the rise of electronic media. Once there were book and movie reviews; now there are event reviews, for example. We call these emerging niche forms of nonfiction writing "micro genres," and they remind us that it's probably important to recognize the increasing range of nonfiction out there and to help our students experience it productively. Embedding is a great way to do that. Interviews, especially of the Q&A variety, are an example of a micro genre that's growing in availability and use. For example, what better to embed in a reading of *The Giver* than an interview with Lois Lowry, its author? Or consider how Peter Sipe, a teacher at Boston Collegiate Charter School, regularly reads obituaries with his class. He thinks it exposes them to a genre that has a useful way of storytelling — retrospective, generally appreciative — but that also shows theme and variation. The funny obituary or the critical obituary are fascinating case studies. In any case, Peter has ensured that his students are prepared to read nonfiction outside the common formats and to wrestle with unfamiliar styles and conventions.

## Nonlinear Layouts

Nonfiction texts include a wide array of text features and structures: captions, sidebars, illustrations, and section headings, just to name a few. Many of these result in information that is not presented in sequential order — the kind of order where a reader clearly proceeds, without question, from page one to page two and so on. In many nonfiction texts, there is no clear point where students should switch from reading the core text to reading the caption under the picture, or reading the potentially distracting sidebar, or looking at the graphic that illustrates one of the key principles in the article. Nonfiction page layouts are more likely than fiction layouts to be nonlinear, often requiring students to "zigzag" across the page to follow the natural flow of text. Each of these factors can be its own special source of distraction and confusion.

That many features of NNNF are not automatically assigned a sequential place in the text leaves a lot of choice up to students — choice they may not be used to having in their relationship with a text. If a student sees a sidebar or a caption, he could choose to read it before the main body of the text, after reading the main body of the text, or at any point in between. It also means that he might forget to read it altogether, or that he might read it at an illogical time — a time that causes him to miss a key connection in the text. What's more, even if a student reads the sidebar at the right time, he may struggle to process two ideas at once, forgetting about the original narrative or failing to connect this "extra" material to it. Nonlinear text requires multitasking.

A fairly significant body of research has recently emerged describing the challenges and costs of constant multitasking. For example, one article in the *New York Times* described the experiences of today's students, many of whom are constantly distracted by the multitasking pervading their electronic lives.[11] With so many texts being transmitted and received at any one time—text messages, Facebook posts, tweets, instant messages, Snapchats, and emails, all of which compete with homework and reading—it's often hard to choose among them. In fact, many students simply choose not to choose; instead, they bounce among them. The result is a tendency to be passive in the face of so many choices, with a sustained focus on homework and reading the sure loser.

In fact, scientists are finding the effects of multitasking on the brain to be stronger than the effects of watching television. Paying attention to multiple information sources at one time dilutes focus from any one most important thing. In such environments, notes a professor at Harvard Medical School, "[Students] are rewarded not for staying on task but for jumping to the next thing,"[12] an approach that makes sustained concentration and analysis a harder task. This means a lower absorption rate for students.

**Figure 3.1** A magazine article with a complex visual layout

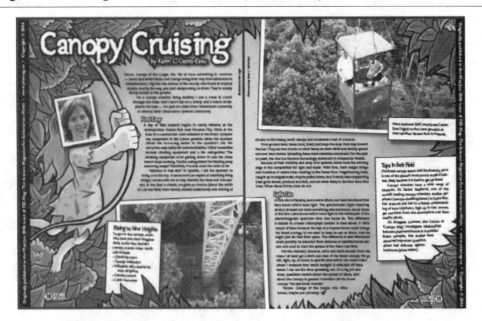

Nonfiction texts, with their variety of flashy features, often replicate this phenomenon. For example, consider the text "Canopy Cruising," an article from *YES*, a science magazine written specifically for students (Figure 3.1).

The article looks almost like a web page, exploding with visual distractions and implicit decisions: When should students read the sidebars, "Rising to New Heights" and "Tops in their Field," for example? The first contains a description of how scientists get into the forest canopy. Is this relatively low-information text box worth the distraction from the central narrative that reading it would create? If it helps students think about the canopy, when, in the course of reading the article, would be the most useful time to read it? And how should students make that determination? In fact, the purpose is often to distract—to sell the nonfiction by making kids look at something else, something "more enticing."

Surely there are some rules to follow (only switch after a full paragraph rather than midsentence, say), but much of the skill of navigating such a complex visual layout is subjective. Having engaged in years of reading nonfiction, sophisticated readers may not even attend to the informal set of rules they use to maneuver nonlinear text formats. But developing readers don't have those years of experience under their belts.

Add to this the anxiety many students feel when they don't know how and when to read an ancillary text—and the fact that nonfiction page layouts are more likely to feature multiple columns, interrupted by visuals in various places—and the result is students' not being entirely clear on what to read next. When it comes to nonlinear layouts, developing readers require explicit instruction (or, at the very least, general guidelines) for what to attend to and when. It's sometimes a first instinct to "clean up" reading materials so that they are more linear and familiar for students. In reality, it may be better to give students articles exactly as they were written and formatted to provide students with ample opportunities to practice maneuvering nonlinear layouts.

## Action Steps to Address Micro Rules, Micro Genres, and Nonlinear Formats

- *Begin introducing "real-world" versus "school-ready" texts* by sixth grade (at the latest).

*(Continued)*

(Continued)

- *Teach students that the art of "selective neglect" is part of the art of reading NNNF*—choosing to ignore things by necessity.

- *Flag—and possibly name—examples of the micro rules* for students when you see them in text. Practice reading nonlinear texts with students, especially texts with ancillary elements such as sidebars, so that students are comfortable and familiar with these situations.

- *Be "meta" about strategies you* use as a sophisticated reader to decide when you read each section of the text and additional features.

- *Provide students with a default strategy for deciding when to "jump"* to an ancillary text—at a subheading or after the last complete paragraph are viable rules of thumb. Regardless, students should know to break to read a sidebar only at the end of a paragraph.

## Reading Nonfiction, Reconsidered

When it comes to making nonfiction stick, working to develop a solid knowledge base is one of the greatest predictors of reading success, particularly in areas of history and the sciences. If teachers want to ensure future reading success for their students— not just in scholarly pursuits but in life in general— they need to prepare their students for the jungle of nonfiction forms, conventions, and formats that exist. Beyond choosing solid foundational texts and secondary pieces to supplement them, teachers can strategically embed texts and intentionally ask overlapping questions, thereby modeling the kind of relationship experienced readers should have with a text—one that is active, rather than passive, one that engages with the main idea and doesn't get overwhelmed by minutiae.

In the next chapter, we'll move on to the fourth key idea raised by the Common Core and central to teaching reading: how writing works in synergy with reading.

# NOTES

1. College Board, *Test Specifications for the Redesigned SAT,* 2014, https://collegereadiness.collegeboard.org/pdf/test-specifications-redesigned-sat.pdf, 9.

2. Daniel Willingham, "School Time, Knowledge, and Reading Comprehension," *Daniel Willingham* (blog), March 7, 2012, http://www.danielwillingham.com/daniel-willingham-science-and-education-blog/school-time-knowledge-and-reading-comprehension.

3. Donna R. Recht and Lauren Leslie, "Effect of Prior Knowledge on Good and Poor Readers' Memory of Text," *Journal of Educational Psychology* 80 (1988): 16–20.

4. Willingham, "School Time."

5. Anne E. Cunningham and Keith E. Stanovich, Early reading acquisition and its relation to reading experience and ability 10 years later. *Developmental Psychology* 33 (1997): 934–945.

6. Willingham, "School Time."

7. E. D. Hirsch Jr., *The Knowledge Deficit: Closing the Shocking Education Gap for American Children* (Boston: Houghton Mifflin, 2006).

8. "Arctic Fox," *Earth's Endangered Creatures,* http://www.earthsendangered.com/article.asp?ID=36.

9. Liam O'Donnell, "Tech Trash Tragedy," *Odyssey* 13, no. 6 (September 2004): 38.

10. Gary Ferguson, "Living the Wild Life," *Boys' Life* 91, no. 12 (December 2001): 28.

11. Matt Richtel, "Growing Up Digital, Wired for Distraction," *New York Times,* November 21, 2010, http://www.nytimes.com/2010/11/21/technology/21brain.html?pagewanted=all&_r=0.

12. Ibid.

# Writing for Reading

### MODULE 4.1: READING CLASS CYCLES

The more writing that students do, the better off they are in terms of both writing ability and reading comprehension.

### MODULE 4.2: WRITING IS REVISING

Revising, as opposed to editing, is substantively more difficult and more important in improving writing in a meaningful way.

### MODULE 4.3: ART OF THE SENTENCE

Through prompting students to write a single, beautiful sentence, teachers can impel students to think seriously about things like word choice and complex syntax.

### MODULE 4.4: BUILDING STAMINA

To prepare students for the kind of writing they'll do in college and beyond, help them put in writing "road miles" now.

### MODULE 4.5: MONITORING AND ASSESSMENT VIA THE STACK AUDIT

Stack Audits can help teachers and school leaders assess sticking points in writing instruction by comparing student work.

Chapter 4

# Writing for Reading

Recently, Gillian Cartwright of Uncommon Charter High School in Brooklyn introduced her ninth-grade students to the play *Fences* by August Wilson. In one lesson, Gillian and her students read scenes 2 and 3 from the second act aloud. Students engaged the text actively, with their pencils up, making notes throughout. Their task was to note literary elements and devices that they thought would help them make sense of the themes and characters. Gillian paused briefly after reading the scenes to inquire about some of the elements and devices they'd decided were "worthy of analysis." Two or three students shared specific lines from the play; Gillian expressed eagerness to hear more and then set the class to writing: "You're going to do a four-entry Lit Log," she said. This meant they were to choose four of the literary elements or devices they'd identified from the scenes and, in a writing "log" they used regularly for this purpose, discuss how those elements and devices worked and what they meant. "You can choose to divide the scenes any way you'd like. You'll be writing for eighteen minutes. Go." And then they were off. For *eighteen straight minutes,* every pencil scratched busily across the page as her students reflected on Wilson's great (and challenging!) play—analyzing different moments in it, from different angles and perspectives, citing different literary tools the author had used, but always in writing.

---

## See It in Action

Watch Gillian Cartwright's class write about and discuss *Fences* in clip 7 at teachlikeachampion.com/yourlibrary.

---

When it was time for the student-directed discussion that followed, one student opined, "It seems like he [Troy] doesn't care anymore, and he's being selfish. But, on page 77 when he was talking to himself and he had that little speech, he said, 'I'm gonna build a fence around what belongs to me, and I want you to stay on the other side.' Right there, he's talking to Death, I feel. It's not that he's being selfish; he's scared. We all know that at the end of the day, no matter what he does, he loves Rose." Another student questioned this analysis, however: "I have a question for you, Allie. You said that Troy is more scared than selfish. Since he's a prideful man, why would he be scared and not try to keep his family together?" And so it went: students engaging each other directly, using evidence from the text and wrestling with specific lines. All of this without a single comment from Gillian herself for more than six minutes.

It was impressive stuff, but Gillian wasn't done. After the first round of discussion, Gillian did something that surprised us. She asked her students to revise what they'd written in their Lit Logs based on the discussion they'd just had. Before jumping into a second round of discussion, students used the first round to refine their initial written thoughts.

Gillian's lesson yielded quite a bit of insight for us—and not just about *Fences*. The discussion was certainly remarkable, but her use of writing is what struck us most, in large part because we thought it had created the conditions that allowed for a high-quality discussion to thrive—deep, sustained reflection on the text by every student in advance, for example. But her use of writing had other benefits too. Consider, first, just the amount of time Gillian devoted to sustained uninterrupted writing: eighteen minutes. That was far more time than we typically observe students writing in most classrooms, but not, we also realized, nearly as much time as students would ultimately need to be able to spend framing ideas in words in uninterrupted concentration as they cranked out papers in college. Eighteen minutes of uninterrupted writing would help students build incrementally the stamina they'll need as successful students. In an age where concentration is increasingly fractured and divided by the pings and pop-ups of a thousand electronic devices, this is no small thing. As one college professor we spoke to put it, "Technology is quickly destroying our ability to focus, to pay attention to details, to appreciate the contemplative aspects of reading." In this class, there was practice sustaining focus — on a text, no less.

The placement of the writing within the class period yielded another insight. Gillian required students to write directly from the text *before* they discussed it. During the discussion, students contributed in a meaningful way as and when they felt it was appropriate, without prompting from Gillian. That autonomy was impressive, but their written ideas were autonomous in another way: they came directly and exclusively from their own fully independent reading of the text, rather than from what they had heard in discussion. The ideas that framed their contributions weren't — at first — based on what they'd learned about the play from Gillian or their peers; they were, of necessity, their own.

The revisions that students were asked to make after the discussion sparked another epiphany. In Gillian's class, students were accountable not just for participating in the discussion but for using it to improve and refine their own ideas! Think about that for a moment. We often set the goal of students "participating" in discussion. Mere participation is nice, perhaps, but it's hardly a perfect incentive; it's all about talking and not about listening. No wonder kids sometimes participate by saying things apropos of nothing. They're chalking up their participation points, sometimes at high cost to the continuity of the discussion. And what about the quiet, reflective deep thinker who all the time is ruminating on the play's themes? Where do we credit that participation? Further, consider that so often class "discussions" are more like arguments. For example, in a typical class, the two students we quoted discussing *Fences* might have begun a disagreement about whose interpretation was right that devolved into a "Who's right?" and "Who is on whose side?" tug-of-war. When there's no clear purpose to a discussion beyond being a part of it, it's easy for students to assume that the purpose is to "win" it, but Gillian subtly gave students a far more useful goal. The goal of discussion in her class was to gather insights that would be useful in refining students' own ideas, in writing, later on. So the second round of writing not only reinforced the idea that revising is an integral part of writing and thinking but also made the discussion part of this process: it's purpose was to learn from others rather than to be "right."

Writing, Gillian's class reminds us, is immensely valuable. The task of taking complex ideas and describing them in precise vocabulary and deft syntax is one of the most cognitively demanding tasks students can perform in the classroom. For this reason, Doug spent a chapter on it in his book *Teach Like a Champion 2.0*. But what Gillian's class reminded us of was something more. In her classroom, the strategic use of writing made reading and discussions of reading—the other core activities of English class—more rigorous, focused, productive, and engaging. In short, it made them better. Writing is a deeply valuable endeavor in its own right, but it is also an endeavor that works in synergy with reading in specific ways.

In this chapter, we will explore some of the synergies between reading and writing in more depth, focusing not only on how and why writing is valuable but also on how it can aid us in building top-level readers specifically—though of course the converse will, we hope, also be true, and we hope also to provide some ideas on how more intentional approaches to reading can make students better writers. (Ideally, the chapter on Close Reading did some of that already.)

First, though, let's take a look at some of the reasons why writing is so important and why doing more of it, in direct response to reading, is one of our four Core of the Core ideas.

Written ideas, it should be acknowledged, have special stature and gravitas, particularly in the humanities. Long ago, before credit cards and the Euro, when you traveled, you could use only money coined in the kingdom where you were at the time. Regardless of the amount of money you had, if it wasn't in the "coin of the realm," it wouldn't help you much. To this day, ideas, interpretations, and analyses are similar. They get full faith and credit only if they are expressed in the coin of the realm, which, in college and in much of professional life, means *in writing*. Written responses are the way students demonstrate their depth of understanding. In almost any college classroom—certainly in the humanities—it is the format in which mastery is finally expressed and in which ideas get the fullest credit. Even if you do "get it," if you can't put it in writing, cogently and coherently, it simply doesn't count as much. So students need to take their verbal discussions and, as Gillian's did, lock them down in written language as a matter of habit.

But writing is not just a means of formalizing ideas, of locking them down with nuance and precision in specific language and syntax. It is also a means of developing and nurturing them from their first tiny roots, one of the primary ways thoughts are generated in the first place. Think about your own experience as a writer. How many times have you started writing and weren't sure where you were going? As you wrote, the ideas developed. Maybe they came out faster than you could edit them. Maybe all of a sudden you had a new idea that surprised or even astounded you. In all likelihood, you revised constantly—but probably not in the systematic way revision occurs in classes, with a rough draft, revision, and final draft. You revised as you wrote, even in your class notes, and over time, the processes became indistinguishable. To write and to revise, at once, was to think.

In reading class, writing is not simply an end product, then; it is a tool for critical thinking. Students need to be able to use writing to formulate and develop ideas. They need to practice thinking as they write, letting ideas emerge from provisional notions even if they don't know the full shape of them when they start. This process doesn't necessarily come naturally. Sometimes it's important to practice writing a first draft, not a final one, where the goal is to let ideas flow, not to finalize them. But it's also important to see the revision process as something that happens with all writing, all thinking, not just drafts of the essays you turn in. In terms of idea development, it's often the habit of constant revision during our *least* formal writing that is most valuable, and this is far less frequently addressed in schools.

Some of the synergies between reading and writing, then, are relatively straightforward: both rely on facility with language and syntax, for example. To write a sentence that makes a nuanced comparison of complex ideas with precise word choice and adept syntax is to prepare to read someone else's sentence of a similar quality. If reading is the process of deconstructing sentences—sentences written with subtle and sophisticated syntax to convey such literary elements as mood, tone, and perspective—then students who are proficient at constructing such sentences are often best prepared to succeed at reading them. And of course, when students write, especially if they examine choices carefully and develop the range of grammatical or stylistic structures they can use, they are most aware of the connection between stylistic choices and authorial intent. After all, the authorial intent is their own. But as Gillian's class—and so many others we observed—taught us, there's more to it than that. The synergies between reading and writing go much deeper, into the structure of lessons, for example, and what activities we do in what order, and this is the first topic we discuss, in Module 4.1.

| MODULE 4.1 | Reading Class Cycles |
| --- | --- |

Writing is often an "end" activity. In most disciplines, an essay or paper is a conventional and rigorous capstone to a unit or the study of a book. So too in the day-to-day sense, a typical class involves reading and discussion, perhaps, and ends with some writing to put it all together. This is especially true in reading classes, where we typically read (before or during class), discuss, then write. That's the cycle: read-discuss-write. Generally we have spent much of our careers thinking about the benefits of this template, and many of our teachers within Uncommon Schools did excellent work finding ways to make reading class more writing intensive. In each lesson, they made it a habit to include rigorous writing prompts that asked students to write about what they read and discussed. This helped them make sense of the lesson and developed the quality of their writing through constant application.

In a typical lesson, students would have read for forty-five minutes (together as a class as well as independently), during which time the teacher paused class to pose questions for students to answer verbally. Some of those questions might have supported basic comprehension; others aimed to prep students for answering analysis-based writing prompts completed at the end of the class period. The idea was to use discussion as a scaffold for high-quality responses to rigorous prompts. By the time the class was finished with reading and discussion, students might have had five minutes (ten on a really good day) to thoughtfully develop high-quality written responses. Although such a coupling of reading and writing did add rigor to classes in many ways, it also had some weak points.

For one thing, we've learned over time that there are limitations implicit in a single period of sustained writing, completed after one extended period of sustained reading. First, when students always complete their daily reading before writing—or save writing until the end—they are left with little time to write responses, and certainly not enough time to develop quality responses. What happens at the end is most likely to get squeezed, and that was almost always the writing. This, we recognized, required a shift in how we allocate our class time.

Big chunks of reading followed by a single block of writing also allowed misunderstandings to spiral. One of writing's most useful aspects is that it makes thinking visible and so helps reveal misconceptions by making them clear and tangible, on the page in front of both teacher and student. But if students read eight or ten pages from *Mrs. Frisby and the Rats of NIMH* before writing about the text, it's more challenging to determine why they misunderstood events than it is if they had had time to jot down explanations periodically.

Most important, when writing comes at the end, after not only a stretch of reading but a stretch of questioning and discussion, the accuracy of the data that writing presents on student understanding is eroded slightly because what students write is drawn from both their own reading of the text and the subsequent discussion by their peers—and their teacher. When a teacher in this classroom collects end-of-session writing assignments, it is impossible to determine whether students with strong answers were outstanding readers or good listeners who might plausibly be compensating for gaps in the understanding they gleaned directly from the passage by using the insights their peers offered during discussion. Certainly at some point we want students to combine their own insights with the best of what their peers thought, but our responsibility as reading teachers is to ensure that students can create meaning directly from reading, on their own and without the support of a roomful of peers. Therefore, we have to assess both with some frequency—initial understanding by each student directly from the text *and* final ideas informed by the community of ideas in the classroom. This might seem like a trivial distinction, but it is not. Some of our smartest students are able to compensate for lack of critical reading skills with good listening skills, and the two are not the same.

The challenge of assessing what students understand about a text directly from their reading of it and disentangling that from what they may glean via other sources is what we refer to as the "Reading CFU Gap." We think it is one of the most important and underacknowledged challenges of the reading classroom.

## CLOSING THE READING CFU GAP

CFU stands for *Check for Understanding.* You can read more about it in *Teach Like a Champion 2.0*, where it gets two full chapters of discussion, but for our purposes here we will explain it as the legendary UCLA basketball coach John Wooden did. Wooden, who, as some people know, began his career as an English teacher and continued to see himself as a teacher throughout his career, once said that the most crucial task of teaching was to distinguish "I taught it" from "they learned it." The core of teaching is recognizing (and then acting on) whether your students truly understood the theme of the story, for example, not just whether you told them what it might be or whether they heard it mentioned during discussion.

Reading poses special and complex challenges when it comes to mastering this crucial skill, because, as we mentioned, students can derive understanding from two sources: the text itself and the content of subsequent discussions about the text. Only one of these is an indication of the ability to read independently, however. The other can be a "false positive." Consider how that plays out in a typical reading class sequence, depicted in Figure 4.1.

In this class, the teacher has just read the first page of *Oliver Twist* with her students. After the initial reading, maybe half the kids get it, while the other half don't (or might

**Figure 4.1**  A Typical Reading Lesson

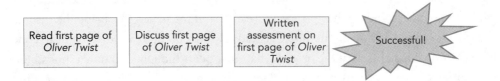

not), at least in part because they're overwhelmed by the language. The class dives into a carefully planned discussion, after which many of the students who didn't initially get it begin to grasp the key ideas. However, now the teacher can't be sure whether students "got it" from carefully reading the text or from carefully listening to their peers. She doesn't know whether they can actually read Dickens or simply follow discussions of his writing. This challenge is often compounded by the fact that a handful of the strongest students can often drive a discussion with their insights. This is a mixed bag.

It's great that many students now understand the opening scene; it's great that they've used their peers' ideas to do that. These are good things. But they are not sufficient. It's *not* great that many of those students still may not be able to generate full understanding from the text on their own. And, most of all, it's not great that we may be inclined to think that many more can do this than actually can and that we may not know from the discussion exactly who can do what. You want engaged, enthused, deep-thinking readers driving discussion, but you also want to be sure that all students are able to generate solid meaning themselves. After all, generating meaning directly from a challenging text is the harder of the two tasks, and in many ways it is "the" college skill—the student is assigned the text, and he or she is expected to come to class or respond in some way based on initial mastery. But this skill is not typically taught in college. Either you have it before you arrive, or you spend a lot of time in tutoring centers and office hours trying to catch up.

To more accurately measure student understanding and progress, it's important to insert at least two assessment points into the process of reading and analyzing a text: first, a point that helps us determine whether students were able to independently establish sufficient meaning from the text; and second, a point that helps us evaluate the quality of their processing after further interpretation and analysis from a variety of sources and perspectives. A strategic placement of writing before discussion, even in the midst of reading, is the most effective way to do this. The typical sequence of activities in a reading class might be reengineered as illustrated in Figure 4.2 to address the Reading CFU Gap.

**Figure 4.2** A Reengineered Reading Lesson to Address the Reading CFU Gap

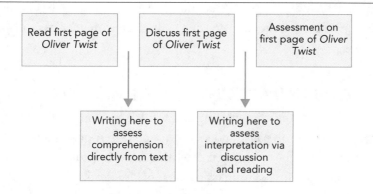

In *Teach Like a Champion 2.0*, Doug discusses a technique called Front the Writing—arranging a lesson so that writing falls earlier in the process than it might otherwise—both to increase the amount of heavy cognitive lifting students do and to support better CFU. Because reading teachers constantly have to balance reading "road miles" with writing "road miles," Front the Writing is slightly different in reading class. (You will read more about road miles in chapter 5.) Yes, writing should come before other activities, but the type of writing students do and the activities that go after the writing vary depending on where you are in your reading and your purpose for writing.

Let's assume that aside from developing students' vocabulary, there are three primary activities in every reading class: reading, writing, and discussion. Teachers of the most successful reading classes intentionally set the length and placement of these components so as to maximize their synergy. Let's look at some of the most effective combinations.

## READ-DISCUSS-READ CYCLE

Because this chapter is about writing in a reading class, we're going to focus here on tools you can use to insert more writing into the process of moving students toward deep understanding of a text—and toward being able to achieve that deep understanding on their own when necessary. Our suggestion is to write more frequently and in between the stages of the process of interpreting a text. However, it's important to point out that we are not offering some kind of universal rule, a mandate that students have to write first every time you want to discuss what they have read. Sometimes in the course of reading a text, especially a complex one, teachers will pause the reading to ask some questions to solidify students' understanding. Sometimes they'll jump right to discussion. But we are suggesting that students write with more frequency and consistency as part of their daily work of responding to texts and, as we'll get to at the end of this section, that teachers frequently do what Gillian did with her class and ask students to write twice.

## READ-WRITE-READ CYCLE AND STOP AND JOTS

Often the first step in embedding writing and using it to support reading is to include prompts that ask students to pause and jot down a quick response, followed by a speedy return to the text. Our name for this type of writing is the **Stop and Jot**—a quick write or a short journal entry—with the primary purpose of idea development. The Stop and Jot is an academic system you can use to help students establish meaning through writing. Stop and Jots allow students time to process and react without significantly interrupting the flow of the narrative or text.

Stop and Jots are effectively used across grade levels. Sam DeLuke of Troy Prep Elementary School explains that in elementary school classrooms, they're useful for solidifying literal meaning before moving on to a more analytical question. The Stop and Jot questions cause students to think carefully about what they understand about a text before tackling a tougher question; they also provide teachers with important data about how much to support students before releasing them to more rigorous thinking and writing. Teachers at Sam's school include their Stop and Jot prompts in students' class-work packet with space to write. Here's an example:

How does the author want the reader to feel about the Forest of Sin when he says "It was like being among the dead men in an enormous empty green cathedral"?

_____

_____

_____

Patrick Pastore, principal of Rochester Prep Middle School, describes how his teachers use Stop and Jots with older students. "A Stop and Jot is a great opportunity for students to complete a short burst of writing to punctuate important moments in a lesson. It helps students lock in key understandings or collect their thoughts, and at the same time it provides teachers with a data collection point without the time commitment necessary for an extended response."

**Figure 4.3** *Miracle's Boys* Stop and Jot

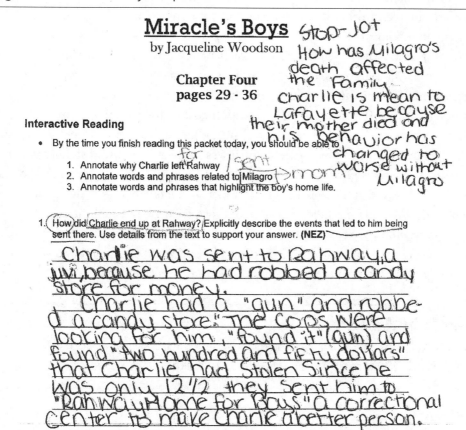

# Miracle's Boys Stop-Jot
by Jacqueline Woodson

How has Milagro's death affected the family.

### Chapter Four
### pages 29 - 36

Charlie is mean to Lafayette because their mother died and his behavior has changed to worse without Milagro

**Interactive Reading**

- By the time you finish reading this packet today, you should be able to
  1. Annotate why Charlie left Rahway / for / sent
  2. Annotate words and phrases related to Milagro → mom
  3. Annotate words and phrases that highlight the boy's home life.

1. How did Charlie end up at Rahway? Explicitly describe the events that led to him being sent there. Use details from the text to support your answer. (NEZ)

Charlie was sent to Rahway, a juvi, because he had robbed a candy store for money.
Charlie had a "gun" and robbed a candy store. The cops were looking for him, "found it" (gun) and found "two hundred and fifty dollars" that Charlie had stolen since he was only 12 1/2 they sent him to "Rahway Home for Boys" a correctional center to make Charlie a better person.

Figure 4.3 is an example of a fifth-grade response to a Stop and Jot question from one of Patrick's teachers, Alison Neufeglise. The Stop and Jot was included to confirm understanding of how the characters in *Miracle's Boys* had been affected by the death of Milagro, which they'd discussed in a previous lesson, before students began the day's reading.

Stop and Jots can be useful for CFU, but, most important, they allow students to think in writing—to support understanding of the text. Because Stop and Jots are quick, teachers can embed several into their daily plans. With regular practice, students are socialized to pause and reflect intentionally about the text in writing. They develop more refined ideas. Students begin to see themselves as active participants in the process of comprehension—a process that relies on writing and thinking, rather than something their teacher does for them. The simplicity of the Stop and Jot is also an important attribute. What you do every day is arguably more important than what you do on your most artfully planned day. Stop and Jots make it easy to build the constant habit of thinking in writing about the text.

Kelsey Clark, an eighth-grade reading teacher at UP Academy Oliver Middle School in Lawrence, Massachusetts, leverages this idea. She has systematized Stop and Jots so that students do them often (multiple times per lesson) and with the same general procedure each time. This reduces the transaction cost of transitioning from reading to writing and back to reading, and her students do it seamlessly. In a recent lesson, she included three Stop and Jots, each of which was characterized by a carefully planned question, a brief period of student writing or annotation, and a quick follow-up discussion to ensure that all students grasped key concepts. Then they dived back into the reading. Within the predictable Stop and Jot system she's established, Kelsey also includes variations, such as where and how students will respond ("Jot a sentence in the class packet or a margin note directly in the text"), and whether or not they discuss with a partner as they write, in order to support pacing and engagement.

---

### See It in Action

Watch Kelsey Clark's systematized Stop and Jots as her eighth-grade students read *Girl, Interrupted* in clip 8 at teachlikeachampion.com/yourlibrary.

---

Because the purpose of Stop and Jots is to use writing as a tool to think, it's important to communicate to students that the standards of quality might be different than those for other types of writing they'll do in class. You might explain, "During a Stop and Jot, your goal is to make sense of the text; pausing to write will help you do that. Grammar and spelling are important, but not as important as getting your ideas on paper. Sometimes I'll ask you to go back and make edits, but most of the time we'll get right back to the reading so we can do more polished writing later in class."

In most cases, writings used to "think on paper" are designed to be imperfect, often used as a means to an end. They are intended to prepare students for more analytical writing at another point in class — the crawling before the walking, so to speak. They also allow students to listen better during subsequent discussions, as their ideas are already written down and they don't have to try to remember them while their peers are talking. It's not that such writing is never revised and turned in; it means most often it isn't. Like the jottings on napkins and envelopes that have captured the kernel of a new or brilliant idea for time immemorial, Stop and Jots serve their purpose simply by allowing for idea development, and they can often be left at that. They (and other formative writing prompts, which are all part of the Everybody Writes technique described in *Teach Like a Champion 2.0*) aren't supposed to finalize interpretations of the reading so much as prepare for what comes next: discussion and more reading. Thus, although the teachers we've observed often glance at them to assess where students are as they write, they don't usually collect them.

As students gain autonomy in their thinking, they'll ideally begin initiating Stop and Jots without teacher prompting. Student-generated practices include marking up a text with notes in the margin, writing a quick self-generated summary at the end of a particularly challenging text, or posing a question regarding the author's tone between paragraphs while reading. These are useful behaviors to look for to assess the degree to which students have internalized writing as a thinking tool: Do they grab their pencils and scribble notes of their own volition as they are reading or listening to discussions? If the answer is yes, we think that's a very good sign.

## READ-WRITE-DISCUSS CYCLE

As we discussed earlier, you'll sometimes want your students to come to a hard stop just after reading a passage. Using a Read-Write-Discuss cycle means asking students to write a response directly from a text—a response that is longer, more outward facing, and more analytical than a Stop and Jot. We call this type of writing an **Open Response**, and its primary benefit is that it mirrors more formal types of writing. Students are asked to write directly from a text without relying on the insights of other students and the teacher, but in formats closer to what they will ultimately have to produce in "formal work"—an essay, final paper, college paper, and so on. Open Responses allow teachers to CFU about what students get (and don't get) about their reading.

Without an intermediate discussion, and by actively circulating to assess, teachers can directly identify what students were able to independently interpret from their reading. The discussion that ensues is therefore more targeted. Teachers can determine the level of student understanding from their Open Responses, and use that knowledge as a starting point for discussion.

In the Read-Write-Discuss cycle, writing supports and is supported by discussion. Students write to develop and refine their ideas before sharing with the rest of the class. Solidifying their ideas in writing helps students engage in a genuine discussion, enabling them to actively listen to peers' answers and evaluate them before responding—rather than spending the "discussion" rehearsing their original thought in order to be ready when it's their turn to share.

An effective writing prompt in this cycle requires students to do more writing and more analytical thinking than they would do in the Read-Write-Read cycle. Generally, these prompts are open ended. Typical Open Responses vary in length, from a few sentences to a paragraph (depending on the age and ability of your students). In writing your prompt, it's important to consider how it will help shape the discussion that follows. Having a clear plan for discussion will ensure that the writing is more valuable for your students. Does it lead to multiple interpretations that students must defend and justify? Is there one correct interpretation? Will the discussion focus on multiple pieces of evidence gathered by students, leading to that interpretation? Your answers to these questions are the starting point for thinking deliberately about the questions you ask students to write about. Include a balance of different types of questions and execute them with intentionality.

## Open Response Prompts

Here are some examples of Open Response prompts based on *To Kill a Mockingbird* and *The Tale of Peter Rabbit*:

- Harper Lee paints an absurd picture of Simon Finch. Choose a detail that shows this and explain.

- Simon is a *foil* to Atticus. Explain at least three ways Scout shows us that they are different.

- The narrator writes, "whom should he meet but Mr. MacGregor." Explain what this means. How did Peter feel in this moment? Use details from the story in your response.

- The author explains that Peter's jacket had brass buttons and was quite new. Explain why that detail is important to the events in the story.

Notice that Open Response prompts usually ask students to refer directly to the text and use specific evidence or details. Although they can be used to CFU, they also frequently assume that students have literal comprehension of the story and are now ready to analyze a character or event more deeply. For example, students responding to the second prompt have a clear understanding of both Simon and Atticus, as well as the definition of *foil* and how authors use them in stories. In order to fully develop their ideas in response to any of these prompts, students usually write multiple sentences.

Beyond thinking about how your prompts might frame later discussion, having a clear sense of what your students understand (and don't) can help you determine where the discussion and the writing prompt should begin. Tracking, Not Watching as your students write—being intentional about choosing exactly what you're looking for as you circulate (see *TLaC 2.0* for more on this technique)—can help you do this. By reading students writing as they work, you gather valuable data that helps determine your next steps in class. If a significant number of students have misconceptions in their responses, your first step is to clarify through rereading and questioning. When your students begin to demonstrate clear understanding through their writing, you can determine which students you might call on during discussion more intentionally. We often call this hunting instead of fishing. Often when we call on a student, we don't know what he or she will talk about. We're fishing. Anything could come out, and that's fine...sometimes. When you preview written responses, you can choose to call on students who can share key insights with clear evidence, or a student whose response can build off of what classmates shared. Or you could ask multiple students to present pieces of evidence in support of a common interpretation. Alternatively, you could decide to call on a student who made a common error or on students with contrasting interpretations to present contrasting viewpoints, and then ask other students to weigh in. Either way, reading written responses as they happen and using them as the basis for a discussion (often through Cold Call or Pre-Call) can make your discussion more productive.

The success of this process—observing student writing to help plan for discussion—is due, in large part, to planning an exemplar student response. This response allows you to provide immediate feedback to students and to help determine which students you'll call on as you facilitate discussion.

## Stop and Jots versus Open Responses

Both Stop and Jots and Open Responses are designed to be formative as well as evaluative. By prompting students to write about the text, both types implicitly require students to think more carefully about what they've read and to prepare for quality discussions. Teachers can use writing from either type as data about what students do and do not understand.

*(Continued)*

(Continued)

However, Open Responses are typically more evaluative than their quick-write counterparts because they're designed to be polished and analytical. This allows teachers to check for a deeper level of understanding. Stop and Jots allow students to gather and note their initial thoughts—thoughts that will be helpful later in forming a more developed argument. When Stop and Jots are used as CFUs, they are generally for checking students' understanding of literal or basic comprehension of the text.

## READ-WRITE-DISCUSS-REVISE

Tweaking the Read-Write cycle to include time for revision is a seemingly small adaptation that pays large dividends for young writers and readers. It's easy to underestimate the power of this simple change in terms of how it shapes not only the written work of students but also discussions about reading. It is, to us, one of the most important, useful, and—fortunately—simple ideas in this book.

Recently, Julia Goldenheim used this approach in a particularly effective way with her seventh-grade reading class.

### See It in Action

Watch Julia Goldenheim's Read-Write-Discuss-Revise cycle in clip 9 at teachlikeachampion.com/yourlibrary.

In the midst of reading *The Winter of Our Discontent* by John Steinbeck, Julia paused her class to draw their attention to one key line in the novel. She prompted students to write about what the line reveals about the character Joey. After several minutes of writing, Julia's class used specific textual evidence to discuss not only what the line showed about Joey but also how it conflicted with their initial understanding of his character. Following the Read-Write-Discuss cycle, Julia asked her students to *revise* their writing based on evidence and viewpoints gathered from the class discussion—specifically, how this line from the text complicated their initial assessment of Joey.

Asking students to revise based on the content of discussion in a cycle of Read-Write-Discuss-Revise encourages them to actively listen to peers—to engage in collegial discussion in a way that allows them to synthesize information and adjust their views and opinions. It gives them a purpose for discussion—to harness useful ideas—which is more valuable than simply trying to "win" with their arguments.

But revising is more than just a tool to bolster discussion. The act of revision forces students to refine their initial analysis. Writing to refine is among the most rigorous and important tasks we can ask of our students. Consistently asking students to revise their writing supports them in effectively polishing their writing and ideas. Further, asking students to revise based on insights from the discussion causes them to listen better during discussion. It socializes students to listen differently—they must listen actively for ways to develop their initial ideas.

The revision itself may be done informally, by having students revise their written responses based on the class discussion. Alternately, a more formal option involves having other students or the teacher provide written feedback, then asking students to revise based on both the discussion and feedback. (See more in Module 4.2, "Writing Is Revising," for specific guidance on revision.)

Uncommon Schools teachers regularly structure student lesson materials as a way to prioritize and strengthen the Read-Write-Discuss-Revise cycle. For an example, see the box "Ellie Strand's Read-Write-Discuss-Revise Template." (See the appendix or teachlikeachampion.com for a downloadable template.)

---

## Ellie Strand's Read-Write-Discuss-Revise Template

### *Everybody Writes 1:*

Explain how Orwell uses the following line to develop a central idea of the chapter:

> Again the animals seemed to remember that a resolution against this had been passed in the early days, and again Squealer was able to convince them that this was not the case.

_____

_____

_____

_____

_____

_____

*(Continued)*

---

*(Continued)*

**Notes from Discussion:**

_____

_____

_____

_____

**Everybody Rewrites 1:**

_____

_____

_____

_____

_____

_____

## Charting the Evidence

Uncommon Schools teachers often post and keep a record of the key points raised during discussion particularly at the elementary school level. The system, referred to as "charting," allows students to see (and write) the most important ideas brought out in discussion. They can use key words, phrases, and ideas from the chart when they go to revise their own work. Charting is also a valuable way to model for students what it looks like to take good notes in a discussion—a skill that will serve them well in college and beyond.

Arranging their materials this way also streamlines observations. Designing materials and student work space so that responses appear in the same, consistent place every time makes it easy for a teacher to find the data she needs (see *TLaC 2.0* for more on the Standardize the Format technique). In each phase of the cycle, she knows exactly where to look to gather data efficiently about students' understanding. In the first response, she can quickly assess which students understood the reading and which students struggled to independently grasp and interpret it. The Notes from Discussion box helps her readily gather information about how well students are following the discussion and distilling important insights and reflections from their peers. In the beginning, structured handouts or packets serve as models for students. Over time (especially with high school students), you'll likely move away from using handouts to asking students to record answers and track discussion in their own notebooks or journals.

## READ-DISCUSS-WRITE CYCLE

Although it's usually best to place the writing directly after reading as often as possible, there are benefits of the Read-Discuss-Write cycle worth considering. This cycle allows students to glean additional insights from the reading through discussions with their peers, before crafting their own responses. These insights may come in the form of paraphrases, clarification of key vocabulary, evidence that supports a particular point of view, or context or background knowledge and can help "prime the pump" (see Module 4.4, "Building Stamina") by giving students insights, evidence, or ideas to draw from when writing in response to a text for extended periods of time. And of course sometimes it just makes sense to vary your approach a little. So we're not arguing here in all-or-none terms, just observing that the Read-Discuss-Write cycle tends to be the default in many classrooms, and its limitations warrant a bit of caution to prevent overuse.

## RE-CYCLING

As you imagine a cycle playing out in your class, perhaps you see a long stretch of reading followed by writing, discussion, and revising. Perhaps you imagine that cycle as nearly an entire lesson. That's fine, but, reading classes can also be structured to use multiple iterations and variations of the Read-Write-Discuss cycle during class. "Re-cycling" like this is one of the keys to maximizing the effectiveness of these cycles.

---

### Ideas for Re-Cycling

Depending on the time in your class period, you can embed two or three Read-Write-Read cycles and one or two Read-Write-Discuss cycles. For your most important (or rigorous) prompt, be sure to add revision to one of the cycles.

*(Continued)*

---

Typical Read-Write-Discuss Cycle: Repeat 1x–2x per class

- Read 10–15 minutes
- Write 5–10 minutes
- Discuss 10–15 minutes
- Revise (at least once) 3–5 minutes

"Re-Cycling" Shorter Read-Write-Discuss Cycles: Repeat 5x per class

- Read 2–3 minutes
- Write 1–1.5 minutes
- Discuss 2–3 minutes
- Revise (at least once) 1 minute

Writing is often squeezed out by the other activities in reading class. By including a variety of short cycles within the course of one class, you guarantee that students have time for writing (and revision). This is important for increasing the road miles that students accumulate for both reading and writing.

An additional benefit to including multiple cycles is that moving from one short activity to the next—all in pursuit of the same objective—creates what we call the "illusion of speed," which increases energy and engagement.

## See It in Action

Watch one of Jessica Bracey's Read-Write-Discuss cycles in clip 10 at teachlikeachampion.com/yourlibrary that she uses to allow students to reflect on their reading in writing. This is just one of several cycles that Jessica uses throughout a class period, which helps her create the "illusion of speed."

Take one of Jessica Bracey's lessons, for example. In it, Jessica and her fifth-grade students were reading a novel, *Circle of Gold*, together. After about five minutes, Jessica paused to pose a question about the novel: "What is the plan, and what does this reveal about Tony?" Rather than take one or two hands and then return to the reading, as many teachers would, Jessica instructed her students to write their response directly into their Reader's Response journal. It's worth mentioning that students were working on question number 87 in their Reader's Response journal, and given that they'd done this eighty-six times previously, it was no surprise that every single student in the class immediately plunged into a thoughtfully written response task. After three minutes of writing, Jessica asked for hands so that she could call on students to share their responses. Their enthusiasm to participate was striking—every hand shooting up into the air, several students practically knocking their desks over in their desire to participate. Preparation builds engagement, it seems. The first student Jessica called on shared a thorough and accurate response. The quality of his work reflected the time Jessica had given the class to refine their thoughts in writing. In fact, it was good enough that most teachers would have ended with that successful response. Instead, Jessica called on a second student, asking her to "discuss, para-phrase, push it even further." Her student did exactly that, drawing on and extending her classmate's initial response. The causes of this are worth considering. Almost assuredly, one cause was this: because her answer was written down, she did not have to try to remember it while her classmate was talking. She could listen and use her processing capacity to analyze and compare the two answers rather than remember her own.

After five minutes of high-quality discussion driven by their writing, Jessica's class then cycled back to the novel to begin another cycle of Read-Write-Discuss. In fact, her lesson consisted of a series of these relatively shorter cycles of Read-Write-Discuss repeated multiple times. This is interesting because teachers who use a Read-Write-Discuss cycle might, as a default, do it only in large chunks of 20 minute each, say. And certainly there are times when that slower pacing would be most appropriate. But Jessica brought energy to her class and illusion of speed by breaking the class's core activities into smaller chunks with more frequent switches. This helped students remain energetically engaged.

Of course, there's far more to writing than where it's placed in relation to reading and discussion and how often it's being done. In the next module, we'll look at one important truth about the written word, one that any good writer knows in her bones: writing is revising.

"I have rewritten—often several times—every word I have ever published," Vladimir Nabokov once noted. "My pencils outlive their erasers." Oscar Wilde did him one better: "Books are never finished," he said. "They are merely abandoned." The best writers are never done; for them, writing and revising are constant partners and often indistinguishable. Interestingly, though, our approach to revision in the classroom is more limited; we expect students to write their formal papers in drafts, but there's often less of a place for revision in their day-to-day classroom lives. In our own daily writing—our emails to colleagues, our notes to our spouses—we begin revising even before we realize we have a draft. As the words emerge on the page, the cross-outs and carets do too, and this distinction is important. Yes, we want drafts with essays, but we also want students who are "impromptu revisers," who use writing as a tool to refine and develop their informal thoughts. And these habitual wordsmiths are also, we think, likely to be most attentive to the difference between "would be" and "will," say, or "forest" and "woods." Students who develop that kind of ear for language are more likely to be successful and attentive readers. Ideally we would create a culture of revision: an indelible connection between writing and refining, rephrasing, or reshaping, even, perhaps especially, in informal modes of written expression.

In thinking about how to build a culture of revision in the classroom, it's important, for starters, to distinguish editing from revising, two processes that are often conflated but that are different in demonstrable and important ways.

In an interview with Doug, Judith Hochman, founder of the highly lauded Hochman Writing Method, described the difference between editing and revising. Editing is the process of making technical corrections to a piece of writing. It includes addressing errors in capitalization, punctuation, and grammar or lack of clarity in syntax. Revision, by contrast, is the process of rewriting sentences, adding, dropping or reframing ideas, and choosing more precise words. One is polishing what is written; the other is rewriting it.

Generally, for writing instruction to be effective, teachers have to make a habit of constantly looking at and reworking what students write, through both editing and revising. But, as Hochman points out, revising is much more rigorous. It's where the work really happens—where an idea is framed, distilled to its core elements, and brought to life.

Editing is important, but revision is critical. Still, many of us don't distinguish between the two. If you let students choose — that is, if you put a block of text in front of them and say something like, "What suggestions do you have to improve it?" — they will generally choose to edit rather than revise. Offering advice like "You need a capital letter" is easier than saying "Rework that sentence to use a subordinating conjunction" or "Make your verb more precise and active" or "See if you can find a word that captures the relationship more precisely."

Teachers, too, may gravitate toward the simpler work of editing. The potential reasons why are diverse. They may not have a set of common criteria for revision — "rules and tools" like those for editing, which are usually established through basic writing instruction in every grade ("Make sure your sentences and proper nouns start with capital letters"; "You need a comma and conjunction to join those two independent clauses"). It's also easy to focus on editing because it's easy to differentiate between correct and incorrect. And carefully editing a written piece provides a sense of accomplishment — students make their writing better in a tangible way. For all these reasons, teachers, like students, may often choose to edit rather than revise.

Editing might make writing more correct, but it doesn't necessarily make it better, sharper, crisper, or more memorable. Revising is about refining, developing, and clarifying ideas, whereas editing is about cleaning up and formatting them. One way to help teachers do more of it is to equip them with common revision criteria and consistent prompts to ask students. After all, even those teachers with excellent revision skills might struggle to codify their knowledge into common actions students might employ. In the following pages, we attempt to build a framework and establish some criteria so that revising can be easier and more productive for more teachers.

## TYPES OF REVISION

Even with revision, there are variables to consider. Are you trying to help students develop *this* idea about *this* text? (For example, "Now that we understand the simile better, revise your response to explain why the author might have included it.") Or are you trying to develop their writing in a way that's relevant in this *and all* future cases? (For example, "Now can you revise to show instead of tell?") Another question: Is the revision a teaching point relevant for everyone in the classroom, or is it private feedback from me (teacher) to you (one student)?

These questions imply two *types of revision* and two *settings* in which students might complete their revisions:

**Types of Revision**

- **Specific:** revision guidance that helps students refine an argument about a specific text or point (revision to develop our interpretation of a particular text as readers)
- **Universal:** revision guidance that helps students improve their ability as writers more generally—use active voice, show don't tell, include action verbs, and so on (revision to develop our capacity to express all *future* ideas in writing)

**Settings for Revision**

- **Private:** revision on your own, reworking your own text
- **Public:** revision as a group looking at a common writing sample and then (often) applying the lessons personally

You would likely use different combinations of these types and settings, depending on your goals for the lesson (see Table 4.1). We argue here not for one best type but for balance and intentionality. Doing both types of revision in both settings is probably optimal!

Even in the classes of top teachers, some of the types and settings for revision outlined in Table 4.1 receive more attention while others are given short shrift. A teacher with a particular passion for literature might be at greatest risk for focusing a bit too often on specific revisions, for example.

But assessing which approach to take can be thorny for other reasons. When we evaluate a student work sample, for example, we're really measuring two things: (1) the student's ability to comprehend and interpret the text, and (2) her ability to articulate that interpretation in writing. In a weak work sample, we attribute misunderstandings to challenges of interpretation or comprehension—often a correct assumption. But it's also plausible that the student did comprehend the text, but her writing deficits prevented her from clearly articulating that understanding.

A revision prompt like "Describe the similarities and differences in one sentence. Start your sentence with the subordinating conjunction ('Although both paragraphs describe...')" can be a helpful tool for gathering more data. If it turns out that the student can't successfully answer the prompt after being given a structure to support her articulation, then it's time to reread and pose questions—to figure out where her understanding has broken down.

**Table 4.1** Variations for Revising

|  | | Type | |
| --- | --- | --- | --- |
| | | Specific Revision (Revising to develop our interpretation of *this* text as readers) | Universal Revision (Revising to develop our capacity to express all *future* ideas in writing) |
| **Setting** | Private (Revise on your own, reworking your owntext) | "Revise your original answer to include at least one challenging idea from today's discussion."<br><br>"Go back and revise your topic sentence to make sure it includes at least two specific adjectives to describe Steinbeck's characterization of Joey." | "Revise your sentence to start with a subordinating conjunction."<br><br>"On your paper, choose two sentences that are best as one complex sentence and combine them."<br><br>"Revise your answer, using only the most significant/relevant piece of evidence." |
| | Public (Revise as a group looking at a shared text) | "Let's help Alicia clarify what she means by 'the people on the other side.' Let's all write an improved version of that sentence now."<br><br>"How can Alicia reinforce her claim about Anne Frank with another piece of evidence from this passage?" | "Find at least one phrase that Alicia can eliminate to avoid the repetition of ideas."<br><br>"Review Alicia's word choice. Identify two words that we can replace with college-level vocabulary." |

# See It in Action

Watch Julie Miller as she provides clear revision instructions to her twelfth-grade students in clip 11 at teachlikeachampion.com/yourlibrary. As her students write in response to a question she's posed about Junot Díaz's novel *The Brief and Wondrous Life of Oscar Wao*, she circulates to observe and give feedback on their responses. Following her observations, she provides two pieces of feedback for the group—one that's specific, the other universal.

## Make the Time to Revise

Because revision is a primary skill in developing both writers and readers, teachers should allocate time for it frequently. The approach you use will often be based on the areas for improvement you observe as they're writing in class. However, you can also be strategic about the focus of revision over the course of a week, unit, or even year. Consider the following list of skills and conventions you might explicitly teach:

- Use active voice
- Avoid repetition/remove all unnecessary words
- Add more/better/more specific evidence
- Use smaller chunks of text to quote; write into and out of them
- Add an appositive
- Add a subordinating conjunction (for example, *after, although, while, until, unless, even though*)
- Use technical/college-level vocabulary
- Combine sentences/ideas
- Include transitional phrases
- Use specific nouns

Prioritizing this list and choosing to focus on modeling and practicing just one skill at a time will help develop students' capacity to independently revise their own writing. Each skill becomes one more tool in their revision toolkit. By the time they're in college, they're equipped and ready to revise their own papers in a meaningful way.

## Preliminary Revision Exercises

Adept writers use a relatively consistent set of tools to expand and develop their ideas within sentences. They enrich a sentence by adding an appositive, for example, or by adding a new clause via a subordinating conjunction. One great way to improve students' ability to apply those ideas to their responses when they write is to help them practice their sentence skills periodically. For example:

- Ask students to add on to their simple sentences by using *but, because, or so.* You can teach them the purpose and meaning of each of the conjunctions just one at a time and then ask students to practice using the words regularly in their writing so that they continue to improve with time.

- Ask students to add detail to a sentence by adding an appositive (a parenthetical phrase that describes the noun in more detail) to elaborate on one or several nouns in a sentence.*

- Ask students to reread their work and strike out every unnecessary word.

- Challenge students to choose three words in their responses and upgrade them to make them sound more "college level."

*The first two exercises on this list were developed by Judith Hochman for her Writing Revolution program.

## POSITIVELY FRAME REVISION

An added benefit of making revision a standard part of writing is that it both helps students understand its importance in the life of a writer and socializes them to revise without prompting. You can intentionally invest students in revision by explaining that it's part of their growth as writers. Use aspirational phrases ("Revise our verbs like best-selling novelists"; "Check to make sure you've used collegiate vocabulary"; "Eliminate repetition to be as precise as a scholar publishing for a journal") to connect the revision they're doing in fifth-grade reading class with the adult writers they'll become. Share with students the purpose behind revision so that they can start to think about their own process as writers. ("Great authors always revise their work to improve it. That's why we are so careful and thoughtful about our own revision.")

## INCREASE THE POWER OF PUBLIC REVISION WITH SHOW CALL

Teachers often ask their students to read their writing aloud in class. This practice is important for establishing a culture where peers can celebrate and learn from one another's strengths and areas for growth. However, because teachers also tend to use a student reading aloud as a starting point for suggestions and revision ("Great. Now that we've heard Damari's answer, let's tell him some things he could do to make it better!"), the potential power of this activity is diluted by practical challenges. It's hard for students to give Damari good and specific guidance because it's hard to remember the details of a response that they've heard only once. Even if a student did remember it, it's not likely that his or her classmates would. In short, it's hard to get to specifics and to articulate what can be changed when the only visual students have of the written piece is in their head.

**Show Call** is a powerful tool that we think can help. It is, more or less, a Cold Call of a student's written work (see *TLaC 2.0* for a full description of both Show Call and Cold Call) in which, after a round of student writing, you take the written response of one student (or a pair of students) and display it on a document camera for the class to view as a group. This approach also enables you to deeply and efficiently analyze a piece of student writing (and, we note, to celebrate it as well as engage the process of improving it). Students can make direct and specific comments about one another's work. You can mark up the displayed response for the whole class to view so that you can record the group's feedback or model a particular revision. It's also powerful tool for accountability. When students are aware that their work might be shared publicly, they're more attentive to the quality of the work they're producing. Or the quality of their revisions, as you could just as easily Show Call those (as in, "Great, let's see what verb Jonathan chose to make stronger").

In a recent lesson at North Star Academy Vailsburg Middle School in Newark, New Jersey, Julia Goldenheim set the bar for excellence in her classroom using a Show Call. During one round of student writing, she noticed that many students were making a similar error: failing to use specific adjectives in an argument statement about characterization.

---

### See It in Action
Watch Julia Goldenheim set the gold standard for Show Calls in clip 12 at teachlikeachampion.com/yourlibrary.

---

After giving that feedback to several students, she asked one student whether she could "borrow her paper," and placed it on the document camera in the front of the room. She then addressed the class, saying, "I'm going to pause your writing. I've been giving similar feedback, and I'd like to share an example that highlights what most of us are doing. I'm going to read you the argument sentence from Amber's response. It's pretty good right now, but let's make it even better." Julia then read the student's argument sentence to the class: "In *The Winter of Our Discontent* by John Steinbeck,

Steinbeck uses imagery to communicate Joey's characterization by using figurative language and diction."

Her argument sentence *was* pretty good. Amber had written a solid, well-structured sentence that included the title and author of the work as well as techniques the author had used to communicate characterization. But it didn't meet the expectations for excellence that Julia had established for her students. Or perhaps Julia just believed in always making ideas better, no matter how good they were. So Julia asked students to offer guidance to make the sentence even stronger. After the end of the Show Call, all students went back to their writing with clear guidance on how they could revise their "good" work to make it even better.

For maximum accountability, try Show Calling students' work to show revisions they have made. It's a great opportunity to spotlight students' efforts to revise, and to illustrate how writing improves because of revision instructions you've given. When the teacher displays the revised work in a Show Call, the revision efforts become concrete, tangible, and subject to positive reinforcement.

As we hope is obvious, a key aspect of Show Call is being adept at expressing the normality of sharing one's work with peers, often by noting that the challenges students faced were common to many in the room. It can also help to use Show Call as an opportunity to celebrate and share exemplar work. In some cases, you might exclusively talk about what's so excellent about a piece of writing. In this way, Show Call can quickly become positive. In many classrooms we know, students eagerly ask if it can be *their* turn to be Show Called that day.

## HOLD STUDENTS ACCOUNTABLE FOR FEEDBACK

Sometimes the revision guidance we provide isn't in the moment, but outside of class. Teachers spend hours — maybe even days — pouring over stacks of essays and furiously jotting feedback for students to use to improve their writing. But what do students actually do with that feedback? Lauren Catlett, principal of Troy Prep Middle School and former writing teacher, devised a clever solution for ensuring that students use the revision guidance she writes into their rough drafts of essays. Lauren describes three steps that students are required to take before they start revising their drafts using her feedback:

1. Circle each piece of feedback and label it with a plus sign or a delta to indicate whether it's positive or something that needs to be changed.

2. Identify and record trends on a feedback chart so that you can track your progress. (This helps students see what their growth areas are and gives them very tangible

ways to improve, and it also allows the teacher to easily see who might need tutoring on a specific skill.)

3. Summarize the teacher's feedback in a paragraph.

When students follow these steps, the teacher's feedback becomes more than just comments for students to gloss over (or ignore) when papers are turned back. Instead, that feedback becomes revision fodder for which students are accountable. If you work hard to give students written feedback, they should work at least as hard to use it.

In the end, there's a lot more to revising than moving commas, capitalizing words, and correcting grammar. At its best, revising has to do with reworking sentences to more clearly and insightfully communicate thoughts, ideas, or arguments. In the next module, we'll take a look at how to work with students to write artfully crafted sentences.

| MODULE 4.3 | Art of the Sentence |
|---|---|

Writing instruction in many English and reading classrooms tends to skip a key step. Teachers spend a fair amount of time on words, building vocabulary that supports writing. From there we often teach the rules for writing grammatically correct, complete sentences. Next we progress to writing paragraphs: write a paragraph with a topic sentence, three sentences with supporting detail, and a conclusion. Next the paragraphs are linked in an essay. But the resulting essays often reveal a significant gap in the process: the sentences students write, though often correct, are largely unimaginative and often wooden ("I think X. I think Y"), insufficient for the hard work of describing the complex relationships of complex ideas.[1]

The essays our students write are limited, in short, because their sentences aren't very good. There is far more to a sentence than whether it is grammatically correct, but our students often have limited proficiency with writing's fundamental unit of expression. In fact, one of the most common definitions for the sentence is "a complete thought," but often students do not have the ability to control its syntactic elements: to subordinate one thought to another; to express the possibility but not assuredness of an outcome, to allude briefly to a previously discussed idea. When your writing consists primarily of simple sentences beginning with the subject, the range of ideas you can capture is limited.

**Figure 4.4** Student sample work that comes across as wooden

> The mood of the novel right now
> is so Suspensful based on the plot
> events. First, Albert went out to see
> to find Ruth. Second, there is a very
> bad lightning storm.

It might help here to look at some actual student writing. Consider Figure 4.4, a student work sample in a response about the mood of a scene from the novel *Lily's Crossing*.

Figure 4.4 is a classic example of wooden writing. ("First, X. Second, Y.") The sample in Figure 4.5 illustrates an increase in complexity, but still contains elements of woodenness characteristic of the writing of many emerging writers. This student expresses some scholarly understandings of the novel *The Curious Incident of the Dog in the Night-Time*, and uses higher-level vocabulary to express her ideas. She lacks, though, the writing tools to develop her ideas into a truly well-written response. The wooden sentences and

**Figure 4.5** Student sample work that contains elements of woodenness characteristic of the writing of many emerging writers.

2. Let's assume that someone has told Christopher, "You should not do things that would make your father angry." How has Christopher interpreted this differently than most people would? (Address literal thinking.)

> Christopher has interpreted this different-
> ly than most people would by Christophers
> egocentric thinking. I say this because Chri-
> stopher is just think about his self he is not
> thinking about if his father found out he was
> in his father would think. I also say this
> because Christopher says "I would move them
> and then I would move them back. And he wou-
> ld never know I had done it so he wouldn't
> be angry. This reveals that Christopher is no
> thinking from his father's perspective.
> Christopher is also not thinking from his
> father's point of view. Most people would say
> Christopher is being egocentric person in this part o-
> the story.

**Bonus:** explain what Christopher means in the paragraph when he is talking about the "Double Bluff."

repetition interfere with this student's ability to articulate a response that reflects her true level of understanding.

Imagine that these students had been taught (or prompted to use) slightly more sophisticated sentence structures—for example, by combining similar ideas in one complex sentence or contrasting ideas with a transitional phrase, such as *whereas* or *although.*

Sophisticated sentence structures (for example, using transitional phrases or subordinating conjunctions) liberate students from the confines of their limited mastery of syntax and allow them to precisely formulate their arguments. You'll probably also note the role that more sophisticated vocabulary can play in helping students as they shape powerful sentences.

A technique that helps address student writing deficits is **Art of the Sentence** (AOS)—asking students to synthesize a complex idea in a single, well-crafted sentence. Having to make one sentence do all the work pushes students to use new grammatical forms, structuring their sentences in new ways and diversifying their syntax and word choice (see *TLaC 2.0* for more on AOS).

Part of this has to do with scarcity. If you are packing for a trip and have a dozen suitcases to fill, you can leave plenty of space in each. Just toss everything in. But if you have just one bag, you must cleverly tuck small items into larger ones and roll bulky items into tight spirals to fit the space available. Sentences are similar. If you can use an unlimited number of words to express an idea, there is no pressure on your technique. But if you have just one sentence with which to capture an important and complex idea—well, then, as with that suitcase, you must roll and tuck ideas deftly into the corners of the sentence.

With regular practice making a single sentence do the work, students improve the quality of their writing and increase the range and complexity of tools they can use to capture ideas. But just as important, as this chapter is about the synergies between reading and writing, this has an important effect on student's ability to *read* complex sentences and syntactic forms. Consider how often students when reading will seize on the meaning of a part of a sentence—a clause or a phrase within it. They understand the phrase but miss the syntactic cues in the rest of the sentence that make it mean something else entirely: a "despite" or a "but in fact" that sets an idea up to be rejected. Writing your own complex sentences that describe not only an idea but also the relationship of multiple ideas is one of the best ways to hone the skill of unpacking such sentences when written by others. In fact, we think that AOS is one of the single best tools you can use to build reading skills.

As is true of any form of art, students become skilled at composing sentences by studying the masters, copying the masters' specific stylistic tools, gradually adapting others' tools for use in their own work, and ultimately fine-tuning their own style. The first time you ask your students to write a single well-crafted sentence, chances are that they'll struggle. Calling attention to carefully written sentences that surface in student reading—in books, teacher-drafted examples, and peer-drafted examples—is an important first step. ("Let's take a look at this complex and carefully crafted sentence. What do you notice about its syntax/organization?" "How did the author show contrast in this sentence?" "Let's look at the verbs in this sentence. How do they help capture the author's ideas?")

Students don't always realize the complexity or beauty of a sentence until it's been pointed out to them; and they need specific, replicable criteria for what makes a sentence beautiful or well wrought if they're going to churn out their own artful sentences. So in addition to increasing awareness of excellent sentences written by others, teachers can equip students with tools for copying and adapting the sophisticated structures they've observed in authors' sentences—and in so doing, elevate their own writing. Three types of prompts can support and push students to write better sentences.

## THE SENTENCE STARTER

The first type of prompt, the **sentence starter**, provides students with specific words or phrases to, well, start their sentences. Providing students with a single sentence starter forces them to apply a more sophisticated syntactical structure to their own writing. The act of writing a single sentence becomes more rigorous because students are forced to think not just about *what* they want to say but also *how* they'll say it.

---

### Sample Sentence Starters

You can arm your students with an arsenal of rigorous writing tools by introducing multiple syntactical structures over time. For example:

- Describe the settings of the first two pages of chapter 2. Start your sentence with "Babbitt juxtaposes..."

- In one sentence, explain how Ramona's actions affected her sister. Start your sentence with, "After Ramona..."

*(Continued)*

---

(*Continued*)

- Explain Fern's and Mr. Arable's differing viewpoints on how to treat the runt of the litter. Start your sentence with, "While Fern believes . . . "

- Describe the opening to Kurt Vonnegut's "Harrison Bergeron." Start your sentence with "In Vonnegut's satiric portrayal . . . "

- Describe the Mongols' success in establishing a centralized empire in Eurasia. Start your sentence with "To the extent . . . "

Sentence starters support a focused postwriting discussion because they cause students to think more deeply within the frame you've provided rather than glossing a broad range of ideas. Take, for example, the first prompt listed in "Sample Sentence Starters." Because of the starter, we can infer that there are two very different settings described in the first two pages of the chapter. Without the sentence starter, it wouldn't be clear whether students are supposed to describe one setting, two settings, or how the setting changes. By using the starting phrase, "Babbitt juxtaposes," students are implicitly asked to focus on the author's intentional side-by-side description of very different settings. This prompt asks students to analyze setting—and the fact that it's intentionally created by authors—more deeply than they would if the teacher simply asked them to describe one or both of the settings. Students spend their time analyzing rather than developing general or surface-level responses. The teacher's sentence starter helps shape the direction and depth of the discussion that will follow the writing.

Undoubtedly, there are times when you want students to share unique interpretations and analyses. But it can be daunting to sift through all of them when you have planned a particular target for discussion. And it can be unproductive when your goal is to deeply discuss one (or two) key ideas.

## SENTENCE PARAMETERS

**Sentence parameters**, a second type of prompt, are specific words, phrases, or structures you give to students to use anywhere in the sentence. Your choice of parameter depends on your goals for students' reading and/or discussion and what you'd like them to practice as writers.

Using sentence parameters, you might ask students to include a specific word or phrase. ("Use the phrase 'internal conflict' in your sentence.") This is particularly effective for providing opportunities to reinforce vocabulary words, especially technical vocabulary words important in reading (*irony, conflict, characterization,* and so on).

---

## Sample Sentence Parameters

Here are a few ideas to get you started setting sentence parameters for your students:

- Explain how and why Templeton supported Charlotte in her plan to save Wilbur. Use the word *motivated* in your response.

- Explain the conflict Steinbeck develops in the opening to *The Grapes of Wrath*. Use the phrase *antagonistic relationship* in your response.

- Describe the introduction to Kurt Vonnegut's "Harrison Bergeron." Include this phrase: "Vonnegut juxtaposes _____ and _____ to show _____."

---

Sentence parameters can be used to provide practice opportunities with grammatical structures you've taught. For example, after teaching appositives, Sarah Benko, an eighth-grade teacher at Democracy Prep, directs her students to use appositives in their written responses about character. This small grammatical structure helps students more clearly demonstrate their understanding of text and its characters. Here's a prompt from one of her student work packets: "In a single artful sentence, analyze Mariam's character and describe a key event that reveals this characteristic. Include an appositive phrase in your sentence."

Sentence parameters can be used in a number of other ways to support students in writing better-quality sentences. You might help them be more concise by providing a parameter such as, "In twelve words or less explain . . ." You can help them improve sentence complexity by giving a prompt and parameter that force them to combine or contrast multiple ideas. ("In one sentence, explain Ralph's and Jack's different reactions to the meeting. Use a conjunction to show contrast.")

Although the benefits of sentence parameters overlap with those of sentence starters, they also allow more student autonomy in how the sentence takes shape.

# NONDENOMINATIONAL PROMPT

The third type of prompt is the **nondenominational prompt**, which is a general prompt for a single great sentence. The benefit of this type of prompt is that it offers students the most autonomy to express their ideas.

---

## Sample Nondenominational Prompts

Here are some examples of nondenominational prompts.

- In one carefully crafted sentence, describe a central theme of this short story.
- On the basis of today's reading, describe the impact of the Stamp Act in a single well-written sentence.
- In a single beautifully written sentence, explain the contrast of the settings between chapters 1 and 2.
- Write a sentence summarizing the key discussion points on today's discussion about...

---

The biggest challenge in using nondenominational prompts is that the resulting sentences can be low rigor and poor quality if students haven't been equipped with tools for crafting top-quality sentences. The best time to use nondenominational prompts is after students have had some practice with sentence starters and sentence parameters—prompts that provide them with structures and tools for writing quality sentences. Before using nondenominational prompts, like the ones above, be explicit about your criteria for an "excellent" or "beautiful" sentence, so that students have a clear set of quality guidelines to follow. Here's a list of criteria we saw posted in the classroom of one high-performing teacher:

- Start with something other than a subject noun, pronoun, or definite article
- Include carefully chosen words
- Pay particular attention to the verbs
- Strike out unnecessary words
- Precision matters
- Respond directly to the prompt

Of course you could adapt this list to fit the needs of your students. In addition to its primary benefit of setting clear expectations, we found it powerful for establishing a common language that students could use when drafting and reviewing their own sentences as well as for sharing feedback on sentences that their peers have drafted.

Recently, we observed Rachel Coffin's eleventh-grade English class, in which she used multiple AOS prompts to help students develop high-quality "mini thesis" statements analyzing the rhetorical strategies Virginia Woolf uses in "Thoughts on Peace in an Air Raid." In the first round of drafting, Rachel asked her students to state their purpose in one well-written sentence (a nondenominational prompt). Then she asked her students to revise their sentences using a sentence starter ("Although Woolf mentions gender inequalities, . . ."). Rachel then Cold Called a few specific students to share the revised examples they'd drafted. Finally, she asked them to rewrite yet again, using a batch of twenty or so strong verbs she'd posted, such as *urges, encourages, prompts,* and *sways,* as sentence parameters.

The sequence of writing and revision Rachel asked her students to do modeled for them the careful thought and intentionality required to draft quality thesis statements. By asking them to use specific structures (the subordinating conjunction *although,* and strong verbs), she's helping build their tools for writing more sophisticated sentences on their own. Rachel also sent a powerful message about the importance of revision as part of the writing process.

---

## When to Use Art of the Sentence

To increase the rigor and quality of thinking and discussion, AOS exercises can be inserted into any reading class cycle (discussed in Module 4.1). The sentence starters and parameters you provide should support students in writing and talking about texts. AOS can also be used in standard parts of your lesson—parts that come before the reading and writing cycles begin (Do Now, Exit Tickets) or after the lesson (as part of a homework assignment). Here are some specific times you might find AOS particularly useful in a reading class:

- Developing thesis statements. Writing an entire paragraph or essay with an accurate answer and details takes a long time to do well—quite

*(Continued)*

---

(*Continued*)

possibly requiring more time than is available during class. Asking students for one well-written thesis statement allows you to efficiently Check for Understanding of key ideas. Later on, students can develop their responses by identifying and analyzing supporting evidence. A well-designed thesis statement also sets up students for a more powerful paragraph or essay.

- During explicit vocabulary lessons and spiraled review. As we develop students' word knowledge, there's no better practice opportunity to apply and problem-solve with those newly acquired words than to use them in a single carefully written sentence.

## TWO APPROACHES TO AOS IN READING CLASSES

In reading classes, intentionality with AOS is particularly important. There are two approaches to using AOS over time to strategically increase writing skills. And for reading instructors, using both is critical.

### Modeling, Scaffolding, and Autonomy

In the first approach, teachers cycle continually and sequentially between three different phases: modeling, scaffolding, and autonomy.

- Modeling

  Whenever you introduce a new grammatical or syntactical structure, show students models of exemplar sentences that adhere to that structure. Slowly introduce starters and parameters to push students' writing and thinking.

- Scaffolding

  Once you've gone through exemplary models, add complexity and challenge over time by providing fewer starters, using more parameters, and introducing nondenominational prompts.

- Autonomy

  In the last phase of this cycle, encourage use and adaptation of familiar structures with nondenominational prompts. Students will independently begin to insert and apply structures that you taught and practiced in earlier phases.

## The Stew

We call the second approach "the stew." The key idea here is to vary approaches to keep writing challenging and engaging. It's important to sprinkle in nondenominational prompts and opportunities for adaptation based on grammatical structures students have learned—even when you're still modeling one grammatical structure and scaffolding another one or two.

This approach is particularly useful to teachers and students who may be using AOS and the writing cycles for the first time. The stew doesn't require an overhaul of your current approach to teaching writing or reading; it is simply a way of helping students focus on the sentence as an integral part of developing as writers.

When you've got only a sentence to make your point, every word counts. And nothing shows a student's comprehension of a subject—or of a newly learned piece of linguistic mechanics—than writing it out in one tight, clean sentence. By prompting students to write a single beautiful sentence, teachers can impel them to think in a serious way about word choice, syntax, and other sentence features.

Of course, writing one beautiful sentence is only the first step toward writing a beautiful paragraph, essay, or paper. In the next module, we'll look at ways to help students build writing stamina—stamina they'll need to do longer-form writing in college and beyond.

| MODULE 4.4 | Building Stamina |
| --- | --- |

Let's return for a moment to Gillian Cartwright's lesson on *Fences*. Her use of writing worked to make discussion more effective, for several reasons: Every student entered discussion with written ideas, thought through in advance. They knew their goal was to harvest their peers' ideas to improve their own responses, so they sought to learn, not "win." And they could listen carefully because they didn't have to try to remember their own thoughts while others spoke. But one other factor made all of this possible, and although it appears relatively mundane, it is critical: her students' writing stamina. Gillian announced that they would be writing for eighteen minutes straight, said go, and watched as every pencil snapped into action, action that was sustained for the whole eighteen minutes.

Our ability to use writing in the classroom, with all of its benefits, relies on students' ability to sustain writing for significant periods of time (think of the essay portion of the SAT or a typical exam in college). Reading, too, relies on the ability to sustain concentration on a single task for an extended period of time. But what happens when you ask students to write, and they don't? Or can't?

**Building stamina** is our term for the tools teachers use to help students incrementally increase the length of time during which they are able to engage in sustained, focused writing, especially in response to a text-based question. Students who haven't developed stamina might start writing but peter out quickly. They might tell you "I'm done" after the first minute or so. They might use a series of stalling tactics we call the "slow play": writing the first part of a sentence, laboriously erasing every bit of pencil lead, rewriting it, erasing again or pausing to think, now adding a word, and so on. A student intentionally or unintentionally slow playing can turn a writing block of several minutes' duration into unproductive time, so it's important to put structures in place that prevent students from using stall tactics—tactics that ultimately impede students' ability to develop stamina in their writing.

So while we don't necessarily think that the first time you say, "Eighteen minutes of writing in your Lit Logs. Go!" you'll get the response Gillian did, we *do* think that with a little bit of intentional work building up your students' stamina, you can get there quickly. And when you do, we'll be there cheering for you!

## STRATEGIES FOR BUILDING STAMINA

In a fifth-grade lesson at North Star Vailsburg, Eric Diamon was strategic in helping build students' writing stamina. Eric asked students to write for a total of eight minutes on four questions, spending two minutes per question. He used a timer to support this expectation, marking the start of the timed writing task with a clear cue, "Go!" While students were writing, Eric actively circulated, ensuring that students were writing the entire time and on the right question, and gathering data to inform both revision and discussion.

### See It in Action

Watch Eric Diamon work with students to build writing stamina in clip 13 at teachlikeachampion.com/yourlibrary.

After the end of the timed writing, Eric asked students to shake out their hands, noting that they'd written for eight minutes, "not as long as normal." In watching this lesson, we learned several key strategies for intentionally building students' stamina as they write:

*Writing Wire-to-Wire.* Students write straight through for a particular extended period of time, from the very first second to the very final one.

*Priming the Pump.* Allowing students to do a lightning-quick brainstorm of ideas before writing on a challenging prompt can help them hit the ground running.

*Using the Pace Car.* Providing students with additional time cues not only builds stamina but also helps students pace themselves in their writing.

*Valorizing Student Writing.* Use Precise Praise (see *TLaC 2.0*) for specific writing elements that you want to see other students replicate (for example, complex sentences, sophisticated vocabulary, clear organization).

## Wire-to-Wire Writing

In order to get students to write wire to wire, teachers use a timer and project the time publically. Doing so sets the expectation for students to write straight through from beginning to end. Incorporating a timing component and expecting students to write for the full time is the first step in ensuring that students are able to write for increasingly longer periods of time. Initially (either because it's early in the year or you're just starting to focus on stamina), the intervals for which students are asked to write should be small, gradually increasing with practice (throughout the year, as well as from grade level to grade level).

To ensure that students truly write wire to wire, teachers might consider Brightening Lines — making clear the beginning and end points between activities (see *TLaC 2.0* for more on Brightening Lines). For example, "Ready, set, write!" or "Pencils in the air; write on two; one, two!" clearly signal to students that they should immediately begin writing. These signals communicate a sense of urgency that then translates to a productive timed writing task. You can also convey reflectiveness by using these same prompts, but in a slowly suspenseful or whispered tone. Similarly, using a short countdown to conclude the timed writing task will signal to students when to wrap up their writing. It also ensures that they've sustained writing to the final wire.

## See It in Action

Watch clip 14 at teachlikeachampion.com/yourlibrary as Lauren Latto establishes clear expectations to set her students up for successful Wire-to-Wire Writing in response to their shared text, *Romeo and Juliet*. Just after students finish reading the play's tragic finale, Lauren sends them to write. You'll notice that she provides them with a choice of three equally rigorous writing prompts; this choice makes it more likely that students will be able to sustain their writing for the allotted time.

### Priming the Pump

Priming the Pump addresses what students will write about as they are expected to write for longer periods of time. Some students may be physically able to write for extended periods; but they don't have the key insights, evidence, or ideas to write about to appropriately fill the time. Having students do a lightning-quick brainstorm of ideas before writing on a challenging prompt (for example, "What are you going to write about, Kiree? Nadia? OK, let's go!") will help students quickly exchange ideas—ideas that will support them in their writing. As students' stamina increases, this scaffold should eventually decrease and disappear.

Another way to Prime the Pump is to give students the chance to read through their margin notes, starring those notes that will help them answer the question. Doing so supports students in both brainstorming independently and incorporating relevant evidence into their answers.

### Using the Pace Car

The Pace Car not only helps build stamina but also supports students in their pacing. Providing a Pace Car means cueing students when they should continue on a different portion of the writing. In some cases, this may mean providing a certain time frame for each question (as in Eric Diamon's lesson), or it may mean pacing students at different points in the writing (for example, "You should be done with your introductory paragraph by now").

The Pace Car is particularly useful for verbose students who may need to tighten their responses based on the time that they have available to them. It may also be useful for students who don't have as much to write, ensuring that they spend a sufficient amount of time at least attempting to write on a particular question or section of a longer response.

Pace Cars can be verbal or visual cues, with the time interval written on the board. Eventually (and in the upper grades), the Pace Car may be removed so that students learn to effectively pace themselves. As with Wire-to-Wire Writing, actively circulating to visually monitor where students are in their writing is an important way to hold students accountable for maintaining the pace and to help you gather data on how much time they need for their writing.

## Valorizing Student Writing

Taking time to publicly celebrate your students' written pieces, thus incentivizing students to produce quality writing, is part of building a culture of excellence. There are many ways to shine a light on students' top-quality work products. We'll describe a few here, and we're sure you'll think of many others. You might ask a student to read her work aloud so that the rest of the class can listen and appreciate how carefully it was constructed. You could also ask permission to read the work yourself, and read it with the same fluency and expression (and maybe drama) that you would the work of a published author. Or, you might Show Call a piece of work to describe the beauty of its construction point by point.

Blazoning one student's work gives students the opportunity to learn from their peers' writing. It also sends the message that your classroom is a place where quality work and the celebration of others are valued. It's not necessary to read or Show Call an entire essay; choosing particularly well-written excerpts can be just as powerful. Many teachers display exemplary work written by students. Consider posting a note by the work that specifically points out what's strong about it. In doing so, you honor the work by showing you've taken the time to read it carefully; you also provide replicable ideas for other students to use in their own future writing.

## BALANCING QUALITY AND QUANTITY

In discussing the idea of stamina we want to be clear about what we are arguing. Of course, there are times when good writers do not plow straight through their allotted writing time, when pausing and reflecting are critical to the process. Often, slow writing is the best writing. Art of the Sentence is a good example of this. There, we want students to consider every word and methodically work through challenging syntactical structures. Such types of writing are high in focus and often slow in rate.

We also stress the benefits of stamina, however, because it is a condition necessary to implementing many types of writing we ask students to do as *readers* specifically.

Writing activities that require students to think things through in writing are especially productive in response to reading—before a discussion, say, or after a tricky passage so you can check every student's understanding. We want to train students in the ability (not to mention the willingness and desire) to write for sustained periods of time so we can insert Stop and Jots, Open Responses, or even sustained reflection in a journal (think of Gillian Cartwright's eighteen minutes here). These activities require students to hit the ground running, to turn a blank space into written words that begin hammering notions into complete thoughts, to remain busily engaged all the way through.

That it is also useful for college-bound students who will later draft longer papers, and writing in-class essays in an hour's time is a fringe benefit. Build stamina as a habit, a capacity. Then, how much you use or expect it in any assignment is up to you. Once your students can write steadily for two or twenty minutes at a clip, whether you require it or slower forms of writing, where pencils may and in fact should stop is up to you.

We've talked about how, to best prepare students for the kind of marathon writing they're sure to encounter in college and beyond, it helps to get them a number of writing miles under their belts before they get there. In the next module, we'll look at how to most effectively gather and utilize data from student writing to best inform instruction.

## MODULE 4.5  Monitoring and Assessment via the Stack Audit

If you're asking students to do more writing—and you're really serious about the quality of student work—it's important to have tools that allow you to monitor and assess their progress—and yours. Show Call, discussed earlier, is a great tool for that, and one that also reinforces accountability for students to do their best work. One other that we think is especially useful—one that's used between classes—is the **Stack Audit**—a systematic process of reviewing student work to gather data that helps inform instruction.

A Stack Audit works by taking a subset of student work from a class, and analyzing the work samples, and then recording observations (in most cases, both strengths and weaknesses) to help identify trends. From those trends, teachers can develop action steps to address the most pervasive gaps in student understanding. The Stack Audit has at least two benefits despite its terrible name: it allows you to focus on specific types of writing in your classroom, and it allows you to enlist the insight and ideas of your peers.

## HOW THE STACK AUDIT WORKS

The name *audit* implies scrutiny and compliance, but really it's a tool that thrives in (and ultimately builds) a climate of mutual trust and respect. The goal is to understand what we do and how to improve aspects of our everyday practice. It can be done to focus on a school, a department, or a single teacher.

Let's start with a whole-school example. A principal or a group of English teachers might gather the homework everyone had assigned over the past two days, or the in-class writing prompts everyone had used, or the Do Nows from all of that day's lessons. The participants would put all the work in a stack in the middle of the table and take ten or fifteen minutes to silently read and reflect, each person pulling two or three from the pile, making some notes on strengths and weaknesses, then putting them back and taking a few more. Everyone would basically be working on a T chart: What were the best things people were doing that could be replicated across the school? What were some problem points they could fix? Afterward, they'd go around the circle and share their observations about bright spots — thirty seconds each to share one thing, and on to the next person. Around and around. Then the same for trouble spots. Someone would keep a list. Finally the group would look at the list and decide on a few points they thought were priorities. They'd write up a set of notes, essentially a how-to guide for whatever the topic was: better writing prompts or Do Now questions. Whatever the topic, the notes would focus as much on strengths as anything else: "Here are five great things I saw; hope you can use them."

Another variation is to collect not just what the teacher assigned but what students actually wrote. If you were interested in writing prompts, for example, you might collect the answers every student wrote in your class on a given day. Instead of looking at what every teacher assigned for homework, you would look at what every student in a class or in several classes completed for homework. Again, it would all be in a big pile in the middle of the table, and away you'd go. As we did with one group, you might find some surprising things: that kids were rushing through their work to try to get it done, say. You could then discuss solutions. At one school, for example, teachers found that writing on homework assignments was sloppy and hasty. Students worked hard in class, but then went home and rushed through their work, using sloppy ungrammatical sentences. A wave of reforms swept the school: teachers read exceptional homework to classes, posted exemplars, and set more rigorous standards for what "done" meant. They assigned shorter but more rigorous homework with clearer expectations for what quality looked like. Two weeks later, a follow-up Stack Audit showed incredible results.

Of course you can also do a Stack Audit as an individual teacher. You might look at all of the writing your students did from class on a given day, or the essays they'd written or their Do Nows, going through them by yourself or with a few trusted colleagues to add insight and make observations.

Recently, we sat down with a group of principals who had collected sixth-grade essays in response to paired texts from each of their schools. This Stack Audit, led by Paul Bambrick-Santoyo, Uncommon Schools chief schools officer for high school, reviewed high-, middle-, and low-quality examples from three different teachers.

Surprisingly, the differences between students of varying levels within the same class weren't nearly as striking as the differences in student work from different teachers. For example, in one class, all levels of students had strong evidence from the text that was clearly explained. But across the board, their thesis sentences were weak. In another class, students' thesis sentences were strong and they cited strong evidence; but their explanations of the evidence were weak. After a thirty-minute Stack Audit, principals developed a clear list of actionable steps for teachers to improve the quality of their students' writing over the course of the next six weeks.

This experience emphasizes that while Stack Audits can and should be done by individual teachers with student work from their own class, it is also important to periodically review student work with others. Doing so causes you to look at student work in a more objective way. Stack Audits are a lens for seeing the truth about student writing and reading.

---

## Tips for Running Efficient Group Stack Audits

- Use a timer to keep participants disciplined about the amount of time they spend reviewing student work and sharing.

- In your notes on each work sample, jot down two to three strengths and unlimited weakness/growth areas/gaps.

- Go around the circle for feedback multiple times with a facilitator charting comments and tallying what repeats.

- Develop action steps for the top two to three needs, and plan them into the lesson (what can be done in tomorrow's lesson, next week's lesson, and so on).

## GATHERING AND ACTING ON DATA FROM A STACK AUDIT

Each time you do a Stack Audit, you're analyzing a data set that provides you with information about your students' writing strengths and deficits. In order to use the information you gather, think intentionally about what you're really looking for and what type of student work will provide you with a reliable and useful data set. Here's a list of different data sets you might analyze, as well as the corresponding questions that you might focus on during the Stack Audit:

**Top students' work:** What are the strengths? What do we need to do to push their work to the next level? What can we do to help other students achieve this quality of written work?

**Work samples from students of varying writing ability:** What are the consistent trends for areas of strength and areas of growth? What elements do the middle- and low-quality samples need to include in order to look more like a high-quality sample?

**Work samples from students in more than one grade:** What are our targets for progression of student work through the grades?

With your colleagues, you'll likely determine other data sets that are useful in your classrooms. Over time, it's important to use a variety of different types of data sets, so that you're getting a reliable picture of all the students in your class (or school).

Using the information gleaned from the Stack Audit, you can adjust your instruction in a variety of ways. If you conduct a Stack Audit after the first day of teaching an objective, it can help you make planning decisions about how you'll approach the subsequent days. Stack Audit data can help you make decisions in class about which student's work you'll Show Call. If you've identified a particular trend for an area of growth for your students' writing, Show Calling work that highlights this area of growth is a great way to provide a model or provide public feedback that all students can use to make their writing better. Stack Audits are also a perfect opportunity to get feedback from colleagues on your students' writing ability. Leverage your colleagues' strengths; if you notice that their student samples are strong in a particular area where yours may be lacking, find out how he or she is approaching instruction differently, and incorporate these ideas into your own lessons.

When it comes to teaching writing, no two teachers and no two lessons are created equal. Stack Audits can help individual teachers—as well as groups of teachers and school leaders—assess particular sticking points in writing instruction. Adjusting one's teaching on the basis of data collected during a Stack Audit can help improve reading instruction in a meaningful way.

## Writing for Reading, Reconsidered

Reading and writing are inextricably linked— in life and in the classroom. The better students write, the better they'll read. More specifically, the more intentional writing practice students get, the more tuned in they'll be to the choices authors and other professional writers make. Rather than consider reading and writing distinct disciplines, teachers would do well to acknowledge their common nature and work toward leveraging their synergies.

Up to this point, we've really dug deep into the Core of the Core— those fundamental principles of the Common Core we believe to be undeniably valuable, regardless of any one perspective on how those principles play out in practice. In part 2 of the book, we turn from foundational principles to the fundamentals— those essential elements of the practice of literacy instruction that offer deep synergies with the Core of the Core.

## NOTE

1. The ideas about AOS in the introduction to Module 4.3 have been influenced by Marie L. Waddell, *The Art of Styling Sentences: 20 Patterns for Success*, 3rd ed. (Hauppauge, NY: Barron's Educational Series, 1993).

# Part 2

# The Fundamentals

SO FAR, WE'VE LOOKED at the different ways teachers can implement four "Core of the Core" ideas in the classroom. By having students read harder texts, Close Read rigorously to establish and analyze meaning, read lots of nonfiction, and write in direct response to written works, teachers can go a long way toward ensuring their students' preparation for and success in college. Still, in and of themselves, those four ideas do not a competent and successful reader make. There are other important and often foundational skills necessary for success in reading.

In this second part of the book, we'll look at those pieces essential to rigorous and thorough reading instruction. We'll focus on a combination of fundamentals—things like increasing vocabulary and sharpening expressive reading skills—and the process of developing positive habits and systems to make classrooms more effective and efficient in supporting student success. Fortunately, these essentials also offer deep synergies with the ideas in part 1 of the book.

# Approaches to Reading: Reading More, Reading Better

## MODULE 5.1: APPROACHES TO READING

No matter the approach, meaningful reading is accountable, expressive, and highly leveraged.

## MODULE 5.2: ACCOUNTABLE INDEPENDENT READING (AIR)

Great teachers prepare students to read on their own productively, accountably, and efficiently.

## MODULE 5.3: CONTROL THE GAME

Controlling the Game is a systematic approach to having students read aloud—ensuring that they are engaged, following along, and always ready for their turn to read.

## MODULE 5.4: READ-ALOUD

Modeling fluency, growing background knowledge, building a bank of vocabulary and syntax, and instilling a love of literature are all benefits of reading aloud.

# Approaches to Reading: Reading More, Reading Better

Consider, for a moment, how much reading you were required to do in college. Almost assuredly there were days when the time you spent reading stretched into hours. Some classes probably required a book a week or a daunting array of journal articles—possibly both. Maybe you glanced at the syllabus and asked aloud, *"Five* articles by Tuesday?!" Did your professors not understand that you were taking more than one class at a time?

The message was clear: you had to read a lot if you wanted to understand whatever discipline you studied and meet the standards of economics, chemistry, political or literary theory. Extensive reading gave you knowledge, context and perspective, an ear for how the discipline talked. It was required not just to "pass" but to earn a degree and enter society. But we don't really need to convince you of that. If you are reading this book, the importance of reading probably requires little explanation. Extensive reading gave you what you needed to succeed, but it was not easy. You needed lots of practice to prepare you.

Almost ten years ago now, our first graduates from Uncommon Schools reported back from college campuses and described a version of this struggle. They encountered not just difficult reading but daunting quantities of it day after day. The extent of the reading pushed to the limits even those who graduated with flying colors. But not every one of our graduates did finish college. For many, reading loads were one reason why.

Other chapters in this book describe steps you can take to make sure students read better, more perceptively, and across all formats of text. Still, we should also remember that quality reading requires *quantity* reading. Students must read not only well but also widely and extensively.

Running is a decent analogy. If you want to be a distance runner, you have to put in the miles. Sure, you can improve your results by refining your strategy and studying up on the science of training. In the end, though, there is no way around the fact that success requires a lot of road miles. In the case of reading, we sometimes refer to this as "miles on the page." Quantity matters.

This observation points out two challenges. The first is that most students don't read as much as they should, both in and out of school. A few years ago, for example, a colleague of ours followed a sample of students through their day at New York City public schools and found that, on average, students were reading for twenty minutes per day. *Twenty minutes!* What's even more disheartening is that almost 40 percent of students did not read at all during the school day. Of course, this assumes that during the time students were reading, they were reading well and attentively, which is no sure thing.

Surely, 20 or 40 or 60 minutes of reading a day doesn't cut it. In fact, even if students read for twice what those numbers suggest, it would still not likely be enough.

Getting young people to read more has perhaps always been a challenge, but today there is increasing competition for students' attention, both in school and at home. Some of the world's brightest people spend their lives designing devices and applications to make everything that could possibly distract students instantly available almost every moment of the day. The buzzing, pinging, and flickering reminders cause students (and many adults) to disengage not only from "mere" reading but also from the sort of sustained, uninterrupted reading that the most demanding texts require. According to the Bureau of Labor Statistics reports, the average American teenager reads outside of school for an average of four minutes per day on weekends and nine minutes per day on weekdays.[1]

Fascinated by our colleague's finding following some of New York City's school children, we set out to measure the amount of time spent reading in classrooms of a sample of middle school teachers from a variety of schools we worked with. The average was seventeen minutes per hour for English and reading classes. The rest of the day it was assuredly lower. More important, seventeen minutes was significantly less than the amount of time teachers *thought* they were reading. This points to the second challenge: we may read less than we think we do in our classrooms. The time that we allocate to "reading" is in fact spent talking about reading, say, or talking about topics brought about by reading. Less often is that time filled with actual reading; how many road miles students really log with reading is an open question.

We have discussed this finding with teachers at our workshops. They often observe that we all suspect that if we could simply make our students read more—a lot more—and love reading more, much of the reading gap might be eroded. Yet this is not so easily done. There are student barriers—students often don't want to read, or we don't really know how well they are reading—and teacher barriers. One teacher at a workshop noted that his own perceptions were an issue. He didn't feel as though he was teaching if *all that students were doing was reading*. When his students read in class, he lived in fear that an administrator would walk into his classroom.

In this chapter, we reflect on tools that teachers can use to maximize road miles: to help students read more, enjoy reading, and accrue the benefits of extensive reading. We'll start with a look at three different approaches to reading: reading independently, reading aloud, and listening to oral reading.

## MODULE 5.1 — Approaches to Reading

Of course, teachers must balance the amount of reading students do with the quality of the reading they do. Three different approaches are worth considering. The way these three approaches are implemented—and the balance among them—can have a dramatic impact not just on the amount of miles students cover but also on the quality of their reading—even their love and passion for reading.

There are clear benefits to giving kids robust opportunities to interact with text in each of the three approaches we discuss, but each also has limitations. As we look at these benefits and limitations, it's important to remember that it's not a competition. The goal is not to identify the best format for reading but to recognize synergies that can allow us to use all three in conjunction—to give students the most meaningful and productive interactions with the texts they read.

## STUDENTS READING INDEPENDENTLY

Reading independently is ultimately how students read on exams, in college, and in their adult lives, so it is especially important to give them lots of practice in doing so. On both sides of the Common Core debate, there is clear consensus that all kids should have ample opportunities to read independently, which is why in countless schools and homes across this country, parents and teachers alike stress the importance of making sure that students have a book in their hand as much as possible.

At the same time, there are limitations to reading independently, and some of these limitations go unacknowledged. Most significant, there is very little accountability for readers when they are reading independently. Readers, especially our most struggling readers, often practice reading poorly by inscribing errors when they read independently. They might decode vowel sounds poorly, drop word endings, or skip over words they don't know. They might read quickly or idly and fail to process the meaning of the words. As a result, they don't effectively practice—or get better at—reading, and they miss opportunities to make meaning out of what they read. Independent reading, for all its strengths, is also, well, independent. Part of the pleasure of reading—sharing the story as it unfolds—is tacitly sacrificed.

## STUDENTS READING ALOUD

One way to address the limitations of independent reading is to design it for greater accountability (more on this in Module 5.2). Another is to balance it with other approaches to reading. Giving students, *especially* developing readers, frequent opportunities to read aloud in addition to reading silently is a great way to do this, though students' reading aloud also has benefits and limitations.

On the plus side, when students read aloud, they are able to practice fluency, decoding, and most of all prosody—the art of using rhythm, intonation, and stress to connect words into meaningful phrases. This, you might say, is a hidden skill, relevant even—perhaps especially—for older students who read complex texts for which the ability to create such linkages can be a key to unlocking the text's meaning. Having students read aloud also provides rich and constant data to teachers on the quality of their reading. Without reading aloud, we know far, far less about the quality and skill of the reading students do. With that constant data come opportunities for immediate—and therefore highly effective—corrections.

Most important, having students read aloud connects students with the pleasure of reading. A classroom where expressive reading by students is the norm, where students take pleasure in books—pleasure that is visible to their peers and therefore infectious—is a classroom where students change their relationship to reading. In that classroom, students come to understand why every culture on Earth tells and loves stories.

However, there are downsides to students reading aloud. One is the challenge of what the students who are not reading are doing when one student is reading aloud. Are they staring out the window? Looking at the text and pretending to read? Teachers are, in fact, often instructed not to have students read aloud in class for this reason. This strikes us as throwing out a very valuable baby due to some easily addressed issues with the bathwater. Later in the chapter, we will discuss modifications and adaptations that can address this challenge.

Another limitation of student oral reading is that it may not fully prepare students to read on their own. In fact, it can result in student reading that is more focused on expression than comprehension—reading during which it is all but impossible to stop and reflect. These issues, generally, are remediable via adaptation, and simply require *balance*—that is, the use of student oral reading in combination and synergy with silent reading.

## STUDENTS LISTENING TO ORAL READING

The third approach to reading is reading to students. It is often the "forgotten" approach among the three, especially for older students, and it too presents a set of benefits and limitations.

A clear benefit is that when teachers read aloud to their classes, the best reader in the room breathes life into the text by modeling fluency, creating meaning, and adding drama. Reading aloud to students also communicates a love and a passion for great books. Perhaps most important, it allows students to access a text well beyond what they can read on their own, enabling them to familiarize themselves with more complex vocabulary, rhythm, and patterns of syntax. Although many educators recognize this benefit in regard to younger students, the benefits of reading to older students is much less often considered. For example, scientific writing, as we discuss in our chapter on nonfiction, has its own unwritten rules and stylistic conventions—the way, for example, some clauses are meant to be parenthetical and de-emphasized. Reading part of an article from a scientific journal to your students would help them hear those rules and conventions, as well as make it more likely that subsequent reading will accurately capture a text's tone and meaning. This may be the best way we can think of to address the nonfiction micro rules we discussed in chapter 3.

The downsides of reading aloud to students are more clear-cut. Reading aloud involves teacher modeling, not actual student practice. The teacher embeds meaning in her own expression—meaning that students may not infer on their own. Everyone has to read at the same pace—and from the same text.

## MEANINGFUL READING

Given the benefits and downsides of the three approaches to reading (listed in Figure 5.1), the goal then is to use each of them in a strategic way which ensures that we can maximize its benefits but also minimize its limitations. Recognizing these benefits and limitations, this chapter outlines a set of concrete actions teachers can take to improve both the quantity and the quality of reading that students do—to ensure that our students log as many high-quality road miles as possible.

For independent reading in the classroom, we use **Accountable Independent Reading**, an approach that helps ensure that independent reading is accountable and of high quality. For students reading aloud, we call our approach **Control the Game**, subtly engineering how you call on students to read aloud in a way which ensures that not

**Figure 5.1**  It's important to understand and master all the benefits and limitations of these three approaches to reading

### Types of Reading

| | Reading Silently | Reading Aloud | Being Read To |
|---|---|---|---|
| **Benefits** | • How students read in on exams, in college, and in their lives.. <br> • Replicable in any setting. | • Provides rich and constant data. <br> • Opportunity for immediate correction. <br> • Connects students with the fun of reading. *Maximize the Benefits* | • Best reader in the room models & creates drama & meaning. <br> • Learn vocabulary and syntax more complex that what they can read on their own. |
| **Limits** | • There is low accountability. Readers practice reading poorly. This effect is most pronounced with the weakest readers. | • Can lack "leverage" I.e., If one student is reading, what's everyone else doing? <br> • Doesn't fully prepare students to read on their own | • Involves more modeling than practice. It can prepare students to engage with texts without being able to read them. *Minimize the Limitations* |

only the primary reader but all readers are benefiting. And finally, for students listening to oral reading, we keep our approach simple and call it **Read-Aloud**. Ultimately, the goal of each approach is to get students to engage in **meaningful reading**.[2] Meaningful reading has three key qualities: it is accountable, expressive, and highly leveraged. We will define each of these characteristics here.

## Accountable

*Accountable* means that teachers are able to reliably assess whether students are actually reading (rather than, say, sitting and looking at the pictures or daydreaming) and reading effectively (attentively, and for some readers, correctly and not reinscribing errors such as ignoring suffixes or guessing incorrectly at words they don't know). Much of the reading that students do in schools fails to meet this criterion. Control the Game and Accountable Independent Reading both address accountability, ensuring that students are meaningfully engaged in the reading they are asked to do, both independently and aloud in class.

## Expressive

When students read fluently and with prosody, they demonstrate the capacity to embed meaning in words as they read, to demonstrate in their inflection that they are processing the words at a level beyond the most basic. We're not talking about Sir John Gielgud here, just nonrobotic reading with demonstrated recognition of punctuation and periodic recognition (via emphasis) of key words and syntax.

Although expressive reading is insufficient to the final task of achieving a full and rich understanding of a text, it is a highly efficient indicator of basic comprehension. In the standard definition, fluency consists of automaticity (the ability to read at a rapid rate without error) plus expression (the ability to group words together into phrases to reflect meaning, emphasize important words, and express tone and register). You could argue, however, that fluency consists of automaticity plus expression plus expressed evidence of comprehension. That is, a student reading a text expressively is (to the practiced ear) presenting data on her comprehension of it: Does her voice reflect register, tone, or mood? Does she recognize which words deserve special emphasis? Does she demonstrate how the punctuation shapes the rhythm and the meaning? In short, fluency isn't just fast reading, but reading with meaning made audible. Although all three approaches address fluency, both Read-Aloud and Control the Game enable teachers to model fluent reading and students to practice.

## Highly Leveraged

The third critical element of meaningful reading is leverage, the extent to which all students are reading. If one student is reading aloud and her classmates are listening passively, there's a leverage factor of 1. It's a highly inefficient activity. However, if one student is reading aloud and twenty-nine students are silently but accountably reading along with her at their desks, you have a leverage factor of 29. Twenty-nine people reading makes for a highly efficient and worthwhile activity. Control the Game—a technique we'll discuss later in the chapter—maximizes leverage by allowing individual students to practice reading aloud while the rest of the class is still reading.

Similarly, if you have a class of thirty students reading independently at their desks, you can't be sure that all thirty are being leveraged; perhaps only your highest readers are. Making the subtle tweaks to your approach to independent reading described in this chapter can also increase the leverage of independent reading.

The three approaches to meaningful reading described in this chapter—Accountable Independent Reading, Control the Game, and Read-Aloud—ensure that students log lots of high-quality road miles. Lots of road miles means that students get the practice they need to become successful independent readers—readers who move from learning to read, to reading to learn. We will now dive into *how* to achieve meaningful reading using each of these approaches.

| MODULE 5.2 | Accountable Independent Reading (AIR) |
|---|---|

The vast majority of high school and college classes require students to complete and absorb extensive amounts of independent reading. They also require students to both discuss and write cogently about what they have read—sometimes moments, hours, or even days later. Almost every assessment serving as a gateway to college admission is built on a student's ability to read, retain information from, and comprehend a text independently. In those critical settings, students have to make sense of what's read without their classmates' or teacher's help.

Recognizing the need to increase the amount of independent reading students do in preparation for college, many classrooms utilize sustained silent reading

(SSR) — essentially designated times for students to read, quietly, from books of their choosing. Whether called DEAR (Drop Everything and Read), FUR (Free Uninterrupted Reading), or any other clever acronym, the idea is to get students more reading road miles by letting them read books that interest them. There is often little in terms of assessment or accountability surrounding this free reading time; it's just time spent with books.

On the surface, programs like DEAR offer a compelling solution. They get more books in more kids' hands and get more teachers, schools, leaders, parents, and students reading. In Marilyn Jager Adams's analysis of reading research, she notes that "if we want them to read well, we must find a way for them to read lots,"[3] and we agree wholeheartedly. Yet general SSR methods can focus on reading quantity to the detriment of reading *quality*. Enter Accountable Independent Reading (AIR).

Accountable Independent Reading involves students in reading texts independently (and silently post grades K–1) — and allows teachers to assess whether effective reading is actually happening. Much of the reading students do in schools fails to meet these criteria. And, unfortunately, the students reading the least are often the ones who need to read the most. Some flip idly through pages, gazing at pictures, while others read lazily or poorly, practicing and reinscribing weak habits as they go. This kind of "reading" fails the accountability test.

The key to making AIR effective is preparing students to read on their own productively, accountably, and efficiently. To effectively bring AIR to your classroom, you want to encode success in reading independently, then start to increase both difficulty and length to build stamina.

First, let's take a look at some of the barriers we face in making sure that independent reading is accountable — and consider how to overcome them.

## BARRIERS TO ACCOUNTABLE INDEPENDENT READING

Given the necessity of effective, independent reading, teachers would be doing their students a disservice if they failed to provide them with extensive opportunities to practice reading on their own throughout their school careers. However, attempts to increase independent reading can quickly butt up against three key barriers: accountability, stamina, and the report-back lag.

### The Accountability Challenge

The first barrier teachers face in ensuring successful independent reading is the *accountability challenge*. As we've already noted, when students read independently, it's hard to be completely sure whether they are actually reading. Or whether they are practicing effective habits or inscribing poor ones. Or that independent reading is not functioning regressively — that is, as an activity that causes good readers to get better by practicing effective habits, and bad readers to get worse by reinforcing bad habits (for example, dropping word endings, reading hastily, not attending to punctuation). Practice doesn't make perfect; practice makes *permanent*. It's *perfect practice* that makes perfect.

What can we do to increase the amount of perfectly practiced reading that students do? To prepare students for successful independent reading, we can systematically build opportunities for successful practice that also include effective and efficient ways to constantly test for mastery — especially before adding complexity and/or further autonomy. We are preparing our students for a marathon, not a sprint, but well before anyone can run a marathon, he's got to be able to run a mile.

## The Fitness Challenge

The second reading challenge shares the stuff of running challenges — namely, stamina. The *fitness challenge* has to do with a student's ability to read long and challenging texts. One former student noted, in reflecting on his first, struggle-filled year in college, that he simply wasn't able to read the fifty or sixty pages of challenging text assigned per class per night that his privileged peers often were. This was nearly his undoing. Students not only need to gradually grow more autonomous as they read but also need to build their stamina to read and concentrate for long blocks of time, a task made even harder by the highly distracting world we live in today.

A colleague who is a marathoner once described the challenging monotony of marathons by saying, "The hardest part of running a marathon is doing the same thing over and over without stopping for three hours (four or five for the mortals among us). The real challenge has less to do with running; it would be hard to play the tuba or even talk to a friend nonstop for three hours." Students need to encounter gradually longer stretches of reading to get in better and better shape as they inch closer and closer to the college marathon. Even though giving students long, sacred blocks of DEAR may seem to address this challenge, if students aren't held accountable for that reading, then it's unlikely that they are building stamina for actual reading. Building stamina for reading has a distinctive wrinkle: you have to understand and remember what you've read.

## The Report-Back Lag

Unlike a marathon, which is over once you cross the finish line, reading requires that you remember it well enough to write or talk about it in a meaningful way. And you may have to retain the insights and understandings gleaned from your reading for minutes or hours or days before someone asks you to reflect on it. Difficulties around the length of time between the time something was read and the time it needs to be recalled make up the *report-back lag*.

Simply reading the seventy-five assigned pages of a biology textbook as part of your Biology 101 course assignment is not enough. You need to be able to make sense of what you've read and be able to recall it later, whether on an exam or in a later lab experiment. The report-back lag poses a significant challenge when asking students to read independently: not only do they have to actually do the reading, but they have to comprehend it and remember it at a later time.

Now that the challenges teachers face in getting students to read well by themselves have been defined, it's time to dive into how to surmount them.

## ACCOUNTABILITY TOOLS FOR IN-CLASS AIR

Several key tools are useful for making independent reading accountable, enjoyable, and successful. The accountability tools that follow address the barriers that we face when giving our students meaningful and productive opportunities to read independently.

## Limit Text and Gradually Increase

AIR should begin with limited text—reading in short intervals, under the watchful guidance of a teacher—before gradually moving toward longer stretches and extended reading assigned for homework. It's better to start by reading smaller chunks with greater accountability and comprehension than to read more text at lower quality. For developing readers or very hard texts, you might start with chunks as small as a single sentence and build up to a paragraph. The goal is to make a habit of reading independently and reading well, even if that means starting with and confirming comprehension after just a few lines of text. Starting with limited sections of text enables you to assess comprehension more accurately and consistently at more frequent intervals. Even very small doses of independent reading with seemingly modest goals can result in high amounts of student error at first—all the more reason to start small and scale up. The goal is for students to become socialized to reading *well* every time they read, at least as much as it is to increase the amount of time they read.

To build stamina over time, increase the amount of independent reading done in class. Lengthening the amount of text for AIR does not necessarily mean you should simply look to add a paragraph or a sentence each day. Gather data through questioning and observation, ensuring that written work demonstrates that students comprehend what they read independently before you add longer chunks of text. Before assigning longer independent portions, it's important to keep a pulse on pacing and accuracy.

### Find a Focal Point

As students read on their own, consider providing a **focal point** before you dispatch them to read whatever chunk of text you've assigned. For example, you might say, "As you read this next paragraph independently, look for three details that describe the setting of our story" or "Take one minute to read the next paragraph on your own. I'm going to ask you what Theo learns about his mother in this paragraph, so make sure you're looking for it." Tell students what they should look for before they start reading. As is true of any skill, mastery (in this case, students' comprehension and readiness to take on longer reading) can be gauged only through a reliable Check for Understanding. Assigning a focal point gives you a reliable measure.

A focal point allows you to see whether students comprehended a key component from their reading and were reliably able to absorb the details that make strong comprehension predictable. Almost everyone can think of something vague to say after they read a paragraph; what you want to know is whether students can *answer a specific question*.

Further, this method allows students a reference point for metacognition—another step toward intellectual autonomy. After they read, they can ask themselves, "What *did* Theo learn about his mother?" "Where was the conflict?" If they can't answer, they know they need to reread.

---

### See It in Action

Watch clip 15 at teachlikeachampion.com/yourlibrary as Patrick Pastore incorporates a moment of Accountable Independent Reading while working through *The Catcher in the Rye*, giving his students a clear focal point: "When you're done, I want you to be able to tell me how Holden and

Childs disagree about what happened to Judas." You'll notice that he adds accountability to these comprehension questions by Cold Calling on students to answer and adding a few follow-up questions. When a student who has been Cold Called gets it wrong, he prompts him to "Check the text and reread."

## Set Time Limits

Beyond assigning how much to read and what to read for, teachers can do a lot for the long-term growth of AIR by giving students **finite time limits**—limits that are tight and manageable but also sufficient and scalable. Initially, providing one to two minutes to read and mark up a few sentences gives students who work at different speeds the opportunity to finish, while not providing so much time that the fastest readers get distracted as they wait for the rest of the class to finish. Again, the goal initially is to read *well,* so the incentive should not be to rush. Following an independent reading chunk with an oral or written Check for Understanding can confirm that students comprehend the main takeaway of that portion of the text. And you can always dig deeper with additional written questions for your faster readers.

As any teacher of thirty students can tell you, there will be a wide range of comprehension in AIR across a classroom. Some students will read quickly, but not understand much. Others will read slowly and have a firm grasp on comprehension. And still others will both read slowly and have trouble comprehending the text. Given the range of possibilities found in any one classroom, you'll want to think about how to best differentiate AIR tasks to support and meet the needs of all students. Another way to gather data on the spectrum of reading skills in your class is to allow a finite period of time for students to read, without indicating how much text they have to read. Instead, have them use a hash mark to indicate where they are when time runs out ("When you hear the timer, mark the spot you've read up to"). Doing so allows you to assess the varying speeds with which different students move through content.

Over time, of course, you'll want to gradually release students to read longer chunks of text, for longer periods of time, with less scaffolding. As students progress, try including questions for analysis and slowly eliminating focal points before AIR—but only after your students have reliably demonstrated their ability to establish meaning of key elements of the text. You should also strive to systematically increase the amount of independent reading that students complete in class.

### Assign an Interactive Reading Task

Add a level of accountability to your focal point by giving students an **interactive reading task**. For example, you might ask students to "Read to the bottom; write 'conflict' in the margin next to the place where we learn what the conflict is" or "Meet me at the top of page 104, and be able to describe the conflict that develops. Have at least one piece of evidence underlined to support your answer." The result is a double line of accountability: one which ensures that students have actually read independently, and the other which shows that students have understood what they have read.

The data you gather from observable markups can then inform discussion. You might choose students to Cold Call or Show Call (project their text markups on a document camera, as described in *TLaC 2.0*) on the basis of margin notes you have observed (for example, "Let's take a look at how Joaquin marked up his text. Notice that he underlined two pieces of evidence of our setting. Who had a different piece of evidence?"). While this helps support students who may not have identified the conflict in this selection of text, it also supports students more broadly by giving strong examples of interactive reading from their peers.

---

### See It in Action

A great catch phrase for helping set reading milestones came from watching Daniel Cosgrove, with his students at Leadership Prep Bedford Stuyvesant Middle Academy, while reading Roald Dahl's *James and the Giant Peach* with his Guided Reading Group. In clip 16 at teachlikeachampion.com/yourlibrary, watch as Daniel sends his students back to AIR with the phrase, "I'll meet you at the top of page 91." This phrase is especially useful because it reminds students, in a warm and supportive way, that they will be accountable. Asking students to meet you "at the top of page 109" or "at the break on page 34" also allows you a simple way to expand the length of reading beyond a paragraph without wasting time trying to communicate where the AIR portion begins and ends.

---

### Confirm and Scaffold Comprehension

Following periods of AIR, confirm comprehension through both written and oral checks (for example, "In one sentence, describe the contrasting settings that appear in the opening paragraphs of *Tuck Everlasting*"). You may also consider having students read back chunks of text as evidence that supports their answer, as in, "Read back the part that demonstrates how the author uses figurative language to describe the contrast between the two settings."

Consistently checking comprehension for AIR is essential to ensuring meaningful reading. Written checks are even more accountable because every student in the class must complete them. They also better allow you to scaffold for different reading levels by varying the types of written comprehension checks. Initially, for struggling readers, your comprehension checks should be more about establishing the literal meaning of a passage. For more advanced readers, you may want to include additional comprehension checks that ask them to analyze meaning. Logistically, both of these comprehension checks should be available to all students. You might just have students first answer the "establish meaning" question before posing more challenging questions—giving faster students an opportunity to answer harder prompts. This is also useful because sometimes our fastest readers aren't actually reading carefully enough; the comprehension checks can cause them to go back and reread to confirm their own understanding—a useful college prep habit to develop.

## On "Silent" Reading

As you release students to their independent reading, the classroom should be silent. And while that means establishing a strong culture of discipline among the students in your classroom, it also means establishing strong habits of discipline for yourself. Remember to try not to talk while your students are reading—if you repeat the directions, say, or make comments loudly enough for public consumption, you run the risk of disrupting comprehension.

## AIR FOR HOMEWORK

Over time, AIR should become increasingly independent and autonomous. This should include accountable independent homework reading. Much like AIR in class, AIR outside of class should begin with small chunks and should stress accountability first and foremost. Remember, *high-quality* reading is what we want. Gradually, the amount of nightly reading should increase.

AIR assignments should not be confused with independent reading that students do nightly in books of their own choosing—and presumably in books at a reading level that is unlikely to cause them to struggle. For example, at Uncommon Schools, elementary students are asked to read independently at home for fifteen minutes per day—and up to thirty minutes independently in the upper grades. Although reading is tracked by parent-signed reading logs, this does not prove that students *comprehend* what they read, but it does help establish a lifelong habit of reading.

Accountable independent homework reading, by contrast, builds in an accountability check for comprehension. Checks serve as a means of holding students accountable for what they have read outside of class and help address the report-back lag, requiring them to remember what they have read after a brief passage of time. They also provide students with appropriate practice with the expectations of high school and college—being held responsible for reading done independently at home.

Comprehension checks can take a number of forms—classroom discussion, written assignments, or quizzes to name a few—and can vary in length at the teacher's discretion. A closed-book reading-check format—which includes three to five written-response questions that are specific enough to require careful reading and that are relatively straightforward if such reading has been completed—is one effective way to hold students accountable for out-of-class reading. The idea behind a reading check is to ask a quick-to-administer sample of questions about the text to see if students understood key aspects. You aren't trying to ask about the whole chapter; you're just asking enough questions that you have pretty reliable data.

Also, just because you give a reading check does not mean you need to grade or score it. If you graded on a variable-interval schedule—grading every second or third one or ten students' papers each time—you'd get a decent sample and build a healthy habit of accountability for simply doing the reading. That said, it is better (1) to use a simple reading check that you *can* grade every time than a more complex one that you can't, and (2) to discuss the answers afterwards so as to fill in gaps any students may have, before moving forward. As with any Check for Understanding, the data you get from student answers will help drive instruction and determine the effectiveness of the independent reading done outside of class. In later grades, significant chunks of reading should be done outside the classroom.

The accountability tools described here work in conjunction with each other to help build students' independence in logging high-quality miles on the page. Each of these tools can be gradually released across the course of the year as more and more students demonstrate that they are ready to successfully read independently. But even once that independence has been established, giving students opportunities to practice reading aloud is still crucial. Enter Control the Game.

Control the Game is about leveraging time spent reading with students. It is a systematic approach to having students read aloud so that they follow along and are always ready to read themselves. Being in favor of healthy doses of oral reading as a class dissents from much of what many schools of education would advocate. Very few, if any, graduate schools of education in our country would spend time training its teachers in how to support students' reading aloud effectively, yet this is often the first topic we cover in our reading workshops. Inscribing such a "basic" skill of teaching reading can free up teachers to focus on what is most important: checking for comprehension, facilitating a rigorous discussion, and circulating to Check for Understanding when students are writing.

Rather than engage in philosophical debate, we merely observe that a public meaningful read, fully leveraged, is one of the major muscle groups of top-performing classrooms. The approach described in the coming pages was first outlined in the original edition of *Teach Like a Champion*. It has stood the test of time and remains here (with updates) because it includes bite-sized techniques that teachers can use *tomorrow* to improve fluency and decoding, while supporting reading comprehension. Not only that, it can also make reading aloud more fun and manageable for both students and teachers. The techniques in this section describe the intentional moves teachers can make to ensure that all students are benefiting from a shared reading.

## CONTROL THE GAME SKILLS

In Control the Game, when one student is reading, everyone reads, and reads accountably. Here are a few ways to get the most leverage out of reading as a class to ensure both high-quality and efficient practice.

## Keep Durations Short and the Reader Unpredictable

When you ask a student to read aloud during class, that student is the "primary reader"—but he should not be the only reader. While the practice the primary reader gets in fluency and decoding is critical, the actions and focus of all other students are also critically important, as they must become "secondary readers." Reading short segments maximizes the concentration of the primary reader. It allows students to invest real expressive energy in reading, to focus intently, and sustain fluent and even dramatic reading. This yields higher-quality oral reading and makes the lesson more engaging.

Further, moving quickly among primary readers keeps a lively pace. It makes the lesson feel energetic, rather than tedious and slow. Knowing that segments tend to be short, may end at any time, and may shift to them at any time (that is, aren't predictable) keeps students from tuning out. If a teacher moves quickly from one primary reader to another, students focus more closely on the text to follow along. This is doubly true if they don't know who the next primary reader will be. A teacher who announces that she'll go around the room in a predictable order (as is often done in "round-robin" reading) gives away a lot of her leverage. Students can tune out until their turn is near and again when their turn has just been completed.

Short durations also allow you to take better advantage of a crucial form of data. Every time you switch readers, you gather information about your leverage. When you say, "Pick up please, Charles," and Charles jumps in with the next sentence without missing a beat, you know he was reading alongside previous readers independently. Ideally, you want this sort of seamless transition every time you switch readers. Switching frequently allows you to gather this data more frequently and broadly. The more data you collect, the more information you have to help ensure both leverage and engagement with the text. If your data suggests otherwise (that is, if one or more students aren't ready to read when called on), it may be necessary for you to revisit your expectations and perhaps backstop with a reminder, support, or consequence.

## See It in Action

Watch in clip 17 at teachlikeachampion.com/yourlibrary as Nikki Frame kicks off a Control the Game reading of *A Single Shard* by Linda Sue Park. She begins the reading herself to model fluency and support comprehension. The first reader omits a word and then corrects himself; Nikki gives positive feedback to encourage this important habit of good readers, "good self-correction." She calls on the next student to read: Brett, who is not where he needs to be in the text. She gently tells him, "Gotta be there, that's two" and calls on a new student to read. "That's two" indicates to the student and the rest of the class that Brett has just received a small consequence (a two-dollar deduction from his weekly "Scholar Dollar" paycheck). She then slowly circulates to his desk, shows him where he needs to be in the text, and warmly whispers "OK, get ready." She calls on him again to read, and he seamlessly picks up the narrative.

When you identify your primary reader, *don't* specify how long you want him to read before he begins. Simply ask him to start reading. "Start reading for me please, James" or "Pick up please, James" is a far better thing to say than "Read the next paragraph for me, James." The unpredictability of durations ensures that other students in the class don't know when a new reader will be asked to pick up, giving them a strong incentive to follow along carefully. Unpredictability encourages attentiveness from secondary readers.

Keeping durations unpredictable also allows you to address a developing primary reader in a noninvasive manner. A primary reader who struggles mightily with a long paragraph risks losing the engagement and concentration of his or her peers, as well as potentially losing track of the narrative thread, all while reducing leverage. When you've committed to a full paragraph, you lose your ability to cut a primary reader's session short and have him or her try again with another passage without its becoming obvious to other students. If you don't specify the length of the read, you can shorten or lengthen as you need to, in the interest of both the primary reader and the rest of the class.

Holding on to your ability to choose the next reader also allows you to match students to passages more effectively. Teachers who effectively Control the Game often plan in advance which students will read which sentences or passages, and for how long.

This allows teachers to match struggling readers to shorter, less complex chunks of text and more advanced readers to longer and trickier passages. This effectively differentiates the task of reading aloud in a way that best supports all readers. Struggling readers aren't accidentally mismatched with an overly challenging chunk of text, potentially undercutting quality road miles or disrupting comprehension. Gradually, as all readers get stronger, the goal is to lengthen the chunk of text read for all readers. Retaining unpredictability of the reader and the duration of the reading makes for better leverage and better reading for all.

## Reduce Transaction Costs

A *transaction cost* is the amount of resources it takes to execute an exchange—be it economic, verbal, or otherwise. If it takes you three days of driving to different stores to find the best price on a TV, your transaction cost is high (three days of your time)—possibly higher in dollar value than the potential savings you'd get from buying the less expensive TV. When you manage finite resources like time and attention, as teachers do, transaction costs are both critically important and easy to overlook.

A transaction cost is implicit in every transition in the classroom—especially in transitions you make frequently, such as moving from one reader to the next. It's important to recognize their significance. A transaction that takes more than a few seconds steals reading time and risks disrupting concentration, thus affecting how well students follow and comprehend the text.

Make it your goal to transition from one primary reader to another quickly, with a minimum number of words—and ideally in a consistent way. "Susan, pick up" is a much more efficient transition than "Thank you, Stephen. Nicely read. Susan, will you begin reading please?" We see Jessica Bracey use the smallest transaction cost possible when she simply prompts with a student's name, "Daniel," indicating that one turn is over and the next has begun with just a simple name (see "See It in Action"). The first transaction reduces the amount of time students are *not reading* threefold because it is more than three times as quick as the second example. Because it causes less interruption, it also keeps the narrative thread more vibrant and alive in students' minds. It also allows you to step in and use it at almost any natural pause in the text.

## See It in Action

Stepping into Jessica Bracey's fifth-grade classroom—a classroom where all thirty students are leveraged—in Newark, New Jersey, is one great way to understand the power of Control the Game as they read *Circle of Gold* by Candy Dawson Boyd. Watch Jessica in clip 18 at teachlikeachampion.com/yourlibrary. After one student struggles with a small chunk of text, Jessica briefly cues the next reader simply by saying his name. After three students read aloud, Jessica jumps in to model fluent reading (as well as to maintain the pace and support comprehension, as she reads a line twice for emphasis). She calls on a few other students to read, and along the way supports students in decoding and fluency.

In this three-minute clip we see the way that Control the Game, when expertly executed, ensures that students are reading along, have the opportunity to practice both decoding and fluency with support, and comprehend what they read.

## Use Bridging to Maintain Continuity and Model Fluency

**Bridging** refers to a teacher's reading a short segment of text—a bridge—in between primary student readers. In a typical sequence of bridging, a teacher might allow John to read for three sentences and then read one sentence herself. Then she might allow Mary to read four sentences and read two sentences herself before asking Nikki to read for six sentences and reading a few more herself before passing off to Jane, and so on. The benefit of this method is that it moves the story along quickly and keeps the narrative thread alive, while supporting and maximizing comprehension by interspersing teacher-quality expressive reading.

## See It in Action

Watch Rob de Leon bridge for his students as they finish reading *The Mouse and the Motorcycle* by Beverly Cleary. Clip 19 at teachlikeachampion.com/yourlibrary opens with some fluent reading by one of his students. Thirty seconds later, Rob chimes in to read. The emotion and suspense he conveys in his reading are awe inspiring. And when he has to tell them "And we're stopping right there; close up your books," the response from his students says it all: "Oh, man!"

Generally, the harder the text, or the more diverse your class's skills, the more you might consider bridging. If you feel that you need to bridge very frequently in order to sustain comprehension, the text you are reading may be too difficult for Control the Game reading. Consider it for Read-Aloud.

## Spot Check

The idea of spot checking came out of watching Rob de Leon teach reading to third-grade boys at Excellence Boys Charter School for Boys in Bedford-Stuyvesant, Brooklyn. In one example, Rob kicked off his reading of *Phantom of the Opera* by leaving a word out at the end of his first sentence: "Carlotta had the …," he read, snapping quietly on the word "the" to alert his students that they should fill in the blank. On the day in question, only a handful of his boys chimed in "leading role" exactly on cue. So Rob started over: "Ooh, some boys weren't quite with us. Let's try that again. 'Carlotta had the …'" and all his boys chimed in with "leading role!!" demonstrating that they were now following along. This device allows Rob to quickly and simply assess leverage. When you're reading along with kids using Control the Game, you're establishing a system for efficient and accountable reading; it's useful to make sure that students are with you by having them read one word as a whole class.

## See It in Action

In clip 20 at teachlikeachampion.com/yourlibrary, Eric Snider shows lots of spunk as his class reads Ray Bradbury's "Dark They Were, and Golden-Eyed." While bridging, Eric briefly snaps to cue students to read several words ("winds," "family," "cold") to ensure that they follow along when he reads.

### Rely on a Placeholder

As champion reading teachers move between reading and questioning their students about what they read, they often use a quick and reliable prompt—a placeholder—to ensure that their students recognize the transition and react promptly. It's called a placeholder because it ensures that students retain their place in the text and can immediately transition *back* to reading after discussion. "Hold your place. Track me," announces Patrick Pastore, modeling for his sixth graders how to point to the spot where they left off reading *Esperanza Rising,* close their books partway, and meet his eyes to show that they are ready to discuss. After a brief discussion of why Esperanza and Miguel react differently to a train ride, he instructs, "Pick up reading please, Melanie." In less than two seconds, she and her classmates are back into the book at almost no transaction cost. "Finger in your book; close your book," intones Rob de Leon as he prepares his students to discuss *Phantom of the Opera*—and to end that discussion and return to the book efficiently. We have observed other teachers use similar prompts, such as "finger freeze" or "pen to page to hold the spot" to cue students to keep their place when reading is interrupted for questioning.

# CONTROL THE GAME, FLUENCY, AND DECODING

One of the greatest benefits of Control the Game is that it allows students to practice fluency, decoding, and express comprehension, while allowing teachers to assess and support them. All teachers (literacy and otherwise) need to have tools to support students in continuing to accurately decode and develop fluency—especially given that teachers in the upper grades, who often aren't explicitly trained in how to teach phonics and decoding, are often teaching students who have skill gaps or who are reading difficult and challenging texts.[4] Without Control the Game and an intentional focus on increasing students' opportunities to read aloud, occasions for both student practice and teacher support can become few and far between.

Although many teachers think of fluency and decoding as skills that are most relevant in the early elementary grades, the opposite might be true as well. In fact, literacy expert David Liben recently observed that what most characterizes our weakest readers is not their "inability to think critically" but rather a lack of fluency. "Fluency does not guarantee comprehension, but a lack of fluency guarantees almost all the time a lack of comprehension, especially with more complex texts," he said.[5] Developing students' ability to comprehend the full amount of information carried within the text relies on an "expressive ear"—an ear that can extract meaning from subtext, tone, register, innuendo, and analogy. Complex texts rely heavily for their meaning on the portion of the argument carried by these subtextual elements. Unlocking those forms of meaning must be continually practiced and modeled throughout the grades and perhaps especially in the later years.

Given the restrictions on the time we have to explicitly teach fluency past second or third grade, it is vital that all teachers are adept at modeling, requiring, and reinforcing fluency at different points during instruction. In the upper grades, fluency and decoding will rarely, if ever, be the explicit objective of a lesson, but should be constantly practiced and implicitly taught by giving students ample opportunities to read aloud. The best way to do this is to use Control the Game so that all students in the class are fully leveraged.

## Control the Game and Fluency

We define *fluency* quite simply as a reader's ability to read with automaticity and expression, in order to comprehend what they have read. In addition to the tools described earlier in this module, one of the most powerful elements of Control the Game is the influence it has on creating a culture of reading in a classroom. Not only does it support accountability for reading in the same way that AIR does, but it also allows a teacher to both implicitly and explicitly shape student beliefs about reading. In classrooms where Control the Game is used effectively, reading is done joyfully with expression and care, modeling expressive reading and asking students to do the same.

Just as reading aloud expressively is good for students, so too is prompting students to read expressively by calling their attention to text features, dialogue tags, and vocabulary that can give them cues for appropriate expression. Such prompting causes them to practice looking for the meaning in words and to pay attention to syntax and punctuation. To make oral reading more systematically expressive, try the strategies we describe in the next paragraphs.

### Capture the Mood

Identify (or ask students to infer) the kind of expression they should impart to the passage based on the general mood or on the affect of a specific character. Then ask them to apply it. In terms of general mood, it might involve asking a student to try to capture the tension of a key scene in the way he read it. In terms of a specific character's affect, a teacher might say, "Wilbur is upset, Diamond. Can you read that sentence in a way that shows that?" or "How is Wilbur feeling right now? What emotion is he feeling? Good … can you show me that?"

Asking students to capture the mood of a scene or character conveys to students that *how* they read a text matters. It also directly supports student comprehension. You can help students do this by calling their attention to dialogue tags and their role as "stage directions." "The passage says, '"I don't want any," Mr. Malone said sharply.' Read that again so his words are sharp." You can also model the applicable tone in your own reading by intentionally bridging around a dialogue tag and asking students to apply it to the sentence they are reading. Sticking with this example, you might say the word "sharply" in a sharp tone of voice that students could then imitate.

### Important Words

Ask students to identify the two or three most important words in a sentence (or the two or three most important ideas in a passage) and place special emphasis on them. You may also choose a key descriptive word (from the surrounding passage or even a vocabulary word) and ask students to read the passage in a way that emphasizes that word. For example, a teacher asked her students to read aloud from a scene in C. S. Lewis's *Prince Caspian*. After the first reading, she noted, "Look back a few sentences. It says the children are feeling gloomy as they sit and wait for the train. Can you read that again to show that the children are feeling gloomy?"

It can be especially rigorous when your line of questioning forces students to infer from subtler clues what tone or mood the words should carry. This is especially useful when using layered reading—reading a complex text multiple times and in different ways (for example, independently and aloud). "Who can tell Danielle what kind of tone to use in reading these lines? Why do you say that?" You might even add, "Can anyone read it another way?" before asking Danielle to model the tone in her reading. Ask students to provide other possible interpretations of a line that a student read and to model those interpretations in their expression.

### Check the Mechanics

Developing readers see punctuation, but often do not grasp what it is telling them to do in terms of meaning or inflection. Making explicit references to punctuation and asking students to demonstrate their understanding of it in their oral reading is a useful way to build this important habit. ("There's a comma there. Remember to pause." "I want you to pause and breathe whenever you see a period." "Don't forget that the quotation mark means that Pony Boy is talking.") The importance of syntax—the relationship of the pieces of a sentence and its effect on meaning—is often lost on weak readers. The idea that the word *though* or *besides* sets the rest of the sentence in contrast to the initial phrase is a critical part of effective reading. Asking students to identify which words told them that a sentence was a question or which words told them that the two ideas were in contrast helps them improve their fluency and therefore their comprehension.

### Lather, Rinse, Repeat

Not only should we have students reread frequently to support comprehension or Close Reading, but we should also consider asking them to reread for fluency. Once students have successfully decoded and established the meaning of words and phrases in a sentence, ask them to go back and reread specifically for fluency. As with Close Reading, even adult readers may need to read a complex passage or a sentence multiple times before it finally makes sense to them. Asking our students to do the same to improve fluency is an important way to support comprehension. By consistently enforcing your expectations and giving students multiple opportunities to read and reread a text, you can encourage students to build lifelong habits that make them fluent readers who love great (and complex) books.

## Control the Game and Decoding

Teachers who don't teach decoding as part of their curriculum (read: post third grade) often don't think about it (or perhaps wish they had the tools to better support students below grade level). It can be a blind spot for some upper elementary, middle, and high school teachers, as it appears to some to be a mundane, "lower-order" skill that should have been established in the earlier grades. However, because its mastery is a prerequisite to all reading comprehension, decoding is vital. Incomplete mastery of decoding can persist well beyond the elementary grades and detract from the overall academic success of even apparently advanced students.

A certain proportion of reading errors are due to carelessness, haste, or sloppy reading habits. For example, weak students may habitually leave the -s or other ending sounds off of words, even though they "know" they are supposed to read them. These errors remain important to correct, nonetheless. They still interfere with comprehension, and, to paraphrase Mark Twain, the student who *does not* read words correctly has little advantage over the student who *cannot* read them correctly.[6] Reading carefully is a very important habit to build, and you can build it through systematically addressing decoding errors using the tools described here.

Given the bedrock importance of decoding, teachers should strive to correct decoding errors whenever it's viable to do so, no matter what subject or grade level they teach. Reducing the transaction costs of your correction is arguably the single most important factor in your success overall. Except in cases where your lesson objective focuses on decoding skills (which is never the case for non-reading teachers), *you should strive for the lowest possible transaction cost in making corrections.* Consider these two corrections of a student's decoding error:

- Teacher 1, student reading the word "inspection": "You said in-SPEAK-tion. Can you go back to the beginning of the sentence and read that word again?"

- Teacher 2, student reading the word "inspection": "In-*SPEAK*-tion?"

The difference between these corrections may seem trivial, but is in fact huge. The time it takes to say the first phrase — the transaction cost — is at least *five times* greater than the transaction cost of the second. Every extra word the first teacher says takes time and disrupts the flow of student concentration on the narrative. Thus every extra word potentially disrupts comprehension. If you used the second phrase to correct, you could make three or four interventions in the time you would spend on just one with the first phrase.

Like the second teacher, strive to make a habit of using the simplest and quickest intervention when correcting decoding errors. If you are consistent in the manner that you do so, your students, too, will get in the habit of self-correcting quickly and efficiently. This requires rigorous economy of language and a systematic approach to fixing decoding errors without having to explicitly double down on phonics instruction across grade levels. That's why our discussion of decoding lives here: it addresses the need to balance high expectations around correcting for decoding with the relentless pursuit of road miles. The following tools help consistently support students in effectively decoding what they read, while maximizing road miles and maintaining comprehension.

## Mark the Spot

Reread the three or four words immediately prior to the word which the student was unable to decode, inflecting your voice (usually by extending the last syllable or two of the last word) to show that the student should pick up there. For example: Student reads, "He ran *though* the door"; teacher corrects: "He ran . . . " This correction provides a minimal prompt and helps the student learn to self-correct by briefly highlighting the mistake she has made.

## Punch the Error

Repeat the word a student misread back to him, replicating and putting emphasis on the part where the error occurred (for example, "Is that word in-SPEAK-tion??" "CARE-pet??" "You said 'cat'—try again"; student: "Catch"). Like Mark the Spot, Punch the Error also encourages students to self-correct. A subtle difference is the use of inflection on the exact error, more directly calling attention to what a student needs to fix. Of all the decoding corrections described here, Punch the Error and Mark the Spot usually carry the smallest transaction cost, assuming that students know how to self-correct when you have called their attention to an error.

## Name the Sound or the Rule

Naming the sound a letter should make is one direct way to correct a decoding error. When naming the sound, you might identify the sound a vowel is making, especially whether it is making a long or short sound, and ask students to apply it. (For example: "[That's a] long *a*"; "Long vowels say their name"; "Read that again: long *a*"; "That has a bossy *e.*") Or you might identify the sound a consonant is making, especially whether a *c*, *g*, or *s* is making a hard or soft sound, and ask students to apply it. (For example: "[That's a] soft *c*"; "Hard *c* like *cat*" or "Soft *c* like *city*"; "Hard *g* like *golf*" or "Soft *g* like *gym*.") You could also consider naming the sound a group of letters is making, then asking students to repeat and apply. (For example: "-*tch* says 'chuh'"; "-*ea* here says 'ee.' [Try it again.]") If there's a clear and identifiable rule, remind students of it and ask them to apply it. (For example: "*e* at the end makes the vowel says its name"; "*ph* makes the *f* sound.")

## See It in Action

In clip 21 at teachlikeachampion.com/yourlibrary, see a montage of Patrick Pastore making a variety of corrections as his students read *The Westing Game* by Ellen Raskin. He names the sound: "the *gh* sound makes an *f* sound in this case," and the students corrects himself: "laughter." Patrick also punches the error: "not *discuss* but ..." But this time the student doesn't accurately correct: "discuse?" which causes Patrick to intervene again: "*ui* makes an *i* sound," resulting in the student reading the word "disguise" correctly. This series of corrections highlights the importance of minimizing transaction costs while at the same time causing students to do as much of the decoding work as possible.

Naming the sound is useful because it references rules that students can then practice applying when reading independently. The student is responsible for applying the rule to the word. With frequent practice, students will be better able to apply the correct rules more consistently when reading aloud or independently.

For non-reading teachers, it is important to collaborate with reading teachers in order to familiarize yourself with the decoding rules that students have learned. Having these rules at the ready will help minimize transaction costs and support students in quickly decoding words. Any tools or visuals that may support decoding (for both students and teachers) should be posted across classrooms as well.

## Beware the Echo Correction

Because decoding errors often indicate a broader lack of knowledge or skills, reinforcing general rules and ensuring that students practice decoding are effective antidotes. However, many teachers and parents who correct decoding errors ask students to make what is known as an "echo correction"—to repeat the correct word without asking the scholar to decode it on his own. However, unlike other methods, echo correction *does not actually ask the student to decode*. Students can "read" the word correctly merely by repeating the pronunciation you've given them. They can fix the error without looking at the printed word or doing any cognitive work. It's far more useful to name the sound or rule. In so doing, teachers treat the cause of the faulty decoding, rather than merely treating the symptom by essentially giving students the answer.

Still, in some cases you may choose to make an echo correction, as it makes for a very low transaction cost. Echo corrections may be worthwhile when you're reading an especially important section of a text and can't afford even a minimal distraction. Otherwise, echo corrections are best used for sight words or for proper nouns that may repeat throughout a given text.

### Speed the Exceptions

Decoding rules always have exceptions. When a word does not conform to standard rules, identify the correct pronunciation quickly and directly. (For example: "That word is written 'bury' but pronounced 'berry.' We'll just have to remember it"; "That word is *through*.") If a student should know a word's distinctive pronunciation (that is, it is a sight word or has recently been discussed), quickly identify it as an exception. (For example: "That's one of our sight words"; "That word doesn't follow the rules, but we studied it yesterday"; "We'd expect the *e* to make that say "g-IVE" [as in *hive*], but this word is an exception.") What differentiates these interventions from the echo correction is that you call student attention to the fact that the word is an exception to a rule. In so doing, you make students aware of the words that don't conform to general rules. Ideally, students are then more likely to remember these exceptions (or at least that they exist) when they encounter them independently.

### Chunk It

It can also be quite useful to ask students to **chunk** difficult words by recognizing familiar patterns and words-within-words. For example, if a student struggles to read the word *hopeless*, you might say: "Do you see a part of that you already know?" or "The first four letters are a word you know" or "Cover the *-less* and read what you have." When asking students to chunk a word, it can help to affirm and reiterate what the student got right, focusing him on the problem "chunk." (For example, "You got *hope*, but the second part isn't *-ing*.")

Use Positive Feedback

For developing readers especially, it's also important to use **positive feedback**—quick and simple positive reinforcement when students read a word correctly. This not only encourages students but also lets them know explicitly that they got it right. Because correction of mispronunciation and misreading may not be consistent for them, struggling readers may not know when they've read a word accurately. *As students continue reading,* say "Yup," "Perfect," "You got it," "Nice," and so on. It can also increase efficiency by reducing the amount of time students spend pausing and wondering whether they've gotten a tough word correct. Obviously you want this method to speed, not slow, your reading. You can minimize transaction costs by making your feedback phrases both quick and consistent. Too much variation can draw too much attention to your words.

## See It in Action

In clip 22 at teachlikeachampion.com/yourlibrary, watch Bridget McElduff's math class. You will see a student struggle over the words *examine* and *thermometer* several times. Bridget normalizes error for the student by having all students repeat the word *examine,* while also giving encouragement: "You got it"; "Try it one more time from the top now that you've got it"; "This is a word we say a lot, so don't you worry, we're going to get it right."

The fluency, decoding, and Control the Game techniques described here go a long way in supporting students in effectively reading aloud during class. Beyond AIR and reading together as a class using Control the Game, there is one final approach that master teachers utilize to improve student perceptions of and relationship with the written word: Read-Aloud.

The final approach to reading is the simple art of teachers (or parents) reading aloud *to* students. Read-Aloud can and should be one of the most joyful parts of the students' and teachers' day—an opportunity to relish and savor the beauty of books. We have always been advocates of Read-Aloud and recognize it as both a dying art as well as a crucial aspect of literacy. We recently asked a room full of teachers why people don't do it as much across the grade levels. One teacher responded, "I'd like to, but I don't feel like I'm teaching when I read to kids"—an astute answer that reflects how a lot of people feel about their lives in the classroom.

This section on Read-Aloud is less about how to do it (although we will touch on this a bit) and more about why. The "how" of Read-Aloud is often quite simply just to do it, no matter what grade or subject you teach. Too often we think of Read-Aloud as something done in early childhood classrooms with beanbag chairs and lots of primary colors on the walls. Still, every classroom—all grades and all subjects—could benefit from a healthy dose of Read-Aloud. It should be an integral part of any successful reading program in order to

- Expose students to texts (and ideas!) significantly above their reading level
- Model fluent reading for students
- Instill a love of reading and a love a literature in our students

In order to accomplish these goals, across grades, it's important to consider where you might be able to incorporate opportunities to read aloud across the day or week, and not just in elementary school, where it seems a natural fit. In middle school, this may be systematically done during homeroom by reading and non-reading teachers alike, or it could serve as a routine to open reading class. In high school, teachers could use as many opportunities as possible to model fluent, artful reading, whether it be a Shakespearean sonnet or a passionate delivery of Dr. Martin Luther King's "Eulogy for the Martyred Children."

Regardless of what form it takes, where it fits into the schedule, or who is doing the reading, the benefits of Read-Aloud remain the same. Yet, on both sides of the achievement gap, the older a child gets, the less that child is read aloud to—both at home and in the classroom.[7] This means that even in families where students were read aloud to as toddlers and young children, when they reach middle school, they are likely being read aloud to significantly less, if at all, both at home and at school. It is therefore even more critical that Read-Aloud remain an important part of reading instruction across grade levels. In this section, we will outline each of the goals of Read-Aloud and how they may be achieved.

## EXPOSURE TO COMPLEX TEXTS

On the too-infrequent occasions that teachers do read aloud to students, the text is often too simplistic. Read-Aloud is a unique opportunity to breathe life into texts that students are unable to read independently, so as to make those texts accessible. Reading difficult texts aloud exposes students to complex sentence structures and vocabulary and builds background knowledge, all of which help them develop as readers and writers. What's more, it's often the really complex and engaging stories that kids love the most. When you read a complete text aloud, you pave the way for students to read it themselves.

## DEVELOPING SYNTACTIC CONTROL

Reading challenging sentences relies on the ability not only to track the connection of ideas within them but also to hear the way that the syntax of the sentence connects the ideas. For example, hearing a line like this from *Mrs. Frisby and the Rats of NIMH,* "In her worry about moving day, in watching the tractor, the cat, and finally the rats, Mrs. Frisby had forgotten that she had set out originally to get some corn for supper," you hear the way the syntax of the sentence connects the ideas, pushing some together and subordinating others. You have to intuit that the phrase "in watching the tractor, the cat, and finally the rats," is a series describing the things that Mrs. Frisby has done earlier that morning, but also that it is a digression in the sentence, almost an appositive to describe her worry about moving day.

One of the biggest benefits of reading aloud is that students are exposed to and come to know what the artful syntax in beautiful sentences—varied, rich ornate sentences—sounds like. Introducing young ears to the complex and nuanced syntax found in more challenging text prepares students to incorporate different types of sentences in their own writing. Developing syntactic control—the capacity to use forms of grammar to build sentences and construct ideas with flexibility and fluidity—does not come without a strong model of what those sentences look and sound like. Being read to also develops students' ability to track ideas written by others, by providing them with robust exposure to how those ideas are presented in often complex and convoluted forms.

All of these things require an ear. They require constant exposure to complex texts that model just how rich and varied a sentence can be. Students, meanwhile, are drinking up the larger story of the sentence, of all the forms it can take and the things it can do. So it's important not just to read to kids but to choose complex texts, often above the level that they can access independently. The power is in having them hear syntax that would be slightly beyond their reach and allowing them to more easily construct meaning out of it on their own.

## BUILDING VOCABULARY

According to Isabel Beck and her colleagues, "The source of later vocabulary learning shifts to written texts — what children read. The problem is that it is not so easy to learn from written context. Written context lacks many of the features of oral language that support learning new word meanings, such as intonation, body language, and shared physical surroundings. As such, the text is a far less effective vehicle for learning new words than oral language."[8] Read-Aloud unlocks the complexity of language by providing more audible examples, setting the stage for students to better make sense of the variety of syntaxes and structures they will encounter when they read independently. When we read aloud words like "sympathetically" and "oddities," or that there was a breeze "carrying the moist essence of spring" in *Mrs. Frisby and the Rats of NIMH*, we are helping students hear artfully crafted sentences that develop both word knowledge and an ear for language and all its beauty. When adults remind themselves to read slowly, students can think about the words and process them with a bit more time, allowing them to linger over particular scenes or savor compelling new words or phrases.

In *The Read-Aloud Handbook*, Jim Trelease outlined how the vocabulary that students are exposed to in books is far superior to vocabulary heard in conversation.[9] According to Trelease, the "Basic Lexicon" consists of five thousand words that are used all the time. Eighty-three percent of the words used in conversations between kids and adults come from this group of words, and this doesn't change drastically as a child ages. On top of these five thousand words, there are an additional five thousand words that are used less often in conversation. These ten thousand words make up the "Common Lexicon." Beyond this group are *rare words*. According to a study in the *Journal of Child Language*, the conversations between adults and ten-year-olds consist of seventeen rare words per thousand (less than 2 percent).[10] In contrast, a children's book has thirty rare words per thousand (3 percent), an adult book has fifty-three rare words per thousand (5.3 percent), and a newspaper has sixty-eight rare words per thousand (6.8 percent).[11]

Initially skeptical of these staggering statistics (and wondering if our spoken language may be robust enough to perhaps beat the 2 percent average), we took a look at some of the most basic children books we might read aloud to our kids: board books, designed as much for babies to chew on as to be read aloud from. The first book we picked up included the words "scamper," "scurry," and "delight," words that we of course know, yet rarely if ever use in conversation. It's clear that frequent exposure to texts read aloud goes a long way in exposing our students to a variety of words that they may not otherwise hear.

Vocabulary develops word knowledge in advance of their ability to decode words. Therefore, when students hear new words read aloud to them, though they may not immediately understand their meaning, their exposure to these words supports their ability to eventually read them independently. When students have the opportunity to encounter the words themselves, they have already been exposed to a preview (or several previews) of the word. Consequently, students *know* words before they read them for first time, and are then able to decode them more effectively ("Oh! *Exemplary!* I know that word"), because they are familiar with the word and how it sounds when read aloud. When students initially struggle to decode a word and then that lightbulb goes off— "Ex … ex-OAT … ex-AH … exotic!"— it is because they know these words to begin with. *Decoding a word you don't know is a much more challenging task than decoding one that you already know.* The best way for students to learn lots of words is to be frequently read aloud to from a variety of complex texts. Exposure to complex texts builds their vocabulary for the long haul—not to mention being highly synergistic with decoding and early success with reading.

## INTRODUCING NEW GENRES AND BUILDING BACKGROUND KNOWLEDGE

Reading aloud is a way not only to develop your students' ears for another challenging genre (for example, long-form nonfiction articles, which carry their own distinct rhythms) but also to build background knowledge. For low-income students especially, it is vital that teachers better support the development of background knowledge, as they are competing for seats in college against students with an array of experiences that have helped them build a broad background knowledge base.

Reading aloud from articles and texts that enable students to experience a world beyond their own is an effective way to address the background knowledge challenge. Reading aloud from scientific articles and primary sources is a great way to build background knowledge, vocabulary, and exposure to other types of complex syntax so often missing from the texts that students read independently. You might specifically consider selecting texts for Read-Aloud (either entire books or excerpts or articles) that serve as a way of building background knowledge for your primary text. This may allow you to read a text that is too far above your students' reading level, but that has important information to help build the background knowledge they need to access other texts.

## MODELING FLUENT READING

Beyond exposing students to complex texts, Read-Aloud is important for letting students hear fluent readers, so that they have a model of what expressive reading sounds like and can work to emulate it. It is important to model expression and linger over words with pleasure, both to convey our passion for reading and to enable students to access and engage with the text. For students who may struggle with listening comprehension, adding drama to your Read-Aloud can be the difference between comprehending a text and tuning out.

### Highlight Points of Emphasis

In order to effectively model fluency, you might consider reading the text in advance to determine which words to emphasize and where to add emotion. An advance reading also will enable you to convey more meaning when reading aloud in front of students because you yourself know where the story is headed. A common mistake that teachers make in reading aloud to students is neglecting to practice. Simply picking the passage that you want to read for your students is not enough. Pick it and pre-read it—that will let you read it with flair.

Reading is like making music. The notes and rests have different lengths, implicit in both how they are written and how they are interpreted. In the first sentence of this paragraph, for example, the words "making" and "music" run together slightly more than the other words for most readers. Most strong readers would group those words for emphasis and rhythm, making the sentence's meaning shift subtly as a result. As with music, some of the meaning is made visible by punctuation, while other aspects are less obvious. When you read, help students recognize how the music in reading is played by conscious grouping. Seek to model stringing words together in fluid groups—the longer the better. Look, for example, for words in prepositional phrases to stick together, for a drop in the voice and a slight acceleration for a parenthetical (which occur more frequently in nonnarrative nonfiction texts). Also consider identifying especially important words in a passage and emphasizing them. Important words are often identified by italics, capitals, and underlines, but you might also consider other textual aspects to highlight based on either plot or genre. For example, one Shakespearean we know proposes that the best way to read the Bard is to find and focus on contrast words and emphasize the tension between them as you read.

### Show Some Spunk

Modeling expressive reading is one of the best gifts that a parent or teacher can give to his or her children. You need only to compare two classrooms in which two teachers read expressively or dryly, and you immediately see the differences in both student engagement and comprehension. The clip from Rob de Leon's classroom that we referenced earlier is case in point. Modeling expressive and dramatic reading (we call it **Showing Some Spunk**) may involve some risk-taking—especially if you're not inclined to drama. You will not only show kids how to unlock the expressive parts of language but also make it safe for them to take the risk of reading with spirit and enthusiasm when they engage in Control the Game reading.

Showing spunk is equally important whether you are reading *War and Peace, Owl at Home,* "A Summary of the Oxygen Cycle," or the directions to a word problem. In fact, students may have the least developed "ear" for the latter two examples and may therefore get the most out of hearing those read aloud fluently. A particularly important time to Show Some Spunk is at the start of a longer section of oral reading or when starting up again after a break for discussion. Reading the first few sentences yourself models and normalizes expressiveness and helps engage and sustain interest in the text by getting it off to an exciting start. The verve and energy you bring to oral reading will be reflected in your students' oral (and silent) reading through increased fluency and joy for reading.

---

### See It in Action
Watch Taylor Delhagen Show Some Spunk with his high school students in clip 23 at teachlikeachampion.com/yourlibrary.

---

We strongly encourage you to practice Showing Some Spunk in advance. Unless you were a drama major in college, reading with confidence and pizzazz—the kind we see in Taylor Delhagen's clip—can seem quite daunting. One of our favorite bloggers from the United Kingdom, Jo Facer, wrote a piece on how she really hesitated to read aloud with confidence in front of her students. She writes:

> As the years went on, I'd found reading aloud becoming easier—if I'd taught a text before, for example, I would feel more confident and could put more energy into the reading. Yet mere familiarity was not enough. Last year, I decided I needed to do more. Over the course of the summer, I practiced reading aloud daily—poems, short stories, newspaper articles—whatever I happened to be reading at the time. I rehearsed. I improved. In September, with my year 10 class I've written previously about, this exercise was invaluable. With reluctant readers, I found for the first time that I could engage them with the sheer entertainment of me reading. I found myself putting on voices, dramatically pausing, and even *walking around the room at the same time as reading* (and, most impressively I feel, at one point crawling around the room, while simultaneously demonstrating a narrator's slide into madness in "The Yellow Wallpaper").[12]

The practice that Facer describes not only helped her students unlock greater meaning from the text but also made reading more fun for both her and her students. Sure, you can do this with lots of experience—your tenth reading of Hamlet is more likely to come more naturally and with more spunk than your first. But why not expedite the learning for you and your students by practicing it in advance? For some teachers, the dramatic flair may come naturally. But for most of us, it requires advance thought, planning, and practice. This means that you should read in advance with a fluency lens any article, passage, or novel that you are going to read aloud in class. Incorporating these fluency techniques on the fly can be challenging, but being intentional about planning can make a big difference—between a successful lesson and an unsuccessful one, and in helping students unlock both enjoyment and meaning from a text.

## INSTILLING A LOVE OF LITERATURE

The telling of stories probably began before the invention of the wheel. Stories have existed as a centerpiece of every culture on earth since the beginning, in large part because they are such a source of pleasure. People love stories, and hearing them read or told aloud, with all of the drama and suspense and humor invested in them, is a source of joy and fulfillment. Stories have endured because people love to hear them.

This is important to remember, because older students especially often aren't very connected to that feeling of joy. They're just like many of us probably were when we read Shakespeare on the page for the first time. The material may have seemed dry, dull, and incomprehensible. Only when someone brought it to life in a performance did you begin to realize that the plays were funny or terrifying (or both). Reading aloud makes that connection for students—they "get it," often for the first time in their lives. People read not because they have to but because they love to, and reading aloud to students makes this love self-evident. As Jim Trelease says in *The Read-Aloud Handbook*, "Each read-aloud to a child or class, we're giving a commercial for the pleasures of reading."[13] In a world where kids are constantly exposed to commercials for everything under the sun, we need to invest in the campaign for books.

Getting our students to love to read can oftentimes be as simple as choosing a text about which we or our students are passionate, and taking the small risk of showing some of that passion in our reading of it.

If a teacher shows love for (or interest in, or fascination with) the text that he is reading, it is highly likely that his students will, too. Given that books read aloud to students influence their own book choice, it is important that teachers carefully consider their text selection. To instill a love of literature, texts should authentically be favorites of the teacher's, as students can certainly sense insincerity. For most of us, it is not hard to rant and rave about a favorite book, and this passion will come through. Also consider making your Read-Aloud texts available to students in the classroom library. A teacher's favorite book will often become the students' favorite book as well. Although your Read-Aloud book will often be above your students' reading level, at least a portion of your students will even then be able to take it off the shelf to enjoy for themselves. For all students, though, it should be a text that they can access through their listening comprehension skills.

---

### See It in Action

In clip 24 at teachlikeachampion.com/yourlibrary, Maggie Johnson, an eighth-grade reading teacher at Troy Prep Middle School, starts a stretch of Control the Game reading of Harper Lee's *To Kill a Mockingbird* by Showing Some Spunk. In doing so, she models what it looks like to read with the kind of fluency and expression that conveys (and even enhances) meaning. When Maggie calls on Arshe, he reads without much expression. With a hint of challenge in her tone, Maggie then asks for some drama: "You can give me a little more than that …" Arshe rereads with a lot more emotion, and Maggie and her students laugh appreciatively. Even though they're knee-deep in a challenging text, students don't forget to enjoy reading with fluency and expression.

---

Becoming passionate about books and recognizing that reading can bring pleasure are especially vital for older students who haven't experienced success in school. For many students, reading may have been a point of frustration in the past. Helping them see what joy and pleasure reading can bring will unlock a barrier to achievement. AIR and Control the Game are important in giving all students the practice they need to become effective readers, and Read-Aloud is important in giving them a model for what effective reading looks like, as well as instilling a passion for literature so that students want it for themselves.

> ## Approaches to Reading, Reconsidered
>
> Before you're allowed to drive, you have to take driver's ed, drive with an instructor, and then put in a certain number of road miles practicing with an experienced driver. Come to a complete stop. Parallel park. Back up in a straight line. Little by little, the supervision that surrounds a novice driver lets up; once a driver finally passes the road test, she's proven her skills— that she can operate a vehicle skillfully enough to do it on her own, and interact with other drivers safely and courteously. Reading isn't a whole lot different. With proper instruction, modeling, and abundant road miles, students can gain the skills necessary for the accountable, independent reading necessary for success in college— not to mention informed citizenship. In the next chapter, we'll take a look at the different ways teachers can work to build student vocabulary.

## NOTES

1. Bureau of Labor Statistics, "Economic News Release, Table 11: Time Spent in Leisure and Sports Activities for the Civilian Population by Selected Characteristics, 2014 Annual Averages," June 24, 2015, http://www.bls.gov/news.release/atus.t11.htm.

2. Doug Lemov, *Teach Like a Champion* (San Francisco: Jossey-Bass, 2010), 255.

3.  Marilyn Jager Adams, *Beginning to Read: Thinking and Learning about Print* (Cambridge: MIT Press, 1990), 5.

4.  National Center for Education Statistics, *The Nation's Report Card: A First Look: 2013 Mathematics and Reading* (NCES 2014-451) (Washington, D.C.: Institute of Education Sciences, US Department of Education, 2013), http://nces.ed.gov/nationsreportcard/subject/publications/main2013/pdf/2014451.pdf.

5.  Liana Heitin, "Literacy Expert: Weak Readers Lack Fluency, Not Critical Thinking," *Education Week,* May 28, 2015, http://blogs.edweek.org/edweek/curriculum/2015/05/literacy_expert_weak_readers_lack_fluency.html.

6.  Twain said, famously, "The man who does not read good books has no advantage over the man who can't read them."

7.  Jim Trelease, *The Read-Aloud Handbook* (New York: Penguin, 2013), 37.

8.  Isabel L. Beck, Margaret G. McKeown, and Linda Kucan, *Bringing Words to Life: Robust Vocabulary Instruction* (New York: Guilford Press, 2013), 3.

9.  Trelease, *Read-Aloud Handbook.*

10. Donald P. Hayes and Margaret G. Ahrens, "Vocabulary Simplification for Children: A Special Case of 'Motherese'?" *Journal of Child Language* 15, no. 2 (1988): 395–410.

11. Trelease, *Read-Aloud Handbook,* 16.

12. Jo Facer, "Reading Aloud," *Reading All the Books* (blog), January 24, 2015, https://readingallthebooksuk.wordpress.com/2015/01/24/reading-aloud/.

13. Trelease, *Read-Aloud Handbook,* 4.

Chapter **6**

# Vocabulary Instruction: Breadth and Depth

## MODULE 6.1: EXPLICIT AND IMPLICIT VOCABULARY INSTRUCTION COMPARED

Teachers aim to introduce a large number of words, as well as instill deep word knowledge.

## MODULE 6.2: EXPLICIT VOCABULARY INSTRUCTION: THE DAILY WORD ROLLOUT TO ACHIEVE DEEP WORD KNOWLEDGE

Four steps help great teachers teach deep word knowledge.

## MODULE 6.3: IMPLICIT INSTRUCTION: BUILDING VOCABULARY DURING READING

To ensure that students' vocabularies grow in a meaningful way, it is crucial to be intentional about building vocabulary during reading.

## MODULE 6.4: MAINTENANCE AND EXTENSION

Great teachers are thoughtful and intentional about creating and using systems for students to meaningfully revisit vocabulary words.

Chapter **6**

# Vocabulary Instruction: Breadth and Depth

Successful reading relies on a reader's capacity to understand both a large number of words as well as the subtleties and nuances of those words, even when words change their meaning according to the setting. To have a commanding vocabulary is to master both breadth and depth.

Effective vocabulary instruction is one of the greatest challenges facing schools and teachers, in all grades and disciplines. Teachers must prepare students to master both breadth and depth, in production *and* reception of language—in writing, speaking, and reading. Not only that, but in the case of students who are not exposed to a stream of advanced words from an early age, teachers must seek to close a gap of, conservatively, several thousand words. According to E. D. Hirsch Jr., students need to learn forty-three thousand words on average to be on track to graduate from college.[1]

As if that were not daunting enough, the depth of students' knowledge of those words matters as much as the number. Isabel Beck and her colleagues report in their landmark book *Bringing Words to Life* that depth of word knowledge among students is a *better*

251

indicator of long-term success than breadth.[2] Successful students must comprehend the exact nuance of a word that serves as the lynchpin of a sentence or a passage, even though it is impossible to predict which word acts as that lynchpin.

Teaching vocabulary is, in short, a daunting challenge that requires far more strategy than memorizing a few definitions or presuming, erroneously, that we can simply teach students to reliably infer meanings from context. It requires instilling knowledge of a wide variety of words and the nuances of those words, as well as the ability to recognize and react to their constant shape-shifting tendencies.

The first step is to think of vocabulary instruction in two parts: **Explicit Vocabulary Instruction** and **Implicit Vocabulary Instruction**.

Explicit Vocabulary Instruction is the direct teaching of words via discrete lessons or activities. The teacher discusses the meaning of certain words before working with a text in which they appear or, in some cases, regardless of whether students will read them in the immediate future. Words in Explicit Vocabulary Instruction are chosen in advance, presumably because of their importance, utility, or relevance to the content of class. For example, you are reading Kurt Vonnegut's short story "Harrison Bergeron" and start the day by teaching the word *satire* because it will be so useful to discussing the story.

Implicit Vocabulary Instruction is the teaching of words via strategies to be used when unfamiliar words are encountered within a text. It is comprised of the approaches teachers take to increase the likelihood that students will learn new words, or to increase how much knowledge they gain from encountering words they are partially familiar with while reading. The words taught in this type of instruction are determined by the text. You read "assuaged" in the first pages of *To Kill a Mockingbird* for example, and have students pronounce it and briefly define it in the margin.

There is a bit of a debate among educators as to which form of vocabulary instruction teachers should use, with advocates arguing for the benefits or insufficiencies of each. Some argue that reading widely is the best way to learn vocabulary, for example, while others argue for systematic mastery of lists of critical words. We believe they are both necessary—and both insufficient by themselves—so teachers should do both. More to the point, there are critical ways in which most teachers can do both *better*, and this is our key point. Just about every teacher teaches vocabulary, no matter the discipline, but precisely because of its familiarity, teachers tend to teach it the way it has always been taught. Fortunately, relatively minor changes can make vocabulary instruction far more effective across disciplines.

There is a difference between knowing a word generally and knowing it deeply. The latter would involve, for example, mastering its subtleties of use and adapting it to match the context. One of the most common experiences of teaching vocabulary is observing students misapply words and, in so doing, showing that they do not yet truly understand them. A student tries, for example, to use one of her new words and speaks about excerpting a slice of pizza from the pie. She thus tells us that we didn't manage to convey the idea that *excerpt* doesn't mean simply "to take a piece of something," but that it applies in situations where a section of print or visual media is taken from a larger document.

A primary goal of Explicit Vocabulary Instruction is to model for students the depth of knowledge that is involved in mastering words: to own a word is to know not just its definition but its different forms, its multiple meanings, its connotations, and the situations in which it is normally applied. Explicit Vocabulary Instruction models this for students by making a case study out of certain words and their application. Its goal is depth, and it requires studying fewer words better. It is a deep dive into a limited number of words—sometimes just one or two—rather than a cursory introduction or gloss-over of long lists of terms.

This represents a departure from what happens with vocabulary instruction in many classrooms. As Beck, McKeown, and Kucan note, many teachers rely on the "synonym model" for explicit instruction.[3] There is a list of words—perhaps ten at a time. Students memorize an analogue for each: *astute* equals *clever*; *mimic* equals *imitate*.

The problem with this model, Beck et al. note, is that while the meanings of *mimic* and *imitate* overlap a great deal, the subtle differences between the words are in fact what matter most. A student reads the word *mimic* in a story where, say, one character mimics another behind his back. The meaning of the passage hinges on the fact that *mimic* means to imitate in a pejorative and mocking way; it is the implication of mockery that communicates the gist of the passage, in this case the nature of the relationship between the two characters. When we rely too heavily on the synonym model—or even basic definitions alone—we risk allowing our students to miss these subtleties. Knowing words without fully mastering them has a negative effect on students' reading comprehension — to miss the nuances of words is to miss the nuances of texts. Inevitably, we will sometimes have to use synonyms or simplified definitions in teaching, but Explicit Vocabulary Instruction provides an opportunity to go beyond that: to teach words to mastery and to demonstrate that the meanings of words are richer than simple synonyms can express.

The goal of Explicit Vocabulary Instruction, then, is mastery of a word such that students can accurately use it in multiple contexts, flexibly adapt the word into its different forms, and understand the connotation and degree of the word in a text. Part of this goal is not just to master each specific word but also to help students think about all words this way — to learn to expect and therefore see depth and nuance in all words.

While teaching vocabulary deeply, directly, and systematically is critical to developing the kind of word knowledge that supports rigorous textual interpretation and strong literary discourse, it isn't sufficient by itself. Students need to learn *hundreds, perhaps thousands* of new words per year to be ready for college. The limits of classroom time and cognitive processing make it unlikely that Explicit Vocabulary Instruction alone could ever close this gap. Trying to remedy the vocabulary gap by explicitly teaching that many words would likely to take an immense proportion of any teacher's time — and, quite probably, fail to result in long-term, durable word knowledge. Realistically, teachers can hope to teach perhaps two or three hundred words per year through Explicit Vocabulary Instruction. On average, that's one or two words per day. Over thirteen years of school, that's about 2,275 words. But faced with teaching a little over 40,000 words, according to Hirsch's numbers, even ten times that rate wouldn't do the trick. In order to significantly increase the number of words students learn, we need to leverage the power of reading and help students learn more words during reading.

If Explicit Vocabulary Instruction is, roughly, a set of tools to teach words directly, Implicit Vocabulary Instruction is a set of tools designed to increase the rate at which students learn words encountered during reading and absorb them into their functioning vocabularies. Because it happens while a class is reading a text — and therefore also pursuing other objectives — one of the goals of Implicit Vocabulary Instruction is to do this with the least disruption possible.

Two other points are worth clarifying here. First, although broad and extensive reading is critical to developing vocabulary, Implicit Vocabulary Instruction involves specific actions to increase the rate at which words are learned as compared to reading alone. Second, it relies on actions other than using "context clues." Even though students are in fact often able to infer the meaning of some words from context, this does not necessarily

**Figure 6.1** When you teach words explicitly and deeply and you also help students broaden their vocabulary through Implicit Vocabulary Instruction, you help them improve both their depth and their breadth of word knowledge

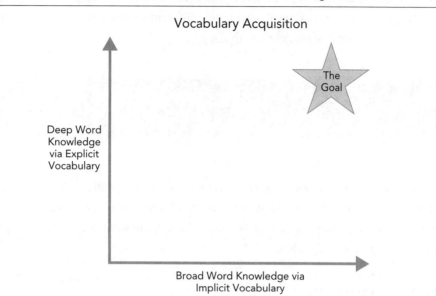

mean that it is a generalizable skill and that students can learn words from context with reliability.

We've tried to capture the relationship of breadth and depth of word knowledge in Figure 6.1. The first goal is to introduce students to a large number of words, especially through wide reading, with Implicit Vocabulary Instruction to reinforce. This is represented by the horizontal arrow. As students learn more words, at least at a basic level the line grows longer.

At the same time, we also seek to instill deep word knowledge, even if with only a smaller number of words at first. This is done through Explicit Vocabulary Instruction, represented by the vertical arrow in Figure 6.1. If you chose just a few words and students mastered them deeply, you would lengthen that line.

Over time, however, a third goal emerges: to increase the proportion of words in students' vocabulary that they know deeply. This goal is represented by the star in Figure 6.1—illustrating that students learn a larger and larger proportion of the words on the *x*-axis at the full depth of the best-known words on the *y*-axis. The idea is that, as students practice and gain experience studying the nuances of how words work, the vertical line "opens up" and encompasses more and more words on the horizontal line.

Students expand their knowledge of word depth and apply it to more and more words, ideally at an increasing rate.

This is all well and good on a theoretical level, but how does it play out in practice? Over the next few modules, we'll look at the different ways teachers can increase both the breadth and depth of student vocabulary.

| MODULE 6.2 | Explicit Vocabulary Instruction: The Daily Word Rollout to Achieve Deep Word Knowledge |
| --- | --- |

Explicit Vocabulary Instruction should take place frequently—daily is common, perhaps even preferred—and should focus on a limited number of words, often even a single word or perhaps a pair of words. It follows, in general, a four-step process, beginning with **word selection**.

## STEP 1: WORD SELECTION

Here's a simple but critically important fact about words, one that we cited in chapter 5 but that bears repeating: the number of different words that occur in printed texts far exceeds the number of words that occur in spoken discourse. Given the opportunity to write, we choose words carefully and precisely. The formality and permanence of the endeavor, not to mention the ease of parsing, cause us to select words more intentionally. We use words we might not consider when speaking. The result is that many of the words critical to understanding written text occur very rarely in spoken language.

Consider the data we referenced earlier from Jim Trelease's *Read-Aloud Handbook*: a typical children's book uses almost 31 rare words per 1,000. That's three times more rare words than adults use when they speak to children (9.3 rare words per 1,000) and also almost twice as many rare words as adults use when speaking *to other adults* (17.3 per 1,000). As students grow older, the rare words premium for written language increases. A book written for an adult audience uses 52.7 rare words per 1,000.[4]

Beyond telling us that it's important for students to read a lot to develop their vocabularies, these statistics tell us that the words that make reading challenging *generally don't occur in spoken language*. Functionally, they are nearly exclusive to written discourse. Therefore, it is critical to focus vocabulary instruction on those words that students won't hear through conversation.

One of the most powerful ideas from *Bringing Words to Life* is that words have differing levels of utility.[5] Beck and her colleagues identify a three-tier hierarchy that is useful when deciding which words deserve "instructional attention." Tier 1 words, they say, are those that are simple and familiar. They occur in general use and are therefore not really worth teaching. Tier 3 words are technical vocabulary that's specific to a particular discipline or subject (for example, *chromosome, thoracic, fiefdom*). For general vocabulary instruction, Tier 3 vocabulary occur too rarely and specifically to have maximum return.

The most useful words to teach, they say, are those in the middle: Tier 2 words. Tier 2 words are highly useful, appear primarily in print, and are likely to appear in multiple contexts or with varying meanings (for example, *chameleon, inflection, disparate*).

We find Beck's framework for choosing words compelling—our teachers use it all the time—but we often see educators cite words that are too simplistic as examples of Tier 1 words, words like *bike, ball,* and *person.* The problem with this kind of conceptualization of Tier 1 words is that it fails to rule out any words that teachers might actually teach in vocabulary lessons. It's more useful to consider examples of words that might commonly be taught but that could be replaced with harder words because they commonly occur in verbal discourse rather than printed text. Words like *imagination, communication,* and *realize,* we argue, are still Tier 1 words. Students are likely to learn them and hear them in everyday discourse. Words like these are perhaps better reinforced via implicit vocabulary methods (which you can read about later in the chapter). Explicit Vocabulary Instruction, then, is more appropriate for more robust words that students are less likely to hear every day.

## Which Tier 3 Words to Teach in Reading and English Classes

A recent visit to Beth Verrilli's senior English class revealed that even twelfth graders aren't too old for a word wall, in this case a word wall reminding them of the Tier 3 technical terms they'd learned so as to talk about literature in the most technical way. It was titled "How Do English Scholars Talk about Literature?" and contained words like *aphorism, catharsis, anaphora, metonymy,* and *synecdoche.* Almost all of the words on the wall would be considered domain-specific, Tier 3 words. It's vital that all teachers prepare

(Continued)

students of all grades to be able to both talk and write about literature with scholarly technical vocabulary specific to literary analysis—in much the same way that a science teacher would prepare his or her students to use scientific vocabulary when conducting experiments.

Because Tier 1 words don't typically pose a problem for even emerging readers, and words limited to specific domains tend to be covered in depth within those domains, reading and English classes, we think, should spend the lion's share of their time on Tier 2 words—the kind of words readers will grow into, the kind they'll use in college and in life.

Because a deeper dive into words implies a greater time commitment, word choice becomes even more important when selecting which Tier 2 words to explicitly teach. Here are some types of words to consider for Explicit Vocabulary Instruction:

- Words that appear in a text you are reading, that students may not know, and that are critical to understanding it.

- Words that relate to the content or themes of the novel or other content being taught. For example, when reading *Esperanza Rising,* you might consider teaching the word *exploit.* Although the word does not appear in the novel, students might use this word to describe the treatment of Esperanza and the other child migrant workers.

- Words that relate to other vocabulary words that can be compared, contrasted, or used as a group (for example, *tyranny* and *oppression; embellish* and *exaggerate; glance, gaze,* and *gawk*).

- Words that enable students to upgrade their word choice, replacing common words used in a book discussion or literary analysis. For the word *good,* for example, they might use *acceptable, favorable, satisfactory,* or *pleasing*; for the word *bad,* they could instead use *evil, wicked, atrocious, dreadful,* or *inadequate.*

## STEP 2: ACCURATE AND STUDENT-FRIENDLY DEFINITION

Once you've selected a word (or perhaps several, depending on the grade level), provide students with a definition that is both simple and clear. It should not contain jargon or phrases that students are unlikely to understand. For example, telling students that the definition of *banal* is "devoid of freshness or originality" may not be as helpful as rewriting it slightly to "lacking in originality"—still accurate, but much more digestible for students. Although ensuring that a definition is **student-friendly** is important, it's just as important that a definition remain as accurate as possible (see the "Pitfalls to Avoid When Writing Student-Friendly Definitions" box).

When a word has multiple definitions, start with the one that is most applicable in the context of your reading and/or the one that will be most frequently used in other contexts (for example, "*Serene* describes a situation or setting that is quiet and calm"). A cautionary note: crafting definitions that are both accurate and student friendly is one of the most challenging and overlooked aspects of vocabulary instruction, so please don't jump over this step hastily!

## See It in Action

Watch Akilah Bond, Colleen Driggs, and Gillian Cartwright demonstrate the importance of accurate and student-friendly definitions in clip 25 at teachlikeachamption.com/yourlibrary. As they introduce the words *sigh*, *scarce*, *eradicate*, and *counteract*, each simple moment illustrates the importance of carefully planned and crafted student-friendly definitions.

Many teachers commonly seek to "arrive" at a definition as a last step in their vocabulary instruction. For them, teaching a new word means asking, "Who can tell me what *destitute* means?" and having students try to infer the meaning from there. To be more rigorous, vocabulary instruction should, in most cases, *begin* with an accurate definition, focusing instead on application (Figure 6.2).

Using words with richness and precision is a rigorous form of problem solving. But the problem solving can begin only once students know a word's basic meaning. If instruction begins before students have a clear definition, they spend their time guessing at its meaning. Time spent guessing a word's meaning is far less productive than time spent using and applying the word's meaning in increasingly complex situations. For example, consider whether it is more rigorous to have students answer the question "What do you think *clandestine* might mean?" or instead to answer "How is *clandestine* similar to and different from *surreptitious*?" or "How could camouflage help you do something in a *clandestine* manner? How could you use something that was 'blaring' to do something in a *clandestine* manner?"

**Figure 6.2** Two diagrams showing less rigorous and more rigorous vocabulary instruction

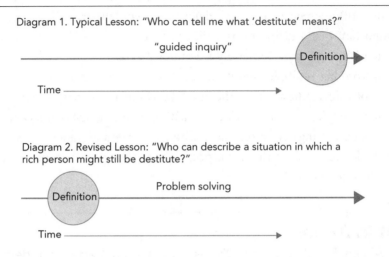

Diagram 1. Typical Lesson: "Who can tell me what 'destitute' means?"

"guided inquiry"

Definition

Time

Diagram 2. Revised Lesson: "Who can describe a situation in which a rich person might still be destitute?"

Definition

Problem solving

Time

## Pitfalls to Avoid When Writing Student-Friendly Definitions

Writing a simple, clear, and accurate definition is a vital part of planning for your vocabulary lesson. Unfortunately, many great vocabulary lessons are undercut by a poor-quality definition. Here are some common pitfalls to avoid when writing your definition:

### Oversimplification

We often give students definitions that don't accurately capture the full meaning of a word because we focus on making it simple or student friendly. For example, a teacher might commonly define the word *heed* as "to listen," but to *heed* implies that one follows the guidance or request of some authority. A more appropriate definition would be "to listen and obey."

### Inaccuracy

Teachers might give a definition that makes sense as a substitute for the vocabulary word as it is used in a given context but that does not reflect the actual meaning of word. For example, a teacher reading with her class came across the following sentence: "The mother tried to *insinuate* that the teachers were to blame for her daughter's problems, but the heroic principal told her politely that he would not tolerate this type of rudeness toward his hard-working staff." The teacher defined the word *insinuate* as "a verb meaning to suggest"—a fitting definition for the context. However, this definition could lead to misunderstanding, as illustrated in this sentence: "I'm going to *insinuate* that you can improve your grades by coming in on Saturday."

## Size

The definition has too many parts to be useful or accessible for students. For example, a teacher might define *puny* as "of lesser size, strength, or significance; appearing weak, especially in stature."

## Inaccessibility

The definition includes words that students don't already know, or it is overly abstract. For example, the dictionary definition for *privilege* is "a right, immunity, or benefit only enjoyed by a person beyond the advantages of most." Better to define it as "a benefit given to a person or group of people"—simpler, yet still accurate.

## Wrong tense or part of speech

The definition is in a different tense or part of speech than the word. For example, a teacher defines *sporadic* as "occasionally." The word is an adjective, but the definition is for the adverb form of the word. Better to define it as "occurring occasionally."

Once you have drafted an accurate, student-friendly definition, it's also important to think about how to make it "sticky." In *Made to Stick,* Chip and Dan Heath define ideas that stick as those that "are understood and remembered, and have a lasting impact"[6]—certainly something we want for the vocabulary words we teach. Making words stick for students increases the likelihood that the word enters their working memory, as well as their speech and writing. Here are a few tricks to make words stick.

## Model Use

An important part of giving students a clear and accessible definition is to model how the word can be used in a sentence. Modeling provides a familiar context for students. For example, "*Tame* means to train a wild animal. Circus trainers would tame wild elephants before they put them in a show so that they could perform without hurting anyone." Examples provide important context and start to model for students how the word might be used in multiple ways.

## Add a Visual

Using a visual image for students to associate with a new word can help them remember not just the word but also nuances of its depth and context of use. Consider using pictures that demonstrate a literal illustration of the word (for example, "What in this picture establishes a tone of *serenity*?" or "I chose this picture as an example of *serenity*. In it you can see a woman meditating. She's sitting with her eyes closed thinking deeply. What else about this picture shows *serenity*?") or that serve as a backdrop for a memorable story that includes the word (for example, a photograph of a squirrel eating out of a person's hand to illustrate the word *tame*). You can use the picture both to remind students of the word's meaning and as a cue encouraging them to apply it. Posting vocabulary words along with their visuals is a useful reminder to students and will increase the likelihood that they use the words in their writing.

## Act It Out

You can also have students act out a word (for example, "Show me what you would look like if you were *furious*" or "Who can *swagger* across the room?") or have students develop gestures to help them remember words. This is useful not only for making the definition sticky and accessible but also for encouraging play with words. You can then help students recall the word by giving them the gesture.

# STEP 3: PARAMETERS OF USE

The first time you tried to use a hammer, you might have bent a nail or two by striking it not quite squarely. Or perhaps you hit your thumb. Using new vocabulary can be similar. What teacher hasn't asked a student to use a new word, only to see him use it in an awkward and erroneous manner: "I *exterminated* the clothes from my bedroom floor," "The lion crept *clandestine* through the tall grass"?

As when one is using any new tool for the first time, it helps to have some guidance. When those new tools are vocabulary words, students need clear and specific guidance about how to accurately use and apply these new additions to their proverbial toolkit. Building good habits from the outset is easier than breaking bad ones. Four **parameters of use**—common use, word partners, forms and prefixes, and similar/different words—can help students drive straight nails.

## Common Use

It usually helps to start with an explanation of how a word is commonly used. You might say, for instance, "*Eradicate* is often used to describe an effort to completely eliminate something harmful. For example, a doctor might spend years trying to eradicate polio," or "You would talk about an animal being *tame*, but not really a person. To do so would imply something animal-like about the person." Explaining common use (and asking students to practice it) allows students to have better access to and command of new words.

## Word Partners

Along with explaining a word's most common use, it's helpful to describe words that often appear with—either preceding or following—the new vocabulary word you are teaching. Be sure to introduce the kind of partner words—often prepositions—without which a word isn't accurately used ("*Foist* is a verb, and people often pair it with the word *upon*"). Word partners help ensure that students appropriately use new words in speech and in their writing.

## Forms and Prefixes

Be explicit about the alternate forms a word might take, providing examples of how and when to change its part of speech. Be relentless when asking the same of your students in their practice. (For example, "*Serene* is an adjective that describes a calm, quiet situation. You might also see the word *serenity*, which is the noun form. It's the thing. I seek it. I seek *serenity* when I go to church or when I want peace and calm and quiet.") Knowing the variety of forms a word can take is helpful not only in ensuring proper usage but also in supporting both depth and breadth of vocabulary development. If a student knows the different forms that *occupy* can take, for example (*occupation, occupied, occupies, unoccupied, preoccupied*, and so on), and how those different forms may be used in different contexts, she will have better command of the word and will have discretely increased the number of words in her vocabulary. Understanding the change that adding a prefix can make increases the likelihood that a student will be able to recognize, define, and understand multiple forms of the word in a text.

### Similar To/Different From

Help students understand the shades of meaning words can have by explaining (or asking students to explain once they know the definition) how a word is similar to and different from the new vocabulary word. For these purposes, choose a similar word and intentionally describe the similarities and differences. (For example, "*Serene* is similar to *quiet* because *serene* things are always quiet, but quiet things aren't always *serene*. You could be quiet and tense or worried or angry and some people feel *serene* even if there's noise around them.")

In many cases, the discussion of the relationship between these two words is the perfect time to highlight the differing degrees of the meaning of words. For example, a person who is feeling *glum* is not experiencing as strong an emotion as someone who is feeling *sorrowful*. If you opt to use similar words to support the rollout of your vocab word of choice, consider the following:

- The similar word should be a word that students are already familiar with, but ideally one with depth and rigor.

- The two words may share a definition at the most basic level (for example, *gaze* and *glance* are both types of looks).

- The similar word may have the same basic meaning but differ in degree (for example, *glum* is not as strong as *dejected*).

- Plan how to clearly articulate what the two words have in common, but also why they should not be used interchangeably (the more concisely you can explain this, the better).

- Ideally, the similar word will be the same part of speech as your vocabulary word.

Carefully describing a new vocabulary word with the four parameters of use helps students begin to grasp and understanding new words deeply—and, ideally, develop a passion for learning them.

## Beware the Synonym Model

Of course, introducing similar words alongside your chosen vocabulary word is different from the "synonym model" of instruction—a model in which words are introduced as a pair of words having the same definition. Introducing word pairs as synonyms can oversimplify their precise definitions, inhibit accurate application, and hinder reading comprehension. Beck and her colleagues describe the flaws in the synonym model of teaching vocabulary, saying, "Although handy for providing a quick anchor point for a word, [the synonym approach] is a bankrupt way to teach word meaning. Building an understanding of language comes through developing knowledge of both the similarities and the differences among words and the precise roles they can play."* In this light, similar words should be used as a way to build both breadth and depth—not as a replacement for deep teaching.

*Isabel L. Beck, Margaret G. McKeown, and Linda Kucan, *Bringing Words to Life: Robust Vocabulary Instruction* (New York: Guilford Press, 2013).

## STEP 4: ACTIVE PRACTICE

The last step in any successful vocab lesson—**active practice**—is the most important. As Beck et al. discuss, we learn words by using them and seeing them, over and over, in different settings. Vocabulary instruction becomes most rigorous when it puts students in situations where they must apply their nascent knowledge of a word in challenging ways, or even problem-solve ways to use words in new settings. Further, as Brown, Roediger, and McDaniel point out in *Make It Stick: The Science of Successful Learning*, rigorous recall—remembering and problem solving at the same time—builds strong *and lasting* memory.[7] Doubly so when active practice causes students to say and hear a word—and its correct pronunciation—multiple times. Triply so when it's intellectually challenging.

At our vocabulary workshops, we frequently ask participants how many times they think students need to say, hear, or read a word before it enters their functional vocabulary. The answers we get have ranged from as low as four times to as many as twenty-five times. Because of a wide number of variables (for example, interest in the word, student absorption rate for a particular topic, variability across words and students), there isn't really a way of knowing *exactly* how many times a student needs to use a word before he remembers it forever. Even so, we know that the answer is definitely not one time. To better ensure that a vocab word will be remembered and used in the future, give students a myriad of quick exposures after introducing it. For each Explicit Vocabulary lesson, plan five to seven quick questions (both verbal and written) that provide students with opportunities to interact with the word. It's not simply about exposure. Active practice should give students opportunities to practice mastering both meaning and usage.

## Active Practice to Master Meaning

Mastering meaning involves students using a word to illustrate its degree of meaning with fluidity, expertise, and a depth of understanding. There are four different ways you can ask students to practice mastering meaning, both verbally and in writing. You can ask students:

1.  When a word would (and would not) apply: "Would it be accurate to say that Aunt Alexandra is acting like a *tyrant* in this scene? Explain."

2.  To combine multiple new words: "Could a *tyrant* ever be *humble*? Tell me why or why not."

3.  To narrate the story: "Can a group ever exert *tyranny* over another group? How? Explain how a group of people in *To Kill a Mockingbird* make decisions that are *tyrannical*."

4.  To define a change: "How is it different to state that Aunt Alexandra is being *tyrannical* as opposed to, say, *bossy*?"

Many teachers tend to have consistent types of questions and prompts for their students (for vocabulary and otherwise), so this list is helpful in starting to expand your repertoire in planning active practice questions. When we shared (and practiced!) these questions with teachers and leaders in a recent workshop, several teachers gave the feedback that this variety of questions has not only improved students' mastery of meaning but has also made vocabulary instruction more interesting and engaging for them as teachers.

## Active Practice to Master Usage

Asking students to practice accurately helps prevent misapplication of words. To build positive new habits (and avoid the need to unlearn bad ones), it's a good idea to have students practice a variety of uses. There are two ways to do this:

1.  Change the form: "In its adjective form, we would say '*tyrannical*.' Would Atticus agree that Aunt Alexandra is *tyrannical*?"

2. Create a sentence with the word and/or other parameters: "Write a sentence in which you describe Aunt Alexandra looking '*obliquely*' at Scout. Be sure to describe what Scout has done to earn such a glance."

It's quite a common practice to ask students to create sentences with new words. Using additional parameters adds rigor and helps ensure that students are learning to use a word correctly.

## Three Keys to Active Practice

When practicing, be sure that students are accurately applying the word. It is not uncommon for an eager student to lose the meaning of a word in her earnest attempts to apply it wherever the definition seems to fit. Whether it's to master meaning or usage, there are three important keys to getting the most out of active practice.

### Say the Word

The first key is to ensure that students actually use the new word in their answers (you would be surprised by how often we forget this!). Instead of using a new word, students will often describe it. For example, if a teacher asks a student to describe a time when he feels *sentimental*, the student might answer, "when I look at photo albums of my baby brother when he was little." That may demonstrate an understanding of the word's meaning, but unless the teacher urges the student to use the word in his sentence—"Looking at photo albums of my baby brother makes me feel *sentimental*"—the student doesn't actually practice using the word, and isn't as likely to be able to use it again.

### Push for Precision

The second key to active practice is ensuring that student answers illustrate their understanding of the word. When asked to use the word *detest*, for example, we often hear students say something like "I *detest* broccoli." Without further explanation, it's not clear whether they truly know what it means to *detest*. In this case, push students a bit further to expand their sentences to illustrate the meaning of the word, as in "I *detest* broccoli because it's bitter."

To ensure that students have to rigorously apply a word and its definition, avoid obvious or mundane questions. Using simple fill-in-the-blank questions or asking questions that require students only to use the word to describe their own experiences can have two negative outcomes. First, the degree of the word may not match the context or shade of meaning (for example, "I was *irate* when my sister got ice cream before I did") because students have grown accustomed to a simple fill-in-the blank formula. Second, students may generate a surface level of understanding of a word ("I *adore* my teddy bear") without understanding its deeper meanings or connotations. To avoid these outcomes, provide prompts that support students' precise use of the word (for example, "Write a sentence about why a mouse would likely *despise* a snake" rather than "Write a sentence using *despise*") or that require combining similar words with slightly different meanings (for example, "Write a sentence in which you describe something you dislike and something you *detest*."). Asking rigorous application questions increases the quality of student practice, as well as deepens their understanding of the word and its definition.

### Make It Right

The final key is for students to practice using different forms of the word—correctly. It is essential to consistently correct inaccurate parts of speech or tenses. Do not accept, for example, "The pond was *scarce* of water." If we accept incorrect forms of new vocabulary words during practice, then students will most assuredly make those mistakes in their writing and beyond the classroom.

The three keys of active practice can support teachers in asking students to rigorously apply their burgeoning vocabulary, and they are useful in giving feedback to students on their practice as they use new words and apply their meanings in a variety of contexts.

## EXPLICIT VOCABULARY INSTRUCTION ROLLOUT SEQUENCE

The order you choose to teach the different components of a vocabulary rollout can be adapted based on the word(s) of the day. For certain words, you may find yourself omitting one or more of the components. It is important, however, to choose a basic sequence and use it consistently. The predictability of the format of your daily vocabulary rollout will both maximize your instructional time and increase student ownership. You'll spend less time explaining what to do and how to do it. Habits lead to efficiency and, in this case, optimizing the focus on studying words. One of the dangers of teaching Explicit Vocabulary in this way is that the lesson runs too long, meaning there is less time left for whatever other reading instruction you might have planned. Teachers who are especially efficient with their time avoid this by carefully planning their

Explicit Vocabulary rollout scripts. In order to make the most efficient use of your time, plan your rollout script so that it includes several key components. You might consider practicing this rollout in advance and timing yourself, ideally keeping the rollout within six to nine minutes and spending as much time as possible in active practice:

1. Define the word and give its part of speech (30 seconds to 1 minute).

2. Give a familiar example (30 seconds to 1 minute).

3. Give a picture/and or a motion (30 seconds to 1 minute).

4. Describe parameters of use (common use, word partners, other forms, similar to/different from) (1–2 minutes).

5. Engage in active practice: six to eight practice questions in which students use the word both verbally and in writing (4 minutes).

To see a completed example of a rollout, you will find one possible rollout script for the word *gullible* in the appendix (and on teachlikeachampion.com).

---

## Another Pathway to Breadth and Depth: Roots and Affixes

Teaching students about roots, prefixes, and affixes is another important way to quickly increase the quantity of student vocabulary. Once students have a handle on a relatively small number of roots and affixes, they have significantly boosted their ability to accurately infer meanings of new words, as well as to deeply understand words. (Anyone who has taken Latin can likely attest to the impact it had on their vocabulary development.) Knowing roots and affixes also helps students grow attentive to a word's etymology and build a breadth of word knowledge. Here are some action steps for exposing students to roots and affixes—and to do so in a way that helps build vocabulary as well as attentiveness to and passion for words:

Provide an example. Give a word that includes a given root or affix. Provide the definition so that students can see how the word parts work together in the definition. For example, "Notice that the word *congregate*, meaning 'to come together,' has the root *greg*, which means 'flock or herd.'"

*(Continued)*

*(Continued)*

Use as part of active practice. Ask students to identify roots or affixes and describe how they relate to meaning. For example, "Why is the root *ped-* in the word *pedestrian*?" "What might *monolith* and *lithograph* have to do with a stone?"

Consider memorization. Although we don't encourage rote memorization as a way to build a depth of vocabulary knowledge, when it comes to roots, affixes, and prefixes, it can be useful to introduce several of these at a time for memorization and provide opportunities for spiraled review.

Use sensitivity analysis. Show students how affixes can be shuffled to make new words. For example, "If we replace *in* with *con* in the word *incur*, the word becomes *concur*, meaning 'to agree with.'"

Use in place of misdirective context clues. When contexts are misdirective (description to come later), support students in determining the meaning of an unknown word based on known roots and affixes. A robust grasp of roots, prefixes, and affixes is beneficial as students learn to independently investigate the meanings of unknown words.

Model etymology. Ask students to identify other words containing a root. For example, "*Telepathy* is sending or reading thoughts and feelings from far away. What other *tele-* words have 'far away' in their meaning?"

Over the last several pages, we've taken a deep dive into teaching depth of vocabulary knowledge explicitly. In the next module, we turn our attention to the different ways teachers can work to expand the breadth of student vocabulary through reading.

| MODULE 6.3 | Implicit Instruction: Building Vocabulary During Reading |
|---|---|

As useful as teaching students to understand the depth of word knowledge is, the importance of teaching and reinforcing vocabulary *during reading* cannot be ignored.

In *The Knowledge Deficit,* Hirsch argues that most of our vocabulary acquisition actually occurs indirectly—through reading, listening, and processing text and oral language.[8] Therefore, in addition to explicitly teaching a few words daily with depth and subtlety, teachers also have to address and reinforce **Implicit Vocabulary**, words that appear over the course of reading. Implicit Vocabulary Instruction helps maximize the likelihood that students will recognize and remember a word they encounter during reading—and increasingly take something away from each exposure. Some words students will learn right away when they read them. Some words they may not learn until many, many exposures later. Fostering attentiveness to those words can be a big help.

To ensure that students make sufficient gains in the number of words they learn per year, it is crucial to be intentional about building vocabulary during reading—on top of the roughly ten minutes spent per day in an explicit deep dive into new vocabulary. The goals of Implicit Vocabulary Instruction are threefold: to maximize the absorption rate of new words by cultivating attentiveness to unknown vocabulary words encountered during reading, to harness the Matthew Effect (discussed in chapter 3, "Reading Nonfiction") by increasing background knowledge, and to increase students' comprehension of the text. Reading experts agree that students need to know roughly 90 to 95 percent of a text's vocabulary words in order to truly comprehend a text.[9] As we increasingly expose our students to more complex texts with more complex vocabulary, Implicit Vocabulary Instruction becomes that much more important.

## PLANNING AND PRIORITIZING WORDS FOR IMPLICIT VOCABULARY INSTRUCTION

As with most teaching tasks, doing a little bit of planning will help you maximize efficiency when it comes to Implicit Vocabulary Instruction. Mark up the section of text you're planning to read; circle all of the words you anticipate to be challenging for your students. Then prioritize those words. Ask yourself:

- Which words deserve the most attention, either because they're crucial to understanding of the text or related to key ideas in the story?

- Which words are students likely to see again, either in the story or elsewhere?

- Which words are really Tier 3 words—words that students are unlikely to encounter again outside the context of the text?

- Where does the word fall with respect to other questions I'm planning to stop reading to ask?

- How quickly will I be able to implicitly teach this word and then return to the text?

Thinking through your answers to these questions (and others) can help you decide which words to address implicitly, and how you'll respond to those words during reading. Once you have planned and prioritized the words you want to teach, it's time to decide *how* you want to teach them — in a way that makes their meaning stick (in some cases) and also supports comprehension by minimizing the disruption to the narrative (in others).

In response to challenging words in student reading, teachers can take four different approaches — all of which can be implemented in different combinations. We discuss them here in order of least in depth/least time spent to the most in depth/most time spent.

## Selectively Neglect

As much as a part of us would love to teach students every word, there are times when it makes sense to simply ignore a word. Perhaps it is too obscure, archaic, or domain-specific to be worth your time. Or perhaps stopping to teach the word would disrupt the narrative at a crucial moment, or there might simply be too many other higher-leverage words to address. After all, if you taught every single word you came across while reading, you might never get to discussing the reason you were reading it in the first place!

Teachers have to selectively neglect a certain percentage of difficult words they encounter, deliberately ignoring them in favor of other words or other teaching goals. For example, when reading *Lord of the Flies* with his students, a teacher might choose to invest in *tirade* and *tumult* via explicit instruction, briefly reinforce *hiatus, tacit,* and *malevolently* via implicit strategies we'll discuss in a moment, and ignore *chorister* and *vicissitudes*. Perhaps *chorister* seems unlikely to appear in other texts, and *vicissitudes* is less useful in talking about the text than *malevolently*. Though these are hard choices, we simply cannot teach every new vocabulary word we encounter, especially when reading complex texts. So a part of reading is choosing when and which words to ignore.

Sometimes fast-forwarding past a word requires a bit more than just ignoring it. For instance, we recently observed Eric Snider of Achievement First Bushwick reading the Ray Bradbury story "Dark They Were, and Golden-Eyed" with his seventh graders. In the midst of a key passage, they came upon a description of a house with "geraniums" outside. *Geraniums* was a word suitable for neglect in this instance; it was not critical to the story, and stopping would have distracted students from other key discussion points. However, not knowing even what a geranium was might have distracted students as much as pausing to define it, so Eric briefly categorized the word for students: "That's a type of flower; keep going." This categorization in lieu of a definition ("a common garden plant with red or white flowers") can allow students to engage the story without being distracted by too much information or too little. It's another way of selectively neglecting a word—giving enough of a gloss of the word to briefly support comprehension without giving a full definition.

You might do something similar with an allusion, like the one Doug came across reading *My Side of the Mountain* with his seven-year-old daughter. A sentence described the forest as being as crowded with animals "as Coney Island." Although *Coney Island* isn't a vocabulary word necessarily, he decided to channel Eric Snider and used a similar approach: "That's the name of an amusement park that would have been really busy," he said, and they picked up reading. Of course, if the details of the allusion had more significance or symbolic meaning in the text, it would be important to describe it with more accuracy or in more depth. Erica did something similar with her son when they encountered the word *parchment* in reading the Magic Treehouse series. Instead of giving a more involved definition of *parchment* as being made from the skin of an animal, she simply gave it a gloss: "it's paper that they used in the medieval times," and they were back in the text. The idea of a fast categorization can be a useful middle ground between completely ignoring a word and giving the complete definition.

## Pronounce

Not all words require a definition during reading. Either it may be obvious from directive context clues, or taking time to define it would be a distraction. In other cases, you might simply want to reinforce decoding; you might think that once students hear the correct pronunciation, they'll recognize the word. In these cases, a quick reinforcement of pronunciation is sufficient. Having individual students (or perhaps the whole class) pronounce a word is useful, especially when you notice students struggling to decode it.

It's important to note, however, that students very frequently mispronounce words, even in copying your model. You might need to say the word multiple times in order to stress accuracy and build fluency. The goal is to make sure that every student practices; they get it right by listening and annunciating carefully, even if that means multiple tries.

# Using Context Clues

Good readers frequently use context clues either to (1) learn a word as they encounter it or, at least, (2) discern enough about a word to prevent it from interfering with their comprehension of a passage. Despite the utility of context clues, however, simply instructing students to use them to figure out the meaning of an unknown word can be a useless exercise.

In *Bringing Words to Life,* Isabel Beck and her colleagues remind us that an author's intent when writing is not to provide the meaning of words. Rather, it is to effectively use words to entertain, persuade, or inform their readers. Beck and her coauthors identify four different types of context, only one of which is useful enough to effectively determine the meaning of a word (appropriately labeled "directive context"). The other contexts are either "misdirective," which would cause a reader to infer an inaccurate definition, or "nondirective," in that they don't provide any information to indicate the meaning of a word. The context could also be too general to be useful in determining the appropriate definition.*

Because the context surrounding a given word is often misleading at worst and unhelpful at best, avoid using context clues as the sole way of teaching vocabulary during reading. If you find a new word that is supported by its context, by all means point that out. For the most part, context clues do not reliably determine meaning; that said, we recognize that using context clues is a skill often required of our students.

In order to maximize students' practice using context clues, select words with a specific, directive context surrounded by other words students know. Doing so will help students arrive at the correct definition of the word. Taking advantage of segments of the text with directive context for a Tier 2 word is the best way both to set students up for successful practice and to support their growing vocabulary. Reading from the novel or text you are studying (or have studied) is a more effective and authentic way of practicing to use context clues than using isolated paragraphs or sentences.

In addition, choose your spots wisely. Help students learn to unpack syntax. The structure of the sentence often lets you know whether two ideas in a sentence cooperate or disagree. You might help students unpack syntax by asking questions like "Does the syntax of the sentence give me a clue?" (For example, "He was typically well behaved, *but* today he was acting mischievously.")

You can also support students in using context clues by using the meaning of the sentence or paragraph that contains the word ("What is the main idea of the paragraph that this word is in?" "Does the meaning of the word you have given me make sense in relation to the main idea?") And, finally, calling attention to the word's etymology by asking questions like "Does the word have a positive or negative connotation?" or "Are there any root words, prefixes, or suffixes that we recognize that can help us determine the definition?" can help students chip away at barriers to understanding.

*Isabel L. Beck, Margaret G. McKeown, and Linda Kucan, *Bringing Words to Life: Robust Vocabulary Instruction* (New York: Guilford Press, 2013).

## Drop in a Definition

Some words are crucial for student comprehension of the text, but aren't really worthy of (or you may not have enough time for) further application. Some words are embedded in text with misleading or misdirective context clues, or are related to other Tier 2 vocabulary that you've taught. For these kinds of words, it's often helpful to "drop in" a definition—that is, to plan a short, student-friendly definition (six or seven words or fewer, ideally) to provide when you encounter the word. For example, when encountering the word *partition* for the first time, you might say, "a partition is a divider between two spaces."

Because time in the classroom is finite—and because time away from reading can often distract students from the story at hand—follow-up beyond the definition should be minimal when you are simply defining a word. That said, you can briefly help dropped-in definitions stick with a few useful approaches, which we describe here.

### Margin Note

The act of writing down a simple margin note for a word makes it more likely that students will remember both the word and its definition. For words that you think are worthy of more attention than just hearing the definition, have students write ("jot") down their definitions in the margin of the text at hand. You would say, for example, "A *partition* is a divider between two spaces. Circle *partition* and write 'divider' in the margin." Initially, you may need to model what students' margin notes should look like before simply directing them to write a definition in the margin (circling the word, drawing a small arrow to the word, positioning the definition, and so on).

## See It in Action

Watch Tondra Collins in clip 26 at teachlikeachampion.com/yourlibrary. Tondra and her students are reading *Twelve Angry Men* by Reginald Rose. When a student encounters (and struggles to decode) the word *unanimous*, Tondra has students circle it and create a stem to the margin note, and asks them to write the definition ("in complete agreement") in the margin. She then asks a brief practice question: "Who do you think the judge is talking to when he says that 'your decision must be *unanimous*'?" The entire moment takes one minute and eight seconds, yet she artfully supports students' decoding, comprehension, and vocabulary development, all with an expert execution of Implicit Vocabulary Instruction.

It's important to plan a short, kid-friendly definition that students can quickly jot down without interrupting the flow of the story. A margin-note definition can just serve as a "gloss" (a shortened version of the definition, used for margin notes) on the more complete definition you give to students. Students can later access this definition for future in-class or homework assignments.

### Call and Response

Another technique you might use to further cement the meaning of a particular word is Call and Response. For example:

Teacher:  A partition is a divider between to spaces. I say "partition"; you say "divider." Partition!

Students:  Divider!

Teacher:  Divider!

Students:  Partition!

## See It in Action

Watch Nikki Frame (reading *A Single Shard* by Linda Sue Park) and Patrick Pastore (reading *Number the Stars* by Lois Lowry) in clip 27 at teachlikeachampion.com/yourlibrary. In both quick clips, Nikki and Patrick briefly drop in a definition to better support students' understanding of the text, and then they quickly return to reading. You'll notice in both of these clips, as we saw in Tondra's clip, that teachers often drop in definitions in response to students' making decoding errors. Although these decoding errors can be a signal that students don't know the word, it's also possible that as soon as they hear the word spoken aloud, it becomes immediately recognizable to them; both of these possibilities are addressed by strong Implicit Vocabulary Instruction.

### Drop in a Picture

For certain words (especially nouns), the best approach might be to show the definition using a picture. When seeing an example of the word is helpful (and perhaps necessary) for understanding its definition, you might introduce the picture, provide a simple definition, and post the picture in your classroom for future reference. This can be far more efficient than trying to give a definition/description of something students may never have seen before (*cistern*, *paddock*, *wharf*, *spectacles*, and so on), especially when a description would not carry much meaning.

## See It in Action

Watch as Jamie Davidson reads *Boy* by Roald Dahl with her students in clip 28 at teachlikeachampion.com/yourlibrary. She implicitly addresses three words in the short selection of text. She has students circle the words *reigned* and *immense* and jot definitions in the margin. She has planned to use a picture for the word *scalpel* by projecting a photograph of a scalpel on the overhead—a beautiful and extremely efficient way to describe the word, given the complexity of trying to do so verbally.

## Define and Practice

For the most important three or four words in a passage, plan short sequences of applications to allow students to practice after you've provided a definition. Prepare in advance a quick vocabulary script to use when you encounter the word, including a brief review of the definition and follow-up questions for practice and application. One of the most important parts of application is that students encounter the word multiple times through questioning. Here's an example:

Teacher: What did we say a partition does to two spaces, Carlos?

Carlos: It divides it.

Teacher: Good, but can you use the word *partition* in your sentence?

Carlos: A *partition* divides two spaces.

Teacher: Good. What's the partition dividing here, Sarah?

Sarah: The partition divides the cabin where Edmund and Caspian sleep from the rest of the ship.

Teacher: Good. Who can tell me what this partition probably looked like, Jasmine?

Jasmine: The partition was probably made of wood.

Teacher: OK — based on the details in the text, how did this partition probably look, Jerome?

Jerome: The partition was probably old and moldy because the author says the cabin behind it wasn't very nice.

Teacher: Good. Let's get back to reading.

Although this might sound like the ideal action for all unknown words encountered in a text, there's rarely time to do this for more than the most important three or four words each day (depending on the length of the reading and instructional block).

---

## See It in Action

Watch Maura Faulkner's fifth-grade classroom in clip 29 at teachlikea champion.com/yourlibrary. While reading *Number the Stars* by Lois Lowry, Maura has her students circle the word *lanky* and briefly describes it as "tall and thin." She immediately asks students to repeat the definition back to her. Then she asks an application question within the context of the novel: "Tell me who is tall and thin? Who is lanky in the text?" and "Find me one more piece of evidence that shows that Annemarie is lanky. When you share out, I want you to say 'I know Annemarie is lanky because ...'"

---

The key to using each approach is to make sure that it's efficient, so that you can return to reading the text as quickly as possible. When you drive, you don't stop at *every* scenic vista or *every* rest stop. If you did, you'd never get anywhere. By a similar token, you don't want vocabulary instruction to interfere with the road miles students are getting each day. Once you've decided how you'll reinforce each word, it's important to carefully plan your student-friendly definitions (in much the same way you do for Explicit Vocabulary Instruction, though more succinctly) for all of the words that you have decided to define, and create application scripts for all the words that are worthy of some practice.

## See It in Action

Watch clip 30 at teachlikeachampion.com/yourlibrary, as Erica Lim and her students encounter the word *sovereignty* in their reading of an excerpt on the city of Constantinople from *The Itinerary of Benjamin of Tudela* by Benjamin of Tudela. She has students "box" the word and pronounce it. Then she defines it and gives an example: "The empire was a *sovereign* nation because they had their own independence from other empires during the time." She then asks several practice questions in which students have to apply the meaning of the word. When students share out, she pushes them to use the word *sovereign* in their answers. She pushes it a bit further, asking students to identify nonexamples of the word *sovereign*. All of this practice takes about three minutes, yet students have several opportunities to use, hear, and apply the word and its meaning.

## CHOOSING WHETHER TO TEACH EXPLICITLY OR IMPLICITLY

When choosing words to teach, you can think about words that will be most applicable in a variety of contexts. Patrick Pastore, a sixth-grade teacher at Rochester Prep, explicitly taught the word *undulating* because the passage his class was reading included the phrase "the hills were undulating." During his lesson, he asked students to describe things other than hills that undulated. After several unsuccessful student attempts, he realized that the word *undulated* is not widely applicable; it probably didn't deserve or require the entire ten minutes of a vocabulary lesson.

The following year, Patrick decided that it would be a far better use of his instructional time to "drop it in" by simply saying "that means that the hills were rolling" during reading. Instead of derailing on *undulating*, it was a better use of time to focus on a word more likely to appear in multiple contexts. This common dilemma that teachers face illustrates the variety of factors we need to consider when determining whether to teach words explicitly or implicitly.

Given the complexity of vocabulary development and reading comprehension, there is no one-size-fits-all approach that can be universally applied to help prioritize which words to teach and how. David Coleman and Susan Pimentel suggest that "when selecting words and phrases for analysis, students and teachers should follow the lead of the text to attend to the most consequential among them."[10] Careful consideration and planning of which words to teach implicitly might cause you to consider teaching a word explicitly in advance instead.

Perhaps in planning and prioritizing words encountered during reading, you come across a word that you feel warrants explicit instruction because it is "high value"—it may shape text discussions or come up in other texts. For these words, you might preteach them in depth, using the explicit framework.

---

## Implicit Vocabulary and Intellectual Autonomy

At a certain point, the legwork of defining difficult terms needs to shift from the teacher to the student. When college rolls around, nobody will be sitting with your students, making sure they've understood all the new words they encounter in the text they've been assigned to read. For this reason, implicit instruction—whereby students take on much of the work of learning new words—is especially important.

As much as possible, but especially in the older grades, students should begin to take responsibility for tracking the vocabulary words they come across during the course of reading. To best prepare students for independent word study, teach strategies that they can use beyond the classroom. Here's one possible plan. Each night for homework, students

1. Copy words from their in-class reading into their word journal. Perhaps you assign two or three of the most important words covered that day in class.

2. Copy the student-friendly definition (provided by you in class) that they have written down as part of their Interactive Reading notes.

---

3. Write a quick description of the context in which they encountered the word.

4. Write a new example sentence that includes and demonstrates the meaning of the word.

As we've discussed, Implicit Vocabulary Instruction is the breadth half of the quest to boost student vocabulary, and it helps students tackle complex texts. Implicit Vocabulary Instruction can increase student vocabulary through the course of everyday reading. Although it requires thorough preparation in deciding which words to teach and how, it goes a long way in terms of preparing students for the kind of independent study that will be expected of them in classrooms of higher learning.

Of course, no good instruction—implicit or explicit—is complete without continued practice. In the final module of this chapter, let's take a look at vocabulary maintenance and extension.

## MODULE 6.4  Maintenance and Extension

You almost never master a word on one occasion. Because the end goal is for students to retain vocabulary (words taught both implicitly and explicitly) for later use in their reading, writing, and speaking, it is important that teachers are thoughtful and intentional about creating and using systems for students to meaningfully revisit these words.

According to research done by David Liben in *Aspects of Text Complexity: Vocabulary Research Base*, students need a *minimum* of six repetitions with a word before they truly learn it.[11] In order to solidify student understanding of vocabulary words, students must use them—and use them *a lot*. Spiraling back involves revisiting words you've already taught, giving students the kind of practice that can ultimately lead to real mastery. We recommend four different approaches to reinforcing and maintaining previously taught vocabulary:

1. Engaging in word play

2. Prompting students to upgrade word choice in discussion and writing

3. Applying words to reading

4. Utilizing the classroom environment

This module discusses a handful of suggestions for spiraling back to vocabulary words that you have previously taught. In the days and weeks after you teach a new word, these approaches should serve as effective tools to help students remember (and remember to use!) vocabulary they've learned.

## USE WORD PLAY

Word play does more than support students in using new words and better understanding them; it conveys a sense of passion, playfulness, and appreciation for vocabulary that is important to communicate to kids (and it is also fun for teachers). By reviewing several words at once, you can ask lots of clever overlapping active practice questions. For example, you might ask students to choose between two targeted words—a tactic that causes them to evaluate similarities and differences between the words. (For example, "Which would you do if you had trouble seeing clearly: focus or gape?" "Which would you probably do if you needed to wear glasses but didn't have any: squint or gape?")

Pose questions that force students to think about the relationship between words, in addition to the words' individual meanings. Connections help students retain the meaning of a word, as well as better grasp its own particular nuances. These questions can be argued with a variety of answers—for example, "Could a *virtuoso* be a *rival*? Why or why not?" "Is there such thing as a *benign tyrant*?" Open-ended questions like these, as in active practice, are useful in providing an additional prompt for rigorously applying a word. They are especially useful when spiraling back on previously taught vocabulary, as you can address more than one word at a time and ask students to rigorously apply the words in a variety of contexts.

Regardless of the types of word play you give to your students, finding ways to systematically incorporate them as part of your daily routines is useful to ensure that you constantly spiral back to vocabulary words you have previously taught. Consider including word-play questions as part of your daily Do Now (a short activity that students complete when they enter class, outlined in *Teach Like a Champion* and *TLaC 2.0*), an oral drill (a questioning routine you might use to review previous material at the start of class), or as part of homework or a word journal (for example, "Write a story about this picture. Use two of these four words"; "Write a story about a tyrannical hermit"). Making vocabulary a rich and consistent part of each of these academic routines can ensure that new vocabulary is maintained and that previously taught vocabulary is spiraled throughout the year.

## See It in Action

Watch as Stephen Chiger kicks off his eleventh-grade reading class in clip 31 at teachlikeachampion.com/yourlibrary. In one of our favorite clips, Stephen introduces three new vocabulary words and reviews previously taught words as well. He gives a variety of examples and clear definitions, uses Call and Response to lock in definitions, and then asks students to describe a variety of scenarios in which one of the previous day's words might apply.

## VOCABULARY UPGRADES

Consistently challenge students to provide vocabulary upgrades in writing and during classroom discussions to make sure that students use the new words they are learning. This will better ensure that new words will enter their working vocabulary. (For example, "What is a more specific word you could use for the word *weird*? Who has a way of upgrading her answer to include one of our vocabulary words?")

Asking students to upgrade the vocabulary that they use in discussion will also better support them in using those new words in their writing. And as always, make sure that students are using new words appropriately. One teacher recently shared with us that she was so insistent that her students no longer use the word *sad* that they began using the word *depressed*. The teacher quickly realized that her passion for vocabulary upgrades caused students to misuse a new word—for example, her students reported being "depressed" that there wasn't pizza for lunch. When you ask students to upgrade their vocabulary, make sure that they are also doing so with fidelity to the definitions.

## CONNECT TO TEXTS

One of the best ways to ask students to use and apply new vocabulary words is to ground your questions in the text. Consider asking students to describe situations in novels that you are reading. (For example, "Which one of our vocabulary words describes how Jesse must be feeling right now? Why?")

In addition, a great way of extending and maintaining vocabulary is to help students identify when one of their explicit vocabulary words appears in a text. Because strong implicit and explicit instruction causes students to be more attentive to words, they will likely find these words themselves. You might consider having students keep vocabulary lists of words encountered in texts—both those encountered implicitly as well as those taught explicitly.

## See It in Action

Watch clip 32 at teachlikeachampion.com/yourlibrary. As they read Shakespeare's *Macbeth*, Beth Verrilli reviews the word *exploited* with her eleventh and twelfth graders with a series of Cold Calls. "Who *exploited* something in *Macbeth*?" "How did Lady Macbeth *exploit* Macbeth's weaknesses?" "One other person who *exploited* something?" "How did Macbeth *exploit* Duncan's trust?" These questions not only help students better understand *Macbeth* but also ask students to apply a vocabulary word that they have previously been taught.

## CLASSROOM ENVIRONMENT

Consider changing the classroom environment to be more conducive to the learning of new words. A word wall is the most obvious and most common way of keeping vocabulary instruction alive for maintenance and extension. Many teachers keep a visual record of all their vocabulary words on a wall in their classroom. The word wall is a helpful tool for students throughout the year; they can use it as a resource to upgrade their vocabulary in both writing and discussion. It can also be useful for teachers to help in planning and asking overlapping practice questions.

> ### Vocabulary Instruction, Reconsidered
>
> For students to communicate effectively, especially at the level necessary to thrive in a college environment and beyond, they need to pick up a serious arsenal of words. It is the responsibility of all teachers to chop away at the student vocabulary deficit in an intentional way—both by taking the time to look deeply
>
> *(Continued)*

(*Continued*)

at a number of specific words and by developing students' general familiarity with more common words throughout the course of actual reading. Through a concerted effort to teach the meanings, uses, and pronunciations of new words both explicitly and implicitly, teachers can give keys both to unlocking complex texts and to becoming excellent writers with a commanding vocabulary.

In the next chapter, we'll turn away from vocabulary to more systems-based strategies. It's amazing what a few intentional and consistent systems for approaching activities in the literacy classroom can do in terms of creating efficiency, productivity, and, ultimately, student autonomy.

## NOTES

1. E. D. Hirsch Jr., "A Wealth of Words," *City Journal,* Winter 2013, http://www.city-journal.org/2013/23_1_vocabulary.html.

2. Isabel L. Beck, Margaret G. McKeown, and Linda Kucan, *Bringing Words to Life: Robust Vocabulary Instruction* (New York: Guilford Press, 2013), 3.

3. Ibid.

4. Jim Trelease, *The Read-Aloud Handbook* (New York: Penguin, 2013).

5. Beck et al., *Bringing Words to Life.*

6. Chip Heath and Dan Heath, *Made to Stick: Why Some Ideas Survive and Others Die* (New York: Random House, 2007), 5.

7. Peter C. Brown, Henry L. Roediger III, and Mark A. McDaniel, *Make It Stick: The Science of Successful Learning* (Cambridge, MA: Belknap Press, 2015).

8. E. D. Hirsch Jr., *The Knowledge Deficit: Closing the Shocking Education Gap for American Children* (Boston: Houghton Mifflin, 2006).

9. William E. Nagy, and Judith A. Scott, "Vocabulary Processes," in *Handbook of Reading Research,* ed. Michael L. Kamil, Peter B. Mosenthal, P. David Pearson, and Rebecca Barr (Mahwah, N.J.: Erlbaum, 2000), 3:269–284.

10. David Coleman and Susan Pimentel, *Bringing the Common Core to Life: Ten Essays on the Anchor Reading Standards* (publication data unknown), 6.

11. David Liben, *Aspects of Text Complexity: Vocabulary Research Base* (Chicago: Bill & Melinda Gates Foundation, 2010), https://docs.gatesfoundation.org/documents/literacyconveningvocabularyresearchbase.pdf.

# Chapter 7

# Reading Systems

## MODULE 7.1: INTERACTIVE READING: AN OVERVIEW

Interactive Reading helps increase student alertness and focus during independent reading, as well as access to rigorous texts.

## MODULE 7.2: PHASES OF IMPLEMENTATION: ROLLOUT, MODELING, PROMPTING, AUTONOMY

A strategic investment in Interactive Reading early on pays dividends in autonomy later.

## MODULE 7.3: INTERACTIVE READING SYSTEM: HOW TO MARK UP A TEXT (AND WHAT TO MARK)

A strong culture of Interactive Reading leads to more productive and rigorous discussions.

## MODULE 7.4: DISCUSSION SYSTEMS: LAYING THE GROUNDWORK FOR HABITS OF DISCUSSION

Discussion behaviors need to be explicitly taught, modeled, and reinforced to become habits.

## MODULE 7.5: DISCUSSION SYSTEMS: BEYOND THE GROUNDWORK

Effective discussions help students clarify their interpretations of a text, identify universal themes, answer essential questions, and change opinions based on evidence.

# Chapter 7

# Reading Systems

Our topic in this chapter is easily overlooked in reading and literature classrooms—often with some justification. Who wouldn't rather think about exploring a text like *The Giver, To Kill a Mockingbird*, or *Charlotte's Web* with students than about procedures for marking up text or discussing an idea with a partner? Of course teachers would prefer to plan the questions to make their students' eyes go wide with insight as they come to understand the results of the Community's best efforts at utopia, or to read aloud the sublime pages in which Charlotte A. Cavatica dies. But systems matter too, and planning to build them into your classroom can make those eyes-wide moments even more memorable—and more frequent.

This is because strong systems make the habits of good readers automatic. They allow you to eliminate potentially distracting logistics so that you and your students can flow simply and smoothly from activity to activity with your minds focused on the text and the ideas you are grappling with, not on how to write what, where, and whether it needs to be in complete sentences. And systems build habits of mind too. Gretchen Rubin, whose book *Better Than Before* is about habit building, puts it this way: "What we do every day matters more than what we do once in a while."[1] Our systems, the things we build into the everyday routines of our classes, set the stage for the moments we value most as teachers — the insights, giggles, and heartbreaks of reading and the relationships with literature that blossom as a result.

If you've read *Teach Like a Champion,* you may first think about systems as encompassing procedures and routines — things like passing out papers or sharpening pencils. But just as important — maybe even more so — are the set of academic systems behind rigorous instruction, many of which are specific to reading classrooms. In high-performing literacy classrooms, simple habits — how your students mark up text as they read and how they hold a discussion that honors different interpretations — allow inspiring and rigorous instruction to thrive.

In this chapter, we are going to go deep into two systems vital for building habits of lifelong readers: Interactive Reading and Habits of Discussion. Both systems contain approaches, procedures, and routines that you can use and adapt to fit your school and classroom. We note, however, that other systems are also deeply important in reading classrooms. In fact, this is in many ways a systems book, and we describe a variety of them elsewhere: systems for writing such as Stop and Jots, in chapter 4, Writing for Reading; systems for the analysis of text passages, such as the literary analysis protocol in chapter 8, Toward Intellectual Autonomy; systems for reading aloud like Control the Game and even for reading independently in chapter 5, Approaches to Reading.

In the following modules, we'll look at two especially important systems and how to install them: how to do a "rollout," model basic steps for students, and maintain ways of doing things over time so that they become lifelong habits. By using these systems, you will better support a more productive and rigorous reading program for your students (and for your teachers if you are a leader). But we also observe that the discussion about installing systems is generalizable: applicable and adaptable to most other classroom systems like those described elsewhere in the book. Ideally, having seen the power of a few key systems, you will begin (or continue) looking to build more of your own.

| MODULE 7.1 | Interactive Reading: An Overview |
| --- | --- |

Think back to the last time you were presented with an important document to read. Maybe it was for work or school; maybe it was a legal document. Before you began, you almost assuredly picked up a pen or pencil, relying on that writing instrument to help you make sense of the document, separate the key ideas from the trivial, and, ultimately, remember what you read. You were using one of the key systems we hope to describe here, **Interactive Reading** (IR)—during which a reader engages with the text by underlining, marking up key points, and summarizing ideas in the margin.

For a long time, we overlooked the power of IR. A visit to Roxbury Prep in Boston changed that for us. While observing classrooms there, we couldn't help but notice how enthusiastically and effectively students "actively read." As their peers or the teacher read aloud or as they read silently at their desks, students underlined key passages and cribbed notes in the margin. The *system* for marking up was consistent—there was a way students had been taught to do it—but each student marked up different things. First one student urgently made notes to herself, then another began furiously underlining in his book. Some idea was bursting in him. This was how he tracked it. No one by this point was telling them to mark up the text. They had internalized the system. IR was part of thinking about what they read. Making note of your ideas in the margins, flagging lines you wanted to discuss later—that was how you made sense of a book at Roxbury Prep.

And students weren't reading interactively only in their English classes. In every classroom at Roxbury Prep, students relied on and teachers reinforced IR. Students circled critical vocabulary and defined it when they could in the margin. While writing about or discussing what they'd read, they directly referenced margin notes they'd made. It had become a habit everywhere in the school, and, quite simply, they were reading like college students. It was clear to us that there was power in this system, that it should become as much a part of reading as turning the page or reading the lines from left to right.

At its most basic level, IR causes students to interact more directly with the text and thus helps increase student attentiveness and focus during reading. It also provides students with tools to break down and make sense of otherwise daunting texts, and in that sense can work in concert with Close Reading to help increase the complexity of text students can read. Consistent use of IR also makes referring to evidence and using specific examples from the text easier for students and therefore increases the quality of discussions and written responses. Flipping through the text for evidence to support a key argument in a paper or a conversation is much easier when the key passages you want to refer to are flagged in advance.

Finally, IR helps make independent reading more accountable, allowing teachers to actively Check for Understanding, something that, without such a system, can be hard to do.

## INTERACTIVE READING AND CHECK FOR UNDERSTANDING

Anyone who's read with students knows that one of the biggest challenges is authentically assessing their understanding as they read. By the time we've given an assessment afterwards, it's late to find out that students didn't comprehend much of what they read. Certainly it makes it more difficult to go back and reread. And even the best assessments can't help us recognize when a misunderstanding begins. For this reason, carefully designed IR can be a powerful tool for providing a real-time window into students' understanding of a text. That is, observing their text markups as they read can give a teacher the means to quickly see how students are processing and even enable them to step in before misunderstandings pile up. In fact, in the early stages of IR we often see teachers design the markups their students do with Check for Understanding (CFU) in mind.

During reading, the tasks you assign for markup with IR can be a way to Standardize the Format, a CFU technique from Doug's book *Teach Like a Champion 2.0*. Asking students to mark up the text and make margin notes in a specific way might look like this, for example:

> When you find Charlotte's thoughts about dying, underline them. In the margin, describe her mood and Wilbur's mood with two adjectives each, like this: [Writing on the board] "Charlotte = brave and calm. Wilbur = worried and scared."

> Or

> When you find Charlotte's thoughts about dying, underline them. Summarize them in the margin under the words: "Charlotte on dying:"

This would allow you to efficiently check in on every student as you circulated while they read. Did they notice the lines right away? Did they grasp the difference in the two characters' feelings about death? Happily, you'd be looking for those key pieces of information in the same place in everyone's book. In a few seconds per student—fast enough to let you get to everyone in class while they read, potentially—you'd know who found the right section of text, how well each child understood it, and even whom you might call on to start the discussion afterwards, either because his or her answer was exemplary or because it was typical of the misunderstandings many students in the class had.

Implicit in this approach is another technique from *Teach Like a Champion 2.0*, Tracking, Not Watching. The idea is that rather than circulating while students are reading to check for basic engagement and follow-through—Are they concentrating and reading?—you are able with IR to go a step beyond and check for specific and important academic actions: for example, a teacher might ask students to "star" lines of dialogue that suggest rising tension between two characters or to circle verbs that contribute to the mood. Their success in doing that tells you not just whether they are busy but whether they are mastering ideas. The great basketball coach John Wooden once advised teachers, "Never mistake activity for achievement." Busy, in short, is not enough. Tracking student completion of specific IR tasks let you look not just for activity but for achievement and possibly even make informed decisions about how best to adjust instruction. Did they spot the clues that tension was rising? To support comprehension, a teacher might decide to reteach or reread a section with the class or particular individuals, or ask fewer, more, or different questions after reading. She might ask students to circle words they didn't know and derive her vocabulary list from that information.

When students interact repeatedly with a text, in short, and make their thinking visible, then teachers can monitor the reading process more efficiently. Discussion, writing, and comprehension are all better off for it. In the next module, we'll look at the main ways teachers can implement IR in a classroom.

| MODULE 7.2 | Phases of Implementation: Rollout, Modeling, Prompting, Autonomy |
|---|---|

The end goal of this system, our visit to Roxbury Prep showed, is for students to internalize and personalize IR. That's how they'll use it in college and probably in their careers. But it starts (as most strong classroom systems do) with teacher planning, explicit modeling and instruction, and, of course, lots of practice. Like many systems, Interactive Reading requires a strategic investment early on, one that will pay great dividends later on. The initial phase of implementation takes time—probably more than you might think you need. Marking up the text can overwhelm new interactive readers, and moving too quickly will cause students to take shortcuts that ultimately undermine the quality of their notes. Conversely, IR notes that require too much time can break the thread of the narrative, interfere with road miles, and feel cumbersome to both teachers and students. The steps we discuss in this module can support the development of a strong IR approach.

## START WITH A ROLLOUT

Students often enjoy learning about IR. It gives them a bit of control over the reading process, and it feels grown up. Starting with a rollout speech—an intentional explanation of and introduction to the system for students—can help ensure that everyone understands the purposes and reasons behind IR. That's often crucial to students' success with and investment in the strategy over time.

### See It in Action

Watch Patrick Pastore roll out Interactive Reading (IR) in his sixth-grade reading classroom while reading *Miracle's Boys* by Jacqueline Woodson in clip 33 at teachlikeachampion.com/yourlibrary. He starts his rollout by defining what IR is. Then he uses the document camera to show an example of his own IR notes. This modeling powerfully demonstrates the how IR can become a lifelong habit.

When drafting your rollout, focus on why IR matters for students. The following is a list of basic purposes you might consider adapting to create your own rollout:

- *College readiness.* For example, "When you read in college, this is how you'll do it! It will help you learn everything you need to learn there. We are going to do a ton of practice marking up our texts so that it becomes a habit by the time we get to college."

- *Comprehension and retention.* For example, "When I read at home, I mark up the text to help me better understand and remember what I read. See ... here's what I was reading last night! I'm excited for you to learn these habits too."

- *Supporting the ability to complete class assignments.* For example, "One of the best things about Interactive Reading is that it will help you in your writing. You can use your notes to support you in finding evidence for our open-ended responses and your homework assignments and final essays, because you will have been marking up your text and finding strong evidence *as* you read. It will also help support strong points in our class discussion."

Sharing these purposes (or adapting the list to create your own) is a useful way of investing students in the "why" behind IR. When students are invested in a system, the system is more likely to operate successfully without teacher support, effectively supporting later autonomy.

## Pen(cil), Not Highlighter

Although it may sound overly specific and oddly particular, a key expectation for Interactive Reading notes is that they be done in pen or pencil. Students *love* highlighters. As soon as that magical marker ink starts flowing, though, it's nearly impossible to stop it. When using highlighters, students fail to prioritize. And because it's nearly impossible to jot a note with the blunt tip of a highlighter, students also often fail to remember what they thought was important in the first place.

## MODELING

After you have rolled out the idea of IR, scaffold IR notes by modeling your expectations. Using "think-alouds" (for example, "We just learned something really significant about Roald Dahl's father in this passage; I'm going to underline it") is an effective way of modeling note-taking for students. Students should begin by internalizing the expectation that they always read with a pen or pencil in their hand; they gain insight into *what* is important by copying their teacher's IR notes.

Modeling with think-alouds helps students understand how to prioritize what is most important — what should be underlined and what should not be. Of course, there's always the temptation to underline more than necessary. Be transparent about the tendency to overdo underlining. You might call this tendency a "sin of enthusiasm." Some teachers, in order to avoid mindless markups, direct students to read with the eraser end on the page and to flip it when making a note. Or you could help students think about why they are underlining by asking them at first to jot a margin note each time they underline to remind themselves why they thought it was important. Or you could just remind them not to overdo it.

We love it when teachers use a document camera (or a one-page copied transparency or photocopied pages of your book) to show students exactly what their own notes look like. The doc cam is also useful to show students exemplary IR notes from their peers. For example, an early lesson could involve Show Calling a few copies of the class novel (if you are marking that up) or a copy of the text you are reading and showing students exemplary IR notes by their peers, asking them to assess how and why the markup is useful.

The goal is autonomy, but it isn't achieved overnight. The number of moments of autonomous IR increase with the age of students and their experience with the strategy. The release to autonomy is a gradual process—first modeling, then overt prompting that gives way to more subtle prompts and eventually to the self-initiated markup that occurs as a natural part of the reading process.

## PROMPTING

After clear modeling, students can be reminded of key times to identify a specific aspect of the text (for example, a literary device, evidence of setting, development of a character trait) that will support comprehension and to underline it in their notes. This is a called prompting. It doesn't tell students what specifically to write, just identifies an ideal time or setting or perhaps topic for markup. In the first months (or even year), a reading teacher's goal is to build the habit of note-taking while reading; early on, the majority of IR notes are likely to be teacher directed. For example, a teacher might say, "As we read this page, jot down the source of tension between Mrs. Frank and Mrs. Van Daan and underline two details that prove it" or "Choose three pieces of dialogue on this page from *Anne* and jot a note about what they have in common" or "You will annotate for mood on these two pages. Two details per page and make notes in the margin." After extensive practice throughout the year, you might ask students to independently identify such text components as setting, characters, conflict, figurative language, and main ideas, with only informal reminders.

## MOVE TOWARD AUTONOMY AND REPEAT

Over time, students should come to read interactively automatically, without teacher reminders or prompts. Throughout the course of the school year (or years), students begin to develop greater independence in their IR: identifying ideas, characters, plot, figurative language, setting, and so on when reading independently. A great way to reinforce this is just to note it when you see it. "Hmm, I see lots of margin notes being made.

I'll be interested to hear what so many of you are seeing!" Or you can intentionally provide time for it. "Let's pause for a second. I see a lot of folks want to mark up this section."

## See It in Action

Watch clip 34 at teachlikeachampion.com/yourlibrary as Kim Nicoll introduces Interactive Reading to her sixth-grade students who are new to the school, and therefore new to Interactive Reading. As they read *The Watsons Go to Birmingham – 1963* by Christopher Paul Curtis, she explicitly models how to underline and use a margin note when they meet the protagonist in their novel. "I would write down "protagonist = Kenny = narrator." She alludes to the habit that they are developing while giving them specific aspects of the text to mark up. "As we're reading, you have your pen or pencil in your hand and you are looking for every single name of a character that we meet so that you can keep track of these characters we're going to meet, and you're looking for the setting."

Later in the clip, you see Kim circulate to hold students accountable when taking their IR notes. It's a good illustration of how intentionally IR is introduced to students, and it compares very well to the next clip of Amy Parsons with her eighth graders, who are masters of IR.

## See It in Action

Watch in clip 35 at teachlikeachampion.com/yourlibrary as students annotate their text, *Forgotten Fire* by Adam Bagdasarian, with minimal directions from Amy Parsons. It's a great example of what IR looks like when the system has been installed and autonomy has developed. She simply pauses to "make sure you [students] capture the details of that scene in your notes," illustrating how thoroughly IR has become a habit for them.

However, foundational IR practices should continually be revisited across the year and throughout the grades. Students should learn to be efficient with their IR (for example, making summary notes more concise) and to take notes without prompting. By the end of elementary school, for example, students should be able to use IR to mark up for main idea, characters and character traits, plot events, figurative language, and vocabulary. By the end of middle school, directions for IR should ideally focus on higher-order thinking skills, such as interpreting symbolism, noting examples of foils and evidence of allegory, and the like. And by high school, students should read interactively with almost complete independence.

## Sample Prompts to Build Autonomy

This table shows several prompts given with a varying degree of scaffolding. Prompts at the bottom provide students with significantly more autonomy than those listed at the top.

| | Interactive Reading Prompts |
|---|---|
| Higher degree of scaffolding/less autonomy | • Circle the word *miniscule* and jot down "tiny" in the margin.<br><br>• "We just learned about similes, so when you see a simile in today's packet, we're going to box it and interpret it in the margin."<br><br>• "Newcharlie just called his brother 'stupid'; this is a clue that he is rude and thoughtless, so I'm going to underline that and write 'rude/thoughtless' in the margin."<br><br>• "Underline that sentence. Write this in the margin: 'Example of irony—he doesn't mean it.'"<br><br>• "Underline that sentence. Write a note in the margin that describes why this is ironic. Let's hear what some people wrote …"<br><br>• "Underline that sentence. Write a note in the margin that describes why this is ironic."<br><br>• "Underline what's ironic here and say why in the margin."<br><br>• "I'll give you a chance to make a margin note here. You might write something about Holden's personality."<br><br>• "That part was really important … I see some people already taking notes … I'm going to stop for a minute and let you take some notes there."<br><br>• "I'll give you a chance to make a margin note here." "What's yours about, Peter?"<br><br>• "I'll give you a chance to make a margin note here." |
| Lower degree of scaffolding/more autonomy | |

One of the biggest challenges with IR, reported by teachers, is figuring out what to ask students to mark up. It's tempting, especially when sharing some of our own favorite works with students, to want to pause and mark up to savor every sentence, but it's important to be disciplined to avoid the "over-markup." In the next module, we'll look at what to mark up in a text and how, as well as how to encourage a culture of IR in your classroom.

Before reading with students, it's often helpful to mark up your own text. Your marked copy can serve as a model for students, which is especially important when students are first learning IR. And it can help you think about or model markup tasks you may want to ask them to try. Over time, your most explicit modeling will turn into more subtle prompting. Even so, you'll still want to have prompts planned to remind students when to make an IR note if you notice they've not done so independently.

## CONTENT: WHAT TO MARK UP

Although IR notes can vary depending on the genre of the text, many types work across genres. We describe some of those here.

### Evidence

Using IR notes to identify evidence is versatile, as it can meet a variety of content objectives. Such notes are also very useful for students when it comes time to assemble evidence for their written work. "Underline the line in that paragraph that is most revealing of Golding's characterization."

### Summary

At the end of a page or paragraph, ask students to jot one or two sentences that summarize what they've just read. Consider doing this when the excerpt is particularly important to the overall understanding of the text or it's a challenging excerpt about which you've planned to pause to ask questions to support understanding. "That was really challenging. Take the next minute to write a margin note to summarize what we read on the bottom of page 33."

## Paraphrase

Like a summary note, paraphrasing is especially important when the excerpt includes a key idea from the text or is particularly complex and may require one or two rereads. A paraphrase is a simplified rewording of a text excerpt—typically a sentence or shorter paragraph—that captures all of the ideas. When it comes to margin notes, you can balance these expectations with brevity. At the end of a complex sentence or paragraph (especially when Close Reading), ask students to paraphrase what they've read. In order to improve efficiency and skill with paraphrasing, you should model and practice this skill frequently: "Underline that sentence. Now let's put it in plain English" or "Put brackets around those two sentences. Read them again and paraphrase in the margin."

## Marks to Reread or Close Read

IR is a tool that can be used to efficiently focus on a critical or complex segment of text for rereading and/or Close Reading: "This paragraph is challenging. Draw a box around it. We're going to reread it more carefully and pause a couple of times while I ask you some questions about it" or "That's a really complex sentence. Reread it to yourself and be ready to explain to your classmates the two key ideas the author is comparing."

## Key Ideas and Themes

For some students, the reading of a novel (or any text taking more than one class period) can feel disjointed. IR notes can help students record and understand the continuity of an extended text. Prompt students to note key ideas as well as recurring themes that appear across a text. Their annotations will increase the likelihood that students will remember them and access them in writing and discussion. For example, "Underline that line we just read. Make a note in the margin. How does this line connect to one of the novel's important themes?"

## Key Vocabulary

As discussed in the vocabulary chapter, it's useful to direct students to circle a word and make a margin note with its definition. The definition should be determined in advance and no more than three to four words when it's jotted in the margin. Instruct students to use a simple and consistent markup for all vocabulary words. "That word is *serene*. It means calm. Circle it and draw an arrow to the margin. Write down the word 'calm' in the margin."

Some vocabulary that is useful to circle and define in the margin might include words that are important to comprehension of the text, words that repeat themselves through-out the text (so that students have the definition recorded in the text for easy reference), words that you've previously taught, or words that have more than one meaning where students may infer the incorrect meaning.

## Objective

The list of potential text markups is not short, and to pause the reading for the markup of every kind every day would be counterproductive to comprehension and detrimental to logging road miles. The majority of IR notes should support students as they work toward mastering the daily objective(s). Objectives target specific skills, but are driven by the text. When planning IR related to the daily objective, it's helpful first to ask your-self, What's most important in this section of the text? And then, What reading skills do the key takeaways from today's text align to? For example: "Underline an example of dramatic irony in today's reading" or "Box the 'crisis' that occurs and how it's resolved" or "Underline evidence that this character is sneaky."

## Final Writing Connection

For IR to translate to strong student work, directions for what to interactively read can be directly related (if not identical) to postreading questions, especially when IR is a new system for students. For example, your IR directions may be "Underline evidence of June's character traits and write the trait in the margin," and the postreading question might then be "What is one of June's character traits? Provide evidence from the text to support your answer." It's important for students to see their notes as valuable tools for using relevant supporting evidence in their answers.

## Genre-Specific Markups

The following are some suggested markups for making IR more genre specific.

| Fiction | Nonfiction | Poetry |
|---|---|---|
| • Theme<br>• Characterization, character development<br>• Plot development<br>• Literary devices<br>• Dialogue tags to support fluency | • Summarize central ideas<br>• Author's purpose<br>• Tone<br>• Main idea | • Figurative language<br>• Mood |

## HOW TO MARK UP A TEXT

We've looked at what to mark up, but the "how" is just as important. What is most helpful is to develop a system for marking the text and make it consistent for students. Keep the types of markings simple, and explicitly teach and model each one. We've listed here a few example guidelines that a school might consider using. Ideally, the system for annotating a text would be consistent across classrooms. The point is to create lifelong habits that support reading comprehension and Close Reading. If students have to learn a different notation for each teacher or at each grade, they will be less successful in forming these habits of effective reading. You might consider using the following markings:

- **Underline.** Use to focus on a very small amount of text—one or two sentences, a phrase, a word.

- **Circle.** This is most effective for focusing on and tracking key vocabulary.

- **Bracket or box.** Use this to reread or focus attention on one or two paragraphs at a time (especially when Close Reading or paraphrasing a smaller chunk of text).

- **Margin note.** This is arguably the most important type of markup. Margin notes should typically be made in addition to the aforementioned marks. Unlike passive underlining, writing margin notes forces students to process and interpret the text. They help students remember why they've underlined, circled, or boxed. For students who are regularly asked to write complete and grammatically correct sentences, the margin note can be a struggle at first. Be sure to model the brevity of a good margin note, as well as the thinking process that goes into turning a complete thought into a margin note.

## See It in Action

Check out clip 36 at teachlikeachampion.com/yourlibrary. In it, Alex Bronson, in her fifth-grade science classroom, highlights a students' Interactive Reading notes in their nonfiction text excerpt as a model for others to learn from.

You should feel free to make adaptations to this system. However, it's critical that the system for marking up a text remain relatively consistent from student to student to ensure that students are using them—and that their markups are clear enough for teachers to use to CFU. All the better if the system is consistent across a school and all content areas. That way, IR can truly become a habit for all students.

---

### Interactive Reading to Ensure Multiple Reads

Amy Parsons, the dean of curriculum at Leadership Prep Bedford Stuyvesant Middle Academy, found that when it came to reading poetry, her students were daunted. Often, she saw her students missing the overall tone and therefore having no chance at understanding the underlying meaning of the poem. She wanted them to slow down and habituate themselves to reading poetry multiple times before they tried to make sense of it, a lesson many adults could also learn. So Amy taught her students to read poems three times:

1. First read: make a mood and tone note.
2. Second read: make a main idea note.
3. Third read: make two notes on literary devices used.

Having a method for attacking poems really helped demystify poetry for her students. To make annotating even more effective, Amy instituted a check

*(Continued)*

---

*(Continued)*

box system, a seemingly tiny and simple thing, but one that turned out to have great big muscles.

By checking one box each time they read, students could track their own readings—and so could Amy. It became harder *not* to read three times than it was to do so. The check boxes made it easy for Amy (and her colleagues, as she rolled this system out across her school) to hold students accountable for something that would otherwise be extremely difficult to monitor. It made rereading visible and manageable, and it pushed her students to hold themselves accountable as well, thereby increasing their lifelong success as readers.

## ACCOUNTABILITY FOR AND ASSESSMENT OF INTERACTIVE READING

When students struggle on comprehension assessments, examine their IR notes. Often students may need more explicit guidance on taking the right kind of notes—guidance that will help them retain important details from the text. This was true in the case of Sarah, a Roxbury Prep student who read on grade level, always completed homework, and stayed focused in class, but regularly failed comprehension checks after independent reading.

When her teacher reviewed her IR notes, she noticed that Sarah made notes about her reactions to the text (for example, "I can't believe that happened" or "OMG!"), but did not make specific notes about the main events that took place (for example, "Byron saves Kenny"). After explicit instruction and extra practice on making quick summary notes, Sarah began performing better on comprehension checks, and her confidence in reading soared. By systematically collecting reading books to assess quality and compliance of notes, teachers can examine IR notes and use them both to assess student thinking and to give students feedback.

## BUILDING A CULTURE OF INTERACTIVE READING

Having a culture of IR means that students can articulate the importance of IR — they understand that it supports them in their reading endeavors, and they are diligent about marking up the text. A strong culture of IR leads to discussions in which students are actively engaged with the text and use their notes to support evidence in their written responses.

To create a strong culture in your classroom, praise and celebrate good IR habits (for example, "Inayah clearly labeled a simile on page 12"; "John summarized the main idea of the opening paragraph in three words!") or displaying excellent notes on bulletin boards (Figure 7.1).

It's also important to frequently remind students of the purpose of IR. After students answered a question correctly in her class, Kim Nicoll at Roxbury Prep reminded them: "Good Interactive Reading equals easy answering of questions. Nice job." It's also useful to display visual reminders for how to mark up the text (see, for example, Figure 7.2). Even at the high school level, students can benefit from posted reminders of how to read interactively.

One final thought on Interactive Reading, this one a cautionary note. There are times in a student's life when he or she must read for speed — that is, under timed circumstances. Generally we think valuing speed over reflection and thoroughness is a poor trade, but the fact is that there are assessment settings where speed matters. In those cases, a deep culture of IR can be problematic. Several schools we know have described watching their students diligently mark up text and extract its full meaning as the minutes on the SAT or a state assessment ticked away. This may be an issue you address directly with students as they prepare for assessments. It's not teaching to the test; it's more a way to make sure healthy habits of reading don't work against students in key moments of their schooling lives.

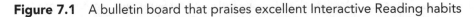

**Figure 7.1**  A bulletin board that praises excellent Interactive Reading habits

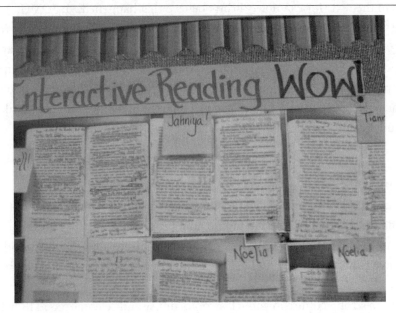

**Figure 7.2**  A visual reminder of how to read interactively

Over the past few modules, we've taken a deep dive into Interactive Reading, whereby students take an active role in prioritizing and pulling meaning from a given text. As promised, in the next two modules, we'll look at discussion systems teachers can leverage to prepare students for college-level discourse. Let's start by laying the groundwork.

| MODULE 7.4 | Discussion Systems: Laying the Groundwork for Habits of Discussion |

The most important habits that teachers can instill in students are those that prepare them for the core tasks of college. In literacy, this of course means reading and writing, but it also means preparing students to have rigorous discussions about texts. Students who are more successful refer to previous comments and add on to or develop or productively disagree with them. Teachers help students do this via teaching moves that teach and model how to do these things, providing ample opportunities to practice, and consistently reinforcing and supporting students to use and adapt them as a matter of habit. We call this process **Habits of Discussion**.

## DISCUSSION BEYOND DEBATE

When you have a discussion, the goal is not merely to talk. Discussions are a means of unlocking deeper meaning and surfacing new ideas about a text. An effective participant comes to understand other people's ideas and uses them to gain new insight into his or her own thinking. The activity doesn't have much value if these kinds of things don't occur. Teachers need to support students to help them develop discussion skills that enable these things to happen.

Teachers face a particular challenge when establishing a classroom culture based on rigorous discussions. During discussions (both in schools and among adults), people often focus more on the debate aspect of discussion than on the consideration and reflection piece. Students (and many adults) tend to approach discussion with the goal of "winning it"—that is, digging in their heels to show that their initial opinions were correct and further entrenching themselves in their opinions without considering opposing interpretations. In effective discussions, however, people change their points of view or recognize the strengths of arguments made by others. The goal is shared collaborative inquiry, not back-and-forth debate or a series of statements on an unrelated topics made in close proximity.

In creating strong classroom cultures — cultures in which students can develop their ideas through rigorous discussion — these issues must be addressed head-on. The Habits of Discussion we'd like students to develop should include the following:

1. Listening to the arguments of others and showing that they heard and understood them

2. Processing and evaluating new information (including conflicting viewpoints)

3. Deciding how new information compares to their understanding of the text

4. Explaining their agreement, disagreement, or changing viewpoint in respectful ways that show that these are not all-or-none categories. In other words, being able to say, "I see your point but interpreted the situation differently"

---

## What Habits of Discussion Are, and What They Are Not

In clarifying the concept of Habits of Discussion, it can be just as useful to identify what Habits of Discussion *are not* as clarifying what they *are*. Habits of Discussion are

- *Pretaught and practiced.* Explicitly teach students when, where, and how to use Habits of Discussion skills and phrases.

- *Concrete and visible.* Sentence starters should be posted for students to see and access.

- *Recorded.* Providing a space and time for discussion and reflection notes will support students in building lasting writing and revision habits that will prepare them for college discourse.

- *Gradually released.* Start with a few concrete skills. Gradually add elements to make discussions more nuanced. Students are ready to own discussion when its quality outweighs all other activities that you could be doing in the classroom (like writing).

- *Intentional.* Discussions should drive students toward a deeper understanding of the text, while at the same time also supporting the development of strong discussion habits.

Habits of Discussion are not

- *Filibusters.* Don't let discussions ramble or time be wasted. Focused student-to-student analysis around a clear purpose is the goal.

- *Soccer or Ping-Pong.* Students don't "possess the ball" (and control the discussion) for long, undetermined periods as they do in soccer. Nor should discussions Ping-Pong back and forth with the teacher. As in volleyball, students should carry the discussion, and when teachers need to jump in help make a pass or a set, they should.

- *The end goal.* The final product of Habits of Discussion is deeper understanding of the text—or perhaps a change in opinion, as a result of evidence—not the discussion itself.

- *A hobby horse.* As teachers, we all have something at which we are particularly talented. Facilitating classroom discussions may be one of those areas, but this should not be the reason that we have discussions in the classroom. The benefits of the discussion need to outweigh the costs.

## ANTECEDENT DISCUSSION ROUTINES AND SKILLS

Although strong Habits of Discussion are the goal, there are some important antecedent steps and routines that need to be consistently implemented early and often; doing so helps enforce high expectations around classroom discussions.

What follows is a brief description of these components (some of which were outlined in the original edition of *Teach Like a Champion*), as well as other vital expectations that, when enforced, allow Habits of Discussion to flourish. These techniques provide the structure necessary for strong Habits of Discussion to develop. By putting these structures in place, we can set our kids free to do the heavy lifting in conversations around a text. The important antecedent systems to establish in your classroom are

1. **Listening:** eye contact, no interruptions, listening gestures

2. **Format Matters:** complete sentences, technical vocabulary, voice

3. **Peer-to-peer speaking**

## Listening Systems

As we've discussed, when it comes to fruitful and productive discussions, listening is hugely important. Here are a few listening systems that set the stage for discussion to flourish.

### Eye Contact

Establishing strong habits around eye contact in discussion is important for the development of other strong Habits of Discussion. Having clear and consistent expectations for eye contact, whether it is with the teacher or a fellow student, is a vital precursor to being able to have an engaging conversation or rigorous debate with another person.

---

## See It in Action

Watch clip 37 at teachlikeachampion.com/yourlibrary as Erica Lim posts a quote from Dan Brown as part of the Do Now on the board ("By its very nature, history is a one-sided account") and asks, "What do we think? To what extent do you agree with this quote?" She first calls on a student, asking students to "track Adrian [eye contact]," then asks for "stronger voice." She then has another student build on Adrian's point. In her classroom there are clear systems for agreeing and disagreeing, and Erica is able to use these nonverbals to push the conversation further, with every comment building on the previous one.

---

### No Interruptions

One of the biggest threats to pacing is interruptions and distractions—questions, requests, and comments that either are off task ("Are we going to be writing in our journals later?") or persist on a topic you are ready to dispense with ("I wanted to read what I wrote about Tabitha"). It's right, normal, and fair to tell students to put their hands down either because someone is talking (you or a student) or because a topic is done ("Hands down now. We won't have time for more questions about Tabitha today.").

Interruptions are often an inherent part of healthy dialogue. In preparing students to eventually engage in hands-down discussion, it is also useful to teach students to wait for a pause before interrupting another person with a new point. This can be a difficult discussion skill to teach, but it begins with setting the expectation that when a student is speaking, all other hands should be down. We recently observed a teacher explicitly praise a student ("Thank you for putting your hand down while Derrin was still speaking") for demonstrating this habit, thereby reinforcing the habit for all.

### Listening Gestures

Explicitly teaching students what it looks like to actively listen is important not only in the classroom but also as a life skill. Beyond nodding, other nonverbals which communicate that you are listening include smiling or other emotional reactions, raising eyebrows, leaning toward the speaker, tilting the head, and the like. Modeling these for your students, as well as explicitly instructing them in how they communicate active listening, is an important step in developing Habits of Discussion.

Of course, there's more to discussion than just listening. And it's not just what students say that matters, but also how they communicate it.

## Format Matters

Two aspects of the Format Matters technique from *Teach Like a Champion 2.0* are especially relevant to healthy discussions. The first is "audible format," the idea that students need to consistently speak loudly and clearly enough to be heard. It's hard to have a conversation when you can't hear half of the comments that are made, so part of building the foundations of discussion is ensuring that students speak up clearly in an audible voice so that others around them can concentrate on assessing their ideas, not on squinting and craning forward to try to hear them.

Using technical and specific language is also important. It's hard to know how to respond to a comment like "He's trying to get them upset" when you aren't totally sure who "he" is and who the "them" are. Using "collegiate format" means asking students to use specific references so that their ideas are spelled out, enabling everyone in the audience to understand them, and technical vocabulary so that their ideas are as precise and clearly defined as possible.

## Peer-to-Peer Speaking

It is important to socialize our students to respond to each other instead of directing their answers to the teacher when discussing a text. This simple adjustment in *whom* students are asked to address has a dramatic impact on effective Habits of Discussion. A teacher's role is to explicitly communicate this expectation and prompt for peer-to-peer discussion.

As we'll discuss in more detail later, prompting can be done either verbally or non-verbally. Verbal prompts like "Tell them, not me" or "Tell your teammates" effectively enforce this expectation. Students (and teachers) are so accustomed to addressing comments to the teacher that it is a very difficult habit to break. Paying attention to the pronouns that students use (for example, "I agree with *you, Pedro*" rather than "I agree with *him*") can also provide a subtle shift for students in thinking about who their audience is. We want their audience to be each other, not just the teacher.

Nonverbal prompts are vital in developing this habit. In addition to nonverbally supporting eye contact, teachers may point to the rest of the class when a student is speaking so that the speaker knows whom to address. Teachers can also strategically position themselves at different points in the classroom to ensure that the majority of the class is being addressed (for example, circulating to the back of the class when someone in the front row is talking). Once the expectations for peer-to-peer discussion have been set, students then feel more comfortable taking on the responsibility of prompting each other as well.

## See It in Action

Watch Erica Lim in clip 38 at teachlikeachampion.com/yourlibrary. In a later example from the same classroom shown in clip 37, you will see how antecedent listening skills result in a rigorous hands-down discussion in a Socratic seminar, with very little prompting from Ms. Lim. Here Erica asks a difficult question of her students, and her kids are struggling. In lieu of jumping into the discussion herself, she gives a nonverbal for someone to jump in. She asks all students to reread specific evidence that one student identified in the discussion. She then prompts students to Turn and Talk with a partner to discuss the evidence. The Turn and Talk here serves as a rehearsal for the group discussion.

### Turn and Talks

When used effectively, Turn and Talks can be a good way to build habits that provide valuable practice for peer-to-peer discussion. In order for you to use Turn and Talks effectively, the following expectations and routines must be rolled out, modeled, and practiced (as with the other systems and routines described in this chapter):

- Assign pairs.

  Set a clear routine for pairing students that you establish in advance. All students should immediately know who their partners are and be able to quickly pair up so that time spent in discussion is maximized.

- Make them brief.

  Turn and Talks need to be tight—a Turn and Talk is a warm-up to a longer discussion. If they are too long, students can begin to feel "talked out" and lose interest.

- Switch partners.

  Ensure that both students have a chance to talk—either by switching halfway through or designating which partner should start the discussion.

- Circulate and Check for Understanding.

  Teachers should actively circulate among students to ensure that they are engaging in dialogue on the question that is posed. This is also a great time to gather data on student understanding of the text—data that can be used to determine who should be called on to start the discussion.

- Share out.

  Asking students to share their partner's answer requires students to actively listen to their partner, thereby improving active listening and discussion skills.

## See It in Action

Watch clip 39 at teachlikeachampion.com/yourlibrary as Erin Krafft from Houston Independent School District installs the Turn and Talk system she will use for the duration of the year. It's a brilliant system that includes sentence starters for students to use and guidance for students on how to agree or disagree within one's partner within the Turn and Talk, enabling more rigorous and productive student-to-student discussion.

## See It in Action

Watch clip 40 at teachlikeachampion.com/yourlibrary as Eric Snider reads "Dark They Were, and Golden-Eyed" by Ray Bradbury with his seventh graders. He efficiently prompts students to Turn and Talk with their partner with the direction "short hair to long hair," indicating which partner should speak first. In the second cut, you see him then reverse the order, "long hair to short hair." These efficient cues help make Turn and Talks a systematic part of the literacy block, allowing rigorous text-based discussions to flourish. As students come out of the final Turn and Talk, he asks them for a raised hand, meaning "I have a strong logical inference."

### See It in Action

Watch clip 41 at teachlikeachampion.com/yourlibrary for another fantastic example of Turn and Talk. In Laura Fern's first-grade classroom, she is using a mentor text to demonstrate how great authors "show not tell." As soon as she says "Turn and talk," her entire room of first graders turns and entirely faces their partners. She circulates throughout the classroom to listen in on their observations and gives a brief reminder to lower the volume. It's an impeccable example of a strong Turn and Talk system in action.

Once strong systems and routines have been drawn around expectations for classroom conversation, students are ready for more rigorous Habits of Discussion—habits that allow for spirited and engaging dialogue around a text. Strong Habits of Discussion enable students to prepare and clearly state their understanding of a text and prepare their arguments for refinement in writing, and enable teachers to effectively Check for Understanding. In the next module, we'll take a look at discussion beyond the groundwork.

| MODULE 7.5 | Discussion Systems: Beyond the Groundwork |
|---|---|

As stated earlier, the final product of Habits of Discussion is not the discussion itself but rather students' having a deeper understanding of the text that they are then able to communicate independently, ideally through writing. Effective discussions help students clarify their interpretation of a text, identify universal themes, answer essential questions, pose questions about deeper meanings, change their opinions, and adapt other pieces of evidence into their existing opinions. These discussions then lead to more enduring understandings, as students are actively involved in helping the class reach new conclusions.

## SENTENCE STARTERS

What follows are the Habits of Discussion that our teachers and leaders emphasize in our schools. These habits need to be explicitly taught, modeled, and prompted for students in order to have discussions about literature that will effectively prepare them for college.

The habits listed here (Table 7.1) work best when the preceding foundations for Habits of Discussion have been established. When a clear process in which students address and respond to each other has been established, the expectations of communication are to engage in dialogue, not debate. This ensures that students will be more apt to direct their answers to the group in a supportive culture.

As you may notice in Table 7.1, providing (and posting) sentence starters for each outlined habit is a good way to scaffold and build these habits for students. They are a valuable tool in supporting students in developing Habits of Discussion. To be most effectively introduced, sentence starters should be visibly posted in the classroom as well as in student materials, and they might also include space for student-generated phrases. Table 7.2 lists examples of phrases you might consider using at different grade levels or at different phases of implementation. This is not an exhaustive list, but it should illustrate the importance of pushing students beyond simply agreeing and disagreeing with their peers' answers.

## PROMPTING

In encouraging strong Habits of Discussion, the teacher plays an integral role in not only explicitly teaching these skills but also effectively prompting students to use them when necessary. Students benefit from reminders that teach them how to keep discussions on the rails but only minimally lead and direct the conversation. Eventually, through clear and consistent prompting, students begin not only to better understand what is expected of them in a discussion but also to prompt each other.

Precision is important in the discussion questions we ask our students. When we ask Close Reading questions, for example, we unpack the linguistic and syntactical pieces

**Table 7.1** Habits of Discussion

| Habit | Description | Sentence Starters |
|---|---|---|
| Paraphrase or Clarify | • Ask clarifying questions of each other.<br>• Rephrase and refine other students' ideas.<br>• Test the logic.<br>• Repeat and add on, build off of students' answers.<br>• Provide evidence and examples. | • "So what you're saying is ... "<br>• "I think what _____ meant was ... "<br>• "Are you saying that ...?"<br>• "What _____ is saying is ..., and I agree/disagree because ... "<br>• "I agree with _____ about _____ because ... " |
| Elaborate or Expand | • After paraphrasing, begin to elaborate on one another's ideas.<br>• Expand your own ideas as a result of prompting (from a teacher or from a student).<br>• Ask other students to expand their own ideas. | • "I want to build on that idea ... "<br>• "I think I can elaborate on _____'s idea ... "<br>• "Can you say more about that?"<br>• "_____, your evidence that _____ is compelling, but there is other evidence that shows ..."<br>• "Why do you think that?" |
| Evaluate | • Evaluate answers as well as a student's evidence.<br>• Suspend your beliefs to process what the other person is saying.<br>• Praise peers' answers. | • "I agree/disagree because ... "<br>• "That really makes sense because ... "<br>• "I understand what you're saying, but ... "<br>• "Do you have evidence to support that?"<br>• "I think there is contrary evidence on page ... " |
| Synthesize | • Be willing to change your mind.<br>• Following a discussion, synthesize your new point of view in writing, using evidence from the text (not just from the discussion) | • "I used to think ..., but now I think ... because ... "<br>• "To summarize the points that _____ and _____ made, ... "<br>• "So what are you thinking now?" |

**Table 7.2** Sample Sentence Starters

| Habits of Discussion 1.0 Phrases Early Grades, Building HOD | Habits of Discussion 2.0 Phrases Upper Grades, Established HOD |
|---|---|
| "I strongly disagree/agree because …" | "I think that's a bit of an exaggeration …" |
| "I partially disagree/agree because …" | "I have a follow-up question …" |
| "I tend to agree/disagree because …" | "I have a more nuanced example …" |
| "I'd like to build/add …" | "I'm torn because …" |
| | "I see a theme developing …" |
| | "I'd like to expand that argument …" |
| | "Going back to _____'s point, …" |
| | "I have a question based on what you said …" |

of a text and study how they make meaning. This requires precise and often direct questions. But in the follow-up questions and prompts to student answers, there are times when less guidance can also be powerful. Sometimes, in response to a question you've asked, a student begins on a productive path, then stops. She thinks she's done, but maybe she hasn't added enough thinking or detail, or provided the right piece of evidence. She might be on the brink of an insight if she can take the next logical step. She is holding back some part of her thinking because she is afraid it might be wrong.

Your follow-up can be specific: "What can you add that clarifies the difference between Kenny and Byron?" That could be effective, but you will have taken over a bit of the cognitive work and steered her in the direction you want her to go. In essence, you will have hijacked the conversation to potentially get to the "right" answer faster. The consequence, though, is that the discussion becomes more teacher directed and teacher dependent. As with correcting decoding errors, you may have helped improve the meaning-making in a specific instance, but you wouldn't be helping students make meaning in future texts. In order to help discussions become more student led, you need a simpler tool in your arsenal. That's where prompting comes in. In prompting, your goal is to get the student to say more (1) at the lowest possible transaction cost and least disruption to discussion and (2) with the least amount of teacher steering possible (see Figure 7.3).

**Figure 7.3** Prompting and transaction costs

| Minimum Transaction Prompt | Maximum Transaction Prompt | Follow-Up Question |
|---|---|---|

**Head nod**
This prompt is the least invasive. It gestures students to keep going with subtlety. Replicates actual cues speakers get (subtly!) in real life and socializes how to react to them.

**"Traveling" Gesture**
This gesture is slightly more explicit. Only a person in authority would give it, though through your modeling, students may start to try it. It's essentially a direction to keep going where the nod might be a more subtle form of encouragement.

**"Say more"**
Least invasive verbal prompt. Merely requests additional discussion. Very few words with no indication whether the answer is right or wrong puts more cognitive work onto students.

**"Keep going"**
Keep going suggests the original direction is worthy. This is positive but also a form of feedback, as it implies that the student is on the right track. "Say more" is more neutral. The student could be wrong.

**"Tell us more"**
Similar to "say more" but more words, which means a higher transaction cost. Introduces the idea of "me"—which reminds students of the teacher's presence versus "say more" which merely focuses on the students' words and thoughts. Using the pronoun "us" conveys the importance of speaking to the whole class.

**"Because?"**
Combine... low transaction cost—a simple, one-word prompt —with a bit of steering. It reminds students about the importance of adding a why at the outset.

**"Why is that important?"**
Similar to "Why do you say so?" but adds a reminder that ideas should be evaluated for importance and relevance. The additional steering in the question would in many cases be beneficial so more invasive prompts are not necessarily bad.

**"What evidence tells you that?"**
While similar to "What tells you that's important?," this is a follow-up evidence-based question. It tells the student to find evidence to support her answer. That's different from letting her follow up in any way she chooses. Not worse—arguably better in some cases—just different.

**"Why do you say so?"**
Provides light steering. Not just more but why. Important to note: this isn't necessarily bad. In many cases it may make the question better. Answering why is likely to be rigorous for students. It also suggests that now is the time to explain the "why." In an ideal world a student would learn to do this on her own so asking this often can be useful.

## Prompt, Don't Steer

The assumption behind prompting is that the student will benefit from further developing the thought she has begun. Therefore, it's important to let her continue with the internal narrative she's having, and not disrupt it. She is moving in the right direction; let her keep going. A low-transaction-cost prompt allows her to keep thinking along the lines she began, without breaking her train of thought. Further, once you've interrupted to add to the argument and steer her thinking, the implication is that another intervention is likely. You've shown your willingness to engage, and she is likely to allow you to do so as much as you are willing. A minimally visible prompt signals to the student that you are *not* eager to step in—that your doing the cognitive work for her is less likely and that she will have to stand on her own two feet. And it leaves her with her thoughts intact, ready to tackle the cognitive challenge.

The goal of prompting is for the student to stand on her own feet—to essentially move forward with the smallest possible nudge to Break It Down (a technique described in *Teach Like a Champion* 2.0), an opportunity to continue thinking down the same path. "Why do you say so?" is a prompt. "Why do you say so? Is there something in Kenny's words that tells you that?" is an effective follow-up question, but it's a question and not a prompt. It steers the student to the right answer. If a student is on the right track, prompt; don't steer.

---

# Verbal vs. Nonverbal Prompts

*Verbal prompts.* Here are some examples of verbal prompts—low-transaction-cost statements that push students to pursue their current line of thinking without further guidance or steering from the teacher:

- "Keep going."
- "Tell us more." (Notice the use of "us" instead of "me" to socialize students to speak to each other, not the teacher.)
- "Say more."
- "Because?"
- "Why is that important?"
- "Why do you say so?"
- "What's your evidence?"

*(Continued)*

(*Continued*)

Notice that some of the prompts are questions, but some are not. They are merely statements—"Keep going." These are arguably the most minimal of prompts.

*Nonverbal prompts.* Of course, even more minimal is a nonverbal prompt. A "keep going" hand gesture, made by rotating the hands, a bit like a referee might signal traveling in a basketball game, can be especially useful. A slight drop of the chin combined with raised eyebrows and a nod of the head can also work. These, of course, have the benefit of being the most minimal. (They also increase the risks associated with prompting [see "Pitfalls of Prompting"]).

## Pitfalls of Prompting

Prompting can be inefficient. Saying "Because . . . ?" or "Say more" to a student can result in a home run—a keen insight or the thinking of a student laid visible. But it can also lead to meandering answers with limited upside, when a more steering question might get you to the high-value target faster. Prompting can yield answers that a student was right to hold back, either because they were way off base or not fully formed. It can socialize students to overtalk as opposed to expand their answers effectively.

To manage these risks, you'll need a plan to get out of the water quickly when necessary. Plan to watch closely and step in with a question, more guidance, or to cut off a "rally killer" if an answer yields little value but lots of talking. It's worth having a few gentle back-pocket phrases you can put into service quickly and easily: "Pause. Let's think about that." "Let's pause and hear from some other folks." "Let me ask a more specific question." Notice the use of the word *pause*.

Using the rally killer as an example, let's say you ask for a piece of evidence that Jonas's perspective is changing, and a student begins a long-winded and meandering rehearsal of everything he knows about the novel. Meanwhile you've got a lesson to teach and tons of text to analyze as a class. But saying "Stop" is a bit harsh, especially when the idea is to discuss one's thinking, after all. It's a misdemeanor, but a well-meaning one. Saying "Pause," possibly followed by "I like your thinking, but I want to let some other folks join in" or "but I really want to focus on the evidence for how Jonas is changing," has a gentleness to it. A pause implies that you might start up again, that you will continue at some point. Which is true.

## Optimizing Prompting

Though it can be valuable and socializes students to develop and elaborate on ideas, prompting without strategy and focus can foster elaboration at the expense of rigor. For that reason, it's worth reflecting a bit more on when it makes the most sense to prompt.

The goal of prompting is to get a student to "self-elaborate," the discussion version of what students do when they self-correct during reading—that is, recognize their own error and fix it without prompting. It's most optimal to prompt with this goal in mind when

- You think the direction of the original answer is sound.

- You think the outcome response will be productive.

- You want to socialize students to self-correct for elaboration.

It's worth noting that you can also make "social" prompts—requests for students to develop one another's thoughts. As with other prompts, these focus on socializing students to recognize times when ideas need developing. This purpose, of course, overlaps with that of sentence starters, but is different in that emphasis is again on low transaction cost and minimal steering. Social prompts can include the following: "Discuss," "Comment," "Expand," "Elaborate," and "Develop." In all of these cases, the request can be made with a student's name—"Discuss ... Peter"—or without. Saying "Discuss" and waiting for a hand or for a student to jump in, in the case of hands-down discussions, is also an option. As with other prompts, these too can be replaced with nonverbals—a nod or raised eyebrows to another student in the room, for example. However, it's worth noting that nonverbal prompts work better when habits have first been built with verbal prompts and gradually replaced.

With persistent use of both verbal and nonverbal prompts, it may be less necessary for students to raise their hands in order to speak. In small-group instruction (for example, Guided Reading, Book Club, Literature Circles), you can start to roll out and practice having discussions without asking students to raise their hands to speak. This requires a shift in expectations on the part of both students and teachers. In order to cue this shift, teachers explicitly inform students of the change in expectations for hands-down discussion. However, raising hands to speak is a very salient habit for students, and cues in body language from the teacher (for example, leaning back in his chair to convey casualness, reaching out hands to students to encourage the conversation to continue, or nonverbally calling on students by nodding) can help remind students of the shift in expectations. For their part, students need to understand the importance of wait time. They also need to know that they too can prompt a peer to respond or engage in the conversation.

Eventually, the expectations for small-group hands-down discussion can also be applied to large-group instruction as well. Using nonverbal prompts is a great way to model and reinforce the expectation for hands-down discussions, which better mimic the type of discussion that students have in college and beyond.

## Reading Systems, Reconsidered

To get the most of reading any text, readers can't be passive. Rather, successful readers engage the written word in an interactive way. They underline and circle and write notes about key questions and ideas. They have the tools necessary to break down arguments and synthesize their own. Having the tools to chip away at the meaning of a resistant text grows more and more important as students come to grapple with increasingly complex ideas, with less and less direction. As teachers, we can help by implementing systems in our classroom that sharpen those tools.

Beyond reading interactively, students gain greater depth of understanding when they are able to communicate effectively with their peers— when there is less debate and more discourse. Strong Habits of Discussion support students in learning to entertain opposing viewpoints and to change their opinions in accordance with fact and reason.

Of course, students won't automatically read interactively, or immediately run their own productive discussions. Just as they would need when first picking berries in the wild or foraging for mushrooms, students should be guided at first, lest they seize on the wrong fruit. In the next chapter, we'll continue this thread of shifting the workload to students and talk about intellectual autonomy.

## NOTE

1. Gretchen Rubin, *Better Than Before* (New York: Crown, 2015).

# Toward Intellectual Autonomy

## MODULE 8.1: FRAMEWORKS FOR INTERPRETATION

Great teachers establish and explicitly teach frameworks — conceptual structures students can use to analyze texts.

## MODULE 8.2: TECHNICAL VOCABULARY

For frameworks to be useful in terms of autonomy, students need an arsenal of powerful words.

## MODULE 8.3: PHASES OF DEVELOPMENT

For teachers to actively foster intellectual autonomy, it helps to think of its development in phases.

## MODULE 8.4: AUTONOMOUS WRITING STRUCTURES

Academic systems for writing should be both low in terms of transaction cost, and high in terms of flexibility.

## MODULE 8.5: AUTONOMOUS DISCUSSION STRUCTURES

By planning and teaching structures for autonomous discussion, teachers can move from being drivers of discussion to facilitators.

# Chapter 8

# Toward Intellectual Autonomy

Good readers learn to develop strong, clear, evidence-based answers, both verbally and in writing, to questions about the books they read. But *great* readers go a step further. They don't wait for their teacher's questions; they frame their own. Their papers pop with insight and pursue a distinctive argument. They begin to wrestle with the meaning of the text—from the author's perspective and from their own—as soon as the words start to coalesce in their consciousness. In their margin notes, they are already rehearsing the paper they will write, the ideas they want to talk about in class. They are independent and autonomous meaning-makers, rigorous and creative, disciplined and distinctive. They generate new insights as much as they develop those they are asked about. They frame questions as much as they answer them.

In her eighth-grade class, Maggie Johnson recently asked her students to read a short excerpt from their whole-class novel, *To Kill a Mockingbird,* and to bracket phrases they thought were worthy of a deeper read.

## See It in Action

Watch this moment from Maggie Johnson's *To Kill a Mockingbird* lesson in clip 42 at teachlikeachampion.com/yourlibrary.

Maggie projected the work of one student on the board (Show Call) — a student who had underlined and marked up a portion of the text where Jem is speaking to Scout: "It's different with grown folks, we . . . " Then she probed the class: "Look at Imani's work. What's she pointing out, and why is it important?" Another student responded, "When Jem says 'we,' he's including himself as an adult or a 'grown folk.'" To which Maggie replied: "Great. Let's hear some other thoughts about this passage."

One of the themes of *To Kill a Mockingbird* has to do with Jem growing up and separating himself from Scout, his younger sister and the narrator, and she watches, feeling like an outsider. What Imani noticed about the word "we" was, indeed, significant.

This fascinating moment is important because it is what we might describe as halfway to autonomy. It's worth noting that Maggie had not drawn her students' attention to Jem's use of the pronoun "we." She could have. It would have been fodder for excellent Close Reading. Instead, she asked *her students* to identify what was important in the passage — what was worthy of discussion and analysis. And Imani rose to the challenge. She identified something crucial. But identifying crucial elements isn't the whole of intellectual autonomy.

In college, Imani will be asked to turn her moment of insight into a ten-page analysis of Jem and Scout's changing relationship, or of the fleeting nature of childhood. So Imani's moment of triumph is the *first step* in a journey — an early and crucial step. Still, it's a step unlikely to lead to the ultimate destination without the intentional and strategic action by teachers like Maggie.

Intellectual autonomy — the ability to make meaning without teacher guidance — rarely comes about without good teaching. Rather, it grows from habits taught and instilled by a teacher — habits that students like Imani internalize, adapt, and reapply on their own. A glimpse of the process midjourney lets us consider how the first steps are made and where a teacher seeking to instill more might go next.

For *some* great reading students, the journey toward intellectual autonomy happens naturally. They may begin to internalize the conventions of various genres, question authorial intent, and notice subtleties in the text without teacher prompting; but, as educators, we're tasked with preparing *all* students for college — not just those to whom intellectual autonomy is second nature.

Intellectually autonomy is student independence with and ownership of the process of thinking about and analyzing text. Usually, it develops after having internalized rigorous tools for executing those tasks and then using and adapting those tools in new ways or settings. It happens over time, with a gradual release of responsibility to students. For teachers this means asking, *Where* do I begin? *What* can I do to develop the skills that support intellectual autonomy? *When* should I start? And *how* do I support *all* of my students in making the journey to autonomy?

We begin by examining some tools we call frameworks.

## MODULE 8.1 — Frameworks for Interpretation

When the goal is for students to do something independently, it can be useful to provide a tangible frame of reference in place of the teacher's normal role of questioning and prompting. For example, we have described how teachers who are trying to foster more autonomous class discussion provide students with an array of sentence starters they can use to respond to one another directly and ensure that their comments build off and make reference to those of their peers. Such teachers have students review the starters, reflect on them, practice them. Then they post them on the wall as a reminder and let students use them with increasingly fewer reminders, in order to build cohesive discussion without teacher mediation. The expectation would not be that a discussion in its ultimate manifestation would involve using only the sentence starters the teacher had suggested. Rather, they would frame ways of thinking about what had been said. Students would use some of what they'd been given, adapt others, and develop new ones of their own.

Similarly, we've seen teachers give students lists of useful things to observe and questions to ask about texts, and let them decide which to use and when. However, whereas most students can quite easily read and "notice" interesting details within a text on their own, they often struggle to develop those observations into a cohesive interpretation of the text—a "reading" in the comprehensive sense that connects observations into an argument. So if the goal is for students to be able to create a reading all their own, a more robust framework is necessary.

For this we suggest **frameworks**—conceptual structures that you can teach your students to use to analyze texts and that you then encourage them to apply and adapt on their own. Frameworks support students when it comes to making sense of texts in logical, methodical ways. They socialize students to think systematically about a text. And they help students distinguish significant details from those less important and to weave those significant details together into a reading. In the end, frameworks allow students to learn the reading skills that, when fully developed, will enable and support autonomy.

So what are these frameworks? They're a bit like the theoretical or philosophical lenses that a seasoned academic might use in approaching a text. You might recall having done at least one postmodern, Marxist, or feminist reading in your college years, for example. These readings were informed by an intentional way of approaching the text, a familiar corpus of questions, common lines of inquiry. You were asked to choose a lens that was interesting—perhaps gender or class—and consistently ask questions about the text based on that line of inquiry. That approach allowed you to generate a unique understanding of the text—one possibly very different from those of others in your class reading the same text but in a different way, and what you learned could be applied again in reading another text. You learned to see gender or class and to make arguments about it as experience helped you see opportunities.

The frameworks we suggest here are different from those you used in college. They are more likely to focus on how a book conforms to or diverges from the conventions of its genre, say, or how the version the story tells about a time in history is accurate or reflects a certain perspective. Even though the frameworks are often different, the idea is still for students to learn to read with their observation focused on a consistent and useful way of thinking about the text.

Approaching a text with a framework both tailors a reader's conversation with the text and facilitates a certain depth of analysis. It helps students "see" the text and process it in a distinctive and focused way. In this module, we'll look at six particularly useful frameworks.

## FRAMEWORK 1: STORY FORM AND VARIATION (GENRE INFORMED)

Teaching students that almost every genre or story type has a set of conventions—basic components of or expectations for the way the story is told that tend to be consistent—can cause them to notice how those components work together to contribute to the experience of reading a text. A story that subtly (or egregiously) rejects those elements is different from one that embraces them wholeheartedly. For example, if we know that coming-of-age novels often end with a reflection in which the tensions of growing up are laid to rest and the protagonist generates insight and perspective upon seeing them pass, we can begin to look at how specific books do that differently, or perhaps set us up to expect a retrospective resolution and fail to provide it. In the elementary grades, you might start working within a story form and variation framework, teaching the five story elements—character, setting, plot, conflict, and resolution—and the aspects of basic plot structure: exposition, rising action, climax, and so on. As students read increasingly complex text, they become more ready to study more nuanced features of the elements (for example, false summits in plot).

Next, you might move on to a study of genres, looking at two or three typical examples and mapping their typical elements: a happy ending, a likeable protagonist, a narrator who tells the truth, and so on. The recognition that different types of text have an expected form and structure helps students notice when the elements vary or diverge from that. Then you might study a specific text in greater depth, comparing it to the model. Remember that ultimately, you are teaching the rules so that students can perceive when they are being adapted, tweaked, updated, or broken. The text you've chosen this time might be a divergent model, and you would study how and why it was different. The goal is for students to say, not "This is a fairy tale," but "This is a fairy tale with an unconventional protagonist who is no simple prince/princess," or, years later, "This is a novel that upsets our expectation for a tidy resolution and asks us to wonder whether things always work out in the end." Then you might move to a "setup" story like Shirley Jackson's "The Lottery," which appears to be one sort of story based on the way the narrative is told—an idyllic small town somewhere in America's heartland populated by sweet but slightly mischievous children—but turns out in the end to be something quite different. (Hint: what you think is a utopia is not.)

This kind of reading would prepare students to read successfully a text such as Jonathan Swift's essay "A Modest Proposal," written in 1729, and which essentially does the same thing "The Lottery" does: disguising its genre by mimicking the conventions of another. Swift wrote what appeared to be a political pamphlet, a type of nonfiction writing common in his time period. It appeared to be a response to the plight of the poor in Ireland at the time and mimicked the conventions of the political pamphlet. For example, Swift began with a statement about the sensible, clearheaded nature of the proposal he was about to make—it's the "modest proposal" of the title—and began by citing statistics and data to build a case. His use of the conventions of the pamphlet thus lulled readers to sleep. Suddenly and quite unexpectedly, they found themselves reading what appeared to be a very forthright proposal to feed poor Irish children to wealthy landowners so that they can be more useful.

Swift's "essay" was, of course, a strident satire of the political beliefs of the sorts of men who wrote such pamphlets and their callousness toward the poor. To study his essay is to understand how a text can exploit conventions to dramatically alter the experience of readers.

One advantage of this framework is that students can find it very appealing to try to "figure out" the tricks an author might be up to, so using it can often be both engaging and rigorous for students. That said, you'll want to hold off on "A Modest Proposal" until eleventh or twelfth grade in all likelihood. Still, there are plenty of examples of genre-benders suitable for earlier grades.

---

## Frameworks and Poetry

Recently, Roxbury Prep's Joe Volpe and his seventh graders embarked on their first journey into Shakespeare with a reading of *Romeo and Juliet*. In this lesson, Joe explicitly taught his students what iambic pentameter is, and why it's used. The objective for the lesson was to interpret Shakespeare's meter and syntax.

Students spent a good portion of the lesson marking lines from Shakespeare plays and using their scansion to fluently read the lines aloud. Several times, Joe grilled the students with questions about iambic pentameter, such as "What is an iamb? Do lines start with stressed or unstressed syllables?" After several rounds of practice and checks for understanding, he paused to ask, "So what does it signal to us when Shakespeare breaks from iambic pentameter?" This question is crucial to building intellectual autonomy. If Shakespeare consistently uses iambic pentameter in all of his plays, as a reader, I should notice when it changes and pause to think about why he's made this decision.

---

## FRAMEWORK 2: IMAGERY, LITERARY DEVICES, AND FIGURATIVE LANGUAGE

Literary devices are the tools that authors use to seed their stories with unique images—to suggest an idea subtly to readers, to imply a connection between unlike things, or to drive an image into their audience's memory with sheer vivid

**Table 8.1** Elements and Devices

| Literary Elements: structures of a text; ones that are always in place | Literary Devices: Discretionary/creative tools to create meaning and emphasize ideas |
|---|---|
| Examples: conflict, resolution, theme, characterization, setting, plot, | Examples: simile, metaphor, personification, hyperbole, irony, foreshadowing, symbol, understatement, allegory, alliteration, allusion, motif |

distinctiveness. Unlike story elements, which tend to be consistent, devices are inherently unique—different in every text, often critical to an author's style and voice. Writers use them to make their writing unique, like literary snowflakes. (See Table 8.1 for definitions and examples of elements and devices.)

Teaching students to use this framework starts with asking them to identify and interpret basic devices, such as simile, metaphor, hyperbole, and alliteration. Over time, you want them to begin connecting the devices that appear in a given text. There are five similes and metaphors here: What kinds of images do they use, and why? When students can make these invisible connections between and among images, they can begin to construct an argument about the role they play more broadly in the text. Eventually, you want students to be able to describe how the devices in a work are different from the devices in other works, and how they reflect an author's particular style or way of telling a story. It's not a huge leap from there to a college paper examining images of light and dark, the symbolism of motherhood, or some other motif in a given novel.

Depending on the complexity of a text, you may ask students to focus on devices in terms of just one element at a time ("Let's look at the devices Golding uses to describe the island and how these and the imagery within them shape the mood of *Lord of the Flies*."). Or you might ask them to look for the use of just one device and how it shapes multiple story elements. ("Many of you have pointed out that in his narration, Kenny often uses hyperbole. Which of the story elements in *The Watsons Go to Birmingham – 1963* does this most directly shape and why?")

# FRAMEWORK 3: KNOWLEDGE-BASED

The insights students have about many texts can be increased through the application of additional information about or perspective on factual topics discussed in the text. Such a topic could be how an event in history is portrayed, how someone's role in society appears, or even how a natural or scientific process plays out in the book. For example, you might ask, of Laurie Halse Anderson's novel *Fever, 1793*, how the book's description of the yellow fever epidemic reflects the true course of such an epidemic or how people at the time probably understood it. You could ask students to look for the accuracy of the depiction of the disease's symptoms or how it was treated. Or, reading Linda Sue Park's novel *A Single Shard,* you could ask students about the book's exacting, detailed and highly accurate depictions of pottery making: Which parts in particular were emphasized? Why were they described so carefully? Why did the author make this such an important part of her story?

Comparing the facts communicated in a story to some other version of them, especially a conflicting version or a factual version derived from reading nonfiction, can allow students to find unique insights about a text: Why *does* one author choose to romanticize the experience of soldiers during the Civil War? What has he left out that another includes to make their lives seem miserable and hopeless? Also important, this framework can enable teachers to use the teaching of fiction more intentionally to build their students' knowledge about the world.

To use a knowledge-based framework, start by providing students with additional texts or a "fact base" from other sources to help them reflect on their primary text. Embedded nonfiction (or fiction) texts (see chapter 3) can obviously be especially useful. Within this framework, students might compare a historical event to its depiction in the text (for example, the Russian Revolution to *Animal Farm*) or explore the portrayal of a condition like autism in *The Curious Incident of the Dog in the Night-time.*

In applying a knowledge-based framework, the goal is for students to question whether the author has provided an accurate portrayal of the facts in question and, as they get older, what distortions emerge and why. More advanced applications of the framework for a teacher reading *Oliver Twist* with her students might involve asking them to reflect on female characters described by Dickens, such as Rose Maylie—pure, chaste, selfless, all-loving—and ask, Did this exaggerated portrait seem feasible to readers in the nineteenth century, or did it seem idealized even to them? How might one venture a guess at the answer?

Ultimately, students should also identify the knowledge that they need in order to evaluate a text, and then decide if they have adequate knowledge or not. The recognition that they don't have enough knowledge to evaluate a text is important; it signals to the students their need to find more information. Providing lots of opportunities for students to read nonfiction and apply it to the fiction (and other nonfiction) texts they read is key to teaching this framework. Asking overlapping questions about both fiction and nonfiction texts (see chapter 3 on nonfiction) is a way to model for students how to use this framework.

# FRAMEWORK 4: AUTHOR'S INTENTION AND POSITION

This framework asks students to observe and question what an author did to elicit a certain response from readers or to consider why a given author writes about a specific topic in such a way. You might describe this second part as addressing the author's purpose, but we choose to sidestep that phrase, as it often refers to a relatively simplistic range of purposes—that is, to inform or entertain. The questions raised in this framework go well beyond that. Asking why an author wrote this piece in the manner he did might mean asking students who are reading *Animal Farm* whether George Orwell is sympathetic to the Russian Revolution, for example, and examining where sympathies or antipathies are revealed. If students are reading "Occurrence at Owl Creek Bridge," this framework might ask them to seek out evidence that the narrator's sympathies are with the Confederate protagonist. Studying how those sympathies are revealed tells students not just about the life and perspectives of the author but how to read a text in a way that reveals something about the author.

This framework often begins with students building attentiveness to their own responses as readers and then drawing on those responses to understand how the author might have intentionally tried to create them. So you might start by asking which characters students felt sympathy with or didn't like, for example, or which characters students *think* an author wanted readers to feel sympathy with, and then how students know that. Next, you might ask if students can identify critical descriptions and scenes and how they awaked compassion or mistrust. Then, as students advance, these questions can become more complex.

At his former school, Jamey Verrilli, currently dean of Relay Graduate School of Education, led his students through a reading of Dr. Martin Luther King's "Letter from Birmingham Jail." They spent the majority of the lesson closely reading important paragraphs. They made observations about the arguments and evidence King used, as well as his use of figurative language and contrast to craft his message. Near the end of the lesson, Jamey turned his questions to the rhetorical strategies used in the letter—the strategies King used to drive home his key points.

One of his students read aloud from the text, "There comes a time when the cup of endurance runs over, and men are no longer willing to be plunged into the abyss of despair." Jamey pointed out to his students that, in these lines, King appeals to ethos and pathos, and then probed them to consider why he hadn't used logos. Students reflected on the question, "Why didn't he go to logical, scientific evidence to nail his point home?" One student opined, "Because it's more powerful to appeal to someone's emotions when you're trying to persuade them to do something." Another student weighed in, "He had to put the ministers in his shoes so that they would truly understand that it's not right to wait [for equal rights]." Jamey then synthesized comments to explain, "If you're going to be in somebody else's shoes, you can't do it with just logic. You need to do it with your conscience (ethos) and your heart (pathos)."

In this lesson, Jamey modeled the author's position framework as he helped students clearly understand King's position. His explicit teaching of three rhetorical strategies (ethos, pathos, and logos) beforehand enabled him to build on the rigor of the lesson by asking students to analyze strategies King used to clearly establish his position and powerfully persuade others to hear and understand his appeal.

In the end, you want students to make a habit of reflecting on how they were affected as a reader by authorial decisions in any text (whether or not the author intended consciously to do that).

## FRAMEWORK 5: CHARACTER BASED

Whereas an author's position framework puts the author front and center, the character-based framework asks students to study a text's characters as an entry point into interpreting the novel. It overlaps with other frameworks, but is useful on its own because of the salience of characters in writing.

Applying a character-based framework begins often with basic questions about a character's traits and motivation. From that starting point, you can move toward asking students to observe how a character has changed. For early elementary school students reading Patricia MacLachlan's *Sarah, Plain and Tall*, you might ask, "What character attribute best describes Anna?" or "Why did Papa put an ad in the newspaper?" or "What made Sarah decide to leave Maine?" Later in the novel, you can ask questions about how characters have changed. "How have Sarah's feelings about living on the plain changed?" "How has the family changed since the beginning of the story?" Most teachers are probably pretty familiar with these types of questions. The opportunity, we think, is to take the framework and go significantly further with it.

Once students attend to characters generally, they can start to classify them. Are they stock characters—painted in broad brushstrokes and conforming to typical roles? Are they simple characters—those whose persona can perhaps be described with an adjective or two? Are they complex characters who don't always behave in the same way depending on the setting or who are a mix of traits and characteristics?

This categorization is important because through regular exposure to character-based questions, we want students to be ready to discuss and understand characters that are portrayed with depth and complexity. A student asked for the first time about Jonas's character when reading *The Giver* might explain that Jonas is brave. While that's accurate, it doesn't nearly capture the richness and depth with which Lois Lowry invested Jonas. "Jonas is brave" reveals little about the constant inner conflict he faces in his role as Receiver and his feelings toward the Community, or the sensitive and passionate side of Jonas, which intensifies as he receives memories. To describe Jonas, or any complex character, requires more than a few adjectives. More likely it requires a full sentence, or perhaps a paragraph. Or perhaps a full paper, as students will undertake in college. In other words, the character framework is richest when it pushes students to describe the complexities of characters that are not simply and tidily summed up.

Students applying this framework need practice to read and reread to understand the complexity, and sometimes contradiction, with which authors create their characters. In chapter 4, you watched a video (clip 12) of Julia Goldenheim's Read-Write-Discuss cycle. This video from Julia's class shows a sequence in which Julia started with a simplistic characterization and then helped students to see greater complexity. In their reading of *The Winter of Our Discontent*, Julia's students had characterized Joey in discussion. In the clip, Julia pointed them to a new section of the text, asking them to reread the new lines carefully and find evidence that further revealed Steinbeck's characterization of Joey. What they found in a careful reading was different from what they had seen before, and Julia prompted her students to apply this new evidence to their previous understanding of Joey, asking, "How does this complicate Joey's characterization?" Students shared insights about how their understanding of Joey had changed. They were finding him more favorable than they'd seen in their initial analyses of his character, but also hard to figure, and Julia solidified their new understanding by asking them to write again, this time to specifically explain how the passage they'd studied contributed to the complexity of his character.

Later in this chapter, you can also see Beth Verrilli discussing *The Great Gatsby* with her students. Their discussion, which takes a full class period, focuses on three distinct and in some ways contradictory aspects of Gatsby's personality. Students end the class making the case for the one that's most salient to them, but the real lesson is that Gatsby is in many ways all of these things at once: an inscrutable and complex being for whom the list of common character traits students used in fifth grade is no longer sufficient.

Characters are also affected by the situations that authors place them in as part of the story, and it's useful for students to read for what we refer to as situational context. For example, a teacher might ask students to compare two characters—Jonas from *The Giver* and Tree-ear from *A Single Shard*—and their responses to adversity. Within this framework, you might ask students to compare a character's response to a given situation with a typical response to the same situation. In Rue Ratray's sensitivity analysis clip (included in chapter 2), he asks students about the culpability of Jonas's father for his actions. Students in his class consider to what degree Jonas's father is more or less culpable than another person lethally injecting babies. Is he less culpable because he lives in a community that has brainwashed him to believe that his actions are merciful for the babies themselves and for the larger benefit of the community? Questions like Rue's are more complex than a typical character analysis question; students must consider a character's motivation and actions, then they must evaluate them in light of the context of the scene or of the novel, and finally, they compare their analysis to the actions and motivation of another person (real or fictional).

Character relationships and interactions can be complex in other ways too. Characters have complex relationships. Take, for example, the relationship between two characters, Isabel and Ruth, in the novel *Chains*. Isabel is the protagonist and older sister of Ruth, a young child who suffers from epilepsy. After the death of their mother, Isabel assumes the role of Ruth's caretaker. The sisters are slaves, and because Ruth is viewed by their master as more of a burden than an asset, Isabel often finds herself fighting to protect her younger sister. Isabel, who is loyal and fiercely protective of her sister, is often punished for disobedience and rebelliousness. She loves her sister deeply, but resents the ease with which she goes through life, and fears that her blithe innocence will lead to their being separated. Thus she resents her most when she is most charming. In short, their relationship is worthy of deep analysis and sustained study. It cannot be glossed in a few words. Similarly, part of the narrative of *Lord of the Flies* is how Jack influences and changes the other boys, bringing out their savagery one by one until just Ralph remains. Students therefore might study how certain characters are change agents. Interactions, in short, are complex, and this framework encourages students *not* to simplify but to explain that complexity.

With lots of practice studying characters, students should be able to recognize whether a character's actions and values are consistent or inconsistent throughout the novel. If the character displays hypocrisy, students should tease out what this might tell us about the author's message. Eventually, students should automatically recognize foils, stock characters, and how certain characters function as symbols or archetypes, playing a role not only in the book but also in helping the author convey a larger message about the world. You can even teach students to question the author's intentionality about why he or she has included a particular character and what the character's role is in the story.

## FRAMEWORK 6: INTERTEXTUAL

The intertextual framework causes students to look at and understand a text as part of a larger body of literature, rather than as a stand-alone work. Interpreting a text in this framework asks students to make connections with other works. It asks students to consider the ways that components of a story or text were influenced by parallel components of another work, or works.

You might approach this framework by providing students with a clear definition of theme, a working definition of which is "the message conveyed by a text that applies to multiple other texts." Over time, you would want to begin comparing how multiple texts addressed a common theme. This could mean asking how two books address the same theme (how *A Single Shard* and *The Giver* relate in different ways the theme that "family is more than who you are related to") or how two books have similar but slightly different themes or arguments about a common idea. (The themes of *A Single Shard* and *The Giver* both have to do with family. How are the themes similar and different?) Of course theme isn't the only way to compare texts. Students could compare the depictions of the life of a soldier in multiple texts. Or the depictions of the "ideal" or "implied" role of women in two novels from previous eras. They could compare different treatments of the same setting or an idea: "Compare how the two stories portray the idea of forgiveness."

Occasionally sharing a framework in advance — We are going to compare this story's portrayal of peer pressure to that of "The Lottery," so read carefully! — can also make students more methodical and observant as they read, knowing that those observations are in the service of finding a cohesive thread.

Building on the character-based framework, students working with the intertextual framework might begin to discuss whether a character alludes to or plays off another character in literature. You might point out to students reading from C. S. Lewis's Narnia series (through direct teaching or background reading) that Aslan, the lion and creator of Narnia, represents Jesus, and the White Witch represents Satan. Students who have read both *The Adventures of Huckleberry Finn* and *To Kill a Mockingbird* might explore the ways that Scout is reminiscent of Huck.

A later application of this framework requires students to define *allusion,* to identify allusions within a text, and to understand how they contribute to meaning. For example, in an independent reading of a short excerpt from *Macbeth,* Beth Verrilli asks her students to identify key lines, paraphrase them, and make inferences. During the follow-up discussion, one of Beth's students explains that she's noticed something significant. "It's a biblical reference to Adam and Eve in the Garden of Eden with the serpent. The serpent is a deceiver and that's what Macbeth is trying to be. He's trying to deceive Duncan so that he can potentially kill him." It's a beautiful moment of rigorous, autonomous interpretation—a moment only possible because of well-planned instruction on allusions and their regular occurrence in literature.

## CHOOSING FRAMEWORKS

We've talked through a number of frameworks you might consider teaching your students, but our list is by no means comprehensive. It includes six frameworks of particular usefulness, but you will almost certainly find others that will support your students' mastery of textual analysis. It's also important to note that, in several cases, the frameworks are overlapping. Each framework can be adapted with a level of specificity relative to grade level, content objectives, and text complexity.

For students to get the most out of frameworks for textual interpretation, there is a certain baseline knowledge they must possess, particularly in terms of working vocabulary. In the next module, we'll take a look at the Tier 3 vocabulary requisite.

| MODULE 8.2 | Technical Vocabulary |
|---|---|

Having a technical vocabulary to describe the foundational ideas within the disciplines of English and literature is a critical—and often underacknowledged—building block to autonomy. It's not just that students need to be able to *use* a term like *dramatic irony*. Having a word for it names it into being. The term helps create the concept in students' minds, teaching them not just how to talk about moments when the audience knows more about unfolding events than do the characters in the story, but to look for and ultimately see it when it happens. Similarly, knowing the term *ambiguity* doesn't just allow students to discuss when the meaning of a moment in text is unclear; it teaches students to look for such moments and to see them as connected to other such moments in the text. Without the word, it's harder to see the underlying event or to talk about the idea efficiently so as to develop understanding quickly and efficiently.

If autonomy is the ability to build and sustain a substantive analysis or discussion of a text without guidance, building a working knowledge of the technical terms of craft is a key step to proficiency. We're not talking about just ten or twelve words, either. Over time, students should have working knowledge of a wide range of terms and ideas. In discussing a satiric depiction of events, students will need to know *satiric/satire* and *depiction,* not to mention support it with a discussion of *allusions* in the text and moments when *understatement* makes the satire biting. Students should be able to talk about a regiment populated with *stock characters,* the *juxtaposition* of a clear flowing stream described near the body of a fallen soldier, and the *paradox* it suggests about nature's beauty and its obliviousness to the events and sufferings that befall humans.

A strong technical vocabulary introduces students to the accumulated history of thinking about how texts work. It defines the core ideas from that history and causes students to be more attentive to them as they occur, making students more insightful as they read. The broader the range of terms at your disposal, the broader and more complex the discussions and perceptions of texts you are likely to have.

One of Ellie Strand's eighth-grade reading lessons is a great example of constant reinforcement and modeling of technical (Tier 3) vocabulary. The whole-class discussion of *Animal Farm* was engaging and rigorous, students effortlessly using words like *allusion, hypocrisy, ambiguity,* and *repetition.* It was clear that this didn't happen by accident; Ellie constantly reinforced important vocabulary by using and referring to definitions and by asking students to "refine" phrases from their conversation by including technical vocabulary. At one point, Ellie spiraled back to a discussion that they'd had about one of President Obama's speeches, asking students about the rhetorical device "We the people . . . we the people . . ." One student responded, "amplification and repetition." Without skipping a beat, Ellie followed with "And that's an allusion to what?" A rigorous, rich, and fast discussion powered by technical vocabulary!

---

## Steps for Teaching Frameworks

Regardless of the framework you utilize, Tier 3 vocabulary will always be important. Here are three steps to getting the most out of whichever frameworks you choose to use.

1. Start by teaching the framework itself.
2. Link Tier 3 vocabulary to the framework.

*(Continued)*

---

3. Teach increasingly sophisticated vocabulary. Vocabulary advances the framework, causing it to evolve as your students become more capable and texts become more rigorous.

So, what should a list of technical vocabulary look like? There's no one right answer, but for context we thought we'd share a photo of the wall in a classroom at Northstar High School in Newark, New Jersey (Figure 8.1). Beth Verrilli shares the room with Mike Taubman, and as you can see, the extent of the technical vocabulary students are expected to know and use is impressive. We can attest to their students' impressive use of and knowledge about the terms, having recently observed Mike's lesson on *King Lear* and Beth's on *Othello*. One result of this, beyond trenchant analysis, is the level of autonomy Mike and Beth can afford students, knowing that the rigor of the conversation will be sustained. For example, Mike regularly plans whole-class, seminar-style discussions in which he is able to step out of the conversation almost entirely for long stretches or perhaps interject only occasionally to acknowledge a "key point" or "smart discussion move" made by a student.

The list of technical terms on Mike and Beth's wall was built up over time, we hope it's clear, with Mike, Beth, and their colleagues adding to it steadily and progressively in grades 9–12. Steven Chiger, the director of literacy at Uncommon's middle and high schools, recently shared a list of key literary terms and their definitions used at North Star High School. First, the document is noteworthy because of the great definitions *and examples* it contains. For example, the entry for *diction* looks like this:

**diction:** word choice

**concrete diction:** words that describe physical qualities or conditions

"The cat rubbed against her knee. He was black all over, deep silky black, and his eyes, pointing down toward the nose, were bluish green. The light made them shine like blue ice." —Toni Morrison

**Figure 8.1** A classroom reference wall of words students use to talk about literature and poetry

How Do ENGLISH SCHOLARS Talk About LITERATURE?

PROTAGONIST
ANTAGONIST
SETTING
FORESHADOWING
FLASHBACK
DENOTATION
CONNOTATION
DICTION
ABSTRACT DICTION
CONCRETE DICTION
COLLOQUIAL DICTION
FIGURATIVE LANGUAGE
METAPHOR
SIMILE
SYMBOL
PERSONIFICATION
IMAGERY
MOTIF
IRONY
MOOD
ASYNDETON
POLYSYNDETON
ALLUSION
THEME
EPIGRAPH
TONE
SUBJECTIVE TONE
OBJECTIVE TONE
POINT OF VIEW
FIRST PERSON
THIRD PERSON
OMNISCIENT
LIMITED

How Do ENGLISH SCHOLARS Talk About POETRY?

STANZA
RHYME SCHEME
END RHYME
METER
IAMBIC PENTAMETER
SONNET
QUATRAIN
COUPLET
OCTAVE
SESTET
VOLTA
APOSTROPHE
SPEAKER
LYRIC POEM
CARPE DIEM
PASTORAL/IDYLL
CONCEIT
ELEGY
CONSONANCE
ASSONANCE
CACOPHONY
EUPHONY
DISSONANCE
CAESURA
BLANK VERSE
FREE VERSE
ODE
EPIC

**abstract diction:** words that describe ideas, emotions or concepts that are intangible or difficult to define precisely.

> "… perhaps all the wisdom, and all truth, and all sincerity, are just compressed into that inappreciable moment of time in which we step over the threshold of the invisible." — Joseph Conrad

Second, the document is remarkable for its thoroughness. It includes 110 terms! You can find our adaptation of that list in the appendix. Finally, the list reminds us of yet another opportunity for schoolwide coordination. Imagine the power of discussions that could be held anywhere in your school if every teacher knew with confidence that every student could use each of these terms to discuss a text!

So far in this chapter, we've looked closely at the tools (or at least a solid list of them!) and the foundational vocabulary necessary for instilling intellectual autonomy in emerging readers. With that base in place, let's turn to the *how* of fostering such autonomy—beginning with phases of development.

| MODULE 8.3 | Phases of Development |
|---|---|

Intellectual autonomy develops over time. Over the course of reading a book, throughout a year, even across several years, students acquire and apply analytical skills with growing confidence and creativity—sometimes intuitively, often through modeling or intentional instruction by a teacher. Over time, the frameworks they use become their own; they use them intuitively and adapt them with fluidity to meet the challenge of a situation or to respond to their own interests as readers and people.

A teacher's goal is to foster this progression of development, and to do so, it may help to think about its moving through three different phases:

1. Guided practice with a teacher-identified framework

2. Independent application of a teacher-identified framework

3. Independent application of a student-identified framework

These phases are neither exact nor inflexible. We describe here how you might apply them with the frameworks we discussed earlier in the chapter, but really they could apply to any method of reading you might choose to use. The core idea is that students execute an analysis using a given framework with enough guidance from you to make sure they know how to do it well. Then they do it on their own with you merely telling them which approach to try. Finally, when they have learned several approaches, it's up to them to choose which to use or how to adapt them. You simply tell them to analyze; their choice of which approaches they use and how is part of their thinking process.

It's worth noting that once you've increased autonomy by moving from one phase to the next, you might move back to an earlier phase to provide more support or guided practice—because students are not as ready as you or they thought or, more likely, because the text they are reading is much more challenging. Dickens, say. Or you might not wait until one phase is "complete," with all students mastering the use of a framework, but rather try to move in and out of phases to increase autonomy and provide support as necessary.

The larger point is that students are much more capable of autonomy when they have tools they can use, combine, and adapt. This lets them experiment successfully, and to do that, they need to be familiar with the tools. Again, we do not think this limits students to the tools you teach them. As they choose to use them, they will also choose to adapt them and find their own way.

## PHASE ONE: GUIDED PRACTICE WITH A TEACHER-IDENTIFIED FRAMEWORK

Before students are ready to choose the most appropriate framework and independently apply it to a text, they'll probably need lots of guided practice with multiple frameworks, ideally applied one at a time. This starts with carefully planned teacher questions and opportunities for students to answer both verbally and in writing.

When reading with students, you may wish at times to be explicit about the framework you plan to use as students analyze the text. In that case, you might frequently remind students that your questions are designed to seek understanding about the text by using that framework. ("Today we're going to try to make sense of the person who's writing this and why she tells the story like she does, so I'll be asking you a lot about her choices.") Pause at key points to help students make observations about the text through your questioning. ("As we read, I'll ask you to make some observations on specific topics.")

As mentioned earlier, you can apply multiple frameworks to a given text. Each one you apply deepens students' understanding of the text by causing them to interpret it in a slightly different way. However, if you work with too many, especially when students are just starting to build autonomy, they may struggle to achieve mastery of the frameworks—or even clarity about the differences between them—especially with richer, more complex texts.

## Moving from Phase to Phase

The release from one phase to another is not unidirectional. It occurs in relationship with a number of variables:

- Complexity of text
- Time in the school year
- Familiarity with the author's voice and style (which depends both on how much of a given book you've read and on how many works by the same author you've read)

Remember, move fluidly between the phases. There will probably not be a day when your students have fully "graduated" from one phase to the next without returning back to one that you've worked in before.

Observations within a framework are bread crumbs leading students to a cohesive interpretation of a text. It's also important to help students make linkages between texts. Recognizing that components of their frameworks reoccur throughout literature is another step on the path to autonomy. ("Can you think of other times in our reading this year when you've seen something similar occur?") It augments their understanding of the framework and causes them to extrapolate their understanding of one text to another.

### PHASE TWO: INDEPENDENT APPLICATION OF A TEACHER-IDENTIFIED FRAMEWORK

Over time, the teacher's role as the driver of analysis can, and should, begin to diminish. Students should begin to establish greater ownership of their own thinking and reading through writing and discussion.

In the second phase of building autonomy, the teacher identifies a framework for students, but asks them to apply it independently. Students exercise increasing autonomy with the shift from teacher questioning at key points to students' being required to detect those crucial moments on their own. A teacher in this phase of autonomy might start class by saying, "In today's reading of *Of Mice and Men,* we're focusing on character, and especially complex characterization as we've studied. Make sure to annotate with observations about characters."

You might be tempted to think that giving students more autonomy would mean less work for you in preparation, but the reality is that achieving successful autonomy often means doing more planning to make sure that the work that students are doing autonomously is productive and rigorous.

Before the lesson, careful planning is important. Here are some (but not all) of the considerations your planning should include: You will want to mark up your own text, so that you can anticipate moments where students should apply the framework. What do you want students' margin notes to look like? How will students exercise autonomy in writing and discussion? For that, you want to plan what, where, and when students will write in the lesson. You also want to decide whether students will take part in a discussion, choosing the format to use for discussion (partners, whole-class), what question(s) you will use to frame the discussion, and what prompts you will use to keep the discussion moving without doing the talking or thinking for students. Finally, how will you hold students accountable for quality writing and discussion?

Here are a few structures that are particularly useful in supporting autonomy in phase two. (We'll describe additional structures for writing and discussion in Modules 8.4 and 8.5.)

## Literary Analysis Protocol

Part of our argument about autonomy so far is that when students practice analyzing texts in consistent ways, the familiarity enables them to read in the highest-leverage ways as a matter of habit. Once those ways of reading are habit, students can change and adapt them with ease and fluidity. Thus building high-quality habits is the starting point of successful autonomy.

Another way to build those long-term habits for approaching text is something we call a **literary analysis protocol (LAP)**, which we've adapted from the work of a variety of teachers over the years. LAP involves choosing an excerpt from the text or novel your students are reading without comment or question beyond something like "Analyze the following passage from *The Giver.*" The tasks involved in "analyzing" are set in advance.

They are the "habit," and in a written response, students would execute the steps you had deliberately designed to replicate the kind of thinking that you hope they will use in autonomous analyses later on (see "Sample Questions and Student Analyses").

## Sample Questions and Student Analyses

1. Identify the characters in the passage—those who speak and those who play a significant role.

   A good answer might say, "This scene involves Jonas, the novel's protagonist, and his younger sister, Lily, who is going to bed. It also describes his father, who is always nurturing, handing the comfort object to his children, and Jonas's mother, who is more analytical, observing the rest of the family."

2. Identify where in the plot of the book the scene takes place (that is, before or after what? Foreshadowing alluding to or referring back to something important?).

   A good answer might say, "This scene occurs early in the novel as Jonas watches his sister, Lily, going to bed. It's a scene that shows more about Jonas's home life and reveals how different and strange the world of the Community is compared to ours. The author describes Jonas's comfort object as a "bear" as if that was some imaginary thing. It implies that bears no longer exist by the time this story takes place."

3. Explain how the scene discusses or reflects on theme(s) or idea(s) that are important to the larger text.

   A good answer might say, "The use of the phrase 'comfort object' reminds me of the term 'family unit.' They are descriptions of things that sound almost normal, but really the things are not what they appear. They're strange and sad. The 'comfort objects' are stuffed animals, but they don't know what animals are called anymore. Earlier in the book when Jonas's 'family unit' was described, it turned out that people don't choose who they marry. They're matched.

And then children are given to them and they aren't their own. So it's like a family, but it's not really a family. Over and over the book describes normal life that's so different and strange."

4. Compare the scene in the passage to at least one other scene in this novel/story or in something else the class has read, explaining how the themes, ideas, and motifs are portrayed.

A good answer might say, "One of the key ideas in *The Giver* is that people are so controlled by the Community. Their families are made for them! But of course they don't realize it. They think they're normal. That's what societies do. They put normal names on the crazy things they do, and that makes people think they're normal."

"This reminds me of the scene, later, where Jonas get his 'job.' That's given to him as well. He doesn't even get to choose, but he just tells the story like, 'of course someone decided what my job is' just like in this scene he thinks 'of course someone assembled my family for me.'"

In this case, the four questions in the LAP are designed to cause students to read closely to get the details and then to connect themes and ideas across the book—and to process their thinking in writing. A student who can do this—identify a key theme in a scene and compare it to the same theme elsewhere—is increasingly ready to build an argument tracing a theme or image through an entire book. The passage could be as short as a single line or as long as several paragraphs. As they complete these—twice a week, say—students are building the muscles they'll use to trace their own themes with ease and comfort. Like other academic systems, the LAP enables students to work at this key task with minimum transaction cost and maximum efficiency.

## Stopping Points to Drive Discussion

**Stopping Points** is another approach you might use that can be applied while using the frameworks we described earlier. The idea is that during a reading of a text, you pause intermittently at strategic points and ask students to make observations regarding the framework you are using to identify topics worth discussing. In other words, you choose the points that are worthy to discuss, and they decide what's important about the places you choose. You might implement this by having them reread the passage. In some ways, Stopping Points is similar to the LAP because you select the excerpt that you want students to analyze, and they have autonomy to analyze it as they see fit, except that here they analyze in a discussion with their peers. That might sound something like this: "Pause. Let's now reread this scene thinking about our character-based framework. Annotate anything that's significant to Jonas's characterization. Jot down one question in the margin worth discussing as a class."

As students work, teachers who most successfully use this system circulate to note the most important observations and/or the most rigorous questions in the class. When the class comes back together, the teachers who circulate have a running record of class insights — insights they can then use to facilitate a discussion driven by student observations. They might start the conversation by asking one or two students to pose their questions or share their observations with the class.

As students reliably generate their own questions and observations at teacher-directed Stopping Points, you can continue to transfer ownership by having students use hand signals to indicate when an important question has occurred to them in the course of reading. This shifts responsibility for noticing the key moment in the text — as well as for generating the discussion question — from the teacher to the students. Our colleague Serena Savarirayan sent us a note describing the use of Stopping Points in an eighth-grade class reading *The Color Purple* she had observed:

Student *(reading aloud)*:  Harpo say, I love you, Squeak. He kneel down and try to put his arms round her waist. She stand up. My name Mary Agnes, she say.

(*Four or five students raise their hands*).

Teacher:  "I see a number of students want to stop here. Stop and jot down a discussion question for the class."

(*Teacher circulates to read responses, and notices that a number of students have written something like one student's question, "What is the significance of Squeak identifying herself as Mary Agnes?"*)

Teacher:  "Ezequiel, your question is great. Read it aloud to the class."

Discussion of Ezequiel's question paired with a Stop and Jot and/or a Turn and Talk would then ensue. Alternatively, a teacher might take several questions and decide with the class which ones are most valuable for further discussion.

Ezequiel's question in the example is interesting. It suggests that students could propose a Stopping Point because they find something interesting—"worthy of analysis," in the words of Gillian Cartwright—or because they have identified something they do not understand fully. Adjusting discussion prompts from "What do you notice?" to "What don't you understand? What remains unclear or unresolved?" can help students embrace the idea that they don't and can't know everything, especially about a particularly complex text, and that what you at first do not understand can often lead to your greatest insights. Part of becoming a sophisticated reader is building awareness of what you don't know and why that might be the case.

---

## A Bridge between Phases

As we discussed in chapter 4, we recently watched Gillian Cartwright and her ninth-grade students at Uncommon Charter High School read August Wilson's play *Fences*. Before reading several scenes, she identified for students a specific framework through which to read the play, directing students to annotate for literary devices and elements. The class read the scenes without further comment or interruption from Gillian; students' read and annotated. But her question also asked them to identify which of the lines in which they noted elements and devices were "worthy of analysis." Before going on to writing, Gillian asked four students to share the quotes they'd flagged as worthy. She did not discuss these. She was merely asking students to describe key points they thought were important. She explained that she often doesn't pause reading for questioning. Instead, she likes to provide students with the mental space to make their own determinations of analysis-worthy moments in the text. Once Gillian provided a framework—literary elements and devices in this case—she allowed students to apply this framework with moderate autonomy to their day's reading.

Gillian relies on several accountability tools to ensure that students' observations are accurate and relevant. First, because she's asked for

*(Continued)*

(Continued)

students to apply the framework via text annotations, she can check their thinking at any time—either through constant circulation while reading, or by collecting them after class. Asking her students to share what they thought was worthy of analysis was another quick moment of quality control before students spent a significant portion of class time writing responses about important quotes. And the writing they did prepared them for a seminar-style discussion—one that Gillian observed and graded.

Gillian's lesson illustrates the bridge between phases two and three of autonomy. Before reading, she provided the framework for interpretation, which is one of the characteristics of phase two. Then she asked her students to apply that framework entirely on their own—in reading and writing—without providing support through questioning, prompting, or feedback. Students' first opportunity to apply and share their interpretations was in a discussion with classmates who were sharing and testing their own interpretations—a way to authentically test the quality of their interpretation. The next step for Gillian's students on their path to true autonomy is to begin to identify the framework they'll use as they investigate the text.

## PHASE THREE: INDEPENDENT APPLICATION OF A STUDENT-IDENTIFIED FRAMEWORK

In the final stage of their progress toward intellectual autonomy, students select whatever frameworks they wish to apply on their own, or they adapt and change the frameworks. They have learned how to read in various ways; now their job is to decide which ways to read they want to use and for what.

You might start, in this phase, with some reflections of the "What are some ways we can think about analyzing this story?" variety. Ultimately, you would ask students to make sense of what they say is important about it, in discussion or writing.

Releasing students to greater degrees of autonomy doesn't necessarily mean that they should interpret entire novels independently right away. You could start by asking students to interpret particular scenes or chapters with autonomy, building them toward the capacity to take on entire novels on their own. As the questions you ask become less directive, *when* you stop becomes more important. It also doesn't mean that once you've crossed the bridge between phases, you can never go back. Because students can apply any framework or analytical tool doesn't mean you can't say, "This is a fascinating book, and I think it will be valuable to read it through our historical [knowledge] framework." This is particularly worth considering, because even with autonomous readers, we want to encourage the use of a wide range of tools, not just the ones that are most intuitive.

In phase three, choose manageable spots throughout the reading and pause for writing and discussion. Doing so allows you to assess students' ability to read solo when you say, "Let's talk about this passage." The task of assessing is more challenging when students can assess any passage in the novel. Another benefit is that students can hear how peers interpret the same passage. The result is that peer-to-peer conversations about the text and student-to-teacher conversations are more accountable and of higher quality.

Planning for student autonomy can be surprisingly time-consuming; it is often more difficult to plan for accountable student independence than it is for a lesson to be entirely teacher directed. In this phase, students should be given extended time for reading and developing an interpretation. It's thus necessary to plan ways to support students in being productively engaged, especially when the work is most challenging.

In some instances, students may apply a framework you didn't plan for, or one that you didn't see yourself. Although these occurrences might be moments of great student insight, they could also be times when it's important for you to correct a misunderstanding. Planning, then, requires you to imagine a range of frameworks and interpretations, as well as how you'll support students when their chosen framework or interpretation just isn't plausible.

The strongest students in your class might use multiple frameworks interchangeably or simultaneously, while other students struggle to identify and apply just one in a challenging text. How can you support all of your students in developing written responses? And how can you facilitate a discussion that includes all student voices, comprising a range of abilities and interpretations?

Developing efficient autonomous structures is critical; they minimize the time you have to spend on setting up routines and expectations. There is a seeming paradox: in order for students to have more autonomy, you need to provide consistent instructional routines and procedures combined with carefully planned structures.

Having a range of structures or lesson routines at your disposal gives you the ability to assess different skills in a variety of formats—all while maintaining efficiency that allows for extended time for students to read, reflect, and analyze. You can create opportunities to promote the autonomous thinking required without having to reinvent lessons every time you do it.

Creating systems that you can leverage over and over are especially useful in making the shift to a culture of autonomy. In the next two modules, we'll look at structures teachers can provide to support rigorous autonomy in both writing and discussion. Of course, structures for rigorous writing and discussion don't exist independently of each other. In fact, structures for discussion and structures for rigorous writing often work together; sometimes they even rely on one another, creating a virtuous cycle—one in which writing leads to better discussion, and discussion allows students to develop and refine their written ideas.

| MODULE 8.4 | Autonomous Writing Structures |
| --- | --- |

When it's time for students to write, systematic ways of writing that are low in transaction costs and high in both rigor and flexibility are ideal. Efficient systems allow more time for student practice, which means more autonomy, more quickly. In that setting, rigorous ways of thinking become strong habits over time. Flexibility allows you to use your approach in a variety of settings.

Many teachers use Reader's Response journals or Lit Logs, venues for writing that, because they are used over and over again, become a habit. This reinforces efficiency no matter how they are structured and formatted. You can see evidence of that in clip 10 of Jessica Bracey's class. It takes just seconds from writing prompt to scratching pencils.

Figure 8.2 shows an example of a school Reader's Response journal from Northstar Academy in Newark, New Jersey. Because the text page number referred to by each question has been provided by the teacher, this journal allows for fast and focused transitions to writing, but it can also be flexible enough to allow teachers to frame any number of types of questions. And with the questions written in advance in the directions, it's easy for students to answer the question in a diligent and focused way. A journal like this normalizes the act of regularly pausing to reflect and write about the text. Over time, however, the questions and page numbers might be eliminated to allow students to write their own questions about or observations from the text. Students could easily recreate this type of structure in their own notebook pages, or you can download a template at teachlikeachampion.com.

**Figure 8.2** Example of a Reader's Response Journal

| Page | Question | Answer |
|------|----------|--------|
| 143 | Think about the Watsons' situation and the fact that they are raising three children. Why might Dad want to drive straight through to Alabama without stopping and staying in motels? | _____<br>_____<br>_____<br>_____<br>_____<br>_____<br>_____<br>_____ |
| 145 | Describe the feeling that the setting creates now that they are in the South. Why do you think the author wanted to create this feeling? | _____<br>_____<br>_____<br>_____<br>_____<br>_____<br>_____<br>_____ |

No matter what form of Reader's Response journals you use, or indeed whether you use them at all, the key is having a consistent place for your students to practice writing. That way, when you ask them to respond to any writing prompt, they already know what to do and how. Taking out their journal and getting stared is a matter of habit. They can be writing within seconds. Every additional second of efficiency in beginning or ending the writing is another second for thinking independently in writing.

Keeping a record of written responses in one place also communicates a sense of permanence, which correlates positively with both quality of responses and cementing of ideas. This record of insights is powerful for students. Looking back at all of their reflections during the reading of a novel lets students see how they've changed since its beginning, how their understanding has deepened over the course of reading an entire work, and how they've progressed as readers and writers. It also provides a record of how they've applied one or more frameworks.

## JOURNALS THAT SUPPORT GREATER AUTONOMY

We've described the benefits of writing in consistent and permanent places in foster-ing autonomy. Reader's Response journals are one way to do that, but there are plenty of other ways to write that allow students to build consistent habits and record their reflections efficiently in one place. Because so many of them build an archive of ideas and thinking, they are especially useful in supporting students' autonomy. Here are a few of the most useful types:

- *Double-entry quotation journals.* In double-entry quotation journals, students ana-lyze powerful quotes, selected by the teacher, from the texts they read. This prepares them to assemble evidence as they write papers. Students can be taught to analyze by making inferences, connections, and judgments.

- *Common-place journals.* In common-place journals, students gather quotations from the reading that are important or fascinating, and reflect on them. This can support students in the transition from answering teacher questions ("Find quotes or evidence to prove X") to framing their own questions ("This quote from the text struck me as important. Why did the author choose this dialogue to develop his characterization of the protagonist?"). This type of journal is similar to the double-entry journal, but supports even greater autonomy because the quotes analyzed in it are determined entirely by individual students.

- *Essential question trackers.* In essential question trackers, students keep a handout with the novel unit or yearlong essential question. While reading, students should record quotes and observations that apply to the essential question. This helps them make connections across scenes and books and draw together the threads of a larger argument.

- *Hypothesis tracker.* As students develop more autonomy, you can ask them to formu-late their own hypothesis about a book instead of giving them an essential question. This allows students to start tracing an idea when it's still unformed. As they read, they test, adapt, and develop their hypothesis. For example, a student reading the first page of *Lord of the Flies* might notice the creeping vines and broken trees and recall that this is similar to the way the Garden of Eden is described in the book of Genesis. They might hypothesize that biblical allusions will recur throughout the book to develop a theme. In the course of reading, they'd look for more of these images ("I've seen this image, and now I'm going to look for similar images") with the understanding that their ideas and understandings will change as they read.

- *Theme or motif trackers.* Students can also keep journals that track evidence of specific themes or motifs. At Uncommon Schools' North Star Academy, seventh-grade teachers will name for students some of the themes of the novel they are about to read, and then have the students identify moments in the text when those themes become evident. By eighth grade, students identify the themes on their own as they read, and annotate (and record) excerpts that reveal the theme they've selected. Similarly, students might use this type of journal to trace a motif, key image, or idea that recurs throughout a text.

During a recent campus visit, a professor gave advice to a group of Uncommon Schools students on preparing for college English classes. He explained that developing a piece of writing over a long period of time and refining that writing diligently is key to developing as critical thinkers. Formulating a unique and complex argument and developing it over time, he said, have more impact than completing a high volume of less reflective writing. Students' journals can support this type of thinking and writing—both of which will be important for their college success.

The last element of autonomy relates to discussion. We'll look at this topic in the last module.

| MODULE 8.5 | Autonomous Discussion Structures |

Literary discourse through peer-to-peer discussion is an essential part of every reading class. It enables students to test the ideas and interpretations they've formulated against those of their peers, and then to revise, refine, and develop them based on the content of their conversation. This is useful in helping students not only achieve academically but also develop an intellectual life both within and outside the classroom, wherein they take interest and even pleasure in engaging ideas. Structures for autonomous discussion establish settings and situations that cause students to talk directly to one another. They play a large role in shaping the kinds of conversations that are most productive in fostering these goals. By planning and teaching these structures, a teacher can shape her role as facilitator, rather than driver, of discussion.

When students are asked to interpret a text independently, there's a range of likely interpretations that will surface. This is usually a good thing, but it is also challenging.

Because so many people are interested in so many things, there's a greater risk of the discussion's going awry or failing to develop any point with sustained insight. This is doubly true when the teacher steps back and lets students run the discussion. All of which is a way of saying that teachers must be careful not to sacrifice rigor for autonomy. When one student's observations are unrelated to those of the next student who shares in class, for example, the class might lose the opportunity to probe an observation, key line, or insight more deeply. When the insights, regardless of quality, are sprawling and disconnected, the conversation remains at a surface level.

In "disciplined discussions," students are socialized to stay inside a certain frame so that they can focus on a given topic in a deep and rigorous way. The idea is that true discussion takes place when a group identifies and rigorously develops key topics at some depth before jumping to new topics. If each new speaker talks about a new idea, it's not so much a discussion as a bunch of people talking aloud in the classroom. The challenge for teachers, then, is to structure discussions so as to retain that focus, especially if they're not going to step in and mediate between every speaker. There is a wide range of discussion structures. Here's a brief description of some that you might use:

- *Discussion pairs.* These are focused, topical "breakouts" directly between two peers. Think of a Think-Pair-Share. Done well, it's crisp and offers almost too little time rather than a little too much. And it has accountability tools to make sure students do high-quality work in their pairs (see the description of Habits of Discussion in chapter 7).

- *Independent work pods.* Small groups of students are asked to answer (or frame) questions about the text and report back to the whole class.

- *Literature circles.* Small groups of students gather to discuss a piece of literature that they've read before class. Teachers often provide a set of discussion questions to guide the groups.

- *Fishbowl discussions.* Half the class discusses; the other half watches and evaluates. The teacher also usually scores and evaluates.

- *Socratic seminars.* These are a form of whole-group discussion, with the teacher offering light direction of topics and evaluating quality of participation. Socratic seminars are meant to simulate the seminar-style discussions students will be required to have in college.

In the next sections, we'll focus on what you can do to facilitate effective discussions within each of these structures so that students can exercise autonomy in a rigorous way. It's worth noting that a quality discussion rests on a strong foundation of Habits of Discussion (discussed in chapter 7).

## PROVIDE A FOCUS

If you want students to focus deeply on a certain topic, you'd do well to start with a focus for the conversation. This doesn't mean that students shouldn't independently analyze a portion of text; they should, especially in later phases of the development of autonomy. But when it's time for discussion, being clear about its focus—what's in bounds and what's off topic—helps students better separate ideas worthy of sharing from those that should be saved for another conversation or explored more deeply in independent writing.

Before a whole-class discussion of *The Great Gatsby,* Beth Verrilli posted three key questions on the board. She described them as "big ideas we came up with when we were reading chapter three." Her wording gave her students agency and ownership over the topics they'd discuss and communicated that their ideas were substantive; it also said, "There are some key things we are focusing on here. We have a purpose."

## See It in Action
Watch Beth Verrilli's class discuss *The Great Gatsby* in clip 43 at teach likeachampion.com/yourlibrary.

Beth explained, "We looked at how [Gatsby] was trying to connect with Nick in an informal, casual way. We talked about how he was also trying to communicate his wealth to Nick, and we wondered whether he was hiding something behind that wealth. Today we're going to focus on Close Reading pages 65–67, the story he tells Nick on the way to the restaurant, and see if it helps us build these arguments even further." Being transparent about the goal of the discussion allows students to steer their comments to relate to those key points. When you set a compass direction, everyone can self-correct. It's also worth mentioning that Beth explicitly told students they would be Close Reading and covering just two pages of the book in a lesson. Doing so not only helped her students focus their comments on a manageable part of the book but also intimated a depth of study that influenced how students participated.

Beth then gave her students one minute to review the pertinent pages with the specific discussion goals in mind. Again, she signaled intentionality and focus. In a sense, she communicated that a discussion has a purpose; therefore, comments are more germane if they address that purpose. She intimated that again as she asked for the discussion to begin: "Of those three arguments, what do you see happening here?" she asked. "If Olivia starts and brings out a piece of text evidence, don't just jump onto another piece of text evidence; make sure we've exhausted all the possibilities with that one."

Throughout the course of the conversation, multiple students weighed in with their opinion. Beth periodically inserted herself into the conversation to ask students to look at a new section of text or a new quote, but always with the same frame that she posed initially. She invited students into the conversation and welcomed their opinions. With her frame and her prompts, she implied, "There are no limits on your opinions; I want you to think independently and deeply. But there are limitations on topics. Until further notice, we're going to stick with this section and how we make sense of it." With a focus clearly in place, discussions become cohesive. Rather than devolving into free-flowing exercises in interpretation, supported by scattershot elements from anywhere, they are organized around the explication of a key section of the text.

Of course, just because a conversation works better with a focus than without doesn't mean every focus has to come from you. To further augment autonomy, you might ask students to propose a topic based on their observations about the text. As the teacher and facilitator, you can vet their proposals and choose the most productive and rigorous for the portion of text the class is discussing. In this way, you both establish limits for the discussion and give students a bit more agency in terms of determining its content.

## KEEP A MAP OF THE DISCUSSION

In addition to providing the frame, you can help students stay within the frame by posting a map of the discussion. Posting the discussion topic and then keeping a running record of the key ideas helps students be disciplined about what they share and provides them with a set of notes useful for rewriting or later refining their responses. It helps them track the course of the discussion and remember the brilliant insights that emerged from it.

Erica Lim's students spent several days reading an essay by Jared Diamond, author of *Guns, Germs, and Steel*. Before the seminar discussion, Erica reframed the general debate her students had prepared for: "On one side we have the progressivists like the authors of our textbook, those who believe that agriculture and history are a march toward progress. And on the other side, the revisionists like Diamond, those who think there is another side to the story and bring it to light." Many teachers would have opened the conversation there, allowing students to discuss which side (that of the textbook authors or Diamond) they agree with and why, based on evidence from the texts.

But Erica gave a second, more focused frame. In the first round of discussion, her students were to focus on argument structure. Students speaking in the first round were expected to describe the authors' arguments and how they were constructed, in order to set the class up for the next round. With this approach, Erica caused students to be disciplined about making text-based statements — describing the arguments in their entirety before taking a stand on which side they agree with. And she provided them a useful framework for analyzing nonfiction writing: read to understand the author's argument and how it was constructed.

The discussion that unfolded was logical and methodical, focused on one piece of evidence at a time and on how that piece contributed to the overall argument. As her students unpacked portions of the argument, Erica posted these key ideas on the board. This record of the conversation is important. It signals to students the value of their comments and serves as a reminder of what has been covered. It is also a shorthand version of complex arguments, helping students see an argument's structure more clearly. And it provides students with a clear and practical note-taking structure — one they can put to good use when analyzing and unpacking texts in the future.

## Before the Discussion

Planning for facilitating discussion requires having a clear picture of key takeaways or outcomes. It could be that you, the teacher, have formed a desired interpretation and collective understanding. The goal of discussion is for students to arrive at that understanding.

Alternatively, you might want students to develop their own understanding. As the facilitator, you recognize and embrace multiple interpretations; students are responsible for justifying and reconciling interpretations as they contribute to the discussion. Over the course of the year, you'll want to have both types of discussions—those with one desired outcome and those with a range of plausible outcomes.

For both types of discussions, careful planning for the takeaways (especially when there's more than one) helps you keep the discussion disciplined and anticipate misunderstandings that might arise. Uncommon Schools teachers plan the map, or chart, of the entire discussion beforehand. Because their

*(Continued)*

(*Continued*)

targets are clear, teachers can intervene when students stray from the frame or express confusion or a wrong interpretation. Teachers who most effectively facilitate discussion might call on another student to clear up misunderstanding or send students back to the text to reread or focus on a key line.

## MODEL REPLICABLE ACTIONS OF HIGHER-LEVEL DISCUSSION

During your class discussions, students should internalize some higher-level actions (beyond basic Habits of Discussion) useful in future discussion. These higher-level actions might include questioning peers during discussion to gain clarity or probe a weak argument, synthesizing multiple comments they've heard, or directing peers back to a key moment in the text to reconsider an argument. Support students by being transparent about the moves you make as facilitator to keep the discussion focused and moving forward. One such move is to steer students back to the text. This is useful when the conversation has strayed outside of the frame or when the conversation has reached an apparent standstill. ("I want to take us back to the piece of evidence that Casey had us home in on. Take thirty seconds to reread line seventy-one.")

---

### See It in Action

In clip 44 at teachlikeachampion.com/yourlibrary, watch as Ryan Miller's eighth-grade history students take part in a disciplined discussion in which they evaluate the veracity of Theodore Roosevelt's claims about America's involvement in the Panamanian independence movement.

During the student-driven discussion, Ryan effectively intervenes at key moments to keep the conversation inside the frame he's provided and to model actions of higher-level discussion. When one student jumps into the conversation with a tangential comment unrelated to the thread of the conversation, Ryan inserts himself to gently prompt the student to respond to some of the key points his classmate just made. At another moment in the discussion, student comments become repetitive, and Ryan asks students to reground themselves in the primary source documents they're studying. In doing so, Ryan provides students with support to maintain focus on the topic at hand, but with fresh perspective and insight based on a rigorous text.

---

## Insert Pause Points

Some teachers insert intentional pause points into class discussions, using them to provide feedback about the content of the discussion. ("The evidence Jasmine provided about Gatsby's motivation to impress Nick was particularly compelling.") Providing feedback on the discussion "moves" that students made is powerful for building students' capacity to engage in literary discussions.

In Gillian Cartwright's ninth-grade English class, she asks students to speak in small seminar groups for six minutes. Then she pauses to solicit feedback from members of the class who had been assigned observation roles. Gillian asks students to start off with positive feedback, so that students know what they should keep doing in the next round of conversation. Students offer feedback to peers like "When the group seemed to run out of things to say, someone would jump in with a question to keep the conversation moving." After three or four points of positive feedback, Gillian asks her students to share constructive feedback so that students can take their conversation from "good to even better to great." Students advise their peers, "Not everyone participated equally. Everyone should be conscious of speaking and allowing others to jump in to ensure more equal voice." Then Gillian herself chimes in with her own feedback: "I want to shout out Richard for starting off with a strong entry point. He started with a logical introduction by describing the scene he wanted to discuss and what led him to that point. Additionally, he was one of the speakers who used the clearest literary terms in his arguments. For example, he said that he saw an internal conflict building."

## Step in When Necessary

Of course, you don't always have to set regimented times to give feedback. In one of Mike Taubman's senior English classes at Northstar Academy, for example, he said almost nothing. His students were doing all the talking. They were having a "college-style seminar" on *King Lear*. The expectation was that they would talk to each other about the text using evidence and strong arguments and that they would focus on developing one another's ideas. He evaluated their discipline, focus, insight, and evidence, and used a specific rubric (one developed by Uncommon Schools' Matthew McCluskey, Sean Gavin, Laura Palumbo, and Rose Bierce) for scoring their comments. (See "College-Style Seminar: Grading Scale.")

## College-Style Seminar: Grading Scale

*A comment earns a ...*

- 10% if a student offers an idea without evidence.
- 20% if a student offers a new idea too soon and analyzes evidence to support the idea.
- 30% if a student responds to a peer's idea by analyzing new evidence.
- 40% if a student responds to a peer's idea by providing an alternative analysis of the peer's original evidence OR offers an idea with supporting evidence after the previous idea has been discussed three times.
- 50% if a student leads the discussion using one of the moves previously reviewed and supports his or her move with analysis of evidence.

*Students need to make at least two comments in the discussion.*
*Students will get two grades for the discussion: their own individual grade and the overall class average.*

During the discussion, Mike never gave his opinion about Lear. He gave students feedback on their discussion to help them stay "inside the box." "Here's what Tanesha just did," he said at one point. "She took two potentially opposing definitions of the idea of truth from the text, and she asked us to define truth or clarify which one we were talking about. That's an outstanding move. So ... what's the answer to her question?"

## Entry Tickets

You're probably familiar with Exit Tickets, but one of Doug's English professors in college required every student to complete an entry ticket before class. Students were asked to write a short reflection on the assigned reading—something they'd observed as particularly interesting—and to end it with a question for potential discussion. At the beginning of class, the professor would choose one or two to discuss during class. A classmate once noticed the prevalence of questionable medicinal practices in a given reading (Doug thinks it might have been a Ben Jonson play, but his memory is hazy at best), which prompted a discussion on the topic that was so interesting that Doug ultimately chose that as the topic for one of his papers.

Through entry tickets, Doug's professor modeled asking students to identify topics that were "worthy of further analysis" and to support their thinking. This application of entry tickets could be used or adapted for middle and high school students.

To ensure quality questions, the first few lessons might involve reading and studying examples of just the questions students had written, with a reflection on how to write them well (and probably lots of revision). Then the first few questions you pick for actual discussion might be exemplars of question quality, which you might analyze explicitly with the class before engaging the discussion. Explaining to the class why you chose certain topics or questions over others also helps them understand what kinds of observations are worthy of deeper analysis.

## Intellectual Autonomy, Reconsidered

When you try to teach someone how to ride a bike, you don't just put her in the seat and push her down a hill. Maybe, at first, you get her to use training wheels. With training wheels on her bike, she gets a feel for riding without getting a feel for falling on the pavement. Then, eventually, you take the training wheels off, but run alongside her until she gets enough forward momentum to keep moving without you. Maybe then you ride together in a parking lot or somewhere without a lot of obstacles, just to give the new rider the feel of cycling unaided. Eventually, the new rider has the skills and confidence to ride wherever geography and legality permit. In a lot of ways, developing intellectual autonomy is similar.

The simple fact of the matter is this: you will not always be there to tell your students to stay on task— or where to look for key points or through which framework to view a certain piece of text. Eventually, throughout their college

*(Continued)*

*(Continued)*

years and beyond, students will need to grapple with complicated arguments through writing and discussion— and they will need to do it on their own. In this light, the best gifts a teacher can give his students are the tools necessary for thinking and writing independently— for taking ownership of the process of thinking about and analyzing a text. He can teach them to ride and point out the way; it's up to them to do the rest.

# Useful Tools

## IDEAS FOR META-EMBEDDING

Here's a list of some good articles and resources about how literature works, which you can use over and over again for meta-embedding (described in chapter 3).

| Resource | Description |
|---|---|
| Cynthia Leitich Smith's website: www.cynthialeitichsmith.com | An "official author site" that includes interviews with authors and many other youth literature resources |
| "Orphans in Literature Empower Children," *USA Today*: http://usatoday30.usatoday.com/life/books/2003-07-02-bchat_x.htm | Exploration of universal elements of stories with an orphan hero or heroine |
| Study: "Images of Poverty in Contemporary Realistic Fiction for Youth": http://files.eric.ed.gov/fulltext/ED437060.pdf | Analysis of images of poverty in youth literature |

| Resource | Description |
|---|---|
| Vandergrift's Young Adult Literature Page: http://comminfo.rutgers.edu/professional-development/childlit/YoungAdult/index.html | Bibliography of readings on young adult literature, booklists, literary biographies, and feminist materials |
| "Young Adult Dystopian Fiction and Its Impact," suite101.com: https://suite.io/megan-b-wyatt/19142s8 | Article about how dystopian literature helps youth see consequences of apathy and indulgence |
| "Fresh Hell: What's Behind the Boom in Dystopian Fiction for Young Readers?" *New Yorker*: http://www.newyorker.com/magazine/2010/06/14/fresh-hell-2 | Article about the popularity of dystopian fiction for young readers |
| "The Tragic Hero in Literature," suite101.com: https://suite.io/beth-ellen-mckinney/30ym2gk | Definition of the tragic hero and a look at three in literature: Oedipus, Othello, and Willy Loman |
| University of Missouri e-themes website: https://ethemes.missouri.edu/ | Links to websites about social injustice and oppression in youth literature |
| "The Parent Problem in Young Adult Lit," *New York Times*: http://www.nytimes.com/2010/04/04/books/review/Just-t.html?pagewanted=all&_r=0 | *New York Times* essay on the presence of "bad parents" in young adult literature (shift from literary orphans) |
| "The Hero's Journey Outline," Writer's Journey website: http://www.thewritersjourney.com/hero's_journey.htm | An outline of the hero's journey in literature |
| "The Tradition of American Protest Literature Probed," *Harvard Gazette*: http://news.harvard.edu/gazette/2006/11.30/17-protest.html | In-depth look at American protest literature |

# EXAMPLES OF EMBEDDING

Here are some examples of embedded nonfiction texts that teachers have paired with their primary fiction texts.

| Novel | Embedding Examples |
| --- | --- |
| *Paddington at the Palace* by Michael Bond | Article on Buckingham Palace |
| | Article describing the Guard at Buckingham Palace/changing of the Guard |
| | Description of Big Ben |
| | Short biography of Queen Elizabeth |
| | Description of marmalade and how it's made |
| | Map of British rail stations |
| | Article on child refugees |
| *Bigmama's* by Donald Crews | Article on midcentury train travel |
| | Description of the rural South (farm life, milking cows) |
| | Article about the Great Migration (implied in the family's having moved north, away from their relatives) |
| | Short biography of Jacob Lawrence (artist who detailed the Great Migration) |
| | Jacob Lawrence paintings |
| | Article on memory and how it works |
| | Description of various family traditions |
| *Sadako and the Thousand Paper Cranes* by Eleanor Coerr | Article on Hiroshima, Japan |
| | Introduction to World War II |
| | Article on the bombing of Pearl Harbor |
| | President Roosevelt's speech to Congress to declare war on Japan |
| | Description of the atomic bomb, with an excerpt from President Truman's speech about his decision to drop the bomb |
| *Miracle's Boys* by Jaqueline Woodson | Biography of Jacqueline Woodson, used to set up the theme of being on the "outside" |
| | Article about totem poles, used to illustrate the concept of Newcharlie's "totem pole of badness" based on racial stereotypes |

| Novel | Embedding Examples |
|---|---|
| | Lyrics to "Me and Bobby McGee" (the song is repeatedly mentioned in text), used to explain the reoccurring theme of escape and freedom from poverty. |
| | Article about orphans in literature (see "Ideas for Meta-Embedding"), used to initiate questions about how the brothers' being without parents might affect the message of the book … and useful in looking at other books with orphaned narrators as well |
| | Passage from Toni Morrison in which she reflects on freedom (quoted in part by Mama in the novel), used to analyze Lafayette's perspective on his own freedom |
| | Lyrics to "Everything Is Everything" (alluded to through an image of a T-shirt in the novel), used to analyze the protagonists' social class and as an example of foreshadowing positive future events |
| *Esperanza Rising* by Pam Muñoz Ryan | Article on the Mexican Revolution, used to establish historical time period and sentiment that leads to Papa's death at the beginning of the novel |
| | Article on behavior of vultures, used to analyze figurative language used to characterize Tio Luis and Tio Marco |
| | Article on women in the Mexican Revolution, used to familiarize students with the concepts of gender roles, powerlessness of widows, and work opportunities for immigrant women in the United States |
| | Encyclopedia entry or article on the phoenix, used to strengthen analysis of Esperanza's characterization of herself as a phoenix |
| | Article on Mexican emigration to the United States, used to set up the immigrant experience in Southern California and living conditions |
| | Article on Mexican repatriation, used to set up text conflict and Marta's motivation |
| | Encyclopedia entry or article on migrant labor |
| | Packet on child labor laws |

| Novel | Embedding Examples |
|---|---|
| | Nonfiction article by John Steinbeck describing his research for *The Grapes of Wrath*, used as a comparative description of immigrant agricultural worker life |
| | Summary of a book about a Mexican American immigrant family involved in Cesar Chavez's rights fight in 1960s, used to discuss the farm workers' movement |
| *Diary of Anne Frank* by Anne Frank or *Night* by Elie Wiesel | Fast facts about World War II, used to build context |
| | Examples of World War II propaganda, used to build context for understanding characters' unique positions on the war |
| | Excerpt on pogroms (mentioned in the diary, not explained), used to develop understanding of bias toward Jews during the time |
| | Biography of Elie Wiesel, or other important Holocaust authors |
| | Biographical info on Dr. Mengele, used to develop understanding of Nazis |
| | Article titled "Life in Hiding," used to highlight the dangers to Jews in hiding, specifically other Jews willing to turn in hiding Jews to the SS in exchange for their own safety |
| | Excerpt from the Jewish Virtual Library on concentration camp tattoos, used to introduce the concept of dehumanization in *Night* |
| | Description of a present-day visit to Anne Frank's house in Amsterdam |
| *To Kill a Mockingbird* by Harper Lee | Speech excerpt by FDR in reference to "we have nothing to fear but fear itself" to give context on the Great Depression |
| | Excerpt from Blackstone's *Commentaries* (for example, "Why is it surprising that Calpurnia taught Zeebo using this book?") |
| | Article on caste system |
| | Article about causes of racism (students had to examine the root cause of racism in Maycomb) |

| Novel | Embedding Examples |
|---|---|
| | Article about hierarchies in the animal kingdom (for example, pecking order) |
| | Article on the Great Depression |
| | Excerpt from memoir about life in a small Southern town by an African American author |
| *The Watsons Go to Birmingham – 1963* by Christopher Paul Curtis | Images/photographs: separate bathroom sign, separate drinking fountains, and so on |
| | Example of March on Birmingham/Children's Crusade news coverage |
| | Jim Crow Laws: summary, example of a Jim Crow Law |
| | The Green Book: summary, actual page from book (1960s travel guide for African Americans that listed safe places to eat, lodge, sightsee, and so on) |
| | Article from 1963 *Popular Science* magazine about installing an Ultra-Glide |
| | Civil rights movement overview (adapted from the book's epilogue) |
| | Dr. Martin Luther King's Eulogy for the Young Victims of the Sixteenth Street Baptist Church Bombing |

# UNIT PLAN WITH EMBEDDED TEXTS
## Rue Ratray and *The Giver*

Rue Ratray, currently dean of curriculum and instruction at UP Academy Oliver, sent us this unit plan from his reading of *The Giver* with his sixth-grade students at his former school. The bolded lines are the days that they read an embedded text. Note that Rue used embedding ten times in the course of reading the novel!

| Day | Essential Question | Chapter in *Giver* | Supplemental Text |
|---|---|---|---|
| 1 | The kids believe in the rules. Agree or disagree. | 1 (Jan 6) | Rules in charter schools |
| 2 | Jonas is relieved that the Elders choose their careers. Agree or disagree. | 2 (Jan 7) | (Identifying components of an argument) |
| 3 | Anonymous/public reprimands are an effective way to maintain order in the community. Agree or disagree. | 3 (Jan 8) | Social manipulation (excerpt from *Switch*) |
| 4 | The Old are treated well in the Community. Agree or disagree. | 4 (Jan 9) | (Identifying components of an argument) |
| 5 | Assessment: Literary Analysis—Comparison | n/a (Jan 10) | *We Real Cool* by Gwendolyn Brooks (mini lesson: Stanzas) |
| 6 | The Community is thankful to be rid of the Stirrings. Agree or disagree. | 5 (Jan 13) | Medicating children |
| 7 | Children in the Community enjoy receiving all privileges in the Ceremony/on the same day as their peers. Agree or disagree. | 6 (Jan 14) | (Identifying the strongest evidence) |
| 8 | Asher is respected in the Community. Agree or disagree. | 7 (Jan 15) | "I'm Nobody, Who Are You?" by Emily Dickinson (mini lesson: Rhyme scheme) |
| 9 | Jonas is lucky to receive this assignment. Agree or disagree. | 8 (Jan 16) | (Evaluating the strongest evidence) |

| Day | Essential Question | Chapter in *Giver* | Supplemental Text |
|-----|--------------------|--------------------|-------------------|
| 10 | Assessment: Analyze argument | n/a (Jan 17) | Text for assessment |
| 11 | Adults in the Community lie. Agree or disagree. | 9 (Jan 21) | (Identifying sequencing of an argument) |
| 12 | Jonas has changed. Agree or disagree. | 10 (Jan 22) | Brain injury and memory |
| 13 | The Giver is wise. Agree or disagree. | 11 (Jan 23) | (Evaluating the sequencing of an argument) |
| 14 | Assessment: Literary Analysis—Comparison | n/a (Jan 24) | "Acquainted with the Night" by Robert Frost (mini lesson: Meter) |
| 15 | Jonas enjoys his special privileges. Agree or disagree. | 12 (Jan 27) | Neuroscience of memory |
| 16 | The Community respects the Giver. Agree or disagree. | 13 (Jan 28) | (Identifying opposing side) |
| 17 | Jonas is jealous of those who do not have to receive memories. Agree or disagree. | 14 (Jan 29) | *The Book of Questions* by Pablo Neruda (mini lesson: Metaphor) |
| 18 | The Giver should have waited to give Jonas the memory of war. Agree or disagree. | 15 (Jan 30) | (Evaluating opposing side) |
| 19 | Assessment: Analyze argument | n/a (Jan 31) | Text for assessment |
| 20 | Jonas loves his parents. Agree or disagree. | 16 (Feb 3) | Parent/child bond |
| 21 | Jonas is no longer a part of the Community. Agree or disagree. | 17 (Feb 4) | (Identifying counterexamples) |
| 22 | Rosemary was selfish. Agree or disagree. | 18 (Feb 5) | Posttraumatic stress syndrome |
| 23 | Jonas's father is cruel. Agree or disagree. | 19 (Feb 6) | (Evaluating counterexamples) |

| Day | Essential Question | Chapter in *Giver* | Supplemental Text |
|-----|--------------------|--------------------|-------------------|
| 24 | Assessment: Literary Analysis—Comparison | n/a (Feb 7) | "Dreams" by Langston Hughes (mini lesson: Repetition) |
| 25 | It is unfair for Jonas to leave the Community. Agree or disagree. | 20 (Feb 10) | Banishment |
| 26 | The Community is cruel. Agree or disagree. | 21 (Feb 11) | (Identifying counterexamples) |
| 27 | Jonas should not have taken Gabriel. Agree or disagree. | 22 (Feb 12) | "The Road Not Taken" (mini lesson: Symbolism) |
| 28 | Jonas and Gabriel find Elsewhere. Agree or disagree. | 23 (Feb 13) | (Evaluating counterexamples) |
| 29 | Assessment: Analyze Argument | n/a (Feb 14) | Text for assessment |

# EMBEDDING NONFICTION: QUALITY-CONTROL CHECKLIST

Before reading a nonfiction text with your students, it's always important to ask yourself, *How do I know the nonfiction I've selected is good? Is it a worthy time investment?* Here are some questions to ask yourself when you evaluate a piece of nonfiction for embedding. Or, better yet, ask a colleague to use these questions to evaluate the nonfiction text you're planning to embed. Doing so can be a useful strategy for starting a deeper conversation about the text before you teach it.

| Questions to help evaluate a piece of nonfiction | <ul><li>How will this text advance and deepen students' understanding of the primary text? What specific themes or topics will it address?</li><li>Why is this text among the most useful and important things to add to students' understanding of the primary text? (In other words, why not choose something else?)</li><li>What content are you seeking to add to the student's overall, long-term knowledge base? Why is this content especially most useful and important to add to students' knowledge base?</li></ul> |
| --- | --- |
| Questions to help evaluate the effectiveness of how you'll use the nonfiction to complement the primary text | <ul><li>Have you explicitly linked the embedded text to the primary text using connecting questions?</li><li>Have you asked text-dependent questions from at least three levels (word or phrase level; sentence level; paragraph level; passage level)?</li></ul> |

# READ-WRITE-DISCUSS-REVISE CYCLE TEMPLATE

Everybody Writes 1:

[Prompt here]:

*[Brief excerpt from text here]*

_____

_____

_____

_____

_____

_____

_____

_____

| Notes from Discussion |
| :--- |
| |

Everybody Rewrites 1:

_____

_____

_____

_____

_____

_____

_____

# SAMPLE VOCABULARY ROLLOUT SCRIPT

**A note to school leaders:** We recommend using a script such as the one here (or one of your own creation) and modeling this rollout live with your teachers as though they were your students. Seeing the vocabulary rollout in action and experiencing it as though they are your students will help teachers understand how to apply this in their own classroom. We also recommend that teachers draft their own rollouts, practice the rollouts with their peers, get feedback on their practice, and then practice again incorporating the feedback. Practicing these techniques is the best way to ensure that teachers bring them effectively into the classroom.

**Step 1: Select Word: Gullible**

**Step 2: Provide Accurate and Student-Friendly Definition**

**Say:** Today's word is **gullible.** Everyone, say **gullible.** When you are gullible, it means that you are easily tricked *and* that you should probably know better. Jot that down in your notes.

**Model use:** So let me give you an example: On a warm, sunny day in the middle of May, my gullible sister believed me when I told her that I had just seen the weather forecast and that it was going to snow that afternoon.

**Ask:** Why is this something that a gullible person would believe?

**Ask:** When I *informed* my sister of this weather prediction, she gullibly said, "Oh really? I had better get my boots out of the attic." How would a person who is not gullible have reacted?

**Use a visual (you may opt to move this step to follow "Supply other forms"):** In this picture, the fortune teller is taking advantage of the man's gullibility. In one sentence in your notes [or taking hands/in discussion], explain why this man may be described as gullible. Be sure to use the word **gullible**, **gullibility**, or **gullibly** in your sentence.

**Act it out (optional):** Show me what your face might look like if you were gullible and I told you that you had just won an outrageous fortune in the lottery. Show me what your face would look like if you were not gullible and I told you that; say, "I am not that gullible."

## Step 3: Describe Parameters of Use

**Supply other forms: Gullible** has several forms. Its adjective form is **gullible**, and it is often used to describe a *person* who is easily tricked. You might say that "the gullible man believed everything that the fortune teller said" or that "the man is very gullible because he believed everything she said." To use it as an adverb, you would use **gullibly**, as in "He gullibly believed everything the woman told him about his future." And if you want to use it to as a noun, you might use a possessive pronoun — for example, "His gullibility led him to believe everything she said."

**Give example:** Because of my sister's gullibility, my father is very *cautious* about the friends that she hangs out with.

**Ask:** Why would my father be *cautious* about my gullible sister's friends?

**Offer similar to/different from comparison: Gullible** is similar to *trusting* because both describe people who easily believe the words or actions of others. **BUT** *trusting* describes someone who is likely to trust, have confidence in, or rely on others (believe in the "goodness" of people); **gullible** suggests that the person believes others without thinking about whether their words or actions make sense — the person accepts information that is not logical.

**Ask:** One of these words has a more negative connotation: **gullible** or *trusting*. Which one?

## Step 4: Engage in Active Practice

**Ask:** Is a two-year-old child who believes in the Easter Bunny trusting or gullible? Why?

**Ask:** Think of another example of someone who is trusting but not gullible. Turn and Talk with a partner.

**Ask:** In your notes, jot down some of the consequences of being gullible. When people act gullibly, how might they feel afterwards? Why? Explain using this sentence starter: "After acting gullibly, one might feel ..."

**Ask: (pick one or two of these; italicized words are review)**

- Which character in our novel could be described as gullible? Why? Give one example of his or her gullibility.

- What is something that a gullible person might be *persuaded* to do or believe?

- Is an *oblivious* person more or less likely to be gullible than others? Why?

- How might someone *intimidate* a gullible person?

- Is it difficult or easy to *boast* to a gullible person? Why?

# READER'S RESPONSE JOURNAL TEMPLATE

| Page | Question | Answer |
|------|----------|--------|
| XXX | [Prompt here] | |
| XXX | [Prompt here] | |
| XXX | [Prompt here] | |
| XXX | [Prompt here] | |

# LITERARY TERMS AND DEFINITIONS

This list is adapted from the one developed by our colleagues at Northstar Academy in Newark, New Jersey; theirs included 110 terms and definitions. We chose fifty of our favorites. Check out teachlikeachampion.com/yourlibrary for the full list.

1. **allegory:** story that can be understood literally and symbolically

2. **alliteration:** repetition of initial consonant sounds within a series of words

3. **allusion:** reference to historical, mythical, or literary person, place or thing

   > Plan ahead. It was not raining when Noah built the ark.

   > Come to the party. Don't be such a Scrooge.

4. **analogy:** a comparison or similarity between like features of two different things; used to help reader/listener understand better: your heart is like a pump for your body.

5. **antagonist:** the character who opposes the main character

6. **apostrophe:** [POETRY] directly addressing an absent person, abstract concept, inanimate object

7. **aside:** [DRAMA] words spoken by character on stage; only audience can hear

8. **catharsis:** [DRAMA] emotional connection or emotional release

9. **climax:** [DRAMA] the highest or most intense point in a drama; the scene of greatest emotion

10. **connotation:** the emotional associations evoked by a word

    > The connotations of *home* might include warmth, family, love, security

11. **denouement:** [DRAMA] resolution; resolves plot elements; ties up loose ends

12. **dialect:** nonstandard subgroup of a language with its own vocabulary and grammatical features

    > "Then when I got home I walked smack dab into the crib door. Hit my eye and scratch my chin. Then when that storm come up last night I shet the window down on my hand." —Alice Walker

13. **diction:** word choice

   ◦ **concrete diction:** words that describe physical qualities or conditions

   > "The cat rubbed up against her knee. He was black all over, deep silky black, and his eyes, pointing down toward his nose, were bluish green. The light made them shine like blue ice." —Toni Morrison

   ◦ **abstract diction:** words to describe ideas, emotions, conditions or concepts that are intangible or difficult to define precisely

   > "... perhaps all the wisdom, and all truth, and all sincerity, are just compressed into that inappreciable moment of time in which we step over the threshold of the invisible." —Joseph Conrad

   ◦ **low/informal diction:** language of everyday use
   ◦ **elevated/formal diction:** language that creates an elevated (high) tone; contains words with many syllables and long, sophisticated sentences

   > "Discerning the impractible state of the poor culprit's mind, the elder clergyman, who had carefully prepared himself for the occasion, addressed to the multitude a discourse on sin, in all its branches, but with continual reference to the ignominious letter." —Nathaniel Hawthorne

   ◦ **colloquial diction:** informal expressions; part of everyday speech, but inappropriate in formal writing

14. **epigraph:** a quotation at the beginning of a poem, short story, or other text that introduces or refers to the larger themes of the text.

15. **exposition:** [DRAMA] beginning of play/story: introduces characters; details setting; sets tone/mood

16. **falling action:** [DRAMA] series of events following climax, leading to denouement/resolution

17. **flashback:** scene that interrupts the action of a work to show a previous event

18. **foil:** characters whose traits highlight the strengths/weaknesses of other characters

19. **foreshadowing:** hint of what is to come, usually negative

20. **hubris:** excessive pride

21. **hyperbole:** deliberate/outrageous exaggeration

> "The shot heard 'round the world." —Ralph Waldo Emerson

22. **imagery:** words that appeal to the five senses

23. **interior monologue:** a representation of an "inner voice" or "thinking in words"

24. **irony:** the opposite of what is expected

25. **juxtaposition:** putting two or more things side by side in order to compare them

26. **metaphor:** implied comparison

> "The streets were a furnace, the sun an executioner." —Cynthia Ozick

27. **meter:** [POETRY] pattern of stressed/unstressed syllables in poetry

28. **metonymy:** a figure of speech in which a closely related term is substituted for an object or idea.

> We have always remained loyal to the crown (crown = royal family)

29. **motif:** recurring ideas, images, topics, or literary devices that can help to develop the theme/s of a novel

30. **onomatopoeia:** the use of words to imitate the sounds they describe, such as "buzz" and "crack."

31. **oxymoron:** combination of opposite terms into single expression

> "jumbo shrimp," "freezer burn," "constant variable"

32. **parable:** brief story to illustrate lesson

33. **paradox:** an apparent contradiction which, after consideration, is true

> "The swiftest traveler is he that goes afoot." —Henry David Thoreau

34. **personification:** attributing human qualities to inanimate objects

35. **point of view:** the perspective from which the narrative is told

   - **first person:** narrator is a person in the story (I, we)
   - **third person:** narrator is not a part of the story (he, she, they)

- **limited:** author is restricted to the minds of a few or a single character
  - **omniscient:** author can enter the minds of all characters
36. **protagonist:** central character
37. **resolution:** [DRAMA] the problem of the climax is resolved
38. **rising action:** [DRAMA] series of events that lead to the climax; the building of tension in a narrative
39. **satire:** [GENRE] poke fun at human weakness with intent to change it
40. **setting:** the time and place in which events in a narrative occur
41. **simile:** comparison of two dissimilar things using *like* or *as*

    The stars twinkled like tiny candles in the black sky.
42. **soliloquy:** [DRAMA] character speaks true thoughts alone on stage
43. **sonnet:** [POETRY] a poem which typically expresses a single, complete thought or idea in fourteen lines of rhymed iambic pentameter
44. **stanza:** [POETRY] group of lines set off division in poem
45. **stock character:** a fictional character based on a common literary or social stereotype
46. **symbol:** a concrete object that represents an abstract quality or idea
47. **synecdoche:** a figure of speech in which a part of something is substituted for the whole, entire thing: "Lend me a hand."
48. **tragic flaw/ tragic hero:** [DRAMA] error in judgment that causes the downfall of a protagonist of high moral standing)
49. **understatement:** deliberate representation of something as less than it is

    "I have to have this operation. It isn't very serious. I have this tiny little tumor on the brain." — Holden Caulfield in *The Catcher in the Rye* by J. D. Salinger

50. **utopia/dystopia:** [GENRE] imaginary society organized to create ideal conditions for humanity/utopian ideal gone awry, leading to conditions that hurt humanity

# Index

Page references followed by *fig* indicate an illustrated figure; followed by *t* indicate a table.

## A

Absorption rate: description of, 120–121; embedding nonfiction to increase, 122, 123–136, 140–143; how what we read impacts, 121–122; increased by batch processing primary text, 141–142

Accountability: Accountable Independent Reading (AIR), 214, 215, 216–223; Gillian Cartwright's tools to ensure students' observations, 349–350; Interactive Reading (IR), 304–305; of students for following feedback and guidance on revisions, 185–186

Accountable Independent Reading (AIR): accountability aspect of, 215, 217–218; accountability tools for in-class, 219–223; barriers to, 217–219; description of, 214, 216–217; for homework, 223–225

Accountable Independent Reading (AIR) barriers: the accountability challenge, 217–218; the fitness challenge, 218; the report-back lag, 219

Accountable tools for AIR: confirm and scaffold comprehension, 222–223; find a focal point, 220–221; finite time limits, 221; "I'll meet you at the top of page 91" phrase as, 222; interactive reading task, 222; limit text and gradually increase, 219–220; remembering to be "silent" during silent reading time, 223

Achievement First Bushwick, 272

Acting word definition out, 262

Active practice: to master meaning, 266; to master usage, 266–267; three keys to, 267–268; vocabulary, 265–268

Adams, John, 107

Adams, Marilyn Jager: her observation on dropping SAT scores of top 10 percent, 7; on providing students with ways for them to read lots, 217

*The Adventures of Huckleberry Finn* (Twain), 27*fig*, 29, 51, 337

Affixes, 269–270

Alcott, Louisa May, 20

*All Quiet on the Western Front* (Remarque), 47–48

Allan, Lindsay, 128

Allusions: allusion questions to analyze meaning, 87; intertextual framework of interpretation and definition of, 337–338

Ambiguity questions, 96

Anderson, Laurie Halse: *Chains*, 106–107, 336; *Fever, 1793*, 331–332

*Animal Farm* (Orwell): author's intention and position framework of interpretation used for, 333; Close Reading burst solos by students on, 109; dramatic irony question on, 89; Ellie Stand's Close Reading burst on, 105–106;

Bierce, Rose, 361

*Bigmama's* (Crews): leapfrog read of, 69–70; nonlinear time sequence of, 33–34; pattern question on, 88; sentence structure question on, 81

Biography nonfiction, 116–117

*The Blacksmith* (Longfellow), 20

Bond, Akilah, 259

Book choice: articles, essays, and excerpts, 46–47; as component of text selection, 45–52; disciplinary literacy and, 51–52; knowledge development and, 50–51; literary significance and cultural capital issue of, 48–50; literary utility and, 47–48; poetry, 46; short stories, 45–46

Boston Collegiate High School, 46, 149

*Boy* (Dahl), 277

Boyd, Candy Dawson, *Circle of Gold,* 176–177, 228–229

Bracey, Jessica: autonomous writing structures used by, 352; *Circle of Gold* lesson using Read-Write-Discuss cycle by, 176–177; video clip on Read-Write-Discuss cycles used by, 176; video clip on using Control the Fame for *Circle of Gold* lesson by, 228–229

Bracketing or boxing text, 302

Bradbury, Ray, "Dark They Were, and Golden-Eyed," 230, 272–273, 313

Break It Down technique, 319

Bridging, 229

*The Brief and Wondrous Life of Oscar Wao* (Díaz), 181

*A Brief History of Seven Killings* (Marlow), 51

*Bringing Words to Life* (Beck, McKeown, and Kucan): caution regarding the synonym model of instruction in, 264–265; on depth of word knowledge as predictor of student success, 251–252; on teaching students to use context clues for new vocabulary, 274–275; on words having different levels of utility, 257–258

Broad word knowledge: goal of acquiring, 255*fig*; Implicit Vocabulary Instruction for, 255*fig*–256, 270–281

Bronson, Alex, 303

Brown, Dan, 310

Brown, Peter C., 265

Building stamina: balancing quality and quantity when, 199–200; description of, 196; Gillian Cartwright's *Fences* lesson for, 195; strategies for, 196–199; tension between building AOS and, 200; video clip on Eric Diamon helping students with, 196

Building stamina strategies: Eric Diamon's approach to, 196–197; the Pace Car, 197, 198–199; Priming the Pump, 197, 198; valorizing student writing, 199; Wire-to-Wire Writing, 197–198

## C

Call and Response technique, 276–277

Canon: benefits of having a schoolwide, 52–53; contemporary youth fiction replacing traditional, 21; definition and meaning of, 21; historic decline of, 18–20; positives and negatives in the decline of, 22–23. *See also* Text

"Canopy Cruising" visual layout, 150*fig*

Carroll, Lewis, "Jabberwocky," 43

Cartwright, Gillian: *Fences* lesson using writing for reading by, 157–160; on finding something "worthy of analysis," 349; inserting pause points during class discussion, 361; video clip on providing student-friendly word definitions by, 259

*The Catcher in the Rye* (Salinger), 220–221

Catlett, Lauren, 185–186

*Chains* (Anderson), 106–107, 336

Character-based framework of interpretation, 334–337

Charlotte Mecklenberg School District (North Carolina), 128

*Charlotte's Web* (White): Check for Understanding (CFU) when Interactive Reading (IR) of, 292–293; examining reading systems to study, 289

Charting the evidence, 174

Chaucer, Geoffrey, 51

Check for Understanding (CFU): contiguous read working as a form of, 65; following an independent reading chunk with written or oral, 221; Interactive Reading (IR) and, 292–293; Open Responses allow teachers to, 169–172; "Reading CFU Gap" challenge, 163–165*fig*; Stop and Jots used for, 172; text markups used for, 303; Turn and Talk technique and, 313–314. *See also* Reading comprehension

Chiger, Steve: "It's Not Just the Questions, It's the Sequence" by, 94–95; list of key literary terms and definitions shared by, 340, 342; "On Writing, Revision, and Close Reading" by, 97–99; video clip on using word play for vocabulary maintenance and extension, 283

Christodoulou, Daisy, 40

Chunking difficult words, 237

Churchill, Winston, "We Shall Fight on the Beaches" speech, 85

*Circle of Gold* (Boyd): Jessica Bracey's use of Control the Fame for lesson on, 228–229; Jessica Bracey's use of re-cycling during lesson on, 176–177

Circling text, 302

Clark, Kelsey, 168

Classroom environment: building a culture of Interactive Reading (IR) in, 305–306*fig*; technical vocabulary (Tier 3) listed on a classroom reference wall of words, 341*fig*; vocabulary maintenance and extension by changing the, 281, 284

Cleary, Beverly, *The Mouse and the Motorcycle*, 229

Clements, Andrew, 24

Close Reading: analyzing meaning using, 83–97; benefits of teachers getting together to practice, 53; Close Reading "burst" track of, 62, 102–111; Close Reading lesson track of, 62–102; as defense against "gist" readings, 60; defining, 60–62; description of, 7–8, 59–60; learning benefits of, 60; marking up text to reread or, 300; as one of the Core of the Core, 5; reconsidering, 111; sequence of questions for,

94–95; by teachers during a workshop, 74–75; toggling required for good, 84, 90*t*–92*t*; zooming required for good, 93–95. *See also* Text-dependent questions (TDQs)

Close Reading bursts: anatomy of a, 107–109; Beth Verrilli's AP English class video clip on, 103–104; choosing lines for, 105–106; consistent practice benefit of, 109; description of, 62, 102–103; epigraphs used for, 106–107; four types of, 104*t*–105; soloing and, 109–111

Close Reading lessons: Close Reading to analyze meaning part of, 63, 83–97; description of, 62–63; establish meaning via text-dependent questions part of, 62, 71–83; layered reading part of, 62, 63–71; process insights in writing, 63, 97–102; processing ideas and insights in writing, 97–99; reading focus used in, 99–102; sequence of questions used during, 94–95; toggling as part of, 84, 90*t*–92*t*; zooming as part of, 93–95

Close Reading modules: 2.1: Layered Reading, 63–71; 2.2: Establish Meaning via Text-Dependent Questions, 71–83; 2.3: Close Reading to Analyze Meaning, 83–97; 2.4: Processing Ideas and Insights in Writing, and the Power of Clear Focus, 97–102; 2.5: Close Reading Bursts, 102–111

Coffin, Rachel, 193

Cold Call technique: interactive reading task using, 222; Patrick Pastore's AIR focal point on *The Catcher in the Rye* use of, 221; similarity between Show Call and, 184

Coleman, David, 280

Colleen's Leapfrog Read, 67, 68–69

College students: challenge of heavy reading loads faced by, 209–210; time spent reading on average by, 210–211

College-Style Seminar: Grading Scale, 361–362

Collins, Tondra, 276

*The Color Purple* (Walker), 348–349

Common Core: exemplars by Lexile vs. Uncommon School canon, 26–27*fig*; reading more nonfiction to prepare for assessments of the, 115, 116; requirements placed on teachers by, 4–5; suggestion that students read harder texts by, 43; Uncommon Schools' *Core of the Core* distilled from, 5–9

"Common Lexicon" vocabulary, 241, 256

Common-place journals, 354

Complexity: narrator, 37–39; of story (plot and symbolism), 40–41. *See also* Harder texts

Coney Island Prep, 128

Connotation questions, 85

Conrad, Joseph, 342

Context clues for vocabulary, 274–275

Contiguous read: description of, 64; leading your students in a, 64–65; various formats for using, 65–66; working as a form of Check for Understanding (CFU), 65

Control the Game: decoding and, 233–238; description of, 214–215; first introduced in *Teach Like a Champion,* 225; fluency and, 231–233; skills of the, 225–230; as system for reading aloud, 290; video clips on using, 226–227, 228–229, 230, 236, 238, 246–247

Control the Game skills: keep durations short and the reader unpredictable, 226–227; reduce transaction costs, 228–229; rely on a placeholder, 230; spot checking, 229–230; use bridging to maintain continuity and model fluency, 229

Convention alignment analyses, 95–96

Convention alignment analysis, 95–96

Core of the Core: Close Reading, 5, 7–8, 59–111; introduction to the, 5–6; read harder texts, 5, 6–7*fig,* 18–55; reading more nonfiction, 5, 8, 115–152; writing for reading, 5, 8–9, 157–204

Cosgrove, Daniel, 222

Crews, Donald. *See Bigmama's* (Crews)

Cultural capital: book choice consideration of literary significance and, 48–50; decline of the canon and loss of, 22–23; description of, 22

*Culture and Anarchy* (Arnold), 19

Cunningham, Anne E., 119

*The Curious Incident of the Dog in the Night-Time* (Haddon): autistic narrator of, 39;

knowledge-based framework of interpretation used for, 332; wooden student writing on, 187*fig*–188

Curtis, Christopher Paul, *The Watsons Go to Birmingham–1963,* 297, 331

## D

D'Addabo, Rachel, 128

Dahl, Roald: *Boy,* 277; *James and the Giant Peach,* 222

"Dark They Were, and Golden-Eyed" (Bradbury): Eric Snider's Implicit Vocabulary Instruction on, 272–273; Turn and Talk system used for discussion of, 313; video clip on Eric Snider bridging during lesson on, 230

Darwin, Charles, 2–3

Davidson, Jamie, 277

De La Salle Middle School (St. Louis), 128

de Leon, Rob: spot checking during *Phantom of the Opera* lesson by, 229–230; video clip on bridging during *The Mouse and the Motorcycle* lesson by, 229

DEAR (Drop Everything and Read), 217

*The Declaration of Independence,* 31

Decline of canon: historic decline of, 18–20; positives and negatives in the, 22–23

Decoding: Control the Game and, 233–238; importance of including in curriculum, 233–234; provide positive feedback for correct, 238; transaction cost of incorrect, 234; video clip on Bridget McElduff's math class, 238

Decoding errors: "echo correction" to correct, 236–237; getting in the habit of self-correcting, 234–235; transaction cost of, 234

Decoding strategies and skills: chunk it, 237; mark the spot, 235; name the sound or the rule, 235–236; positive feedback, 238; punch the error, 235; speed the exceptions, 237; use positive feedback, 238

Deep word knowledge: Explicit Vocabulary Instruction for, 255*fig*–270; goal of acquiring, 255*fig*–256

Embedding nonfiction: aiming inside and outside the bull's-eye, 127–130; ideas for *A Single Shard,* 127–128; to increase absorption rate and build background knowledge, 122, 123–136; keys to planning, 136; lessons on maximizing, 131–136; leveraging Matthew Effect and synergy in, 124–125; pairing nonfiction with primary text for outside the bull's-eye, 125–127; text pairing inside the bull's-eye for, 123–125

Embedding nonfiction lessons: cutting and adapting, 131; embedding with other genres, 134–135; frequent embedding, 132–134; keys to planning embedding nonfiction, 136; meta-embedding, 135–136; overlapping questions, 131–132, 142; Sample Embedded Outline, 133–134

Embedding nonprinted texts, 140

Embedding out loud, 141

Embedding with other genres, 134–135

English language arts (ELA): Close Reading, professional development, and subject knowledge of teachers in, 74–75; "relative decline" of SAT scores in, 6–7*fig*; Uncommon School's "figuring out" reading approach to, 3–5

Entry tickets, 362–363

Epigraphs for Close Reading burst, 106–107

*Esperanza Rising* (Ryan): meta-embedding of, 135; overlapping questions used for lesson on, 131–132; placeholder used during lesson on, 230; vocabulary instruction specific to, 258

Essay reading, 46

Essential question trackers, 354

"Eulogy for the Martyred Children" (King), 239

Exceptions (decoding rules), 237

Excerpts reading, 46

Exit Tickets, 362

Explanation questions, 78

Explicit Vocabulary Instruction: beware of using the "synonym model" for, 264–265; choosing to teach implicitly or use, 279–280; comparing Implicit Vocabulary Instruction and, 253–256;

deep word knowledge via, 255*fig*–270; description of, 252; primary goal of, 253–254

Explicit Vocabulary Instruction rollout: accurate and student-friendly definition, 258–262; active practice, 265–268; parameters of use, 262–264; roots and affixes, 269–270; sequence of, 268–269; word selection, 256–258

Expressive reading, 215

Extended metaphor/allegory question, 89

Eye contact, 310

## F

F&P Levels (Fountas and Pinnel's Guided Reading Levels): comparing *The Outsiders* to *The Adventures of Huckleberry Finn* and *Animal Farm,* 27*fig*; Precisely Wrong and Perverse Pairings results of, 28–29. *See also* Lexile system

Facer, Jo, 245

Faulkner, Maura, 278

Faulkner, William, 6

*Feast of the Goat* (Vargas), 97–99

Feedback: College-Style Seminar: Grading Scale as, 361–362; decoding instruction and providing positive, 238; hold students accountable for revision guidance and, 185–186; inserting pause points to provide discussion, 361; Julie Miller providing specific and universal, 181

Feeney, Nolan, 21

*Fences* (Wilson): building stamina through Gillian's writing lesson on, 195; Gillian Cartwright's application of framework for student autonomy during lesson on, 349–350; Gillian Cartwright's writing for reading lesson on, 157–160

Fern, Laura, 314

Fernando, Megan, 94–95

*Fever, 1793* (Anderson), 331–332

Fiction: text markups of, 302; young adult (YA), 21. *See also* Nonfiction

*Field Notes* blog (Lemov), 46

Figurative language: figurative language questions to analyze meaning, 87–88; figurative/literal meaning question, 85–86; framework of interpretation using, 330–331

Finite evidence questions, 82–83

Finite time limits, 221

Fitness challenge, 218

The Five Plagues of the Developing Reader: archaic text as, 29–33; complexity of narrator as, 37–39; complexity of story plot and symbolism as, 40–41; nonfiction as a sixth "plague" added to, 44; nonlinear time sequence as, 33–37; perspective on text selection context of, 43–44; resistant text as, 41–43

Fluency: capturing the mood element of, 232; check the mechanics as part of, 233; Control the Game bridging skills to model, 229; Control the Game for practicing, 231–233; definition of, 231; identifying the important words for, 232–233; Read-Aloud for modeling, 243–245; rereading for, 233

Fluency modeling: Control the Game bridging skills for, 229; highlight points of emphasis for, 243–244; Showing Some Spunk by, 244–245

Focal points, 220–221

*Forgotten Fire* (Bagdasarian), 297

Format Matters technique, 309, 311

Forms of word, 263–264

Frame, Nikki: video clip on Call and Response technique used by, 277; video clip on using Control the Game during *A Single Shard* lesson, 226–227

Frameworks: choosing your teaching, 338; description of, 327–328; for interpretation, 328–338

Frameworks for interpretation: 1: story form and variation (genre informed), 328–330; 2: imagery, literary devices, and figurative language, 330–331*t*; 3: knowledge-based, 331–332; 4: author's intention and position, 333–334; 5: character based, 334–337; 6: intertextual, 337–338; intellectual autonomy development phases and practice with,

342–352; literary analysis protocol (LAP) used for, 345–347; for poetry, 330; Stepping Points approach to, 347–349; steps for teaching and adding Tier 3 vocabulary to, 339–340. *See also* Reading comprehension

*Frankenstein* (Shelley), 31

Frequent embedding: description of, 132–133; Sample Embedded Outline on *Lord of the Flies,* 133–134

*From the Mixed-Up Files of Mrs. Basil E. Frankweiler* (Konigsberg), 38

Front the Writing technique, 165

FUR (Free Uninterrupted Reading), 217

## G

Gavin, Sean, 361

Generic number rule, 147–148

Genres: embedding with other, 134–135; framework for interpretation informed by, 328–330; markups specific to, 302; nonfiction micro, 148–149; Read-Aloud for introducing new, 242–243; synergy in embedding different nonfiction, 124–125. *See also* Text

Gestures (listening), 311

"Gist" readings, 60

*The Giver* (Lowry): allusion questions on, 87; character-based framework of interpretation used for, 335, 336; comparing Lexile levels of *The School Story* and, 24–25; embedding with an interview with author of, 149; intertextual framework of interpretation used for, 337; Rue Ratray's sensitivity analysis of, 86, 336; Rue Ratray's Close Reading burst on, 107–109

Global-level text-dependent questions: ambiguity questions, 96; convention alignment analysis using, 95–96; description of, 95; intratextual motifs and discourse using, 96; part-to-whole questions, 96

Goldenheim, Julia: character-based framework of interpretation in *The Winter of Our Discontent* lesson by, 335; sequence of questions for *The Pearl* lesson by, 94–95; Show Call used for revision by, 184–185; Show Calls used for *The*

*Winter of Our Discontent* lesson by, 184–185; video clip on Read-Write-Discuss-Revise used by, 172, 335; video clip on Show Calls used by, 184

Golding, William: *Lord of the Flies* by, 27*fig*, 29, 41, 53, 75; vision of "natural" state of humanity by, 75

*Grapes of Wrath* (Steinbeck): connotation question on, 85; continuous read of the, 65; extended metaphor/allegory question on, 89; figurative/literal meaning question on, 85; intertextual discourse on, 96; intratextual motifs and discourse to analyze, 96; the leapfrog read of the, 67, 68–69; line-by-line read of the, 66–67; missing word analysis of, 86–87; part-to-whole questions on, 96; referent questions on, 77; sensitivity analysis of, 86; toggling process for, 91–92; zooming process for, 93. *See also* Steinbeck, John

*The Great Gatsby* (Fitzgerald): knowledge development through reading of, 51; soloing Close Reading bursts using, 110–111; video clip on Beth Verrilli's character-based framework used for, 335; video clip on Beth Verrilli's focused discussion topic on, 357

*Guns, Germs, and Steel* (Diamond), 358–359

## H

Habits of Discussion: description of, 290, 307; elaborating or expanding, 316*t*; evaluating, 316*t*; Format Matters technique, 309, 311; listening systems, 309, 310–311; paraphrasing, 316*t*; peer-to-peer speaking, 309, 311–314; phrases to build in early grades, 317*t*; phrases to use in upper grades with established, 317*t*; prompting, 315–322; sentence starters, 315, 316*t*; synthesizing, 316*t*; what students should develop as part of, 308; what they are and are not, 308–309. *See also* Discussion systems

Haddon, Mark, *The Curious Incident of the Dog in the Night-Time,* 39, 187*fig*–188

*Hamlet* (Shakespeare), 20, 83–84

Harder texts: book choice and selection of, 115–152; Core of the Core on reading, 5, 6–7*fig*; Read-Aloud as opportunity to read, 240. *See also* Complexity

Harvard Medical School, 150

Hawthorne, Nathaniel, 20

Heath, Chip, 261

Heath, Dan, 261

Hemingway, Ernest, 51

Henry, Amanda, 128

Highlighting points of emphasis, 243–244

Hinton, S. E., *The Outsiders,* 27*fig*, 29, 126–127, 135

Hirsch, E. D., 18, 119, 251, 271

Hochman, Judith: on difference between revision and editing, 178; preliminary revision exercises used by, 182–183

Hochman Writing Method, 178

Homework: Accountable Independent Reading (AIR) for, 223–224; Implicit Vocabulary Instruction and intellectual autonomy during, 280–281. *See also* Students

*A Hope in the Unseen* (Suskind), 48–49

Houston Independent School District, 313

"How Do English Scholars Talk about Literature?" word wall, 257–258

"How to Get Kids to Read––Let Them Pick Their Own Damn Books" (blog title), 47

Hughes, Langston, *A Dream Deferred,* 76–77

*Hunger Games* (Collins), 44

Huntington School (England), 54

Hurston, Zora Neale, 22

Hypothesis tracker, 354

## I

"Illusion of speed," 176

Imagery, 330–331

Implicit Vocabulary Instruction: comparing Explicit Vocabulary Instruction and, 253–256; broad word knowledge via, 255*fig*–256; building vocabulary during reading, 270–281; description of, 252; intellectual autonomy and, 280–281; planning

meta-embedding applications by, 135–136; overlapping questions on *Esperanza Rising* by, 131–132; *To Kill a Mockingbird* lesson using Close Reading by, 72–74; video clip on *To Kill a Mockingbird* lesson using different approaches, 246–247

Jones, John, 147

Journals: Reader's Response, 290, 352–353*fig*; types that support greater autonomy, 354–355

Jubilee Public Schools, 128

*Julius Caesar* (Shakespeare), 69

## K

Key line questions, 81, 87

*King Lear* (Shakespeare), 340, 361

King, Martin Luther: "Eulogy for the Martyred Children," 239; "Letter from Birmingham Jail," 62, 66, 82, 89, 101–102, 116, 333–334

Knowledge: book choice relationship to the development of, 50–51; cultural capital of, 22–23; the Matthew Effect, 117, 125; reading nonfiction as best way of building, 115–116; reading skills dependence on, 18. *See also* Background knowledge

Knowledge-based analytical questions, 142

Knowledge-based framework of interpretation, 331–332

*The Knowledge Deficit* (Hirsch), 119, 271

Knox, Henry, 107

Knox, Lucy, 107

Konigsberg, E. L., *From the Mixed-Up Files of Mrs. Basil E. Frankweiler,* 38

Krafft, Erin, 313

Kucan, Linda, 253, 265, 275

## L

Language: challenging vocabulary as generally not occurring in spoken, 256; Close Reading as the methodical breaking down of, 61; figurative, 85–88, 330–331; text written in archaic, 29–33

Latto, Lauren, 198

Layered reading: combining the different reads for, 70–71; contiguous read for, 64–66; description of, 63–64; the leapfrog read for, 67–70; line-by-line read for, 66–67; video clip on using, 71

Leadership Prep Bedford Stuyvesant Middle Academy, 222, 303

The leapfrog read: description of how to use, 67; Donald Crews's *Bigmamma* read using the, 69–70; *Grapes of Wrath* lesson using, 67, 68–69; of *Julius Caesar,* 69

Lee, Harper. *See To Kill a Mockingbird* (Lee)

Lemov, Doug: on entry tickets to facilitate discussion, 362–363; *Field Notes* blog by, 46; *Practice Perfect: 42 Rules for Getting Better at Getting Better* by Erica and, 109; on soloing Close Reading bursts as effective practice, 109–110; on starting a contiguous read, 64. *See also Teach Like a Champion 2.0* (Lemov); *Teach Like a Champion* (Lemov)

Leslie, Lauren, 118

"Letter from Birmingham Jail" (King): asking sequenced, text-dependent questions on, 62; author's intention and position framework of interpretation used for, 333–334; delineation question on, 82; line-by-line read of, 66; as nonnarrative nonfiction (NNNF), 116; paragraph function question on, 89; reading focus approach to Close Reading of, 101–102; summary question on, 82

Lewis, C. S.: *The Magician's Nephew,* 31–32; Narnia series, 337; *Prince Caspian,* 232

Lexile system: Common Care's decision to use the, 25; Common Core exemplars by grade estimate and, 26*fig*; comparing *The Outsiders* and *Lord of the Flies,* 27*fig*; *The Giver* has an example of limitations of the, 24–25; Precisely Wrong and Perverse Pairings results of, 28–29; text attributes determined using the, 24; Uncommon Schools canon vs. Common Core exemplars by, 26–27*fig*. *See also* F&P Levels (Fountas and Pinnel's Guided Reading Levels)

Prefixes: increasing vocabulary by teaching students, 269–270; parameters of use on, 263–264

Primary text: description of, 122; embed nonfiction throughout your, 142, 143; increasing absorption rate by batch processing, 141–142; *Lord of the Flies* taught as a, 122; overlapping questions to connect secondary and, 131–132, 142

Priming the Pump, 197, 198

*Prince Caspian* (Lewis), 232

Prior knowledge. *See* Background knowledge

Private revision setting, 180, 181*t*

Professional development workshops: Close Reading by teachers during a, 74–75; questions on tension between AOS and building stamina during, 200. *See also* Teachers

Prompting: Art of the Sentence (AOS) nondenominational, 192–193; Interactive Reading (IR), 296, 298; Open Responses, 170–171. *See also* Discussion prompting

Pronoun references: challenge of word- and phrase-level questions and, 78; sixth-grade Common Core passage text on tracking, 78–80

Pronunciation instruction, 273

Public revision setting: description of, 180, 181*t*; Show Call used to increase the power of, 183–184

Punch the error, 235

Punctuation, fluency and understanding, 233

## Q

Questions: allusion, 87; ambiguity, 96; Close Reading and sequence of, 94–95; connotation, 85; delineation, 82; denotation, 77–78; dramatic irony, 89; explanation, 78; extended metaphor/allegory, 89; figurative language, 87–88; figurative/literal meaning, 85–86; finite evidence, 82–83; key-line, 81, 87; knowledge-based analytical, 142; overlapping, 131–132, 142; paragraph function, 89; paraphrase, 80*t*–81; part-to-whole, 96; pattern, 88; reference, 81; referent, 77; summary, 82; word pattern, 85. *See also* Text-dependent questions (TDQs)

Quigley, Alex, 54

## R

Rare words vocabulary, 241–242, 256

Raskin, Ellen, *The Westing Game*, 130, 236

Ratray, Rue: Close Reading burst on *The Giver* led by, 107–109; *The Giver* sensitivity analysis led by, 86, 336

Read-Aloud: building vocabulary benefit of, 241–242; description of, 215, 219; developing syntactic control using, 240–241; exposure to complex texts through, 240; finding opportunities to incorporate, 239–240; instilling a love of literature through, 245–247; introducing new genres and building background knowledge using, 242–243; modeling fluent reading through, 243–245; positive learning outcomes of, 239

*The Read-Aloud Handbook* (Trelease), 241, 246, 256

Read-Discuss-Read cycles, 165–166

Read-Discuss-Write cycles: closing the "Reading CFU Gap," 163–165*fig*; comparing Open Responses and Stop and Jots for, 171–172; description of the, 161–163; examining how to insert more writing into the, 165–166; typical reading lesson using, 164*fig*

Read harder texts: challenge of selecting the right text, 15–17; modules on text selection process, 18–55; *Oliver Twist* as example of, 16–17; as one of the Core of the Core, 5, 6–7*fig*

Read-Write-Discuss cycles: comparing Stop and Jots and Open Responses for, 171–172; description and benefits of the, 169; "illusion of speed" created by the, 176; Open Responses used for, 169–171; re-cycling the, 175–177; video clip on Jessica Bracey's use of, 176

Read-Write-Discuss-Revise cycles: charting the evidence during discussion of, 174;

in, 282–283; Format Matters technique from the, 309, 311; Front the Writing technique from the, 165; on the learning value of writing, 159; Not Watching technique from the, 171; Show Call technique from the, 183–185, 199, 200, 222; Standardize the Field technique from the, 292; word-play questions as part of daily Do Now from the, 282. *See also* Lemov, Doug

*Teach Like a Champion* (Lemov): antecedent discussion routines and skills outlined in, 309–314; Control the Game introduced in, 225; daily Do Now outlined in, 282–283; on reading systems as encompassing procedures and routines, 290. *See also* Lemov, Doug

Teacher-identified framework: guided practice with a, 342, 343–344; independent application of, 342, 344–349

Teachers: benefits Close Reading practice by, 53; Close Reading, professional development, and subject knowledge in ELA by, 74–75; giving up text selection autonomy, 53–54; historically concerned with what books students read as part of reading, 18; how universal education movement impacted how reading is taught by, 18–20, 22–23; reinforcement of Implicit Vocabulary by, 271; role in developing intellectual autonomy by students, 326–327; the teaching responsibilities of a reading, 2. *See also* Modeling; Professional development workshops

"Tech Trash Tragedy" (O'Donnell), 145

Technical (Tier 3) vocabulary: classroom reference wall of words, 341*fig*; description of, 338; intellectual autonomy and, 338–340, 342; steps for teaching frameworks and adding, 339–340

"The Tell-Tale Heart" (Poe), 38–39

Text: democratization impact on canon, 18–23; the McGuffey Reader as reading, 19–20; marking up, 299–303; multiple reads of, 303–304; primary, 122, 131–132, 141–143; resistant, 41–43; secondary, 122, 123–136,

140–143; Writing for Reading, 161–204. *See also* Canon; Genres

Text attributes: description of, 23–24; Fountas and Pinnell's Guided Reading Levels application of, 24, 25–29; Lexile framework application of, 24, 27*fig*, 28–29; text selection as more than just quantitative, 25

Text content markups: daily objectives(s), 301; final writing connection, 301; identified evidence, 299; key ideas and themes, 300; key vocabulary, 301; marks to reread or Close Read, 300; paraphrasing, 300; the summary, 299–300

Text-dependent questions (TDQs): analyzing meaning using, 84–89; establishing meaning via, 71–83; global-level questions to analyze meaning, 95–97; paragraph- and stanza-level questions to establish meaning, 76*t*, 81–83, 88–89, 90*t*–95; Participation Ratio vs. Think Ratio in, 72; sentence- and line-level questions to establish meaning, 76*t*, 80–81, 87–88, 90*t*–95; *To Kill a Mockingbird* lesson using paraphrasing and, 72–75; toggling, 84, 90*t*–92*t*; unlocking the power of the microscope using, 75–76; word- and phrase-level questions to establish meaning, 76*t*–80, 84–87, 90*t*–95; zooming, 93–95. *See also* Close Reading; Meaning; Questions

Text markings: bracket or box, 302; circles, 302; margin notes, 302–303; underline, 302

Text markups: Check for Understanding (CFU) using, 303; genre-specific markups, 302; "how" and techniques for, 302–303; video clip on highlights a students' Interactive Reading, 303; what content to, 299–301

Text meaning analyses: convention alignment analyses, 95–96; missing word analysis, 86–87; sensitivity analysis, 86, 336

Text selection: assessing text attributes using Lexiles and F&P Levels, 21–29; book choice component of, 45–52; decline of the canon implications for, 18–23; the Five Plagues of the Developing Reader component of, 29–44;

Woolf, Virginia: "Thoughts on Peace in an Air Raid," 193; *To the Lighthouse,* 36

Woolway, Erica: *Practice Perfect: 42 Rules for Getting Better at Getting Better* by Doug and, 109; on soloing Close Reading bursts as effective practice, 109–110

Word definitions: define and practice, 278–279; dropped-in definition techniques as reminders of, 275–277; providing accurate and student-friendly, 258–262. *See also* Vocabulary; Words

Word knowledge: Explicit Vocabulary Instruction for deep, 255*fig*–270; Implicit Vocabulary Instruction for broad, 255*fig,* 270–281. *See also* Vocabulary

Word-level questions: to analyze meaning, 84–87; Close Reading and the sequence of, 94–95; connotation, 85; denotation, 77–78, 79–80; establishing meaning through, 76–80, 76*t*; explanation, 78; figurative language, 87–88; figurative/literal meaning, 85–86; missing word analysis, 86–87; referent, 77, 78–79; sensitivity analyses, 86; test using sixth-grade Common Core passage on, 78–80; toggling, 90*t*–92*t*; word pattern, 85; zooming, 93–94

Word partners, 263

Word pattern question, 85

Word play: video clip on Steve Chiger using, 283; vocabulary maintenance and extension through, 281, 282–283

Word selection: Explicit Vocabulary Instruction and, 256–257; of Tier 3 words for instruction, 257–258

Words: affixes of, 269–270; chunking difficult, 237; fluency by identifying the important, 232–233; forms of, 263–264; missing word analysis of, 86–87; modeling fluency by highlighting points of emphasis, 243–244; planning and prioritizing for Implicit Vocabulary Instruction, 271–279; prefixes of, 263–264, 269–270; rare, 241–242, 256; root, 269–270; Tier 1, 258; Tier 2, 257; Tier 3

(technical vocabulary), 257–258, 338–342. *See also* Vocabulary; Word definitions

"The Worst Mistake in the History of the Human Race" (Diamond), 83

Writing: Close Reading and reflection through writing and revisions, 97–99; Closed Reading with mastery expressed through, 62; Hochman Writing Method for, 178; processing ideas and insights in, 97–102; Read-Write-Discuss cycle of, 161–177; synergies between reading and, 160–161; *Teach Like a Champion 2.0* on the learning value of, 159; vocabulary upgrades during, 281, 283. *See also* Revising

Writing for Reading: Art of the Sentence (AOS) for, 186–195, 200; building stamina for, 195–200; description of, 8–9, 290; Gillian Cartwright's *Fences* lesson using, 157–160; as one of the Core of the Core, 5; reconsideration of, 204; revising and feedback on, 178–186; Stack Audit for monitoring and assessing, 200–204; vocabulary building for, 187*fig*–188; wooden student writing, 187*fig*–188

Writing for Reading modules: 4.1: Reading class Cycles, 161–177; 4.2: Writing Is Revising, 178–186; 4.3: Art of the Sentence, 186–195; 4.4: Building Stamina, 195–200; 4.5: Monitoring and Assessment via the Stack Audit, 200–204

## X

Xavier University of Louisiana's premed program, 2

## Y

*YES* (science magazine), 150

Yezzi, Katie, 109

Young adult (YA) fiction, 21

## Z

Zooming: description of, 93; for *The Grapes of Wrath* discussion, 93–94; *The Pearl* discussion using, 94–95

# How to Access the Online Contents

- If you purchased a new paperback copy of this book, you will find a unique single-use access code for the video clips and downloadable tools inside the back cover.

- Go to www.teachlikeachampion.com/yourlibrary and click "Activate Pin."

- If you don't have a pin, simply answer our verification question to then create an account.

- Follow the instructions on the website for registration.

- If you have any issues with Your Library account, please contact us at teachlikeachampion@wiley.com.

# How to Use the DVD

## SYSTEM REQUIREMENTS

PC or Mac with a DVD drive running any operating system with an HTML-compatible web browser

## USING THE DVD WITH WINDOWS

To view the content on the DVD, follow these steps:

1. Insert the DVD into your computer's DVD drive.

2. Select Home.html from the list of files.

3. Read through the license agreement by clicking the License link near the top right of the interface.

4. The interface appears. Simply select the material you want to view.

## IN CASE OF TROUBLE

If you experience difficulty using the DVD, please follow these steps:

1. Make sure your hardware and systems configurations conform to the systems requirements noted under "System Requirements" above.

2. Review the installation procedure for your type of hardware and operating system. It is possible to reinstall the software if necessary.

## CUSTOMER CARE

If you have trouble with the DVD, please call the Wiley Product Technical Support phone number at (800) 762-2974. Outside the United States, call 1 (317) 572-3994. You can also contact Wiley Product Technical Support at http://support.wiley.com. John Wiley & Sons will provide technical support only for installation and other general quality-control items. For technical support of the applications themselves, consult the program's vendor or author.

Before calling or writing, please have the following information available:

- Type of computer and operating system
- Any error messages displayed
- Complete description of the problem

It is best if you are sitting at your computer when making the call.

# More Ways to Engage and Learn with Teach Like a Champion

## COMPANION WEBSITE

We invite you to join the Teach Like a Champion team on our website, teachlikeachampion.com, to continue the conversation through Doug's blog, free downloadable resources, and our community forum.

## TRAIN-THE-TRAINER WORKSHOPS

Uncommon School's train-the-trainer workshops prepare instructional leaders to deliver high-quality training on *Teach Like a Champion, Reading Reconsidered,* and

*Practice Perfect* techniques. Participants learn both the fundamentals and subtleties of various techniques through analysis of video clips, case studies, and live demonstrations, then apply their emerging understanding immediately in carefully designed practice.

## PLUG AND PLAYS

Designed specifically for busy instructional leaders, Uncommon Schools' Plug and Plays provide all needed materials for two- to three-hour teacher training sessions on specific *Teach Like a Champion* and *Reading Reconsidered* techniques. Each Plug and Play provides leaders with ready-made PowerPoint presentations with embedded videos of the technique in action, facilitator notes, practice activities, and handouts. View a sample on teachlikeachampion.com.

teachlikeachampion.com